RADICAL PERSONALISM

RADICAL PERSONALISM

Revival Manifesto for Proactive Devotion

Swami Padmanabha

Other books by Swami Padmanabha

Inherent or Inherited?: Bhakti in the Jiva According to Gaudiya Vedanta
Available on Amazon and other Online Bookstores

For further conversation

www.Facebook.com/groups/GaudiyaReformForum
https://SwamiPadmanabha.com

Copyright © Swami Padmanabha, 2023
All rights reserved

Hardcover ISBN 979-8-9883934-1-2
Paperback ISBN 979-8-9883934-0-5
eBook ISBN 979-8-9883934-2-9

Library of Congress Control Number: 2023939614

Cover Design: Juan M. Tavella
Condex@gmail.com

Published in the United States
by Inword Publishers
Mill Spring, NC
www.InwordPublishers.com

Subjects: BISAC: REL032040 NON-FICTION / Religion / Hinduism / Theology

To each of those who,
no matter their tradition,
embody the heart and spirit
of Radical Personalism.

Table of Contents

Part Three — A Deeper Dive

FOREWORD

I FIRST MET PADMANABHA SWAMI IN 2017. As a leader in South America, he was contending with an upheaval that spanned many countries: hundreds of devotees were in crisis, having lost their (and his) *diksa-guru* to improper behavior. To hear from a respected devotee he had accepted as a *siksa-guru* ten years earlier, Padmanabha Maharaja had come to an *ashram* I was also visiting.

Externally, Padmanabha Maharaja appeared even keeled, and his classes displayed his intellectual acumen, knowledge, and attraction for hearing and chanting about Krishna.

Still, I had my doubts, having seen many spiritual disasters and knowing how a guru's misbehavior can irreparably devastate the foundation of even the sincerest devotee's faith in *bhakti*. How was he coping with his own loss? Did he even have time to sort out things internally, given that he was meant to carry the torch of hope and faith for others? I would be shown answers to these and other questions and would come to appreciate Padmanabha Swami more by being with him during another crisis a few years later.

In the meantime, Maharaja soon shone as a leader in the new *sangha*. He nourished the camaraderie and created community in a way that hadn't existed. With genuine interest in individuals, he encouraged and engaged each person in new initiatives he designed. I began to take note of his unpretentious, friendly demeanor. He was unaffected by his position as a *sannyasi* (member of the renounced order) and didn't show a need to have things center on and privilege him. By observing his interactions with others, I understood that relationships—people—were very important to him. Many devotees commented that in his presence they felt noticed, valued, and appreciated.

As far as I could see, Padmanabha Swami was loved and respected by everyone in the *sangha.* He is a rare combination of unassuming but real renunciation, competent intellect, soft heart, and psychological balance. He shows a genuine integration of his humanity with his spirituality.

I remember how he was intent on including everyone. On more than one occasion he asked me to lead *kirtan,* though he is an accomplished *kirtaniya* and the event would have called for him to lead. I had been attending gatherings at this *ashram* for years, however his invitation was the first of its kind.

By this time, Padmanabha Swami had taken re-initiation from his *siksa-guru,* who once shed tears of affection watching Maharaja lead a *kirtan* at a public event. Padmanabha Swami's devotion to his guru was palpable; hundreds of classes were filled with references to his guru, expressing deep gratitude for their relationship and the many things he had learned from him. So when I and others began to see a change in his guru's mood toward this ideal student, we became bewildered. Eventually, his guru publicly rejected him as his disciple.

That this was deeply disturbing is an understatement of grand proportions. Since there is no relationship more important for a Gaudiya Vaishnava, there's no greater tragedy than losing one's guru. Suddenly, Maharaja had lost a second guru.

At the time, Maharaja was living with a mutual friend, and I was seeing him almost daily as he navigated this sudden storm that had led him into the unknown and uncertain. Maybe one can hide behind a persona in public, but when everything is in gut-wrenching turmoil, it's impossible to hide who you are from people you are living with.

I was awed by how Maharaja comported himself. Though stunned and disoriented, instead of laying blame he entered deeply into prayer and repeatedly brought himself into an internal stance of full surrender, seeking to understand Krishna's will for his life. He had a humble, yet unshakeable, confidence in Krishna's unconditional love and trusted that there was a reason for the current situation. Whenever I asked how he was processing some new piece of information or the overall experience, his reply revealed a grave person turning to deep introspection, honesty, and contemplation. As the internet chatter intensified, he demonstrated integrity, forbearance, faith, tolerance, acceptance, and dignity.

The questions I had asked myself years earlier were answered. He must have dealt with his first loss in a comprehensive, mature way; otherwise, he would not have been able to navigate this one, which presented him with more complexities than the first, with the honesty, humility, and grace he showed.

By divine arrangement, this defining life event formed the genesis that churned this important book into being.

In one sense, this isn't surprising. Something that cuts to the quick and strips one of identity powerfully challenges faith and is a forceful instigator to turn us inward to do the work demanded of us. As we face ego deaths and leave behind previous realities and certainties, we must contend with many questions. What troubled us before, but we let slide, can no longer remain unaddressed. What we didn't notice before becomes disquieting now. We are flooded with intensified awareness, and everything seeks resolution, or at least honest appraisal.

Usually, what is specific (even personal) on a very deep heart level has universal application. Maharaja's challenge is a universal one. We have to make sense of setbacks, obstacles, and betrayals that don't make sense. We have to press on through unthinkable sorrows. We have to trust, to courageously look into blinding darkness and find light.

By writing through his process, Maharaja has bared his soul and courageously brought into public discourse topics that have disturbed many Gaudiyas from different *sanghas* for decades. Not only does he take up a discussion about an individual's progress, but he takes on the tremendous task of critiquing Gaudiya Vaishnavism overall with keen observations about how a religion can best progress and avoid pitfalls. This has significance for all of us.

In addition to our individual spiritual project, as Gaudiya Vaishnavas in the current timespan we're also called to respond to institutional ills because we are the stewards of this fledgling theological newcomer to the Western world. It ought not die or be permanently tainted by us. So when we hear about the shortcomings of the institution or its members, such as abuse, betrayals, dogmatism, sexism, fanaticism, bigotry, sectarianism, or simply the insensitive, unwise, or hurtful, we need the courage to look honestly, speak up, and ask unsettling questions. Maharaja frankly poses one at the beginning of this book: Should I stay, or should I go?

To ask the question is a sign of bravery. But for those who have dedicated their life to a particular path the question is terrifying. It is, however, a clarifying, honest one. If we choose to stay after having honestly wrestled down this question, then our priceless, precious gift of faith thickens. We will stay, but at a deeper level and with a different quality of attendance.

I'm passionate about the topics Maharaja has taken up here; they've been on my mind for a long time. They impelled me to action, which I eventually set aside as I gave in to hopelessness. I was spiritually born and raised in ISKCON (International Society for Krishna Consciousness) and maintain my bonds of love there. As well, I maintain a hope that the mission of my spiritual master (Srila Prabhupada) can improve, and I appreciate all the ways it is serving the spiritual lives of many. But for at least three decades I have been deeply disturbed by much of what I've seen and experienced.

In a public letter I wrote and circulated in 1989, I challenged the attitudes that had led to the disempowerment of women, and I pointed out how this had facilitated the abuse of children. Educating others about this issue and forming an avenue of representation for women in ISKCON became a focus for me between 1990 and 2000. Between 1990 and 1996, I edited, published, and funded *Priti-laksanam,* an international newsletter that fostered open public dialogue about issues that were often ignored or intentionally silenced. In 1993, at the Third Annual ISKCON Communications Conference in Radhadesh, Belgium, I presented my paper "Building an All-Attractive ISKCON," calling for more personal dealings in our Society.

I have not been alone in working to reform ISKCON or in giving up out of frustration. For decades, many devotees have been disillusioned and have expressed their unrest and dissatisfaction about numerous individual, societal, and institutional dysfunctions. There have been countless private conversations, angry public discourses, and a variety of papers on many topics. But we have tended to focus a light on one anomaly or another instead of undertaking a comprehensive overview of issues.

Padmanabha Swami has done something unique in *Radical Personalism*, which we can confirm by a quick scan of the Contents page. He has taken a broad look at societal and institutional concerns, scriptural misunderstandings and misapplications, and individuals' psychological hindrances. We soon learn that he is looking to address the obstacles for individuals *and* institutions. This book isn't aimed at any particular group as ISKCON isn't the only organization in the Gaudiya universe—or the religious world—that would benefit from correctives.

As we dive into the book, we find that he explores in candid detail, with insight and compassion, the complex topics that have troubled us, but he's added many more that were lurking at the periphery. It turns out that these ancillary issues, when unpacked, are not supplemental or superficial at all and offer critical insights into how to solve the issues that have long troubled us.

Maharaja hasn't simply named problems. He offers us possible solutions wrest from his soul through deep probing, experience, and introspection.

We may not agree with Padmanabha Swami on every issue, but we must admit that he has accurately identified, on an individual and institutional level, much of what ails us. I've never seen anything that comes close to succinctly, frankly laying out the challenges and possible solutions. On the whole, with this book we've been gifted a comprehensive examination of how to return Gaudiya spirituality to a lived mystical tradition, as intended by Sri Chaitanya Mahaprabhu.

A special feature of the book is how Padmanabha Swami has taken a deep dive into the approaches and contemplations of thinkers of other religious traditions, especially from the more mystical side of Christianity. Along with the insights he has gathered and shares with us, he has brought together quite a thorough examination of theory, common sense, wisdom, and *sastra* (revealed scripture). With *Radical Personalism* we have a considered blueprint for an emerging future for Gaudiya Vaishnavism that we can contemplate, enlarge upon, and apply. Individuals, leaders, and managers can all benefit from Padmanabha Swami's manifesto.

I thank Maharaja and commend him for his vision and for his courage to be vulnerable and publicly share his hopes, research, experience, and perspectives. *Radical Personalism* is a book about caring, penned by a person who cares deeply about people and the future of our tradition. I have been illumined by many of his insights, and even though I have been a *sadhaka* (practitioner) for nearly fifty years, I have found new ways, enlightened ways, to think about my relationship with Krishna and how to approach him.

Radical Personalism can clear muddled thinking; instill hope where it is absent; ignite enthusiasm and determination where apathy has taken hold; encourage honesty and dethrone duplicity; bring light where darkness prevails; inspire us to leave aside the pettiness, sectarianism, and fundamentalism that have gripped various Gaudiya groups in recent decades; and usher in a united and vibrant Gaudiya community devoid of the barriers that currently divide us.

As Padmanabha Swami's book softened my heart, I pray that it softens hearts everywhere. I hope we can lend an inquisitive, empathetic listening and grapple with this book humbly, honestly, and with eyes and heart wide open. We may find ourselves edified and enlarged and our *sadhana* surcharged.

Pranada dasi
(Pranada Comtois)

INTRODUCTION: Should I Stay or Should I Go?

IT WAS ANOTHER RAW DAY on a creative level, arguably one of the rawest during the end of 2022. Despite my witnessing a rich discussion about innovation amid paradox, my expressive skills as a writer remained somewhat paralyzed on that particular day. That's the price of authorship, especially transpersonal authorship, where one attempts to be a mere witness to *someone else* writing the piece through your own pen and heart. There I was, by myself and oozing with vulnerability while facing the unknown, the uncertainty, and the paradoxical that exists in each of us and *always* shows its reflection during creative junctures. There I was, on the frontier of something I couldn't fully comprehend, contending and struggling with a problem I was just beginning to puzzle out. Two short but endless months prior, my life had taken one of the most unexpected challenging turns I could have possibly ever imagined. It was now December 7th, 9:00 PM.

The first draft of this work had been started a few days before. I was relatively pleased with the five or six initial chapters written. However, the introduction had been relegated to the "Utterly Poor and Inadequate" folder. Not knowing what to do about this all-important yet missing piece of my work, before taking rest for the night I ventured into a few pages from a recently arrived book. This particular work had captured my attention, since its premise involved a Christian author who dared to ask the question of whether he should remain a Christian or not.[1] In its first two parts, he presents an elaborate list of points to justify either of these possibilities, which he then unpacks before concluding with a "how" section where he advises how to proceed, depending on the corresponding verdict. Since I was already pretty tired, I was only able to read the first few pages of it, but that was enough for something quite unpredictable to happen. In almost every example given in the author's list, I felt I could easily replace the word "Christian" with "Gaudiya Vaishnava" and make the whole book applicable to my own tradition. That was enough epiphany for one night. I had what I needed to resume this Introduction.

Before sharing the list that I wrote the following day, where I itemize potential reasons for staying or leaving my own tradition, I would like to clarify that this book is emphatically *not* about leaving Gaudiya Vaishnavism. It's about *living* and *loving* Gaudiya Vaishnavism. In other words, this manifesto known as *Radical Personalism* does not ultimately point to any leaving—either loudly or silently—but asks *how* to stay, a question we are invited to wrestle with for the rest of our lives.

This work is for those who already belong, but who wonder how to continue belonging—how to belong *deeply*. It's also meant for those who, although having attempted to fit into Gaudiya Vaishnavism, have not yet found a community or experiences that affirm their feelings of belonging. Thus, this book seeks to nourish potential "leavers" for reasons that actually could have been prevented—whether these are philosophical, social, institutional, emotional, or a mixture of many—while not attempting to use unsatisfactory arguments to force their staying. But to be utterly honest, the main concern of this work is those who remain fervent adherents of their tradition *but for the wrong reasons*. Through such a disjointed membership, these advocates can only make of their tradition something more and more at variance with what it was supposed to be, not only misrepresenting their own lineage but also justifying it with some of the most antithetical reasoning we could imagine. And all of us are one of them, at least potentially. And the result of this playing itself out? Havoc.

Though we want everyone to stay in their own respective traditions, we want them to stay there *only* for the right reasons. That's actual substantial belonging. Whatever goes against this principle can at best be regarded as "fitting in," but never as deep belonging.

Interestingly, the reasons some people leave Gaudiya Vaishnavism—whether as a movement, religious community, or personal path—are healthier than the reasons for which some people stay. Why? Because the reasons these two groups have may be exactly the same, but prompting one to desist and another to persist. For example, a sincere seeker may feel the need to take a distance from Gaudiya Vaishnavism due to having witnessed excessive conformity to the status quo for the sake of position and prestige, while another person may choose to stay exactly because of that. For this reason, this work will not only explore potential causes for leaving one's tradition, but will also try to understand why some members have chosen to continue their journey in this particular school, and how that choice can be informed in such a way that those practitioners continue to stay for the right reasons.

The mystical school of Gaudiya Vaishnavism, a monotheistic branch of devotional Vedanta, is an intricate marriage of diverse elements, and the reasons for one's leaving or staying may be closely tied to one or more of its manifold aspects: cultural, theological, institutional, historical, political, doctrinal, and social among many others. Having been myself deeply associated with each of these features for more than two decades, I ruminated on each of them, took some deep breaths, prayed deeply for a moment or two, and then finally formulated a quick list of reasons to stay and not to stay as a Gaudiya (some of them more related to one group of the tradition than others) as follows:

Why not to stay as a Gaudiya Vaishnava

- Lack of human sensibility and psychological balance.
- Tribal thinking, institutionalism, and various types of fundamentalism.
- Unaddressed abuse of different types.
- Deep cognitive rigidity and poor capacity for dynamic dialogue.

- Not enough appreciation for other mystical schools.
- Not enough appreciation for other forms of nonmystical knowledge.
- Chauvinism, institutional patriarchy, and other forms of discrimination.
- Disjointed relationship with matter, especially with one's physical body and its various needs.
- Toxic nostalgia for past achievements and unwillingness to deal with the modern world's paradigms.
- Over-idealized emphasis on proselytism.

Why stay as a Gaudiya Vaishnava

- The above ten reasons for not staying are not part of the actual Gaudiya doctrine, but rather the result of an immature understanding and application of it.
- Patience, gratitude, and compassion rule the day, despite all else.
- A noble ideal and lifestyle will nourish and accompany our progress.
- A unique level of theological depth and intricate descriptions of post-liberated life.
- The undeniable presence of both past and present saints who embody the essence of the tradition.
- The sweetness of relating to the Lord through the chanting of his holy name.
- Dedicated contribution of wonderful souls who are truly in love with the Gaudiya ideal.
- The maintenance of sacred pilgrimage sites around the world that give shelter and hope to many.
- The life, legacy, and gift of Sri Gaurahari, the founder and deity of the Gaudiya school.
- Holy and deep personal commitment experienced in the company of authentic kindred spirits.

This is my list, offered in the spirit of shared reflection. If you are so inclined, you are invited to write your own.

Needless to say, most of the above "no's" are not limited to the Gaudiya tradition or even restricted to other schools, but basically depict the unrefined psychology and social dynamics of the human race when not duly enlightened. However, we should not minimize those no's at the expense of the yes's, but we should learn to hold that tension so one informs the other in a sobering way. Therefore, I embrace those no's in the mood of acknowledgment and also in the context of embracing the yes's, since I personally choose to stay as a Gaudiya Vaishnava despite the no's, which merely portray the type of practitioner *I don't want to be.* The above list is thus not about whether we stay as Gaudiyas or not, but more accurately *how to stay as humans* while we remain as Gaudiyas. It is about *how to live,* since whether we stay in our tradition or leave it, we have to continue living our lives as humans—as humanly as possible.

I have come to recognize that if we want to have a balanced and healthy community and mentality, both points and counterpoints are required in our equation. Religion is serious stuff. Religion can kill. Religion can also obscure. At its best, religion can change *the* world. But only after it changes *our* world first.

Every religion holds a set of seeds with varying potential. These seeds, watered by the motivations of the leaders and practitioners of the tradition at any given point in history, can sprout into very diverse and even perverse venues—from transfigured mystical voices, to cults of irrelevance, to ruthless totalitarian regimes. As the form diverges from the substance, religion divorces from spirituality and even humanity, and exploitation replaces self-sacrifice. What was meant to be a vehicle of expression and attainment of the highest pursuit of humanity—uninterrupted and unmotivated love of God—becomes little more than weaponized mercy and sanctified hatred. In fact, as Blaise Pascal has said, "People never do evil so completely and cheerfully as when they do it from a religious conviction."[2] And none of this exists exclusively outside of the practitioners of the tradition—*outside of us.* Thus, personal accountability is a critical facet in the health and sustainability of our individual spiritual life, as well as in the trajectory of our tradition.

Spiritual life is, first and foremost, a participatory enterprise. In addition to its collective dimension, the notion of participation also, and significantly, hints at the necessity to actively invest our volition, something that only *we* have the power to offer. Once we have decided to participate, the vital question now facing us is to what degree do we participate? How much of ourselves do we dare to invest in order to make such a life our own and belong to it? In brief, this is what this book is exploring: how to continually actualize a full sense of belonging in relation to the embodiment of sacred infinity—a dynamic, ongoing, and perpetual project.

A FORESHADOWING OF THIS WORK

For almost the last twenty-five years, I have been a monastic practitioner of Gaudiya Vaishnavism. In my earlier days, I was initiated into the art of drinking wisdom from diverse mystical traditions, and through that nourishing exercise I quenched my thirst for truth and became gradually more acquainted not only with the glory and depth of these rich sources, but also with their contemporary shortcomings and necessities in our postmodern world. To my great surprise, not only did I find astonishing correspondences between these schools on a theological level, but I was also met with equally unexpected similarities in regard to how each of these communities, including mine, struggle to sail in their current times, witnessing their heroic attempts to update and upgrade their standing and remain relevant to, above all, themselves. It was the appreciation of such endeavors that foreshadowed this present offering in service to each of these faith traditions and each of its progressive members—whomever they may be and wherever they may roam—in honor of their most commendable contribution.

There is a thorough universality to the issues addressed in this work, issues that pervade not only most religious communities but human psychology in general. And although the focus of my presentation will be the Gaudiya school and its own unique circumstances, I will resort to a broader and more inclusive language with the hope of remaining relatable to other communities with similar dynamics. I am aware that this can be risky and one can end up relating to no one, but I'll take the risk not only for the above reasons, but also since I feel that Gaudiyas themselves need to relate to their own lingo from a renewed perspective. To further accomplish this goal, although I have also chosen to express myself throughout this book in gendered terms of both he/him/his and she/her/hers, staying consistent within individual paragraphs, it should be understood that such pronouns are interchangeable and are not meant to be in any way exclusive of other genders. In this spirit, I will also omit Sanskrit diacritics and, for the most part and unless absolutely necessary to make a specific point, I will be using universal ways of referring to God, such as "the Divine," "the Supreme Lord," "Ultimate Reality," and especially, "the Sweet Absolute."

While this work could aptly be tied to a series of lectures I started in 2022 under the name of *Radical Personalism,*[3] it could also be seen as a further unpacking of some of the implications presented in the introduction of my very first work, *Inherent or Inherited?* Its introduction is titled "A Story about Dialogue, Potential, and Integration of Complexity," and there I describe the present condition of my own tradition as,

> ... *in urgent need of conversation with itself as well as of ample room for freedom of theological thought, in order to transcend the cognitive rigidity and tribal thinking that so much characterizes the approach of the novice.*[4]

Also in that introduction, I delve into Paul Ricoeur's notion of a first and second naiveté. The first naiveté, or simplicity, is experienced by the novice. Out of an attempt to secure initial faith while still unable to discern the finer points of a tradition, the newcomer innocently resorts to varying degrees of sectarianism and zealotry as a way to gloss over the gaps in his or her understanding. If healthy development occurs, this first naiveté will give way to a maturity that allows for integration of apparent paradox and perplexities that were initially side-stepped. This process in turn invites the practitioner to a second naiveté, one born not from ignorance but rather from knowledge and the embrace of a more robust version of themselves as well as the tradition, leading them to consummate their life journey in a truly epic and authentic manner. And while my first book only ventures to explore one single layer of this complexity by contemplating the ontology of the soul in relation to divine love, in the present work I will try to extend my research to other related areas of concern, which are similarly required for us to "return home" with accomplished integrity—an integrity which can only come after due integration. In this way, it is this organic concatenation through which I've found myself stringing my first two works together and through that my whole existence, both of them inextricably informing one another.

The present work, being in itself a manifesto and therefore a living document which presents an original set of premises to be progressively unfolded in an ideal future, does not aspire to be a final word of any sort, but rather a simple contribution to a larger conversation that has gradually emerged in recent years and decades in the Gaudiya Vaishnava community—what we may call now "Emerging Gaudiya Vaishnavism." In connection to this dialogue, the mood of the narrative will be thus: each time I may refer to my own community, I will be simultaneously bearing in mind its individual members, and each time I suggest some refinement in any of its individual members, starting with myself, I will also be aiming at the Gaudiya community as a global entity. May both the Gaudiya community and its individual members—the broader family of Radical Personalists—accept this minor offering at their feet.

Swami Padmanabha

Part One
ORIENTING OUR APPROACH

Why Radical Personalism? 1

To be alive is good; to be more alive is better; to be always alive is best.

– Tao

Before the why of Radical Personalism, let us first go to the when to provide some context.

It all began last year, when 2022 was in its final month and a kindred spirit dared to coin this term in describing my poor self as a "radical personalist." I can tell you, I'm not such a thing. But since the very moment I heard the concept, I became somehow obsessed with its prospect and never-ending intimations—to the point of writing a whole book about it—while feeling irresistibly called to get as close as I can to such an ideal.

Although usually invoked while implying a negative connotation, the word *radical* also has its positive usage. This term comes from the Latin *radix*, which speaks about that which is connected to the root of something else. In other words, whatever is modified by the word *radical* will be that thing to its very core. In this case, the word that is qualified by *radical* is "personalism," which underscores the centrality of individualized existence as the locus and ultimate explanatory, ontological, and even theological principle of all reality.[1] Radical Personalism, then, is personalism to the root, to its very core. Let's further unfold this notion by way of a typical contrast found in the Hindu tradition.

One of the various expressions of Hinduism is popularly known as Advaita Vedanta, which in technical terms could be called Radical Nondualism. While the notion of Dualism portrays a divided reality which does not share a common existential ground, Nondualism proposes that existence shares an underlying unified foundation through which everything is related to its source. In the case of Radical Nondualism, this system conveys the idea that, ontologically, reality itself is actually devoid of any form of variety, personhood, and individual interactions, since according to the Advaitins ultimate truth is not only nondual, but nondual "to the very root"—*radically* nondual. Accordingly, it is no surprise that this radical form of nondualism has been described by many as impersonalism.

In contrast to this particular proposal, Hinduism also introduces us to an alternative pattern, another expression of Vedanta, which although nondual in nature is not impersonal. We can refer to these various schools (which are basically all monotheistic traditions) as Theistic Nondualism, or personalism. While these traditions' premise is also that ultimate reality is nondual in nature, they also contemplate the possibility of eternal individuality, loving interaction, and a diversity that does not compromise the intrinsic unity of the Absolute. Among its many theological expressions across the globe, I describe my own tradition not only as Theistic Nondualism, but more specifically as Radical Personalism.

A brief but necessary disclaimer is required at this point. By saying the above, I do not mean to imply that my tradition is objectively better or worse than any other tradition. While other schools may embody this same principle in their own way, Gaudiya Vaishnavism most comprehensively expresses my theological conception of Radical Personalism. Rather than denying our diversity in an attempt to gain unity, we can celebrate each other's specific perspectives. There is unitive value in a plurality of traditions sharing their unique angle of the same principle—mutual enrichment of each individual's understanding, nuanced in multiple ways by other's experiences. With this intent of mutual nourishment, let us share a few words about how Radical Personalism plays itself out theologically throughout the Gaudiya Vaishnava tradition and, from there, extends itself to each of its members.

As expressed through the lens of Gaudiya Vaishnavism, Radical Personalism is not merely related to the notion of upgrading our individuality as much as we can, but even to the acceptance that, in its ultimate expression, *everything,* and not merely everyone, *is* in fact a person. Not only "people," but planets, mountains, rivers, virtues, ideas—all of them have their personalized representation in their mutuality and foundational existence. A few classical examples of this principle can be found in the celebrated Franciscan notion of Brother Sun and Sister Moon, or in descriptions like the one found in *Srimad Bhagavatam* 10.13.53 where the time factor, karma, desire itself, and the three modes of material nature all adopt personal forms and worship the Sweet Absolute, or when great Gaudiya mystics like Raghunatha Dasa Goswami famously talked to his own mind as an individual person.[2] In other words, there is an every-one in every-thing; there is the possibility of meeting existence subject-to-subject, and therefore we could say that ultimately *reality is always a person.* This is another way of conceiving reality as radically—to its very core—personalistic, as Srila B. R. Sridhara Deva Goswami exquisitely described:

> *Whatever we may experience is conscious, and consciousness always indicates a person. In fact, consciousness and personality are the universal basis of reality. Therefore, the great sages address whatever they find within the environment as if they are all persons—they always take the personal perspective. What we perceive to be dead matter, they perceive to be conscious. With such a vision of reality, they used to address everything within this world as a person: the trees, the mountains, the Sun, the Moon, the ocean. Everything has a personal conception. In the background of what we can perceive with our dull senses, everything that is said to be matter, there must be a personal conception. Without the influence of a personal conception, consciousness cannot reach the stage of gross matter. From the personal conception things*

> *evolve to gross consciousness. It is all personal. Everything is conscious first—then there is matter. Everything has its representation in the original, personal, conscious, spiritual reality. Since everything is a unit of consciousness, everything has personal existence. In the background everything is a person.*[3]

Similarly, the Gaudiya appreciation of God's personhood in terms of Radical Personalism is even more complex, abundant, and comprehensive. Many volumes would be required to do justice to its perspective. Although this is neither the time nor the place to delve into such a specific ocean, the discussion at hand necessitates that we speak something of it as it points to the zenith of theistic Vedanta and offers a full expression of Radical Personalism. I feel comfortable with making such a bold statement because in the Gaudiya school we find an extremely detailed description of how the Sweet Absolute,[4] referred to as Sri Krishna, is as much a person as he can possibly be: a totally diversified supreme individual who becomes so engrossed in loving relationships with each of his devotees that he ends up being unaware of his own godhood, lost in a humanlike fabric known in Sanskrit as *lila*, divine play. This *lila* could be even more accurately depicted as *celebratory movement*, where the Sweet Absolute embraces divine oblivion and self-forgetfulness due to the weight and impact of divine love and, as a result of this, he perpetually acts, moves, and dances in celebration of his own inner overabundance.

It is in this passionate and enigmatic frenzy that God somehow transcends his own godhood, becoming all that he can be in love divine. This particular face of the Absolute has also been referred to as the Supreme Personality of Godhead. The Absolute here is not merely God the Supreme, but God exhibiting the supreme side of his personality at a particular moment in his eternal life. In Sanskrit, *prema* is one of the main terms for divine love, and *su* is a prefix intensify the meaning of a Sanskrit word. If you put the two of them together, you then have *su-prema*, or "excessive love"—a love *supreme*. Thus, we could say that something qualifies as supreme as long as it includes this abundance of affection. And since God himself is not willing to be an exception to this particular rule, the supreme side of his personality is what is the most affected by loving interaction.

If this is not yet enough of a dose of Radical Personalism, Gaudiya Vaishnavas entertain the possibility of going even a step beyond God's individual personality. The Sweet Absolute as Sri Krishna is never alone. He is classically depicted in the company of his greatest lover and female counterwhole, Sri Radha, who personifies God's own love potency interacting with his own self in divine play. Radha's love is so deep and ever-expanding that Krishna becomes haunted by the possibility of relishing an experience of himself from the vantage point of her love—to know himself through a new set of eyes and heart. And this in turn gives rise to yet another expression of his multiple faces, known as Gaurahari, an additional intricate layer in the theological constellation. Thus, if for the above reasons or any others there is a place to describe Sri Krishna (or even the dyad of Radha-Krishna) as the apex of Radical Personalism, we could rightfully say that Sri Gaurahari then constitutes the overflowing of that apex, the meta-climax of all specified experience or, in other words, the ultimate reach and expression of Radical Personalism in the form of God's very existence, life, and eternal unfolding.

Since the form of Gaurahari has all to do with Krishna tasting himself from the vantage point of Radhika (another name for Sri Radha), we can then further connect the notion of radical with the very person of Radhika. It is she who, to her very core and at her very root, is exclusively preoccupied with the highest peaks of divine love, a love which in itself is the very root of existence. She thus becomes the ultimate personification of that love to such a degree that God himself wants to fully relish her experience. In this way Radical Personalism can be another way of referring to and honoring the radical person Sri Radhika, her radical love, and how the Sweet Absolute himself desires to honor that love in his most radical form of Sri Gaurahari. At this highly theological zenith we thus find Radical Personalism exploding into Radhika's Personalism or, in other words, "Radhikal" Personalism.

Here is a simple daily example so we can further glimpse this complex theme. We are hardwired for connection, and we each see the world through the stories we tell ourselves. If we want to successfully connect with each other, rather than *project on* each other, we will have to learn each other's story. This is the very purpose of true dialogue—to step into the other person's story, to see how they see the world. And why is this true? Because this is true for God himself. His most complete connection—to the point of losing himself—was achieved when he stepped fully into the story of Sri Radhika. Again, "Radhikal" Personalism in the context of Radical Personalism. Accordingly, when Gaudiya Vaishnavas look at the evolution of theism in the Indian subcontinent, they clearly recognize a noticeable pattern which goes from nihilism to impersonalism, and from varieties of personalism to the ultimate converging point of Radical Personalism. In other words, they identify a pronounced unfolding from Buddha's nihilistic "zero" to Sankara's impersonal and monistic "one," and from Ramanuja's personal and qualified "one" to Madhva's metaphysical "two." Finally, according to Gaudiyas, this numeric progression explodes and finds its zenith in the 108 shades of Radical Personalism proposed and exposed by Sri Gaurahari through his own example and inner experience.

In order to actualize such an exalted ideal, Gaurahari inaugurated a method called *raganuga*, the following of divine passion. This entails a "walking after" in the service of those particular personalities who embody the specific ideal of divine love one longs to experience. This process can also be referred to as "the path of specificity," since so much of our own will and individuality is to be invested in this reciprocal love project, with considerable detail and nuanced expression of one's entire being—sacred passion having the potential of consuming it all. Given that Gaudiya Vaishnavism portrays an ultra-personal Deity, an extremely individualized ideal, and an intricately detailed methodology and conceptual orientation, a wide gamut of pressing questions naturally emerges: Where do the Gaudiyas stand today, both individually and collectively, in relation to the Radical Personalism they are expected to represent, embody, and long for? Are they—we—walking through the world as fully invested persons, vulnerable and courageous in our exchanges with each other and with our own inner selves? Or are there shades of impersonalism that color our vision and foster our embrace of personalism's antithesis? And in the name and guise of Radical Personalism, is the opposite actually creeping in like a noxious weed, mimicking a desirable plant, spiraling itself around the beneficial plant's stem while looking quite upright in its deceit?

For a Gaudiya Vaishnava, being a Radical Personalist entails not only the *holiness* of acknowledging and integrating our soul's potential in devotion, but also the *wholeness* of offering each facet of our humanity in the service of the soul's potential. That means our physical body and each of its functions, as well as our psychic dimensions, including our thoughts, emotions, and discernments. While conventional religiosity often leads to neglecting one or many of these facets, Radical Personalism attends to each of these dimensions like with any other sacred ritual. In fact, considering that every pore of our being is potentially offerable to God and thereby truly sacred and never profane, perhaps we have an even deeper challenge: How can we be all that we can be today—not tomorrow, but today—as living emblems of devotion, and then facilitate that epiphany in others? What are the fullest implications of being a person, and, even more so, what are the implications of *God* being a person? What is the highest prospect for these two uniquely personal beings when they relate to each other through love, the most personal of all fundamental interactions?

Although the Divine may still be a theological figure for most of us, he is actually a real person—the most real, the most personal, the most alive among all entities. In fact, he is the very source and shelter of all real-ness, personal-ness, and alive-ness. In our corresponding constitution we are also persons; therefore, we must be alive as well, and hopefully alive in every sense that this term allows. Consider for a moment what would be the state of being if the Sweet Absolute and each one of us were to accept the other in a mystical embrace through a hyper-personalized proposal such as Gaudiya Vaishnavism? The result of that could not be less than something alive in its maximum expression—a plentiful abundance of movement arising out of not only a school of thought, but a *living* school of thought, and not only thought but love's embrace. To meet the demands of Radical Personalism, to meet the necessities of reality itself, everything must be alive at this point—vibrant, ongoing, and in constant evolution.

As long as these dynamics cease to exist, the sacred Hindu scriptures will speak of us as "killers of the soul" and multitudes who are "dead, though alive," indicating that tragic moment in which inertia and evasiveness have taken hold of our trajectory. It is possible not only to neglect this principle of Radical Personalism, but also to dismiss it to such a degree that the depersonalized journey begs for a new identity symbol, that of a breathing corpse.

In this way, both for Gaudiya Vaishnavism and for any other tradition that feels a similar call, the real question remains: How can we be all that we can be, both individually and collectively? How can we make our doctrine and practice relevant, experiential, and relatable to ourselves? How can a living school of divine love remain beholden to its infinite potential and not fall prey to the comforts of calcified doctrines? Unable to endure any form of wasted potential, this work looks forward not to a Gaudiya Vaishnavism "As It Is" or even "As It Should Be," but actually "As All That It Can Always Be"—Gaudiya Vaishnavism as an *eternal becoming*.

Awkwardness & Gifts of My Present Situation 2

This being human is a guest house. Every morning a new arrival. A joy, a depression, a meanness, some momentary awareness comes as an unexpected visitor. Welcome and entertain them all! Even if they are a crowd of sorrows, who violently sweep your house empty of its furniture, still, treat each guest honorably. He may be clearing you out for some new delight. The dark thought, the shame, the malice. Meet them at the door laughing and invite them in. Be grateful for whatever comes. Because each has been sent as a guide from beyond.

– Rumi

IT IS SAID THAT GOD COMES disguised as one's life. In a few never-ending months, my own life as I knew it was no longer mine—God had come and taken it over. The most intense and unexpected visit of the Sweet Absolute basically deprived me of almost every aspect of my daily structure, ousting me from the very conception of who I was. Although my tradition teaches that one should honor uninvited guests *as if* they were God himself, it offers little in the way of protocol if God himself does show up on our doorstep. What to do? Let him in, of course. These are the moments for which we long. Yet there was little I could do but wonder and wait. "What will he bring in his agenda? How can I accommodate his plans?" I spent my time listening for answers to my questions, trying to remain open and receptive, to read the day as he intended.

The opening page of God's agenda, in ink that became more visible in time, read: "Nothing to lose ... but everything to gain." Alas, an invitation to the glorious tradition of being "a nothing"! At first glance we might think, " 'Nothing to lose' doesn't sound so bad. It even sounds easy." But as we look deeper, we can understand that to have nothing to lose implies that we have already lost everything, all of it—at least on one level.

Franciscans will refer to it as "poverty," Jesus as "the desert," and Buddhists as "emptiness." We Gaudiyas may invoke the Sanskrit term *akinchana*, which can mean both "devoid of everything" and "he whose only possession is God." When we are nothing—when we are empty—we are in a very special position to receive everything from above. This is confirmed by the Sweet Absolute himself, where he boldly declares in *Srimad Bhagavatam* 10.88.8 that if he wishes to especially favor someone he takes everything away from that person. So, there I found myself, empty and full at the same time, in the most unusual circumstance I could have ever anticipated.

From tip to toe, I was being invited to reframe, rethink, and recalibrate my whole life, since I was suddenly now uninvited from the spiritual family I had been a part of and served in for close to a decade.

The details of my saga would require a separate book, and because they do not serve this current work, I don't intend to go in that direction. What is pertinent to share, however, is that I was thrown into a complete tectonic shift. I was challenged by what was then the most awkward chapter of my life, but was soon to realize I was simultaneously being gifted the opportunity to look at my life and at life itself from an entirely different perspective. Only God is capable of offering such comprehensive paradox. Imagine looking through a pair of glasses with lenses capable of showing you not a whole new world, but rather the same world in a whole new way. That was my experience—a new prescription for sure. It was my turn to view from that (ad)vantage point, to contemplate in a new light not only my very existence, but others' as well, and the world in which I lived, specifically my own spiritual community within that world.

To begin with, one of the immediate epiphanies I experienced was that my personal situation presented not only a challenge for me to grow through, but for many others as well, including those witnessing its unfolding from quite a distance. My condition was in such a liminal state that most of those who viewed me from afar were not able to figure me out. One day I was considered a prim and proper respected member of the group, nicely holding the shape of others' aspirations; then suddenly I no longer fit into any of the classical boxes into which a Gaudiya Vaishnava is typically sorted. Others struggled with my unsettling condition when it became apparent that I was not in a rush to fit into one denomination or another: I was more concerned with *belonging* than with fitting in. While fitting in requires suspending and compromising your individuality in the context of conformity, true belonging embodies almost its exact opposite—it does not require you to *change* who you are, but it requires you to *be* who you *actually* are.

At least we should long to be who we are and all that we can be, and in that sense we should *be-long*. In other words, our belonging is defined by our longing, by who we long to be. As much as we become longing ourselves, then proportionately we belong in the most substantial way. *And this is not only a play of words.*

Perhaps even more bewildering for the long-distant observer was that I was not actively collecting materials to build a new box to crawl into for security and definition—not even a no-box box, or a temporary box that might require a future breaking and rebirth. Many could not understand why I was not nervous, or how I did not disintegrate and cease to exist. I did not feel compelled to "solve" my dilemma. But with conscious endeavor I entered into the mood of radical acceptance, trying to remain open to receive and discern the Lord's will. I encountered that the raw materials *found me* instead, synchronously showing up with perfect timing in the form of very specific situations, insights, and advice. In a way similar to how an artist's materials may speak for themselves, revealing their own value in relation to their source, a vessel expressing form out of chaos slowly emerged and informed my direction.

Of course, order and structure are basic needs for a healthy human psychology and even survival, but when those needs fuel an addictive pattern of subtle control that we resort to in order to avoid anxiety—labeling everything and everyone as soon as possible, including ourselves—then that order and structure become a template for abuse due to the very dynamics of control and manipulation. The underlying narrative of this archetype will say, "As long as I know where everything fits, I am still in control." But we should be aware that when someone does not fit within the confines of our mind-boxes, we are being invited to think outside of the box, to expand our ability to hold diversity, our skill to further accommodate reality and coexist with paradox. If this is not gradually accomplished, we run the communal risk of exclusionary tribalism to the point of ostracizing even ourselves, as well as the implosion of the very structure we sought to protect.

So there I was, challenged and challenging others, although not having any intention to do so, and witnessing yet another layer in the realm of human possibilities where we feel the urgent need to categorize one another and then perpetuate the process through further labeling, preconceiving, and judging in various ways—all of this in the name of relationships, even within spiritual relationships! But as Nietzsche wisely proclaimed, we are still human, all too human. And we actually *need to be*: if we dare not be fully human, we will still feel the need to be in control of situations in order to experience at least a shadow of actual relief while maintaining most of our relationships in a depersonalized zone. In interesting contrast, the ideal of *bhakti*, or devotion, is defined in my own tradition as *sarvopadhi-vinirmuktam*, being totally free from all temporary labels and, by extension, of all labeling. The latter is known in Sanskrit as *maya*, or illusion, which is portrayed in our tendency to measure—label—reality. This is in part the milieu I will try to address in this book, hoping to bring awareness of how, in the context of the notion of Radical Personalism, actual relationships can only exist through a generous investment of our time and energy—our very life—to bring forth their desired fruits in the form of authentic, sincere, and uniquely transparent interactions with one another.

Although uniquely personal, my microcosmic plight can operate like a finger pointing to the moon of a bigger collective framework: the macrocosmic stage where my own community, and most likely communities of others, stands at present, foreshadowing the transformation required to experience a brighter and more sustainable future. The needs of progress know when to knock on our door, and their timely entreaty should be acknowledged by all those who wish to remain in the coils of dynamism. Appreciating past glories and building upon them, without nostalgia, and accepting that what served a crucial purpose yesterday may no longer be effective today, is how to properly serve the past and not become a dead corpse entombed by it. *Today's perfection is tomorrow's imperfection.*

We may find that the very thing which nourished us at one point may suffocate us at another; what inspired our faith on day one may choke that same faith on day two, and therefore mercifully come to us in a different shape according to the necessity of the moment. We should learn to recognize that inspiration as the call of our faith in continual enfoldment according to our progress and, above all else, welcome such a dynamic process, leaving nostalgia for the past in the past. We need not worry about losing the life of a bygone era, because everything is here with us, always present in the now, but adopting a new and necessary shape—or maybe even begging for it. Since life only happens in the present moment, to be present in that present is a present unto itself, one that we can and should offer to ourselves and to everyone else.

The past several decades have witnessed all-too-common attempts to enter the domain of sophisticated theology and detailed descriptions of a whole world of ecstasy and its possibilities offered by the Gaudiya Vaishnava tradition, without first addressing how our understanding of the basics of the tradition plays out in our relationships with each other in our everyday lives. For instance, the very etymology of the word *ecstasy* implies the notion of "departing from the norm," yet how as a community do we deal with a person like me (but not only me) or situations like mine (but not only mine) that happen to be an exception to the rule? Do we know how to functionally respond to those cases which constitute a departure from the norm, in the sense that they do not fit the common boxes by which we deal with the typical Gaudiya scenario? Or conversely, are we expert in saying the proper words and taking the proper actions only when everything fits the demands of normalcy? What do we do when something remains outside of the box, but is still part of the Bigger Picture? To answer these inquiries, a new orientation may need to be put in place.

My main name is Padmanabha, which can refer to someone or something born from a lotus (*padma*), especially a particular lotus which is in itself born from a navel (*nabha*). As a lotus is born from mud but eventually rises above it, my present situation has arisen out of the navel-mud of crisis and uncertainty and seeks to rise above it in a lotuslike fashion, thus giving full justice to the name I once received and hope to still honor by navigating these uncharted chapters of the Lord's agenda. Therefore, it is from this present out-of-the-box vantage point of emptiness/fullness that I feel compelled to share both my awkwardness and its gifts, taking a look at my own tradition from the liminal angle of being an exception to the rule, and from there attempting to share some constructive criticism in service to my own lineage and, as odd as it may sound, hoping to renew my commitment to it through such an exercise.

3 Upgrading My Loyalty by Critiquing My Own Tradition

The prophet is not an outsider throwing rocks or an insider comfortably defending the status quo. Instead, the prophet lives precariously with two perspectives held tightly together. In this position, one is not ensconced safely inside, nor situated so far outside as to lose compassion or understanding. Prophets must hold these perspectives in a loving and necessary creative tension.

— Richard Rohr

As COUNTERINTUITIVE AS IT MAY SOUND, sensitive critique has the potential to embody one of the highest demonstrations of loyalty to the tradition one may be paradoxically targeting. As I've already explained, I write from the unusual—and you could even say privileged—position of not officially belonging to any particular spiritual institution yet remaining dedicated to the Gaudiya tradition. Using this as an advantage, I'm attempting to offer some healthy reassessments from an impartial perspective or, in other words, by remaining equally partial to every nook and corner of my own Gaudiya lineage. Abraham Lincoln once said, "He has a right to criticize who has a heart to help," and in this spirit, being one of its members, I feel the solemn call and duty to critique my own tradition, exactly because I fondly appreciate it and wish to remain one of its contributing constituents.

As with every other religion, the Gaudiya landscape presents us with many outstanding examples of genuine followers who were madly in love with their tradition, but who also criticized it considerably. Just take a minute to look at the different pictures on your Vaishnava altar. As you do, you'll realize how each one of them—including Gaurahari himself, the lineage's very Deity—were nonconformists to the core. However, critiquing one's own system is not a matter to take lightly. By reestablishing the very spirit of the ancient revealed law in novel but substantial ways, they stood in sharp tension with the climate of the times, while providing fresh insight about how to belong to the tradition in deeper and deeper ways. Actual belonging is not something we can negotiate with external forces, but is a force in itself—a flame—that we carry in our hearts. These spiritual revivalists loved their traditions greatly, worshiping the potential and scope their path provided. Therefore, they could not but oppose each element which prevented their lineage from becoming all that it could be. Most notably, as part of their "alternative orthodoxy,"[1] they shared their criticism while strongly embracing the very substance of their tradition. This is the art and gift of our predecessor teachers to all who are willing and able to learn from their example.

I strongly feel the need for such a gift of healthy critique to be expressed in our present times—abundantly. By the grace of such a gift, each of us will be able to praise our tradition in an unprecedented way: not only shouting "all glories!" as loudly as we can in regard to those who came before us, but also, and especially, reflecting on what needs to be done *today* to keep the ancient legacy of our guardians alive and well. Of course, we are to praise the exploits and contributions of our devotional heroes, but they expect much more from us than just that. They want us to ask ourselves what *they* would say and do today. And, perhaps to our dismay, we'll understand that we are the ones meant to express those things at present, to express what our guardians would like to say through us: one voice extending into the next one and continuing to sound to and through the next generation. In fact, this is what an actual *parampara*—lineage of succession—is all about.

Constructive criticism is to be offered in the spirit of gratitude and service, and in a manner that celebrates our legacy and its brilliant prospect. We're meant to sit down and reflect about those things that need to change and those that will flourish more fully in a vitally vibrant environment. Actual praise, as it has already been described, is expressed in a dynamic and fearless tone, devoid of sentimental nostalgia. Similarly, we should be very careful not to overestimate or over-glorify the present condition of our community as an evasive tactic to avoid dealing with whatever problems need to be addressed, because, in the cutting words of Srila Prabhupada, "If one is overestimated, glorification is just another form of blasphemy."[2]

Spiritual bypassing is a modern well-known term which refers to using one's spirituality to escape from facing unresolved issues on a personal, interpersonal, or systemic level. In the book *Spiritual Bypassing*, the author portrays it by expressing how "we'd usually much rather theorize about the frontiers of consciousness than actually going there, suppressing the fire rather than breathing it even more alive, espousing the ideal of unconditional love but not permitting love to show up in its more challenging, personal dimensions. To do so would be too hot, too scary, too out-of-control... but if we really want the light, we cannot afford to flee the heat."[3] A Gaudiya example of such bypassing could be the above-mentioned excessive praise, where we may end up extolling a saintly person in a hyperbolic way at the stake of downplaying other saints' contributions. Although in one sense we can never glorify the Lord's agents enough, in another sense we can over-glorify them, like a young child who brags about his father's "superpowers" in the schoolyard in order to avoid having to deal directly with his contemporary bullies. For the price of some external applause, we can enjoy the perks of our ancestor's contributions, living off of their legacy without responsibly dealing with the present realities of our heritage. In other words, it is possible to exploit past resources in order to remain in our comfort zone, and this in the name of sacred eulogy. However, this is mediocrity at its best, a complacency which rejoices in the glories of the past (an unbecoming attitude) while claiming extreme loyalty to it. For our sake and prospect as individuals and a collective, we are expected to exhibit a healthy degree of nonconformity against such deceitful artifice.

We are not proposing a radical change in the foundational teachings of our tradition, but rather a change of *the eyes* through which we conceive and understand those teachings. To the uninformed eye, these two—renegade modifications in the fundamental principles vs. necessary changes in how we understand them—may appear like twin siblings, while they are almost exact opposites. Thus, the role of authentic critique is to invoke reform in the service of ancient roots and tradition. In fact, while some may think that constructive criticism toward one's tradition is a clear sign of disloyalty—something evident through the number of prophets killed by members of their own lineage—one's criticism may come when one is actually exhibiting the most profound allegiance to the group. Because healthy critique is a constant need, it has to always be present in any life project, as a litmus test for sobriety and sustainability.

Love begins in the fight with imperfection, showing deep care and concern in addressing the things that those whom we love need to become aware of. In honestly reviewing and assessing, we can remain profoundly identified with the ideal of divine love and still be critical in a positive way, as a unique symptom of that very love. This is not the same as sheer anarchy or becoming a rebel without a cause. Rather, it's about identifying a cause that is remarkable enough to elicit rebelliousness for the sake of truth.

A healthy nonconformist is not righteous, angry, resentful, or interested in accusing others of being wrong (and through that proving oneself right). Such a person seeks a conversation where we dare to express, with love and concern, how certain things may not be accurate, up to date, or holding sufficient depth. And there is a very necessary place for that.

In summary, as Radical Personalists we are not to become outsiders who only know how to throw rocks and complain, nor should we be insiders who merely conform to everything because it is ancient. By this we mean to say we should be neither judgmental nor sentimental, but rather involved participants who are able to inhabit a place in between these two domains—remaining inside by our dedication to the central ideal, yet on the outside edge of that inside—where the membrane of the tradition remains permeable and alive to continual transformation, where ancient knowledge intersects with contemporary living practice. In other words, a real insider will turn from primitive insular zealotry to the *outside of his inside.* In so doing he will inform his perspectives and become qualified to critique his own tradition without hating it or leaving it, but offering his examen as a service and symbol of enhanced loyalty.

4 A Living School of Prophets: An Urgent Need for Proactive Revival

The author's thought must have progress in the reader in the shape of correction or development. He is the best critic, who can show the further development of an old thought; but a mere denouncer is the enemy of progress and consequently of Nature.

– Thakura Bhaktivinoda

THERE IS A PLACE FOR RADICAL PERSONALISM in whatever spiritual tradition one identifies with. The notion of Radical Personalism constitutes a profound commitment to, and partnership with, our distinct potential, bringing dynamic life to any tradition with which we have communion and infusing that "aliveness" with the blossoming of individuated potential within its communal body. The more a school of thought values and facilitates such unfolding potential, the more it offers itself as a living school of Radical Personalism.

To the extent that any member of such a living school actively longs for this "aliveness" and consciously embraces the ongoing challenges that arise from such a longing, then to that degree he or she embodies the life of a prophet. Therefore, any genuine mystical tradition holds the potential of being a living school of prophets. Some might think this is too bold of a claim, so let's clarify this idea further.

If we look at the etymology of the word *prophet*, we find that a prophet is essentially a spokesperson, or someone who speaks in the name of someone else. *Ideally*, the spokesperson is someone who speaks on *be-half* of the Sweet Absolute: her qualification is to be a part of—to "be-half" of—the Divine's own voice and its action upon the world. Thus, a prophet comes to be known as an inspired and committed participant in life, through whom the divine will flows unimpeded to the shore of everyone's heart. The definition of a prophet reminds us of a mystic, or someone who has transitioned from mere belief systems to actual inner experience. The shift from an external to an internal experience is the field of activity offered by mystical traditions. If we place ourselves within such a living school, called *sampradaya* in Sanskrit, then we are expected to enter that field of mystical experience and live the way of a prophet.

The prophet and the living tradition are inextricably intertwined, with one informing and forming the other. As any living being possesses particular symptoms that indicate life—dynamic growth, movement, creativeness, maturation, and ever-evolving patterns—so too does a living tradition. The prophet dutifully monitors the health of these symptoms of life within her tradition and acts in ways to hold and assure their continued vitality. And in the same way, she is watchful for signs that indicate the progression toward death: dismissal, stagnation, neglect, deterioration, or ultimate demise, and seeks to diagnose the disease within the collective body by identifying the cancers of insularity, sentimental nostalgia, philosophical misapplication, sectarianism, or passivity that may have metastasized within the body, or system, of the tradition. It is precisely the job of a prophet to shine a light on the insufficiency of the old order,[1] to deconstruct the system each time it malfunctions, and to lead us into a revitalized living sacred space that safeguards the present and future of her living school.

A prophet is expert at discerning what remains essential from what has become irrelevant. There is no need to modify eternal paradigms. That is, the soul will remain as it is, eternal, and Krishna will continue to be the Sweet Absolute for Gaudiyas. Instead, the necessity for progress points to those things that truly beg for upgrade and renovation. That said, the eternal condition of the Sweet Absolute is to become sweeter and sweeter every single moment, and thus we are invited to keep up with these unique dynamics of transcendence. In fact, that's basically what spiritual life is about—a continual becoming as the perfect antidote to avoid all that is unbecoming.

Although this book addresses relative necessities, such as updating the language we employ to convey ancient concepts in postmodern times, it mainly tries to encourage the development of a spirit willing to keep up with the pace of transcendence. Transcendence is unlimited, which means we're called to ever new horizons of understanding. We're to keep pace with an ever-evolving reality that we are part of, with an ever-evolving God we are tied to, and, thereby, with an ever-evolving tradition through which these very principles are revealed to us. Thus, the tradition needs to remain ever-evolving if it's to accurately represent an ever-evolving proposal such as (among other divine portals) Gaudiya Vaishnavism. As it has been beautifully put by Richard Rohr while addressing the Sweet Absolute, "You are infinite in action, which makes me infinite in becoming. This is my divine possibility."[2] Actual being is thus a process of becoming, and not a fixed state—an ongoing journey, never a destination.

In this way, the business of a prophet is to keep up with the pace of transcendence—a pace that is persistent, mysterious, uninterrupted, and *mostly* happening outside of the comfort zone. In such business, the "profit" of the prophet will always come from above, descending as divine grace, like the mythical *chataka* bird of the Vedas, whose life is sustained and exclusively dependent on a pouring which can only come from heaven. If we are to become prophets, then we are to drink—copiously—from this holy fountain of grace. The more we dare to drink, the more we become contributing members to our living school of prophets. While our Gaudiya notion of evolution may not be Darwinian in the full sense of the term, it will be compulsory to keep our own sense of evolutionary spirit in our practice and conception, especially considering the nature of the Absolute and its perpetual unfolding. As much as this evolutionary worldview consisting of "eternal becomings" is in place, we will be able to understand our own gifts and potential, and promote actual growth and transformation.

REPAIR, REORDER, AND RELIGIOUS DENIAL

The subtitle of this work is A Revival Manifesto for Proactive Devotion. Although a vibrant living school of prophets holds the potential for its members to fully embrace and embody Radical Personalism, it is possible to belong to such a school in name only, or to simply be a two-dimensional card-carrying member of the student body without actually being alive or prophetical at all. This peripheral involvement, whether defined by either apathy or naiveté, calls for a proactive revival, a repairing and reordering. There is a saying "evolve or die," and it refers to the inability to move beyond our current dysfunction because we must first address the structure that holds that dysfunction in place. If we do not do so, the worst atrocities won't be those committed in the present, but the future ones.

While the notion of revival clearly points to rejuvenating someone or bringing new life to something in the present moment, the temporal position of proactivism is also in the present moment but with an intimate connection to the future. It is an action in the now that is informed by an anticipation of future events or ways of being. Instead of responding to undesirable conditions *after* they have occurred, being proactive creates the potential of preventing various avoidable difficulties. An accurate example in this regard is that of a hurricane. Although typically considered an act of God, failure to prepare for it when the necessity for preparation is well-known could be seen as a form of sin. In fact, one part of being a prophet includes a *prophetic* side: not precisely in the form of omniscience and foreseeing the future in unnecessary oracular detail, but in developing enough sensitivity to foresee how our present dynamics may play themselves out unfavorably in the near future—and what is required in the immediate—so we can responsibly dispense with foreshadowed problems before they occur. Instead of mere reactive action which only knows how to respond to the past, deep proactive performance often rises from an urgent call for revival. The call grabs us and demands we act, regardless of the discomfort it may cause us or others. A prophet is someone who has the courage to answer this call, proclaim disaster before it manifests, and stand by her own words of alarm even in the face of condemnation.

Proactive devotion encourages this process by first advocating that we acknowledge whatever problem may need to be addressed. Then we try to understand the problem comprehensively, and *only then* do we try to solve it. We never rush to make a problem go away before exhaustively learning what it has to teach us within its various shades and nuances. Albert Einstein is reported to have said, "If I had an hour to solve a problem, I would spend fifty-five minutes thinking about the problem and five minutes thinking about solutions." He realized that the solution lies within the grasp of the problem, and that understanding the problem *solves* the problem almost in its totality. However, such understanding, especially of complex issues, may require considerable time from us, and we should be willing to embrace that holy investment and not hasten the process by spending less time than required to fully apprehend the solution within the problem.

Like many other schools, Gaudiya Vaishnavism is a living tradition. And any living tradition requires renewal, which involves a revaluation of what we deem normal and a further recalibration of it. Insanity has been famously defined as doing the same thing over and over while expecting different results. And while we surely want divine insanity (the ultimate summit of saintly euphoria offered in beatific service), to achieve that we first have to abandon the path to unwanted insanity. If we feel the need for different results, we then need to do things differently. What we need is a further re-cognition, learning to see and rediscover our own selves with new eyes (and everything else by extension) while letting go of unquestioned assumptions and daring to reexamine the depth and intention of our core beliefs. This can be terrifying for many reasons, one of them being the fact that we're looking at the unknown. This fear of the unknown applies not only to our darkest shadows and potential monstrosity but even to our brightest future and prospect as lovers of the Divine. Why? Because when something is unknown to us, beyond our normal everyday experience, it exists outside of our control. For one who has not embraced the mystery of divinity, such uncertainty either freezes our mobility, like a deer caught in headlights, or propels us off the road. Either way we often ineffectively seek to control the unknown by denying it.

Religious denial—denial in the name of religion—is arguably the most comprehensive way for evasiveness to soundly succeed as it cloaks itself in the guise of spirituality. We can stamp God's name wherever we want to justify or hide anything. From the most abominable crimes against humanity to the seemingly innocuous prejudices we have against those who are different from us, this array of hatred and illusion of elitism is somehow made "right" if the malevolent acts are carried out under the cover of God's name. In this way, religious denial becomes one of the most elegant and perfect façades to perpetually justify any falsehood. In fact, falsity itself relies upon denial and disguise. However, religious denial, although undeniably comprehensive, is not absolutely so. Eventually, denial itself becomes the elephant in the room and it keeps growing with the expansion of the false narrative—the story we tell ourselves to make sense of falsity. The more denial we invoke, the bigger the elephant becomes and is joined by other elephants until a whole herd has invaded the room! At such a point, louder voices, insistent voices ringing with truth, are required to be heard above the trumpeting of mad elephants. Otherwise, the emperor parading as if glorious will sit upon the throne, dressed only in his underwear and cloaked by false praise. Without these rising voices calling out the truth cloaked in religious denial, what we are trying to avoid will run us over. Why? Because the part of us that resists the transformation that is being called for is the very part that needs to be offered for the transformation to be complete. *What we resist will persist*—first in our individual experience, then gradually in our shared global history.

Proactivism begins with understanding that history tends to repeat itself. Proactivism is a preventive stance where we face the demands of life voluntarily and take full responsibility to look at those sectors where our ego would prefer to be blind. This ego could be defined as the unobserved self, and as long as it remains unobserved, entire religious communities can end up revolving around its camouflaged ideological bunkers without even a hint of the need to question their existence. As already mentioned, it is this religiousness that potentially presents the perfect stage for denying and hiding, layer after layer, of undigested generational trauma, unaddressed collective wounds, and a myriad of gross and subtle dysfunctionalities—all in the name of divine love. In order to disarm the unobserved self, we "simply" need to become aware of it and thereby render its effect on us impotent. Bringing unaddressed issues to light may be simple, but it is not easy; difficult, but never impossible. And it is the difficulty embraced by prophets who help us not only survive but thrive in our highest ideals.

THE FUTURE OF GAUDIYA VAISHNAVISM

In the concerned eyes of some, it has become increasingly obvious that the Gaudiya Vaishnava global family is missing the mark in considerable ways. While making huge progressive leaps in the past centuries through the contributions of numerous stalwarts, this beautiful tradition presently finds itself navigating very complex waters. The situation need not be attributed to any kind of fault; it may just be the way things have played out over time. Still, contemporary Vaishnavas are being called to enter the rising waters of present-day challenges and find their place there.

Before turning to the second part of this book, where an abundant list of these challenges will be presented, let us share one brief observation that encapsulates the present paradigm of Gaudiya Vaishnavism as a contemporary community not only in the West, but in a westernized East as well. Due to the cultural appropriation of the tradition and its recent transplanting in foreign soil, many of its nuances have been at least partially obscured, and out-and-out misunderstandings and confusions between principles and details have ended up riddling various conceptions of the Gaudiya philosophy. This has resulted in the propagation of misplaced values on a grand scale—a tricky landscape, to say the least. At this time of our distinctive developmental stage, it is the duty of those who have turned within—the "cartographers" of the tradition—to point out that the current map may no longer correspond to the present-day landscape. New roads and bridges remain obscured while others have been washed out or closed or lead to dead-ends. The very terrain itself has been pushed up, shifted, and opened due to the forces of time. In other words, it is incumbent upon those who by the grace of the Sweet Absolute are able to rise out of the box of "conformity for conformity's sake" to push the envelope of their tradition. They must do this not by some artificial or rational pushing or an egoic battle with power, but simply by the expansiveness of their own experiences in divinity, which naturally pushes them against the bounds of those previous structures that no longer nourish but suffocate the natural flow of faith. Without this vital air, there is no actual future to breathe into.

Unlike almost every other species, one of the defining features of the human mind is the capacity to think in terms of the future. However, many times we find that the future being spoken of is only in terms of judgment and apocalypse. This is not the best language to guide history forward or inspire us with purpose and direction. Therefore, the unique ability to inquire into what lies ahead must adopt a new shape and, through it, bring us to a very weighty question: *What is the future of Gaudiya Vaishnavism?*

At least some members of any tradition—its elders—should ponder this query daily and reply to it through their daily behavior and proactive action. In fact, we need to learn how to live and coexist—and even wrestle—with this question throughout our life in a way that it is not tormenting but electrifying and thrilling. This should be part of our vocation, called *anticipatory* Gaudiya Vaishnavism.[3]

However, to even pose the question appears dangerous and alarming for those who have invested their lives to assure that whatever is to come will look exactly like whatever has been. They don't want to change a single thing because what they liked in the past or hold dear in the present may not be there in the future.

This crucial question will also seem risky to those who reply with resigned complacency, excessive idealism, and regressive yearning for the past. These impair their vision and prevent them from seeing any present problem at all. And the most dangerous are those people who acknowledge a number of shortcomings but conclude that "somehow or other the Lord will harmonize everything." This idea is not much more than wishful thinking, and assures that nothing and no one will disturb the coziness of the comfort zone of those who think like this.

Of course, we can also reply to the above question by saying that our future as a community is absolutely irremediable and downright dreadful. This utter cynicism, born from an initial romanticized idealism, is the extreme apocalyptic counterpart of idealism. In fact, you will find no one more cynical than the disillusioned idealist. Nonetheless, this is still the other side of the same coin, flipping between normalized apathy and self-indulgence. This coin will not purchase real membership into a living school of prophets. It does not afford constructive critique, which has nothing to do with either throwing rocks from the outside or embracing the mediocrity from the so-called inside. With so many member-generated obstacles blocking an honest and fruitful exploration, how are we to approach the pivotal question about the future of our tradition?

A simple and sustainable approach is to begin by acknowledging that the future of Gaudiya Vaishnavism lies in our own hands, not in big institutions or megalithic managerial arrangements, nor in unimaginable miracles or enlightened *avataras*. While all these aspects may be there and even help us greatly, at the end of the day it is up to us to decide the only thing we are capable of deciding: how to offer our life in the service of our life-giving tradition. This is how any real journey begins, develops, and sustains itself. The tradition can flourish when there is a very remarkable mission in the mind of each of its members, coupled with their committed words living in their flesh, causing them to move. This proactive action implies a visionary revival, transformation, and constant adaptation according to the contours of our time and circumstances. This is not necessarily an organized religion, but a creative one. However, these processes always begin from a fully responsible individual, and from there, like from the locus of an explosion, expanding until it finally reaches the collective.

We call this Radical Personalism.

Holy Shift! | 5

A radical change must be affected in us if we really want a life worth living. This is the singular meaning of our ideal.

– Srila B. R. Sridhara Deva Goswami

SHIFTS HAPPEN. And whether we see it or not, shifts based on the refinement of conceptualized truths in service to the highest good are always holy without exception, even if they create temporary mass chaos in our otherwise well-ordered life: Holy Shift! But why are such shifts necessarily holy? Because by definition whatever entices us to embody the best version of ourselves must invite a novel paradigm to be incorporated so that our present constellation of paradigms becomes actualized and therefore holier.

The notion of paradigm refers to a framework or worldview that organizes concepts through which we interface with the world. It is our conceptual framework that brings order to chaos by giving each new thing we encounter, or more precisely each new idea of something we encounter, its perfect place in relation to all of the other ideas we have already ordered. It is a living multidimensional model of what we believe to be true, with every entry hyperlinked to every other entry in a sophisticated relational network that informs our behavior.

Because we are continually bombarded with new bits of information, our paradigm is constantly receiving micro-updates that go unnoticed. However, some ideas we encounter through experience or hearing challenge the very core of our foundational order, our sense of self, and the world around us and within us. To integrate these updates into our conceptual framework requires a substantial shift—a paradigm shift—or, in other words, a "reframe-work," a laboring of love to rethink and realign our present cosmovision. For those fully participating in a living school of prophets where the subject of study is Infinity itself, such major shifts are continuously called for and consciously welcomed, fluidly releasing old understandings in the face of new revelation.

Because paradigms are built upon past experiences and impressions, reluctance to acknowledge a present necessity to update our conceptual framework—unrealistically dismissing a call to accommodate a new encounter with truth—tethers us to the past alone, resulting in stagnation and decline. If we become more attached to the stability of our present paradigm than to embracing the truth, then every time we encounter something that does not fit our paradigm (even though we know that "something" to be true), instead of modifying our conceptual framework and all of the subsequent dependent changes, we will "adjust" that piece of truth until it fits and reinforces our belief system. However, such adjustment is tantamount to untruth, since it prompts us to live outside our true and authentic values. What happens instead is that we begin to live a lie—and to believe it.

As already explained, spiritual participation is not about fitting in or making things fit, but rather it is about *belonging*. Paradigm shifts are required to destroy outdated templates to accommodate growth. We ought to welcome them. And interestingly, Thomas Kuhn, the main person who popularized the notion of paradigm shift, has mentioned how these shifts have little to do with logic or even evidence, but with cataclysmic insight and breakthrough. Kuhn further added that these holy shifts become necessary when the plausibility structure of the previous paradigm becomes so full of holes that a complete overhaul, which once looked utterly threatening, now appears as a lifeline.[1] However, if we insist on avoiding these holy shifts and instead attempt to understand even new things in the same old-patterned way, nothing new will ever happen: a new idea held by the old self is never a really new idea, whereas even an old idea held by a new self will soon become fresh and refreshing.[2]

These holy periods imply reorganization, transfiguration, and remodeling, all of which set the perfect stage for the descent of epiphany. In the classic *Bhagavad-gita*, the saintly warrior Arjuna embraces a drastic paradigm shift while having to face his dearest relatives during an unavoidable battle. We can view Arjuna's situation as one that personifies our own dilemmas as we face our greatest attachments. Similarly, the virtuous King Parikshit was unjustly cursed to die in seven days, but he entered the wilderness and embraced the "curse" with a transformed mind. In Christianity, Jesus basically inaugurated his ministry through what is termed *metanoia*, which means "to change one's mind." *Metanoia* is deeply connected with the Sanskrit term *mantra*, which means to transcend your mind by *changing* your mind, i.e., by moving beyond duality and oppositional thinking and from that viewpoint employing your mind differently. Thus, a new way of thinking about the meaning and purpose of our life is the starting point from which all of our service will unfold. Are we willing to rearrange and embrace a whole new set of thoughts, new paradigms and holy shifts that will invite empowerment to our potential being? Since any community develops through the development of the individual, are we ready as a community to embark upon such a holy journey and change our angle of vision? Or do we just push for global transformation while not being willing to change as individuals?

SAMBANDHA: LEARN THE CONCEPT BUT ALSO HOW TO CONCEIVE IT

Another Sanskrit term that is fascinating to consider in relation to "paradigm" is *sambandha*, which is generally translated as "relationship." Etymologically, this word refers to that knowledge which shows how everything in reality (*sam*) is connected (*bandha*) with its source on a nondual foundation—relationship. In fact, one way in which Gaudiya Vaishnavism refers to the Sweet Absolute is as *mukhya-sambandha*, he with whom everyone and everything has a primary relationship. This is confirmed in *Srimad Bhagavatam* 10.85.4, which declares, "Whatever comes into existence, however and whenever it does so, is created within you [God], by you, from you, for you, and in relation to you." In other words, we don't have to create the relationship, but rather find its healthy expression while avoiding misappropriation. In fact, the very notion of *maya*, or illusion, basically refers to living one's life unaware of this intrinsic relationship that *sambandha* speaks about. This is clearly established by the Supreme Lord himself, when he says to Brahma, "Whatever appears to be of any value, if it is without relation to me, has no reality. Know it as my illusory energy."[3] We are not only relational, but we are relationship ourselves. We are not an independent substance: we exist only in relationship. The same applies to the Sweet Absolute, who is the very personification of absolute relatedness. Therefore, our ultimate salvation could be described as the readiness, capacity, and willingness to stay in relationship—that very thing that both we and God are.[4]

This knowledge is the progressive self-manifestation of God's own inner potency (*svarupa-shakti*), and thus cannot be pursued, wrestled with, and captured but rather humbly received, embraced, and followed. That said, *sambandha* refers not only to receiving such knowledge but, more specifically, to the "how's" of such reception. *How* do we conceive the concepts handed down to us; *how* do we relate one concept to another; *how* do we relate ourselves to each concept? Thus, *sambandha* is not about what to think, but *how* to think about what we think—how to constantly remain in fluid adaptation to those things which inform our inner pilgrimage. This Gaudiya notion is perfectly in line with the first step in Buddha's Noble Eightfold Path: right perspective. If a genuine view of things is in proper place, everything will follow accordingly.

Sambandha is not the type of knowledge that bears absolute certainty and proudly leads us to think that now that we have it within our grasp, we own it and know it perfectly and completely. In fact, it's not about *possessing* accumulated knowledge at all, but rather reflecting and ruminating on it, and then knowing what to do with it. It is about not only becoming expert in the practical application of knowledge but also being thoroughly contemplative of it in our initial approach, deriving a rich and well-integrated conception. An everyday example is that in order to be nourished by the food we eat, it is essential to begin the entire process of digestion by *thoroughly* chewing our food. Thorough chewing not only breaks down food into smaller particles, facilitating assimilation and integration of nutrients, but also gives rise to a relish of flavors that satisfies our hunger. This keeps the system happily running and provides energy to fuel actions in pursuit of our goals. In a similar way, *sambandha*, a thorough ruminating, or reflecting on knowledge, gives rise to an irresistible taste that naturally fuels a devotional enacting, or *abhidheya*.

From proper hearing, conceiving, and assimilating one's *sambandha*, then one is inspired to act accordingly; *abhidheya* is that corresponding activity. Since *sambandha* constitutes the essential knowledge of how everything exists in relationship, *abhidheya* therefore constitutes a whole lifestyle that substantiates this principle in full-range motion. Finally, what follows *abhidheya* is *prayojana*, the fullest blossom of the initial *sambandha* and the ultimate fruit and unavoidable result of the previous sequence—perfect divine love. *Prayojana* is nothing but the final consummate integration and expression of all that *sambandha* implies and *abhidheya* embodies. In this way, both *abhidheya* and *prayojana* can be seen as speaking about *sambandha* and its implications. They highlight the essential and initial art of properly *conceiving the concept*.

In part, the spirit of *sambandha* involves being simple but not simplistic. Endless layers of prejudice, cultural baggage, ego filters, dualism, and other ingredients are also part of this complex recipe, and we need to detect each of them as part of our cooking process. When we understand the need to integrate each of these elements into upgraded versions of themselves, we can be delivered from all forms of rawness and become worthy of being offered on life's sacred altar. And, needless to say, a daily and healthy voluntary immolation on that sacrificial altar is always preferable to burning ourselves down to bedrock, often against our wishes, every twenty years or so. That fire of sacrifice is the center around which life fully revolves. At the very beginning of creation, when Brahma was welcomed as its first manifest being, he heard the Sanskrit sound *tapa*, which means fire, inward heat, or, by implication, introspection and upgrade. This inaugural example set the whole model for whoever was to come after Brahma—every one of us.

When we talk about a collective "upgrade" or paradigm shift, we are not speaking about rewriting the wisdom of the ages, altering the eternal principles of religion, or inventing new theological fantasies. Nor are we proposing that this shift *should* be one-size-fits-all advice for everyone, at least not necessarily on the same level, at the same depth, or with the same shape. In fact, if a reframing mandates that each individual should conform to it, then how different is that from any other expression of dictatorship?

The repackaging of external force is still external force. That kind of shift would be as much of an imposition as any system that promotes absolute power over another. Radical Personalism facilitates freedom for personal inspired participation in the spiritual journey by emphasizing how *we ourselves* relate internally to the concepts presented externally—how we process our own ideals. It is not about changing our metaphysics—what we know as real—but about our epistemology, or *how we know what we think we know.*

STARTING A MOVEMENT—AN INTERNAL ONE

As mentioned in the previous chapter, Gaudiya Vaishnavism, among many other mystical traditions, could be regarded as a living school of prophets. And just as life comes from life, a living school comes from a living heart as an organic and mystical overflowing that serves as the sufficient and necessary cause of kickstarting a movement.

It is in this way that Sri Gaurahari inaugurated Gaudiya Vaishnavism as a movement, not as an institution—not even as a religion! With his inner heart deeply *moved* by volcanic ecstasy, he could no longer sit in quiet meditation but had to *move* in yet another form—dancing and singing. He *moved* masses of mesmerized followers to walk and dance behind him. As Gaurahari's inner movement gave rise to an external one, and an ontology formed around his Radical Personalism, similarly, something has to be moving inside of our hearts. It is there that the headquarters of the Gaudiya *sampradaya* resides, and there that we'll find the actual movement we need to embrace as ours. By definition *every movement has to be moving for it to remain an actual movement.* And through that very motion it may—it should—in time shed its own skin to accommodate a noble and ongoing evolution as it aims toward wholeness, sensitive humanness, mature relationships, and regenerative and sustainable ways of conceiving our own practice as crucial aspects of our daily endeavors.

This is the movement proposed by Radical Personalism, upon which the Gaudiya *sampradaya* is founded—the inevitable shifts in paradigm necessary for us to become better participants in this movement, which, again, is always an internal one. It is not a world-conquering movement that seeks to expand membership in terms of quantity at the cost of quality. In a more accurate sense, it is a *non-group group*—a group beyond groupism—where those "two or three" gathered in deeper truth have the potential to create a whole new level of affiliation—of real belonging.

Our hope does not lie in buildings, or in the staff required to maintain them, but rather *in the transformed lives of people,* and it is on that that we can build on. In the Gaudiya school, these prophets are called *saragrahi* Vaishnavas, or essence-seekers. And it is only through such people and through such movement, a movement ignited in the hearts of such people, that we will be able to provide a gateway to the heart of the gift of our own tradition, for ourselves as well as others. In this way, if we want the movement to grow, then our hearts have to grow. The more our hearts grow, the more the movement grows.

The Collective Unconscious of Our Spiritual Lineage | 6

The most obvious, ubiquitous, important realities are often the ones hardest to see and talk about.

– David Foster Wallace

IF WE HAD TO CHOOSE one single outstanding contribution that modern psychology has given to the world, probably that would be the idea of the unconscious. A comparable version of it is found in the Hindu scripture's yogic term *chitta*, which refers to that invisible storehouse where unlimited acquired impressions (*samskaras*) lie and inform most of our present movements. The notion of the unconscious is not limited to the individual but also has its collective expression, as it has been famously delineated by Carl G. Jung: the collective unconscious is that part of the subconscious mind derived from ancestral memory and experience and common to all humankind. In the context of this book, it is common to all members of a particular tradition. Thus, not only do the individual members of a spiritual lineage possess these two types of unconscious, but the very lineage to which they belong is also possessed of them. To be more precise, despite being founded by divine personalities, the institutions that represent a particular lineage are not purely spiritual in themselves, and therefore need to promote a healthy acknowledgment of the shadows of its members. If this is not the case, this dismissed individual shadow will gradually become a collective one. Thus, part of our duty as followers of our tradition is to heal not only our microcosmic psyche and subconscious mind, but that of our macrocosmic tradition as well. Family therapy may now be in order for our Gaudiya community—the salvation of deep healing. Thus, if you were a therapist yourself and Gaudiya Vaishnavism your patient, how would you diagnose its present condition?

For those who are unsettled by the mere idea of a collective unconscious because it is not explicitly present in their tradition's revelation, please consider that referring to other spiritual traditions—or even secular fields of research—which discuss premises not found in one's own school is not necessarily a form of heresy. In fact, although appalling as it may sound to some, we might even *need* to learn from them. In most cases, contemporary findings in areas like science, sociology, history, and especially psychology have tremendous potential to enrich our spiritual practice by helping us understand the world we are living in, and acknowledge, heal, and deal with our own inner topography. We stand to benefit from these disciplines directly, and we also benefit by recognizing how our ancient wisdom traditions can be explained to others—and even understood better ourselves—in the context and through the language of contemporary science and human developments, keeping the ancient relatable and relevant, rather than distant and archaic. To choose not to do so and thus remain aloof from these important disciplines will be nothing but culpable chosen ignorance.

Here, psychology has been especially highlighted above the other disciplines because in all likelihood the most profound psychotherapy will be essentially spiritual, and the deepest spiritual quest will always include some depth psychology. Among other proposals, this important discipline, which has somehow become the new "handmaid of theology," invites any modern spiritual lineage to engage in both individual and, let's say, family therapy, confronting its subconscious to reach a necessary new level of harmony. In this connection, questions arise, with the core focus being: What is it that lies just out of sight in both the individual and collective unconscious of Gaudiya Vaishnavism? What is hidden in its invisible "storage shed," unobserved and swept under the rug perhaps for generations? Once having asked these questions, we cannot un-ask them without being irresponsible. And as Gaudiyas, we especially are called to frame, name, and ask these questions, since Sri Gaurahari, our very Deity and emblem of devotion, began his only written legacy with the word *cheto*, another way of referring to *chitta*, which in itself indicates the unconscious.

From Carl Jung's paradigm of the unconscious came another impressive contribution, the concept of the shadow self. Jung taught that in addition to the aspects that we recognize, accept, and share with the world as our self, both individually and collectively, we also have thoughts and tendencies, fears, and negative emotions that we are ashamed of and feel guilty about, qualities or behaviors that don't correspond to our conceived idealized sense of self. Rather than acknowledge their existence and deal with them consciously, we deny them and press these weird aspects of ourselves that don't fit into who and what we think we are down into our subconscious, where they live quite robustly as the shadows, secretly influencing many of our reactions to perceived threats. If these parts of ourselves remain unaddressed and continually denied, they won't become less active but will continue to insidiously and invisibly inform our movements, whether we know it or not, like it or not.

Concerning how to deal with these unseen forces, Jung invoked the term "shadow work," which is connected to the Gaudiya notion of *anartha-nivritti*. *Anartha-nivritti* involves not only the purification of one's heart, as commonly understood, but also an *awareness* of all obstacles, both conscious and unconscious, that need to be ascertained for the process of purification to be enacted. In other words, *anartha-nivritti* is not merely a stage to pass through or a byproduct of spiritual practice, but rather the *willingness to be aware* of those particular forces that are getting in the way of our practice at whatever stage we as individuals or a community may be. In relation to community, Thakura Bhaktivinoda said that "Those who have been entrusted with the responsibility of being spiritual teachers in the Gaudiya *sampradaya* should try to remove all *anarthas* from their *sampradaya*."[1] Without awareness of obstacles and the shadow work which aims to bring them into the light, and without a clear understanding of the influence of the unconscious to begin with, many of us can easily fall prey to different forms of spiritual bypassing by employing divine concepts to avoid facing pending emotional issues, psychic wounds, and unfinished developmental tasks, thus engaging in *shallow* work instead of shadow work. This possibility was highlighted by Sri Gaurahari himself, who described the spiritual practice as watering the creeper of love, but he also spoke of *anartha-nivritti* in terms of pulling out (*nivritti*) the weeds (*anarthas*) around that creeper. If weeds are not pulled out, they will be watered along with the main creeper, killing the plant in the name of nourishing it. Similarly, if we continue practicing spirituality without being aware of the *anarthas* that need to be pulled out—if we continue without shadow work—our very practice may end up becoming the perfect disguise to increase our *anarthas*. Conversely, shadow work attempts to create the best possible version of ourselves by owning and integrating our shadow as part of our personality. Therefore this process becomes a crucial aspect of our life and practice, since only by completely embracing who we are, including our shadow as individuals as well as a community, there will be no limit to all that we can accomplish.

However, one of the most terrifying adventures to embark upon is that of accepting oneself completely. This shadow work can be particularly scary for any captive soul, since it implies exposing the real enemy—our ego, or false sense of self. In order for the ego to survive, it needs to be in charge and remain in control, and therefore it detests any kind of change or remodeling that could create chaos and undermine its power. By itself, the awareness of one's own shadow is usually enough to keep most people absorbed in a ceaseless guilt trip, whether toward themselves or imaginary outskirt rivals. In fact, for the shadow to be what it is, it must by definition be that part of ourselves we are thoroughly ashamed of.

Unfortunately, rather than teaching their community to realistically confront and integrate the shadow, many spiritual traditions have historically denied it. Some of them have told us to attack those things we are ashamed of, or to hide them, or to confess them. But whatever may be the case, if our shadow is not integrated but *deni-*

grated, it remains an operative and powerfully influencing feature in our daily lives. In fact, one of the biggest impediments to spiritual growth is that we do not perceive our own hidden motivations. Thus, if a tradition ends up officially extending such a massive pattern of denial to every member of its community, we should not be surprised if the global entity that a tradition embodies has also massively grown its own unseen shadow and unconscious. Every time an inner situation is not made conscious, *it appears in the world as an event.*

But how are we to integrate our subconscious and become actual shadow workers? Our soul searching should begin by admitting the shadow's very existence in our lives and community. With the same special attention one would employ to locate a hidden treasure, we should focus on the search for our shadow. This is an essential aspect of our spiritual path and never separate from its pursuit. Also, another effective way to tease out the face of our individual and communal shadow is to notice our emotional reactions to other people, groups, or opinions in general, but especially to those that differ from our own tribe narrative. Gossip, or talking about other people's shadow, is a typical way the shadow expresses itself—not talking to others, but *about* others. It is also recommended to pay close attention to our *inner talk* by listening to the shadow's invisible voice and proposals (yes, not only crazy people talk to themselves!). In this way, by gradually confronting and becoming acquainted with our shadow, rather than suppressing or denying it, we will be able to recognize which patterns require healing. After successful healing, we are invited to integrate the now healthy patterns into our own personality, both as individuals and as a group.

However, before dealing with our unconscious shadow we should first deal with those issues that we are conscious of but still willingly ignore. By first addressing our conscious dimension, we will make "further space" for the unconscious to naturally come to the front of our awareness, being further revealed by God's grace so we can do our part in this heroic task. In this way, only after properly attending to our conscious dimension, we will be able to delve into our subconscious with courage and integrity—first consciousness, then the unconscious. Another popular name for Gaudiya Vaishnavism is Krishna consciousness. This is a telling term that could be taken as implying that we cannot generally become fully Krishna conscious unless we are simultaneously willing to also become conscious of ourselves, which includes becoming conscious of our unconscious. As much as we engage in this exercise, we can point to Krishna consciousness in a sustainable and supported way. Without dealing with our conscious and unconscious dimensions, we can have only Krishna unconsciousness at best.

So how conscious are we of our unconscious? Do we even acknowledge its existence and influence? How much have we avoided facing the details of our own human history as a community? How willing are we to actually recognize our wounded side as a family, our brokenness as a tradition (not inherently in its essence, but in its history)? How successful have we been in withdrawing the projection of our own shadow onto others? How much do we hide our collective shadow in excessive praise of our tradition's past and present glories, diminishing the potency of those glories to mere tranquilizers? Each time we choose the easy way out, the feigned unconscious way out, avoiding the potential and expressed darkness of our selves or our tradition, we attempt to manipulate reality by peddling the fantasy of deceit as if it were truth, and we miss the mark of being a full and wholehearted honest participant in life. This kind of avoidance, living the "life lie," is basically a sin of omission, by which we let something bad happen or continue to happen that we could have prevented or ended but chose to ignore instead. Turning a blind eye does not alleviate our involvement, it simply obscures it, at least in the immediate future. It is commonly assumed that a sin of commission—when you do something you know to be wrong—is more serious than one of omission, of avoidance. But is that actually the case?

Radical Personalism is about humanizing our existence to its very core, holding ourselves accountable in connection to others as well as in relation to larger groups around us. Considering this, the inseparability of our own healing journey becomes apparent and more necessary than ever. In fact, different social-system theories propose that any grouping of people is more than the sum of its parts. It is a system with its own life, an entity in many ways like a person, with a group mind, or *egregore*, which represents a nonphysical entity that arises from the collective thoughts of a distinct group of people. With this idea in mind, let's apply the basic tenets of Radical Personalism and for a moment conceive of the current Gaudiya community as an entity unto itself, with its own personality, needs, and unconscious shadow. As we would treat ourselves with kindness in regard to acknowledging and addressing our individual accumulated and unresolved trauma, we also need to be compassionate and loving as we ask the same question to the personified version of our tradition: Which traumas from the past have not yet been fully admitted and resolved, but rather remain deeply hidden in the unconscious of our spiritual lineage, secretly influencing its present and future shape? Please take all the time you need to seriously consider this question. Bear in mind that trauma constitutes a psychic wound that hardens us psychologically and then interferes with our ability to grow and develop. Trauma is not precisely what happens to us, but what happens *inside of us* as a result of what happened to us.[2]

EMBRACING OUR WOUNDS SO THEY DON'T EMBRACE OUR NEXT GENERATION

Unearthing our collective unconscious as a lineage is not an easy undertaking, and for those engaged in such a sacred exercise, it may closely resemble the burning pain of childbirth. While resilience is a must for every individual, for us to be strong enough to recover from the past we must first allow the past to happen to us—in us—by acknowledging it comprehensively. Only then can we know what we need to recover from. And as excruciating as this process may be, we should have hope and courage. We can remind ourselves how failure and suffering are both to be considered the great equalizers and levelers among humans, while success is generally the opposite. As a matter of fact, entire committed communities can form around suffering much more readily than around the idea of how wonderful or superior we are.[3] As Nietzsche said, "The discipline of suffering, of great suffering—do you not know that only this discipline has created all enhancements of man so far?"[4]

Transformational conflict is a secular notion whose main idea is that any form of crisis is but a veiled opportunity to redefine or reestablish a higher standard of relationship for all involved. In fact, the very etymology of *crisis* indicates to a "decisive turning point." Of course, before this can happen, we must first acknowledge the crisis itself, as painful as that may be, and learn to mourn the loss and weep for the pain of that before we try to resolve it. Those tears will not go unnoticed. In fact, this weeping is the exact middle point between blaming and denying, where we can make use of our wounds to redeem ourselves, as well as others around us, instead of weaponizing our pain through various tones of victim consciousness. Thus, we should learn to embrace the wound, and then sit and cry for it as part of our healing process—*the way to healing is through the wound.* Veritably, as Gaudiyas, we belong to what may be called a "tradition of tears" or, more accurately, a "crying school," where we learn through the process of devotional experience to attain the final goal of being able to sit and cry in divine separation from our beloved Lord. But without this first ocean of tears accounting for both our individual and collective wounds, we cannot actualize the potential held within the healing process to cross the developmental divide and gain full access to the next stage of spiritual possibilities that awaits us as a community in the progress of grace. It is not that we need to heal our jagged wounds, stitched over and seemingly made whole as soon as possible, but rather *our wounds create the process through which we will be healed*—and they will heal us for *as long as it takes*. And when that has happened, we will then be able—as counterintuitive as it may sound—to laugh over our brokenness and weep over our beauty as potential lovers of the Divine.

Although some prefer to conceive of our lineage in terms of what they may call "the language of ascent," a process of ascending and transcending while leaving behind the so-called mundane, the need and invitation of the present-day zeitgeist is written in a different dialect—the language of descent. While the former basically implies meritocracy and the earning of deserved rewards through personal ascent, the latter speaks about willingly, and with full trust, entering—descending—into the dark regions of our consciousness, and exponentially growing from there. As we will explore throughout this manifesto, such growth implies learning to coexist with uncertainty, paradox, and unknowing, all the while trusting the Sweet Absolute's permanent presence in our life. In other words, before heading toward the higher stages of spiritual pursuit, we should begin to journey downward. We shouldn't rush into the domain of (imagined) sheer ecstasy without first doing the hard work of confronting our unconscious motivations and purifying and unifying the foundational levels of our consciousness, thus providing ourselves the fortitude and wisdom to make more tangible the journey into yet higher stages.[5]

If we as a community avoid transfiguring our sorrow, the reshaping of it into an integrated and more mature version of itself, we may end up transmitting those undigested heartaches not only to our immediate peers, but in particular to our next generation. The duty of the present generation is to allow the future generations to deal with their own traumas, and not to pass on unresolved issues, adding to their already complex baggage: the rule here will be "transform it or transmit it." In our present times, perhaps because of a rapid decline in recognizing generational responsibility, there is an emergence—emergency?—of members of the younger generations expressing their unwillingness to swallow the generational trauma of their progenitors. They have plenty of their own generational trauma to deal with.

The Sanskrit term *parampara* refers to the passing down of wisdom and new revelations from one generation to the next. In fact, we could extend the implications of this idea and say that any wisdom imparted through *parampara* is partly the result of the elders' *resolved* traumas, their acquired experience and maturity, extended to younger representatives so they are better equipped to tackle and integrate their own generational issues. Following this line of thought, we could then say that one of the meanings and implications of *parampara* is that a new generation will ideally receive the *resolved* trauma of their elders, so they can better deal with their own unresolved trauma. Conversely, *parampara* is not the passing of elders' unresolved trauma to their descendants. By belonging to any tradition, we surely inherit both treasure and trouble, but we are morally obligated to pass on the least amount of trouble and pay forward the most amount of wisdom we can. If we are greedy for the strength of wisdom that comes from our ancestors but unwilling to provide that to those who follow us ... good luck.

In Erik Erikson's terms, we are to become "generative" persons. This expression does not refer to people who generate stuff, but to those who are deeply concerned with the future generations. Such personalities inhabit all the phases of time simultaneously: learning from the past, living in the present, and looking to the future. It is from this unique generative position that we can generate whatever changes we need to invoke today, in a fearless but fresh voice, with the boldness and originality that so much characterize our glorious ancestry. Thus, our venture calls for us to be both creative and critical, to propose ideas imaginatively, but also ... tentatively.[6] Let's not merely tend the tombs of the prophets but become humble prophets ourselves, through whom God's own voice is urged to speak once again.

THE KUMARA-LILA OF THE GAUDIYA SAMPRADAYA

In terms of geological time, Gaudiya Vaishnavism has only existed on this planet for the last nanosecond. Historically speaking, inaugurated by Sri Gaurahari five hundred years or so ago, the Gaudiya lineage is relatively junior in age to most other world traditions. If, on top of that, we choose to analyze its timeline and condition from the time it left the borders of India and became global, then what we are looking at is a beautiful living school whose age is basically half a century and which, for all intents and purposes, is in its early infancy, not even out of diapers. In Sanskrit terms, we would be speaking of the *kumara-lila* (infancy exploits) of the Gaudiya *sampradaya*.

Like any other tradition, the Gaudiya mystical school is rich with many elders and saints, both past and current. But from the wider perspective of contemporary history and collective unfolding, it is just beginning to crawl and learn what steps constitute progress. And as occurs with any toddler, this chapter of life is itself a charming stage, and should be duly acknowledged, appreciated, and understood by all. As both parents have the right to rejoice in their newborn, they also have the duty to secure her future and gradually anticipate the baby's childhood and teenage years, till she reaches the safe shores of adulthood and eventually attains the grand finale of becoming a revered wise elder. Only then are the initial charm and potential of infancy entirely justified. Babies expose us to something truly miraculous—their latent pristine potential juxtaposed with and tensioned by their extreme fragility and vulnerability. These two combined make for an overwhelmingly enticing prospect. Similarly, a tradition's early years may possess a charm of its own for exactly the same reasons. But its committed members should bear in mind its ideal developmental trajectory. They should not fear its vulnerabilities, but rather be informed and realistic about the corresponding needs in each progressive chapter, so everything flows and converges into a final and glorious climax in each member's heart.

By contrast, dysfunctional caretakers spoil their child by being toxically overprotective and not allowing her healthy exposure to formative challenges necessary for growth. In Freudian terms, what we have in that case is an Oedipus complex, which is applicable not only to individuals, but to groups as well. As described in Chapter 2, overestimation can be another name for blasphemy. Overprotection of a babylike lineage runs parallel to this, giving rise to a traumatized infant who may easily drift into terror, having become addicted to excessive protection. At this point we should ask ourselves: are we so enamored with our own lineage that we have a naive loyalty that blind us to the faults in a particular community? In contrast, we should learn to see current and potential dysfunctionalities and, more so, beyond that, wisely discern the different symptoms of our infant tradition as possibly representing growth that should be tended to appropriately, not something bad that should be hindered. Brian McLaren brilliantly puts it:

> *Wouldn't I be wiser to redouble my efforts to help this fledgling religion learn to walk, stop biting its playmates, and feed itself? Perhaps, then, we should see this tantrum-prone baby's current regressive behavior and temper tantrums as signs of developmental frustration. Perhaps our terrible two-year-old religion is on the verge of a breakthrough.*[7]

In case we choose to invert the angle of vision and see ourselves as infants and our lineage as the parent, then similar templates of naiveté will still play out, as demonstrated by immature affirmations such as "my lineage is the best" or "my guru is better than yours," acting like a child to feign our sense of security. Stuck on this level of group identification, whoever agrees with us and with our religion will be seen as perfect, while everybody else will be seen at best as inferior, but more often than not as threatening, or at least potentially so. In fact, it is during times of crisis that we tend to run toward feelings of embraced security and blanket ourselves there, choosing the line of least resistance. In this way, the capacity to go forward into personal responsibility is constantly challenged by the temptation to revert to lower levels of consciousness and behavior.[8] Although survival instincts and the need for security are natural for every individual and group, not only in early childhood but throughout life, these necessities can become delicate obstacles if by our subconsciously avoiding them and thereby fulfilling them in unconscious ways they turn into unrealistic demands and over-idealized expectations that we project onto people, groups, and situations.

Another charming but potentially taxing aspect of the *kumara-lila* in Gaudiya Vaishnavism is what Thakura Bhaktivinoda called "cultural baggage," by which he meant those influences which arise from the various social units we have been part of and whose values, even as infants, we accepted indisputably. Please bear in mind that this applies not only to us as individuals, but to our lineage as an individualized group, so to speak. While this experience is normal and necessary for any child, as adults we are called to reevaluate each of these principles so that we follow these modes of being with a clear understanding and voluntary acceptance, and not because we have a need to fit in. That need arises when we divisively over-identify with our tribe and are uninformed in our judgements. Does any of this sound familiar?

I pray that the above words are not merely the result of some type of religious PTSD (post-traumatic stress disorder), but a crucial aspect of our healing journey (which could include some form of religious PTSD in some part of its trajectory) as members of the Gaudiya lineage. While these concerns could have been present since time immemorial, life and its nuanced events create the opportunity for us to look at them with new eyes, considerations, and hopes. Radical Personalism does not wait for our tradition to magically upgrade itself, with all the wrongs made right by someone else's effort or the unreliable, sleepy effect of time, but rather to responsibly do the work we have been given. And *that* work begins at home. Thus, first and foremost it should be our intent to act responsibly, each and every one of us, as if we heard the call of our own name in the plural "us" and "you." Only by reforming our own heart, can we look forward to potentially reaching anyone else's heart.

Thus, the collective unconscious of our spiritual lineage needs to be addressed by each of its members according to their sincere capacity, not remaining as passive consumers of the tradition but rather becoming active participants. Each of us should ask ourselves how we can make our own unique contribution, and then contribute. *A sacred lineage is not a product to consume but an ideal to actively serve* by constantly asking these sacred questions and remaining amenable to whatever portal they may open to us. Although scary in the beginning, answering the very queries we have posed will fill our days with prospect, potential, and aspiration. As Viktor Frankl said, "It does not really matter what we expect from life, but rather what life expects from us."[9] Likewise, isn't it true that it's not so much what we expect from our own tradition, but what our tradition—and God himself coming through it—expects and needs from us? We will respond to that question by turning next to the manifesto.

Part Two
THE MANIFESTO

The Manifesto | 7

Humility implies perfect submission to the truth and no sympathy for untruth.

– Sri Bhaktisiddhanta Saraswati Thakura

FOR US RADICAL PERSONALISTS, a question still remains. It burns, scorches, and threatens to consume our whole being. The question is persistent, unending, incessant, and boundless and will probably remain so forever, including as it does all other possible questions, and their ongoing continuous answers. The question is about us. As simple as it sounds, the question touches every aspect of our world:

WHO ARE WE?

We've used capital letters in the above question so that we might give each of the words a new sense and meaning, a new depth and dimension—a new reply, explanation, and solution to this demanding question. This is a question that, at one point, can no longer be addressed with predictable formulas from ideological bunkers. It is a question that can reduce everything to ashes if not answered properly and timely. And the time has come for us to thoroughly take this quest to heart. We are the ones to hear the call from a new direction, to embrace and interpret it from a new vantage point, and to respond to it comprehensively *from an entirely new place*—a place of renewed commitment to our own ideals, a place of rebirth and revival, a fresh, powerful clamor erupting from the very heart of our tradition.

The above question, however, can only be dealt with by Radical Personalists in terms of potential. In other words, the question "*Who are we?*" is synonymous with the question "*What is all that we can become?*" This is so because Radical Personalism plays out the implications of *everything*—questions, concepts, decisions, situations—and does not merely interpret facts literally or superficially. Since a shallow reading of things does not entertain reality as possessing a much greater prospect and content than what we may presently see, such a form of reductionism is to be deemed as yet another variation of disguised impersonalism. For example, a complex set of ideas, like the ones shared throughout this treatise, should not be reduced to a single proposition in an attempt to demote the intricacy of reality itself to a few oversimplified axioms. That process would leave out a tremendous relevant amount of nuance, and our final product would end up a half-baked reality. But we worship a Sweet Absolute—not a small God who makes his devotees smaller in any way, but an infinite God who allows them to be all they can be.

As one of its core values, Radical Personalism attempts to unravel all potential that is latent in reality—a reality unpacked only by insight—and is utterly preoccupied with the proper unfolding and sequential implications of whatever we may be talking about and willing to take full responsibility for its outcome. In other words, let's not just say something and stop there. Rather let's think about where our proposals will end. Let's visualize their trajectory and converging points in the short, middle, and long term. For instance, Native Americans, before accepting any innovation into their tribe, would traditionally play out its implications for the next seven generations. It is through this creative but responsible method that we can judge if our ideas are realistic, sustainable, and worthy of being entertained by ourselves and others. And for these ideas to work, let's take the necessary time to go through that process in our own minds. Let's take the required amount of time to be real persons. Let's become as personal and specific as we can. While Radical Nondualism attempts to make things as homogeneous and nonnuanced as possible, Radical Personalism attempts to make reality as heterogeneous as possible—*as it is*. This has been beautifully portrayed by Thomas Merton:

> *A tree gives glory to God by being a tree. For in being what God means it to be it is obeying him. It 'consents,' so to speak, to his creative love. It is expressing an idea which is in God and which is not distinct from the essence of God, and therefore a tree imitates God by being a tree. The more a tree is like itself, the more it is like him. If it tried to be like something else which it was never intended to be, it would be less like God and therefore it would give him less glory. No two created beings are exactly alike. And their individuality is no imperfection. On the contrary, the perfection of each created thing is not merely in its conformity to an abstract type but in its own individual identity with itself. This particular tree will give glory to God by spreading out its roots in the earth and raising its branches into the air and the light in a way that no other tree before or after it ever did or will do. Do you imagine that the individual created things in the world are imperfect attempts at reproducing an ideal type which the Creator never quite succeeded in actualizing on Earth? If that is so they do not give him glory but proclaim that he is not a perfect Creator. Therefore, each particular being, in its individuality, its concrete nature and entity, with all its own characteristics and its private qualities and its own inviolable identity, gives glory to God by being precisely what he wants it to be here and now, in the circumstances ordained for it by his love and his infinite art.*[1]

As we already mentioned, Radical Personalism is another name for Emerging Gaudiya Vaishnavism, a mothership with inestimable and untold potential to sail the ocean of mundane conception and take us to the shores of post-liberated existence, even during this lifetime. But despite its bright sailing prospect, many of us feel that at present the ship is not forging ahead but is, at best, moored to certain unobserved, deep-seated anchors that first need to be acknowledged. It is these anchors that the following manifesto seeks to address so that our Gaudiya mothership can travel swiftly and safely to the other side—to *its* other side—and be safeguarded not only from merely floating while going around in circles, but from a potentially agonizing sinking. In fact, Emerging Gaudiya Vaishnavism is nothing but the voice of this ancient tradition's very essence, reemerging and reclaiming its own spirit in the present times.

Seen through the lens and theme of Radical Personalism, this manifesto includes points that we deem crucial to enable one's participation and deep belonging in relation to Gaudiya Vaishnavism, and in such a way that the substance of the tradition remains relevant and relatable to both present and potential members. Although presenting concrete situations and prospective solutions, the manifesto's main orientation points toward purpose-finding rather than problem-solving, trusting that the former will naturally shed light on the latter.

Expanding on the initial list shared in the Introduction to this work, we will problematize and articulate the present condition of our lineage from the unique perspective of Sri Gaurahari, the very Deity of the tradition, considering as best we can what his present opinion might be as we ask the following questions: Would Gaurahari join the Gaudiya *sampradaya* in the present times? If so, would he agree with how the tradition is being conceived, presented, and approached? For God's sake, let's never stop this sacred inquiry and collective introspection.

Arguably, this joint reflection is probably the highest form of worship and communion. We Gaudiyas call it *sankirtana-yajna*. Gaurahari's movement entirely revolves around this *sankirtana-yajna*, a method translated as "the sacrifice of collectively chanting God's names." However, this chanting has to be accompanied by collective introspection to be fully actualized and effective—to be all it can be. Without such introspection, this chanting will be reduced to mere musical entertainment. In other words, *sankirtana-yajna* is *synonymous* with collective introspection. How? The Sanskrit term *yajna* refers to sacrifice, which implies the fire element. And according to Gaudiya lore, the very first pronounced word in creation was *tapa* (fire), which invited Brahma, the first manifest being, to close his eyes and see—to enter the space of introspection. In fact, the Sweet Absolute declares in *Srimad Bhagavatam* 2.9.23 that *tapa*/introspection is his very heart and soul and nondifferent from him. In this way, sacrifice, or *yajna*, implies fire, and fire points to introspection. The syllable *sam* in *sankirtana* indicates a group effort, and *kirtana* refers to a practice whose goal is the spreading of the fame (*kirti*) of our tradition and its ideals. Thus, *sankirtana-yajna* essentially implies entering together into the fire of introspection and deeply thinking about how to better spread the glories of our lineage—and such expansion starts in our own hearts. Although introspection takes place in one's inner landscape, such a journey is not traversed in isolation but rather in the company of other pilgrims.

When restricted to the individual, this power of reflection remains limited and rudimentary. It is only in connection to kindred spirits that we can discover our own depth and wholeness. In other words, reflection can be developed only in communion with others. It is essentially a *social* phenomenon.[2] It is *sankirtana*, which by its very definition as a collective engagement tells us that we cannot participate in it by ourselves. If we do it alone, we may engage in *some kirtana*, but not in *sankirtana*. We need each other to make this collective sacrifice of introspection successful, thriving, and, above all, *true*.

As to the *truth aspect* of this exercise, it has been said that "One man who stops lying can bring down a tyranny."[3] In other words, truth and its power can shatter and overpower even the greatest structures of untruth. We Radical Personalists very much feel that as the consciousness rises in a collective sense—as individuals awaken more and more to the necessity of a spiritually congruous lifestyle—religious traditions and spiritual avenues will be called very strongly to dynamically integrate the wealth of tradition with the evolutionary stance of the contemporary individual. They will be called to do this not just for the sake of the tradition's survival but, even more importantly, for the relevant service it potentially has to offer. Sometimes in collective history, just as in an individual's, there are tectonic shifts in consciousness that demand social structures on all levels to rise up to higher ground in order to serve creation. The following manifesto is an attempt to serve this emerging and fundamental necessity. It is an attempt to revive and rethink the substance of mystical devotion in ourselves today, so that tomorrow can wait for us in its proper place.

A FEW KEY TECHNICAL NOTES

Before officially starting this Revival Manifesto, we would like to clarify a few things that will be crucial when trying to grasp the essence of the points shared below. On a technical note, the manifesto's main premises are presented in large type and then briefly explained. Although these main points will be integrated into Part Three, some of them will be explored at a deeper level and therefore contain a shorter commentary in this part of the book.

Also, some of the readers of this manifesto for proactive devotion may feel that most of its points are more conceptual than pragmatic, and this has been done purposefully. Radical Personalism is not as passionate about changing the world—any world—as it is about first *understanding the world.* Before changing through action, we should inspect our present conceptions and be willing to modify them as may be required. In other words, before attempting to implement any practical adjustment, we must first be acquainted with an accurate conceptual framework of those constructs that will then inform our actions. As you read this manifesto, it is imperative to actively keep in mind that we don't need Gaudiya Vaishnavism to change, but we need to change *the way we relate* to Gaudiya Vaishnavism. The content of this manifesto will revolve around this premise, as well as around the very spirit behind whatever action may eventually be required.

It is said that the only constant is change. This is not wholly accurate. Essence, by its very definition, does not change, although the form of it does—and should—according to the progressive understanding we gain through experience. The force of this change of form—or re-form-ation—comes from the dynamically expressive nature of essence itself. In response to an external change in the form of an essence, we are called to update our conceptions so that we remain relatable and relevant to the essence. Consider the following example of the natural reciprocal nature on informing and reforming, a nature that constitutes growth.

Throughout our life, we have been hearing and using the word *love*, but what it has meant to us, the depth and breadth of the implications of this simple four-letter word, has taken many different forms according to our understanding of it at respective stages of our development and within—and due to—various relationships we have had. How many times have we redefined *love* and expressed it accordingly? And we did so not because the principle of love was somehow insufficient, but because the way we were conceiving of love no longer matched our experience of it. Our participation in love and our growth of love were such that our conception of it was no longer sufficient, and our own sense of being called for a new understanding. This informed our approach to love and our expression of it in the external world. But what about those times when, for any number of reasons—fear, nostalgia, laziness—we don't update either our own inner glossary or our external expression of a concept, even though nudged to do so by experience? This wouldn't really be a problem if the world and people in it, including ourselves, weren't constantly changing: if we lived in a vacuum devoid of time and space where standing still was possible without falling behind. But that is not our world. Both our internal and external worlds are dynamic, and we must adapt our orientation to them or we will become irrelevant and dysfunctional. This is where change remains the constant. In a similar way, the essence of Gaudiya Vaishnavism does not change, but because the environments in which it lives does change, we must continually adapt our approach to it so that the form of it can continue to express its essence in relevant and graspable ways.

This Revival Manifesto seeks to highlight patterns observed in our contemporary Gaudiya communities which raise concern and beg to be acknowledged and addressed and which indicate that certain conceptions and expressions of them are out of alignment with the essence of Gaudiya Vaishnavism. But is not intended to point fingers in any direction, to any Gaudiya denomination or individual, much less at the total Gaudiya tradition as a homogeneous whole. This exploration is neither an exhaustive nor a conclusive list of issues, and other persons might recognize different patterns that they see need to be acknowledged, rather than those presented here. And that's all right. Actually, that should happen, since this is an internal and personal process, although with communal and public effects. With this manifesto, we are hoping to open a discussion of these issues so that each one of us can deeply reflect on them, challenge the viability and validity of our current understanding, and discover how harbored misconceptions may be playing themselves out through us in the name of the tradition we are supposed to represent. As much as we align ourselves with the essential premises of our school, our tradition will be properly represented, and in that same proportion we will actually *belong* to the tradition.

In order to spell out this last point even more, and to make the import of this manifesto as actionable as possible, we will explain each of the points below in the context of setting up two contrasting characters. These characters personify two inner voices that operate and usually take turns not only outside of us, but inside us as well. They are the voices of Radical Personalism and Conventional Dogmatism. While the notion of Radical Personalism is not our own creation but rather a way of referring to Gaudiya Vaishnavism in its ideal expression, its personified archenemy and villain in this discussion will be embodied under the name of Conventional Dogmatism. By setting up this contrast we hope to emphasize personal responsibility and thus provide a clearer intellectual filter for all of us to engage with reality, so we can ask ourselves whether we are living out Radical Personalism or its undesirable alternative. As mentioned, the headquarters of our lineage is settled in our own hearts, and it is only from there that Radical Personalism—or its nemesis—can truly emerge.

Radical Personalism is but a synonym for Emerging Gaudiya Vaishnavism, the essential voice of a tradition reclaiming its own spirit through a wide variety of facets and vital ingredients. In their ideal disclosure, all of these features are to be expressed not partially, but *radically*—to their very core. Thus, in order to draw out the value and ultimate prospect of the different points mentioned throughout this manifesto—the various constituents of Radical Personalism—each of them will be given a name accordingly: Radical Wholeness, Radical Guidance, Radical Fluidity, and so on.

REVIVAL MANIFESTO FOR PROACTIVE DEVOTION

Let's begin this fearless inventory and inaugurate our manifesto by setting foot into the decisive entrance hall to Radical Personalism through the opening door: Radical Vulnerability.

Radical Vulnerability

> *As counterintuitive as it may sound, vulnerability is a mandatory prerequisite to courage and the prospect of overarching empowerment. Without the willingness to be vulnerable as a tradition and without the acknowledgement of the tradition's woundedness and possible frailty, we as members of the Gaudiya community will disempower ourselves and deprive ourselves of the ability to grasp any of the remaining points of this manifesto. By allowing itself to be thoroughly vulnerable, however, Gaudiya Vaishnavism can experience its highest reach and required revival. We call this Radical Vulnerability.*

Archetypically speaking, the Fool is the precursor to the Savior. This means that the more we dare to admit our foolishness, the less of a fool we are, and the closer we get to actual wisdom and sacredness.

There is strength in weakness. In fact, weakness is strength's exclusive source. In Radical Personalism, vulnerability becomes empowerment, a virtue, by having the humble courage to confront our brokenness in a committed environment, with healthy and clear boundaries. Actual freedom is not needing to pretend anymore, and the experience of Radical Vulnerability provides such autonomy: we can stop shying away from a full-blooded investigation of our core wounds. By contrast, the voice of Conventional Dogmatism entertains fictitious notions of power, trying to prove itself competent by refusing to embrace its darkest Achilles heel. This dogmatism is nothing but a deadly form of assertiveness and blind certainty, a close-mindedness that amounts to an imprisonment so total that the prisoner doesn't even know he's locked up.[4] This vicious voice is the exact opposite of Radical Vulnerability.

Integrating our imperfection through the privileged portal of vulnerability is not about not being mistaken, but about responding to our failures in such a way that they become part of our final glory and brightest potential. And this is what Radical Vulnerability is all about: the willingness to show up in those demanding moments and shed profuse blood, sweat, and tears, so we accomplish as a tradition all that we are expected to attain.[5] This particular facet of Radical Personalism will be an all-pervading theme throughout the balance of this manifesto, a required theme to be fully embraced in order to cope with any of the remaining points.

Due to its paramount importance, Radical Vulnerability will be further unpacked in its own chapter in the third part of this book.

Radical Wholeness

> *Although being itself a personalist tradition, contemporary Gaudiya Vaishnavism sometimes presents the opposite in the form of various shades of disguised impersonalism. This is expressed through a lack of human sensitivity and psychological balance, which includes emotional atrophy and endless types of unaddressed abuses. We need to become whole and human once again. We need to become individuated participants in our tradition, and especially and gradually we need to become edifying elders. We call this Radical Wholeness.*

In the name of being and remaining transcendentalists, Conventional Dogmatism often urges many of us to neglect our humanity and other expressions of horizontal development (psychological and emotional well-being) in the name of focusing on a concocted idea of vertical development, or moving toward transcendence. Conventional Dogmatism insists on moving beyond the personal toward the transpersonal, but in fact one may be slipping into the domain of depersonalization. For this reason, Radical Personalism will be quick to add that actual transcendence has nothing to do with any type of rejection or evasion, but is all about *accurate integration*. Before attempting to transcend—and even ascend—first we need to descend. First we need to properly ground ourselves as authentic human beings. Everything—and, we repeat, everything—is potential paraphernalia to be engaged in divine service, including our human body, senses, and emotions. Thus, the real challenge for a Radical Personalist is not so much what to reject, but *how to harmonize and incorporate*, how to be wholesome to the core and offer our balanced humanity in sacred service. We do not embrace spirituality to be okay, *but we try to be okay so we can embrace spirituality.* To put it bluntly, we should not try to serve so we can feel something; rather, we should try to feel something so we can serve.

Radical Wholeness could be another synonym for the project of our becoming Gaudiya humanists, whole-makers, people who address their present persona in such a way that their spiritual identity may eventually be established as a result. And for Gaudiya Vaishnavas, that final destination is perfectly divine but also perfectly human—divinized humanity, divine humanism. Thus, human relationships equally matter now and in transcendence. The inner voice of Conventional Dogmatism, however, will plead for a depersonalization of the self, a form of poetic justice through which we inadvertently end up promoting the exact opposite of the personalist ideal we generally speak about. The implications of this distortion in which we don't treat each other as human individuals are appalling and alarming: abuse, misuse, and endless shades of spiritual bypassing. All of these can be healed and restored by a deep recognition of our existence as unique single personal entities.[6] From this wholesome place each of us will develop, eventually reaching the blossoming point of being truly wise elders.

As with Radical Vulnerability, this Radical Wholeness is such a cardinal expression of Emerging Gaudiya Vaishnavism that it gets its own chapter in the third part of this book.

Radical Organization

> *Whatever difficulties we may be experiencing as a community are not necessarily related to our institutions per se, but in most cases to the fallacy of institutionalism. Gaudiya Vaishnavism is to be first and foremost concerned with real people, not with projects. When each individual heart is properly honored and cared for, projects and institutions will then naturally fall into their proper roles and functions. We call this Radical Organization.*

While the previous point of this manifesto dealt with how we should relate to ourselves as wholesome humans, this next item extends a similar reflection in connection to other individuals, who happen to be part of a particular institution. Institutions can be compared to cups, through which we are able to drink milk. While we could drink milk directly from a cow, a cup will generally be helpful and even preferred. Similarly, although transcendental substance does not depend on any institution for its transmission, institutions can often assist. By themselves, spiritual institutions (if it's appropriate to even use such a label) merely constitute the vessel through which the experience of transcendence is ideally extended to others and facilitated for them. However, to pass on anything enduring requires a healthy container. And while outer form will never be equal to inner substance, there is some kind of correlation between these two: *the more sublime the gift, the more delicate the container*. Among other virtues, a delicate container is one which will never take itself too seriously, giving preeminence instead to the inner substance it is supposed to facilitate. When this does not happen, institutions may abandon the original mission for which they were created. They may instead redefine their purpose, insisting that only absolute loyalty to their current shape is absolute loyalty to their founding principles. Then we don't have a delicate container anymore, but a *container in a delicate state*. We have institutionalism or, more precisely, yet another variety of impersonalism.

This subtle refuse of institutionalism is one of the many and main maneuvers that Conventional Dogmatism will present in its desperate attempt to secure its yearned-for throne. By concentrating power and focusing attention on buildings and structures rather than individuals, Conventional Dogmatism deems the institution its very Deity. By extension, the institution's "loyal members" are also deified, and garlanded with power and prestige although they are neither constitutionally responsible to nor held accountable for the people they are supposed to serve through that very institution. When such emphasis is combined with micromanaging people and relationships as well as an acute demand for respect regardless of the propriety of behavior, then we have a lethal recipe for authoritarianism. In contrast, Radical Personalism chooses to build itself on the foundation of authentic personal relationships, and not on legislated bureaucratic control systems. Its duty is not to disempower people (which sometimes institutions end up doing with consummate expertise) but to recognize how any real power lies in its living members, never in structures. If the members of an institution face alienation and isolation, if they become fragmented, disenfranchised, and uninspired, if they do not trust their leaders nor even themselves, then it's time to implement Radical Organization on a new level, where the required empowerment is once again brought back home. Institutions are not mere buildings, papers, bank accounts, and hierarchy systems. Institutions are its members, and therefore *institutions cannot be better than their own members*. Without real people there is no actual project.

Some leaders will always care more about rules, numbers, or reputation than they do about people. This is a type of organizational deformity known as utilitarianism, where if something is useful to the majority, or even a choice minority, then anything can be justified. The proposed solution of Radical Organization is to care about individuals, especially those who won't benefit us in any immediate form, instead of only "serving" those who, no matter how they may behave, contribute to our own separate cause. However, if we choose to be "seduced by empire" and allow institutional codependency to dominate over us, our living the tradition may actually look like *leaving* the tradition. In fact, in the name of committed belonging we may be promoting a thick socio-religious entrapment, where many end up inside a taxing system where they have to work for their superiority, but can gain inferiority in a moment. Mostly everyone joins a spiritual institution looking for an identity, and to further perpetrate that newly acquired identity, loyalty comes next as an immediate byproduct. While all of these elements are fine in and of themselves, they can turn into deceptive devices when wrongly mistaken as the ultimate goal of one's initial joining.[7] In other words, as long as we at best merely seek a religious role in our institution, there will be no urgent need to concern ourselves with deeper, subtler problems. Such an approach will only invoke dis-location, a total lack of any sense of actual deep belonging.

Truth be told, if one expects too much perfection from any spiritual organization, one will be disappointed for sure. The divine substance is immensely vast and impossible to be completely contained and represented by one institution or another.[8] And like most of us, institutions, being damaged and insufficient structures in themselves, tend in time toward corruption and other shortcomings. In spite of this, spiritual institutions do have a role to play in the lives of most; thus we should be ready to repair their brokenness and redefine their roles in order to fulfill the institutions' actual purpose: training and educating; assisting in the development of both devotional and vocational skills; counseling; and, as simple as it may sound yet necessary to say, giving encouraging and down-to-earth friendly advice. This is the concern of Radical Organization, a concern that seeks to upgrade the inner qualities above external status, a concern that seeks not to create card-carrying members of the tradition but *heart-carrying members* who carry their very selves in their hands as a voluntary and enthusiastic offering. This heroic task requires both introspection and self-reform, which separate saints from official religious statesmen. Where do *you* want to belong?[9]

Radical Guidance

> *As sacred and relevant as it has been and will continue to be, the principle of the guru is often addressed and even embraced through a set of misunderstandings, misrepresentations, and false expectations, by disciples and even gurus in some cases. The required recalibration is not so much about the notion of guru in itself but in how we approach and conceptualize it, both in its theory and in how the intricate dynamics of this distinctive relationship play out. We call this Radical Guidance.*

While being authoritarian is closely tied to the previous notion of institutionalism, the principle of true authority not only speaks of a position, but also indicates that genuine affection must actually be present for it to be what it can and should be. Ideally, a genuine guru naturally commands but never demands respect and invites her dear disciples to a loving relationship of eternal trust and service, where both pupil and teacher remain students forever. In this latter form of interaction, we do not find the typical pyramidal system of hierarchy (or even monarchy), but a circular or even spiral way of sharing, where guru and disciple learn from each other and therefore need each other and collaborate in their service to God. This unique form of Radical Personalism lies in striking contrast to the inner voice of Conventional Dogmatism, which mandates a shallow, calculative, and fearful following devoid of any trace of authentic freedom and is thus a denial of personal commitment in the name of self-giving. O Sweet Absolute, please protect us from surrendering to others the responsibility to think for ourselves and making our own decisions![10]

Radical Guidance fully acknowledges the copious debt that a disciple has acquired with her gurus, both past and present. However, it also acknowledges that in her attempt to pay that debt back, the student may have to mostly pay it *forward*, honoring the received gift and legacy in a dynamic, proactive spirit. As our sincerity grows, the object of our love will be further refined and defined—never modified—and a new sense of responsibility and personal initiative will naturally arise as a result: not to merely carry on with the tradition but to *challenge and improve it*, building upon the success of our ancestors and present mentors, embracing creative thinking in the present as they did in the past. Instead of a mere regurgitation of outdated dogma, something akin to spiritual infidelity, Radical Guidance invites each of its members to reconsider their approach to the principle of guidance itself, in terms of both providing it to others and receiving it themselves.

As with many other topics, this particular face of Radical Personalism will have its own chapter in the third part of this book.

Radical Remark

> *Criticism is not, per se, something necessarily offensive. In fact, friendly criticism is an absolutely crucial component for any mature conversation—and relationship—to exist and evolve. Unfortunately, some Gaudiya representatives tend to weaponize concepts like* aparadha *(offense) and even demonize any form of critique as something to be avoided at all costs. Instead, we*

> *should learn the art of constructive criticism, through which we offer and receive advice and perspective in the spirit of selfless service. We call this Radical Remark.*

The Sanskrit term *aparadha* refers to "that which goes against (*apa*) love (*radha*)." It basically indicates biting the hand that feeds us, especially intentionally and with ill-motives. Needless to say, this is something utterly undesirable in all dimensions of life, but especially in connection to divine principles and personalities. However, *aparadha* is something very different from many other things that sometimes are unfortunately labeled as such by the inner voice of Conventional Dogmatism. One of these is constructive or friendly criticism, which entails nonenvious critical feedback and intimate correction instead of scapegoating, defamation, or slander. How can we spot actual constructive criticism? In brief, we could say that in relation to whatever the critic may say: (a) he will sincerely pray not to project onto others things present in himself, and if he learns that he has, he will be open to acknowledge such an overstep; (b) before criticizing others, he will first appreciate various positive attributes in the other person so that his criticism is inspired by a desire to help and augment whatever positive values are already present in the criticized party; (c) he will make sure that his critique is shared with the intention of helping the critiqued person; and (d) he will commit himself to fully supporting the criticized party to help him change whatever has to be changed, so that person can succeed in the desired transformation. This is the proposal of Radical Remark: let's not use others' defects as an excuse to distance ourselves from them, but rather as a way to approach them.

The above pivotal facet of Radical Personalism is not only something permitted, but is an absolute necessity for any deep and honest relationship among spiritual aspirants. By contrast, the more this healthy critique is forbidden and stigmatized, the closer we get to a cultish, dictatorshiplike type of regime, one devoid of free speech, trust, and the necessary liberty of thought and expression that any functional society should always encourage in each of its members. While Conventional Dogmatism will surely object that highlighting freedom may undermine the process of surrender to

God, its opposite will actually be true: the greater the liberty, the more we will be allowed to surrender voluntarily and wholeheartedly. Conversely, the less freedom we are granted, the more our surrender degrades into a heartless and fear-driven avoidance of punishment, which is not true surrender at all. Therefore, even if it seems counterintuitive, if we are to cater to a culture of full surrender, we have to initially facilitate a culture of full liberty.

True to its nature, the voice of Conventional Dogmatism may still resist, this time resorting to false humility as an excuse for not having to examine and discuss others' behavior and shortcomings. It will invoke noble ideas such as guarding ourselves from committing *aparadha*, or not disturbing others' faith or one's own practice by criticizing others. But this is often spiritual bypassing, and we run the risk of making most of our relationships extremely diplomatic and calculated. In reply to this, Radical Remark will remind us that throughout sacred scripture we have been repeatedly advised to properly ascertain each person's situation, so we can relate to and honor them appropriately. In fact, many of those who advocate a wholesale ban on criticism are the very ones trying to evade deserved and healthy criticism of themselves. In contrast to this, Sri Rupa Goswami's *Upadesamrita* (verse 4) insists on revealing one's mind in confidence to others, which would include the possibility of constructive criticism. And he further describes this practice as a *loving exchange* between devotees. By banning all forms of criticism per se, we render these vital practices invalid. Similarly, by not allowing ourselves to get enough critical feedback from others, we may not only deprive ourselves of further improvement but may end up totally dysfunctional beings, just like an overprotected isolated child who has never been exposed to any scenario that may challenge his present views and experience of life. Thus, Radical Remark makes this very clear distinction between blasphemy or abuse (referred to in Sanskrit as *ninda/aparadha*) and that friendly criticism which constitutes an indispensable exchange of trust and affection. It is through the latter that we will be further trained in the art of unconditional love, where we embrace someone not despite his or her imperfections, but *because* of them.[11]

Radical Fluidity

> *Fundamentalism, tribal thinking, and profound cognitive rigidity prevent the Gaudiya community from the dynamic dialogue that so much characterizes not only the modern times, but the vibrant essence of our own ancient lineage. There is an emerging urgent need for a broader focus and an emphasis on broadmindedness and intermissionary solidarity. We call this Radical Fluidity.*

From tip to toe, the Gaudiya tradition fully revolves around the idea of love. Paradoxically, and often without being aware of it, we are usually terrified of love more than any other thing. Why? Because love is the very thing that will fully transform us, and we are scared of decisive change. Radical Personalism is not only about change and questioning our own thoughts, but also and especially *questioning the way we think about thoughts.*[12] Accordingly, Radical Fluidity calls for a sacred exposure of those very elements that prevent our transformation, those unchallenged biases that need to be finally uncovered. This long list upon inventory, if like most, may include our tendency to prefer a simple lie to a complex truth, to reject any idea that may endanger our status quo or way of making a living, to reject inconvenient truths that make us uncomfortable and disrupt our complacency, to believe stories that exonerate us or portray us as innocent victims, to overreact to catastrophes but easily and conveniently miss slow erosions of normalcy, and so on.[13] Biases and assumptions need to be challenged to become truth, truth needs to be further challenged to become wisdom, and wisdom needs to be even further challenged to become revelation. That said, how much do we as individuals, as well as Gaudiyas, need to be challenged to perfectly understand and integrate truth, wisdom, and revelation into our lives?

Fearing its imminent demise and championing justice (not mercy), the voice of Conventional Dogmatism will cry out as primitively and crudely as it can, being totally unwilling to abandon the theological comfort zone, ideological communism, and superiority complex it has developed in relation to other religions and humanity in general. This tumorlike mentality tends to rest in the greatness of the ideal presented by one's tradition, without being willing to do one's part so that the ideal can become fully actualized in *us*. However, Gaudiya Vaishnavism is not a closed system but an open one, willing to exchange with and be nourished by its environments. These include not only other Gaudiya branches, other Hindu schools of spirituality, or other mystical theologies, but even secular disciplines that have the potential to inform and amplify our own appreciation of the tradition we love and live. In other words, we propose a form of what we may call "integral theology," which includes not only theology but spirituality, philosophy, technology, psychology, and history.

Radical Fluidity allows us to benefit from an area like history, which correspondingly will allow us to study and understand the timeline of our lineage like never before. Through the lens of psychology it will see itself engaging in whatever shadow work may be required to heal unsolved generational trauma. It will appreciate and learn from the scientific method and science's permanent disposition toward wonder and a greater and greater alignment with reality. In fact, New Physicists are now saying that love is the ultimate consciousness out of which the whole universe exists. They even recommend meditation and the study of our own subjectivity in order to be a true scientist and observer of reality. If only every religion were as mystical as some of these scientists![14] In contrast, Conventional Dogmatism sometimes wins the day through different forms of theological arrogance, still convincing us that ours is the most complete version of transcendence, to the point of disparaging other traditions as mere perverted reflections or partial expressions of our lineage. And that is on a good day.

Instead of undesired insularity, let the truth speak for itself, however and wherever it may choose to manifest. What is the fear? What do we have to lose by such exposure? If we listen to others and find they don't move our heart or challenge our ideas that are ready to be upgraded, *then where is the harm*? And if these same people, traditions, or disciplines move our heart to the point of inspiring a stronger commitment to the things we already cherished, and if they do challenge our head so that one by one misconceptions are corrected and aligned with an inner truth like never before, *then where is the harm?*

Radical Presence

> *Present-day Gaudiya Vaishnavism is often misrepresented by the fantasy of traditionalism, an entrapment that ensues from using the glories of the past as an attempt to resist present change. This toxic nostalgia and over-attachment to ancient templates prevents us from properly tuning in to the ethics of modernity and its challenges. And it promotes an arthritic sense of dismissal and spiritual obesity, where one's intelligence is no longer required in the here and now, since everything has apparently already been sorted out by our past heroes. To overcome this threatening tendency, we need to be courageous and dare to embrace our contemporary trials by thinking for ourselves and honoring our legacy with boldness, creativity, and vigor. We call this Radical Presence.*

While the past tends to look more beautiful than it actually was, nobody has been able to live in it permanently. Thus, Radical Presence is required, and it's possible only here, in the present moment, the perfect point of any possible unfolding and evolution. Neither God, nor us—nor anything—is a static relic; everything is a perpetual flow, a dynamic pattern of relationships, an event unto itself. If there is any fixed framework in life it is that everything is constantly changing, for better or worse. In Darwinian terms, the eventual survivors are never the strongest, but those who have the greatest capacity for adaptation and change. We can apply this same principle to how our tradition will be able to endure in the future. We do this by transmuting in the present whatever requires urgent revival. In Latin, this is known as *mutatis mutandis*: those things that can be changed *should* be changed. And this will be possible by fully embracing Radical Presence in the here and now.

The very nature of life itself brims like a wild river, meandering eternally, its external paths ever adapting. When certain traditions claim to own the essence of reality, there is an attempt to cement the embankments of the wild river of life which prevents it from winding according to its nature. However, this artificial damming, which goes against the flow of nature, is a sure way to lose the essence. While the preserving traditional spirit is surely a noble one, we have to assure that its essence is never submitted to cementation because, in that case, a cemented river is no longer a river, but a canal. And history shows that without exception even the most orthodox traditions meander and diversify over time, no matter how hard they fight against this reality. Risky "fossilism" will not allow us to embrace the true history of our own tradition, which meandered throughout many generations. Denying our own history is denying our own roots. This denial comes at the price of instability and even delusion. Therefore, embracing a progressive spirit should not be felt as a threat to one's tradition. Rather, it allows us to both embrace the past's true meandering history and preserve its continuous natural meandering. This is the only way to guarantee future access to its essence.[15] Go with the flow.

Although the Conventional Dogmatic in us may have become momentarily shy, by hearing the above set of proposals it's likely to again become nervous, unsettled, and ready for a new dispute, resorting to all sorts of unfounded accusations and claims of heresy. As an argument, this inner voice may insist that a possible outdated model established by previous teachers may be still working nicely and the proof is abundant income and new contributing members. But what if those developments are only external, while the inner spirit of true dynamism remains neglected and stiff? What if a literal reading of reality deprives us of necessary nuance and takes most important things out of context? What if one of the consequences of this outlook ends up in anachronic proselytism, where we attempt to convert others without first considering our present times and challenges?[16] Succinctly, the reply to these questions converges in the following: *facilitating disaster while claiming "revelation."*

As with many others, the past of our tradition is in fact abundantly glorious, but this doesn't mean that there have not been mistakes throughout history that need to be equally acknowledged. As realistic contributing members, we are expected to hear the wrongs of our past, feel the corresponding pain, and try not to minimize them. If we choose to mask our past as a lineage in a veil of religiosity and excessive saintliness, our so-called spiritual life may end up becoming the best possible excuse *not to practice actual spiritual life.* In other words, to institutionalize nostalgia as a superlative kind of faith constitutes an insult to the whole process of spiritual progress. Thus Radical Personalism humbly insists on the need for Radical Presence, so that traditionalism is ultimately replaced by its required converse: vitality, courage, and inspired vision.[17]

Radical Appreciation

> *Depending on how we approach it, our highly refined theological sophistication has the potential to be an encouraging blessing or a damning curse. We can either be unnecessarily arrogant, filled with a sense of moral superiority or even elitist complexes in relation to other schools (group narcissism), or we can be grateful and humbled by the fortune, charm, and prospect inherent in our mystical doctrine. We call this Radical Appreciation.*

We may have access to rich theological depth, but how deeply are we diving into that depth ourselves? While there are traditions that may not be as theologically rich as ours, many of their practitioners in effect go deeper into their mystical explorations than we claim to go into ours. In fact, it is more favorable to go deep into the basics of our theology rather than remain basic in the profundity of it, and sometimes even ironically proud of our grasp without recognizing just how very shallow that grasp goes. We are our own mistake, as Thomas Merton rightfully claimed.[18] This delicate condition leads us to not only "legal" wrongdoings, but premeditated forms of misuse of God's mercy. Due to the latter perversion, the most noble and thrilling form of divine revelation can be exploited and engineered to the point of justifying a hyper-elite oligarchy. The highly refined Gaudiya doctrine is not meant to fuel our sense of moral superiority, spiritual privilege, and religious exceptionalism, and then reinforce those values through the rituals and devotional activities we perform. No. Again, this is the voice of Conventional Dogmatism promoting a formal sense of religious affiliation while falsely denying the mystical side of our tradition. With such an attitude, our beautiful Gaudiya expressions like "servant of the servant" can be used as nothing more than a camouflage to hide our pride, prejudice, and violence.[19]

In contrast, the voice of Radical Appreciation calls for a meek and respectful valuing of the gifts we've received, gifts that will never make us better than anybody else. On the contrary, properly received grace allows us to detect the presence of that same grace in a multitude of other diverse expressions. Truth is to be properly discerned and honored, not judged. An evasive sense of appreciation focuses exclusively on one's upsides and others' downsides. To counteract this tendency, we as a tradition should be humble enough to study our own historical downsides without any need to whitewash and sanitize them, without any need to depict "our people" as being always the good and heroic ones, without any need to live happily ever after within a thick wall of bias. In other words, there is absolutely no need to see ourselves (or others) as something we (or they) are not. And whatever we happen to be is to be acknowledged from the vantage point of modesty and unassertiveness, with all that such acknowledgement implies. As the famous adage proclaims, *better to be rejected for who we are than accepted for who we are not.*

Radical Harmony

> *Because of being an ultra-specified tradition (in terms of its theological details and subtleties about post-liberated life), and also because of the abundance of historical and philosophical opposition to Radical Nondualism, Gaudiya Vaishnavism runs the risk of easily becoming dualistic and rejecting all expressions of nondualism—including the nondualism our tradition should represent. We need to become deeply aware of how nondualism plays itself out in Radical Personalism, and properly embody such a principle through each of our actions. We call this Radical Harmony.*

While Gaudiya Vaishnavism proposes that reality is ultimately nondual consciousness (*advaya-jnana*), this proposal is not entirely synonymous with that of impersonalism, or Radical Nondualism. Similarly, although Gaudiyas include and allow the existence of diversity and individuality even in eternity, their school is not Radical Dualism either, but something that harmonizes these two opposites: we may call it Nonradical Nondualism, Nuanced Nondualism, Unity in Diversity, or as it's traditionally stated, *achintya-bheda-abheda-tattva*, inconceivable simultaneous bipolarity. However, since Gaudiya Vaishnavism possesses an abundant and meticulous description of individualized life in transcendence, it is possible to end up placing too much emphasis on the *bheda* (difference) side of the equation and lose sight of the *abheda* (unitive) side of it. Therefore, it is important to keep in mind that nonduality is the very foundation upon which diversified expression of spiritual life actually happens. Without a strong recognition of such a foundation, there is no possibility for a sustainable spiritual project.

As Gaudiyas have clearly opposed Radical Nondualism throughout history, the voice of Conventional Dogmatism may loudly and immaturely proclaim that we should be equally militant against all forms of nondualism. However, accepting a blanket opposition to all forms of nondualism would then amount to philosophical dualism, which runs the risk of not only bypassing our nondual existential bedrock, but also overflowing into other forms of dualistic thinking that will spring up from a philosophical dualism, such as fundamentalism, tribalism, and narrowmindedness. In other words, the price for rejecting all forms of nondualism is that we may end up becoming a dualistic tradition ourselves and, even worse, perhaps representing a nondual tradition in extremely dualistic terms, not only philosophically, but through a whole dualistic lifestyle. And if on top of this we add the extreme level of theological detail and specificity we find in our Gaudiya tradition but with a heavily dualistic framework, then we will basically bring down the whole spiritual realm to worldly terms. To rediscover and integrate the place of nondual thinking through Radical Harmony will not only protect us from these unwanted shortcomings, but it will also add a necessary dimension of depth and experience to our daily life and practice.

Due to its critical significance, Radical Harmony will be further unpacked in its own chapter in the third part of this book.

Radical Phraseology

> *Our Gaudiya glossary needs to be revised, upgraded, and re-cognized. Not only do we need new words for some of our ancient terms, but we also need to understand how some of those notions coexist and apply in our lives today, if at all. We need to unlearn, relearn, and repurpose our old lingo in the context of modernity. We call this Radical Phraseology.*

Whether we admit it or not, language and words are one of the most influential forces shaping the way we conceive of and relate to reality itself. In fact, words are crucial not only in all our social engagements but, especially so, in the inner dialogue we conduct with ourselves daily. As members of a particular tradition, we have our own distinctive jargon, one which is deeply encoded in our worldview and mental architecture, creating various networks which, from time to time, require a generous rebooting of the system for them to remain relevant and relatable in our modern era. As with any tradition, our Gaudiya school won't be able to evolve to its next stage of unfolding if it is not accompanied by the type of language that will correspond to such necessary unfolding. Hence we have Radical Phraseology. This particular proposal has nothing to do with destroying anything of actual value, but with *reconstructing* value and purpose on the basis of our ancient tradition by mining meaningful relevance obscured by archaic and religious verbiage. Without updating the language and personalizing its import in our lives, deep philosophical expressions remain as shallow as clichés. We need a vocabulary unique not only to our times, but *unique to each soul*: each of us needs to find his or her own individual way of expressing and relating to revelation in a way that remains valid as well as relevant. Each of us needs a *journey language*, a *growth language*, a language that can accurately portray the movements of our inner landscape.

To be sure, the shadow of Conventional Dogmatism inhabiting our psyche will protest against this project ad nauseam, perceiving an extremely intimidating push out of its comfort zone, a zone where concepts and words have a fixed museumlike meaning, a zone which allows for unchallenged complacency and mediocrity to reign without question. In fact, *mediocrity can be firmly and easily established through revelation.* Instead of being rooted in tradition and revelation, we can end up being *rotten* in them. For this not to happen, Radical Personalism insists on redefining our relationship with scripture, its language, and its trademark terminology. The ultimate exclusive purpose of information is to inform and reform us. Information implies someone *in formation.*

One possible example of how to keep our glossary and liturgy relatable is to venture into singing our daily prayers in our local language, as a complement to the classical method. This can help those who do not speak Sanskrit or Bengali to easily connect with the mood and meaning of what they are singing about and, through such a process, make those prayers their own, in their own hearts. Another possibility could be to rephrase expressions of our native language that are outdated when we need to speak about things in the present. For example, instead of saying, "This offensive entity has acted in a demoniac way, and therefore has to urgently purify his evil heart and be submissive, instead of resorting to his false ego," we could reframe it as, "This dysfunctional human being has unresolved trauma, and therefore is in deep need to express his vulnerability and engage in some shadow work, instead of merely resorting to his intermediary identity."[20] Here we have basically said the same thing in two different ways, the latter being more relatable not only to contemporaries but to our own minds, speaking to us more clearly about the essence of the "old" terms and freeing us from all the ways we may still wrongly divorce our humanity from our spiritual practice through the language we use.

This "lingo excavation project," however, is not limited to adjusting mere terms for modern relatability. On top of that, Radical Phraseology points not to only changing our glossary, but to lifting our inner structures out of the comfort zone and learning to reconceive each of the concepts we have learned in the past—not only a rephrasing of them, but a reassessment. While we may not need to change every single word in our Gaudiya lexicon, we may need to reconfirm *that we are properly understanding every single word* in a deep and dynamic way. By suggesting this alternative orthodoxy, we are not being merely rebellious or complacent toward what mainstream Gaudiya Vaishnavism may still insist upon, but actually expressing the exact middle point—and only alternative—between these two. The alternative to overcompliance is not being rebellious, but rather being adventuresome.

Radical Decoding

> *Among the above-mentioned terms that beg for an upgrade, predominant Gaudiya themes such as surrender, humility, obedience, and submission are in urgent need of a higher-resolution version of themselves. These are not meant to be stagnant concepts that can only be expressed in one particular "correct" way. They are extremely dynamic realities that will adopt endless forms according to the time, place, and necessity of the moment. In other words, they must not be ascertained by their external shape and presentation, but always according to our internal disposition. We call this Radical Decoding.*

As with any other spiritual practitioner, a Gaudiya Vaishnava will resort to certain specific terms more than others, and these will constitute, so to say, a "conceptual theme park" he inhabits. In our tradition, words like surrender and humility will lead the way, and therefore we should be extremely careful not to think we already know all the implications behind these sacred terms. As already mentioned, Radical Personalism is all about playing out the implications of everything to the greatest possible degree, and these crucial terms are not an exception to this rule. Thus, Radical Decoding goes hand-in-hand with the above-mentioned Radical Deconstruction, both of which attempt to dethrone stagnation and lack of rigor in our spiritual journey.

The inner voice of Conventional Dogmatism understands surrender as absolute submission devoid of all critical thinking, and it warns us not to question authority and risk becoming (or being labeled as) blasphemers. Radical Decoding, however, will present a much more generous outlook: surrender is always voluntary, an open choice based on love and trust that is never one-sided, but always reciprocal. And since surrender is nothing but the outer expression of our inner faith (and there are many stages to faith development), surrender cannot be a one-act performance, but a *process* that will take time, perhaps even lifetimes. For attributes such as humility, it is more often expressed as a neurosis than a virtue. Humility has nothing to do with imposed obedience and obsessive self-deprecation, but constitutes the natural response when being touched by graceful affection: *I am part of something bigger than myself, and there is reason to celebrate.* Thus, real humility, surrender, and similar other qualities are the reasonable price we choose to pay for the undeserved gift of causeless mercy. This gift is causeless because no matter what we do, we will never be able to fully deserve it. However, this causeless gift is not "cost-less," without a price; the price to pay—the divine currency—is in coins of genuine humility and surrender. But this currency is to be properly decoded, since it will take different shapes of value according to the need of the market, to each particular circumstance in relation to our own hearts. So let's be careful not to over-idealize their perfect expression, and remain open to new ways of connecting with them.

Radical Integrity

> *Gaudiya concepts like the well-known Four Regulative Principles should be fathomed in their full depth and possibilities, and not merely interpreted and adopted as literally as possible. On top of this, these Four Principles are not the ultimate litmus test to define one's standing in Gaudiya Vaishnavism, but a set of human virtues that promote an integrated foundation for an authentic culture of divine love. We call this Radical Integrity.*

Gaudiya Vaishnavism is not a set-for-life formula through which we have finally embraced the correct set of beliefs and practices without any further need for future recalibration. It is not transactional, but *transformational*. While the mere external following of our particular set of vows may be an important beginning point for us as new recruits, it will prove insufficient in more advanced stages. In fact, each of our vows is expected to be renewed regularly—even daily and at every moment—if we are to discover all of their meaningful potential. While some Gaudiyas may follow these moral principles "just in case the whole thing is true," real morality is ultimately based on insight, not mechanical puppeting of the motions. In other words, these Four Regulative Principles have nothing to do with cheap sanctimony or spiritual meritocracy, but with a profound sense of commitment and integrity—Radical Integrity.

Unfortunately, Conventional Dogmatism still wins the day in some cases, conceiving these Four Principles exclusively in negative and thus disempowering terms: *no* meat-eating, *no* illicit sex, *no* intoxication, and *no* gambling. But Radical Personalism is not about *not doing* certain things, but embracing the positive value of everything, especially of what seems to be purely negative. How then do we break down these principles so their ultimate positive content is disclosed to us? Let's take the example of "no meat-eating." Strictly speaking, this principle is not about avoiding eating meat, but about becoming vegetarian and thus *doing* a certain thing instead of not doing something else. But to be honest, this principle is not limited to this either. On a deeper level, it especially points to the quality of *ahimsa*, nonviolence. But now we are somehow back with a negative definition of this principle. What could then be nonviolence's better half? Becoming loving and compassionate. However, fully played out, this latter notion ultimately converges not only in being loving, but in *being as loving as we can.* If we analyze the above sequence, we will discover an immense abyss between this final distillation and the undeveloped and reductionistic notion of no meat-eating. This same criterion can be easily applied to each of the other three principles, which instead of three don'ts actually speak of three positive values expressed in their highest possible degree.

In the case of "no illicit sex," a realistic reading of it refers to the expression of one's sexuality in the context of a committed relationship. This principle is tied with the virtue of purity, which, again, is not something necessarily limited to the realm of committed sexuality (or even full-fledged celibacy). To be *as pure as we can be* lies way beyond these initially simplistic notions. Similarly, "no intoxication" not only speaks about abstaining from intoxicating substances, but embracing the quality of austerity. To be *as austere as we can be* implies abstaining from different forms of intoxication not only externally but also internally. It includes, as well, abstaining from toxic emotional and thinking patterns. Finally, "no gambling" is not limited to an outright ban of your local casino, but to embracing the virtue of truthfulness. And being truthful has little to do with not lying, but with taking shelter in truth *as much as we can*, with its ultimate expression being divine love itself—something quite beyond the mere act of placing a bet. In this way, these four initial don'ts can quickly be upgraded to four subsequent do's, and these in turn will eventually show their ultimate face in the most comprehensive application we can possibly attach to them. As you may already sense, this is not a watering down of the Four Regulative Principles, but a deeper and broader—and a more challenging—way of relating to them.

Following the above criterion, Radical Integrity will rigorously examine the distance between our enacting the letter of the law and our embracing the spirit of it, insisting that we don't contradict ourselves by claiming to follow a principle externally while internally dismissing the defining aspects of that principle. An example of this would be embracing committed sex life with our partner but being violent with her—or even with ourselves—in one way or another. Another example would be avoiding toxic substances but intoxicating ourselves with pride or other vices that clearly go against genuine truthfulness. Similarly, we may be expert at avoiding sins of commission by externally following these Four Principles, but still engage in sins of omission by avoiding to deal with demanding issues that go against our sensibilities, in order to spare ourselves the discomfort of facing them, resulting in an attitude of hypocrisy and an expression of evasiveness. This can be worse than actually breaking one of the Four Regulative Principles, which gives cause for sincere repentance, because sins of omission leave the door wide open for a prideful façade of following these vows, while in reality it hides the constant failing to do so on a deeper level.

Considering the above, it should be natural to conclude that the mere external following of these principles does not constitute any definitive way of ascertaining one's inner standing in Gaudiya Vaishnavism. And this may help us understand why some practitioners may follow all these rules strictly for decades while still exhibiting the extremely poor character of a neophyte. Among other places, these principles are described in *Srimad Bhagavatam* 7.11.8 but not in the context of their representing transcendental qualities. Rather they are attributes that every human being should ideally possess. While these features are supremely relevant to our status as Gaudiya humans, they cannot be entirely correlated with our inner life or even moral quality as human beings. Thus, occasional failures in the external following of these principles are not a "fall down," as sometimes they are unfortunately described. These failures only show how a practitioner sometimes wins the battle, but also sometimes loses. Actual falling down may be compared to leaving the path altogether (or remaining in the path for the wrong reasons), but not to losing one or even many battles while continuing to strive humbly. The founder of Radical Personalism, Sri Gaurahari himself, has emphasized this fact by presenting his own Four Regulative Principles for every devotional aspirant. In his arguably most important instruction and golden rule, Gaurahari invokes the principle of Radical Integrity by claiming that the actual Four Regulative Principles for any Gaudiya Vaishnava are not the ones unraveled above, but *sunichena*, *sahisnuna*, *amanina*, and *manadena*: deep humility, compassion, unassertiveness, and respect, all in the context of spiritual culture. As long as we embrace these, it doesn't matter how many battles we may periodically lose in our trajectory.[21]

Radical Digitality

> *Due to the unprecedented pervasive and subtle reach into the fabric of our contemporary world, social media's potential influence and nuanced implications need to be continually explored, updated, and proactively addressed as a crucial aspect of our spiritual culture, daily life, and practice. We call this organic summoning of a "Fifth Regulative Principle" Radical Digitality.*

The right and duty of every Gaudiya ambassador is to grasp their corresponding zeitgeist and then address its malleable attributes according to time, place, and circumstance. In the present digital age, social media and technology are arguably *the* topics to be ascertained. This is to be done through continual dialogue, since the very nature of technology is to remain in a constant state of update. Thus, ongoing realities demand ongoing conversations so we can remain functional in relation to them, just as when addressing our ongoing inner dynamics. The Four Regulative Principles can be transgressed through social media in many more ways than we could have imagined a few decades ago. These include varieties of addiction (e.g., gaming), dependency on others' opinion of us, showing a false sense of identity to the world, and so on. And since social media amplify whatever problems we already experience, Radical Digitality attempts to confront this complex scenario via a veritable Fifth Regulative Principle.

While the voice of Conventional Dogmatism may stigmatize and even demonize the breaking of the Four Principles, it may conveniently normalize our unfiltered engagement with social media to the point of our breaking those same principles by the way we relate to technology. This might include being untruthful by showing online a false sense of who we are, committing diverse forms of violence in impersonal threads, and so on. In other words, we may normalize (and disguise) what we also demonize. The idea of Radical Personalism is not to engage in either or both normalizing or demonizing, but to find the middle path by proper approach and conception. We can step onto this middle path by first recognizing that even though social media was not originally conceived of as something spiritually uplifting, it has the potential to be so by being one of the unlimited energies of the Sweet Absolute. Nothing is intrinsically bad, because everything is ultimately resting in the Divine and therefore everything can connect us to him. In fact, a prime technological figure like Nikola Tesla would foretell that, at least in his idealistic view, future technological advancements would allow humans to have more free time and energy to dedicate themselves to life's higher purposes. While such a potential clearly exists, for such miracles to happen we need to *align* our potential. If we don't learn to see social media as one of the potencies of God, it will gradually replace what a Supreme Being meant to us. God's omniscience will be replaced by our daily Google search, his omnipresence by technology's unlimited functions and all-pervading existence, and his omnipotence by technology's having a more and more powerful influence on our life and consciousness.

Volumes have already been presented about the intoxicating effects of social media through the stimulus of dopamine and other similar substances in our own body. This already creates very new and strange patterns of thought and perception, and will be especially so for the generations yet to come, who may try to solve existential riddles through mere clicks of a device and develop a false sense of relationship devoid of any actual deep conversation and human connectedness. Deprived of face-to-face relationships, we lose our capacity for empathy and hearing each other—the perfection of distraction. On top of that, the more we surrender to social media without perceiving its sacred potential, the more qualities like memory will become deficient, and our capacity for deep reading, indistinguishable from deep thinking, will be eventually lost. Blaise Pascal would say, "All of humanity's problems stem from man's inability to sit quietly in a room alone." Let's apply this same principle not only to our modern times, but to our spiritual practices, which require a peaceful, focused mind and moments of prayer and introspection for it to be deeply remunerative. To put it bluntly, the cheap predictability of social media is the very antithesis of the contemplative heart we want to develop.

Radical Digitality thus seeks to bring awareness to this all-pervading milieu so that which is potentially unfavorable can somehow play a favorable role in our lives. In fact, the facilities of social media very much resemble the amazing yogic powers depicted in the ancient Hindu scriptures, but in this case, without any demand for severe austerity. Technology is thus a very subtle expression of material energy which, like any other expression of material energy, needs to be respectfully approached for us not to be entangled in it. Both our own attention and social media are but energies of God—and are to be properly honored. However, for this not to remain only a romantic ideal, we can test ourselves and see how much we are using technology with the right spirit by, for example, engaging in reasonable periods of social media detox and seeing if any variant of cold turkey emerges. Radical Personalism embraces sustainability, which in this case means to be satisfied with *a lifestyle that is so plausible that it will continue in eternity*. Since there is no social media in the spiritual realm, we should live our present lives without depending on it as an eternal asset. Consequently, Radical Digitality does not promote perpetual engagement with technology, but promotes a responsible involvement with it *here,* so through that involvement we are taken to the highest technology *there*—divine love.[22]

Radical Individuation

> *In complement to the universal principles consensually followed by almost every member of the Gaudiya tradition, we should also stress the importance of creating a personal* Rule of Life, *or vows and patterns that matter to each of us as individuals. The* Rule of Life, *although differing from one practitioner to another, will be as crucial as* (*or even more so than*) *the global regulations followed by the majority. We call this Radical Individuation.*

Although change is a crucial ingredient of life, change will be different for different people. For example, whatever this manifesto suggests is not something to be equally applied to each member of the Gaudiya tradition. And even if most of us require to upgrade the same specific area in our lives, each of us needs to do that in our own unique and individual way. When it comes to the question of change and how to embrace it, there is no universal template equally applicable to all. In connection with the above universal rules of conduct, they will be embraced and conceived differently by every individual, and what to speak of those personal rules of life that are unique to each practitioner. As diversity and nonduality exist in a mutually regenerative relationship, similarly does the individual and the universal, or collective. The process of a person's sense of unique identity—full with their unique gifts, qualities, and characteristics—rising distinctly from the group is known as Carl Jung has termed it, individuation. The psychological mechanism that pushes this process forward is the integration of the conscious with both the personal unconscious and the collective unconscious, resulting in a person who fully embraces the highest reach of collective values by becoming the best version of themselves—a fully unique person who gives back to their community synergistically and naturally through their successful progress toward individual wholeness. Individuation is different from individualism in regard to belonging and responsibility. While individualism tends toward an excessive notion of personal freedom and autonomy that leaves one feeling isolated from the whole, Radical Personalism supports individuation and therefore creates a healthy acknowledging of each other as unified but also diverse beings. Radical Personalism also creates a serious caring for those things that are to be integrated by any prospective mature individual. In other words, by properly dealing with our own human uniqueness in the context of spiritual practice, we will naturally be prompted to the humanlike individual uniqueness that waits for us in transcendence.

Conventional Dogmatism, remaining true to its nature, protests when hearing this proposal. This inner voice will promote a threatening notion of communism by which the individual ends up being reduced to the needs of the group, and only in that sense is taken as a valuable unit. Radical Individuation needs to speak louder than this, by *re-minding* its wicked sibling that our life project is all about remaining personal *as much as we can*, and this will actually represent the highest fruit for the collective. While this personal *Rule of Life* can be communal, most importantly they are always personal, and need to remain so even while being embraced in the context of a group. This implies that each aspirant is asked to look at where they are in their life *today*, and they are then invited to make a commitment to a particular way of living that makes sense for them as unique individuals. That continues to drive them forward in their inner transformation while calling for a positive, detailed, and balanced structure to guide their life, crafting an *ecology of practices* that inform, nourish, contextualize, and authenticate one another.

How might a Gaudiya Vaishnava *Rule of Life* look? It may ask you to explicitly state your aspirations (for the short, middle, and long term), and on the basis of that, it may ask you to arrange your daily activities in such a way that they fuel and prompt your desired goals in a realistic and sustainable way. Daily practical examples of how to implement this could be to decide regarding times to wake and sleep, amount of food to eat, exercise to be done, fasts to be kept, number of rounds to be prayed, sacred songs to be sung, texts to be studied, sexual commitments (from full abstinence to monogamy), acceptance of spiritual direction, use of psychotherapy or other mental disciplines if required, service commitments to a community, guru, or temple we may visit, service commitments to those in need in the world, times of the day that we will set aside for deeply considering God through prayer, and so on. This personal *Rule of Life* can then be witnessed by someone of significance (guru, spiritual mentor, partner) who will offer friendly advice and support, and it will also be revised as we mature as individuals. This process of Radical Individuation encourages each of us to reflect deeply on what we long for and then frame our day and life in a very concrete, flexible, and powerfully effective way.

Radical Fraternity

> *In terms of communal living and experience, Gaudiya Vaishnavism is invited to broaden its horizons to alternative expressions of "togetherness," where involvement with community life may take new unexpected shapes and dynamics. We call this Radical Fraternity.*

With rising levels of individualism and bizarre online dynamics in the world, the now old experience of community life seems to be at stake for many of us. For others, this uniquely complex scenario offers yet another golden opportunity for rethinking the very essence of communal life and how it can be rediscovered in our present times. Despite our being individuals, communal experience is absolutely crucial for the final success of Radical Personalism in the hearts of each of its members. In fact, a strong sense of community creates a strong sense of individual personhood—true individuals create true community, and true community creates true individuals.[23] Of course, as form and structure can often facilitate, they can also limit and suffocate. Something that was initially nourishing may later choke the very initial purpose it nicely served, creating the need to rethink our idea, in this case, of community. This proposal doesn't call for a debasing of any traditional core values, but proposes an extraction of further intrinsic purpose from the notion of spiritual community. This proposal continues to honor community's original purpose of committed mutual communion instead of complying with the mediocrity that so often infiltrates any human project with the passage of time. In fact, it is the very structures of many spiritual groups that encourage people to act disingenuously and pretend, fostering the development of hypocrites from initially sincere seekers.

Thus, Radical Personalism turns into Radical Fraternity and comes to our help, starting on the premise that community basically means *common unity*, and for that to happen we don't need expansive organizations or massive centralized gatherings. As Matthew 18:20 says, where three or even two of us are gathered together in the name of the Divine—in common unity—there the Sweet Absolute becomes manifest, and we have *created* community. Thus, it's not so much about finding a community as creating and embodying one. We Gaudiyas call this *svajatiya-prasanga*, or deep connection with like-minded brothers and sisters, through whom the music of conviviality is called to overflow. It is a holy ground where we can be tender-hearted to the broken places among ourselves, where we can be both safe and vulnerable. Saint Francis of Assisi would call this "a band of brothers and sisters." It is not a domination system as we may generally think of it, but rather a place where each person will dominate the other through the force of affection, each person equally enslaved by it in a decentralized way, centered on fraternity. A new sense of community.

Taking shelter in our own flock of kindred spirits also bears the name *intentional communities*, or *ashram* in Sanskrit. It is a place where we share with others the sacredness of life, and we do so with clear and committed intentions that may ultimately fulfill our common goals. In fact, to live in an *ashram* doesn't mean inhabiting a particular building, but taking inner shelter in proper company and building an *ashram* within our hearts. It is from those *heart*quarters that we will be able to set up a space where we can afford each other's transformation. There we can together not only communicate but *commune*. We can share participation in a joint ecology of practices while cultivating an enhanced sense of the depths within us calling to the depths of others. We can commit to fostering our sacred shared bonds the way we commit to a friendship—Radical Fraternity. It is contrary to the impersonal and utilitarian approach of Conventional Dogmatism and its emphasis on hard institutions. Radical Fraternity calls for real fraternity as the communal affiliation of the future. It is a principle complementary to that of having a guru and beloved elders in our communities. Our experience of *togetherness* needs to remain deep, personal, substantial, and as sacred as it can be, regardless of what shape it may take externally.

Radical Inreach

> *Taking over the world is not a Gaudiya goal, but taking over our own inner world is. In other words, the changing of one's own heart is the main purpose of this tradition. Sri Gaurahari wants to see transformed hearts, not a counting of heads. Whatever quantity follows that quality is then to be accepted and honored as the will of the Sweet Absolute. We call this Radical Inreach.*

Like any mystical movement, Gaudiya Vaishnavism is also possessed of a clear breadth and depth. Both are to be acknowledged and attended to, but an important hierarchy is to be established. First, as depth, or inreach, is properly embraced, then breadth, or outreach, can follow accordingly. The opposite sequence (initial breadth and subsequent depth) can create a superficial obsession with outreach while neglecting the principle of Radical Inreach, which dictates that we can touch others' hearts only as much as our own heart has first been transformed. Strictly speaking, there is nothing inherently positive about expansion per se—think of colonization, imperialism, or even metastasizing cancer. So we should be careful not to make expansion our very means and goal in life, divorced from inner culture. An over-idealized emphasis on proselytism may easily disguise itself as universal compassion, although in many cases it will only insist on transforming the world as a way of creating new converts to uplift our own weak faith. "If so many people are joining, then I must be in the right place!" Yes, this is the voice of Conventional Dogmatism once again. The bigger the crowd, the more negligible the individual becomes. The greater the outreach, the more possibilities to downplay and deny our need for inreach.

Radical Inreach was exposed by Gaurahari himself as the very genesis of his lineage. His initial inreach took him to a type of outreach which took him to a further inreach. The goal of life is not to preach, since in the spiritual world there will be no one to preach to. But here it can and should be done, and done in a way that will attract us more and more to a further inreach and the ultimate goal of life. This inreach can never be a selfish act, since attaining ultimate personal salvation implies, at least for Gaudiyas, becoming full givers and lovers in the deepest sense of the term. In Sanskrit, inreach and outreach are called *achar* and *prachar*, respectively. While *achar* refers to one's conduct, the term *prachar* includes in it the word *achar* but adds the prefix *pra*, which indicates augmentation. Thus, although generally translated as *outreach*, *pra-achar* actually means "a very special type of conduct." In other words, our own inner behavior is the most powerful and convincing form of outer dissemination. The more our hearts are full with realization to the point of overflowing, the more that realization will sprinkle on others and become something organically epidemic. Radical Inreach thus calls for a deepening of our practice, so that whatever gems we find in the depth-ocean of our prayer and service, we can extend to others. Devoid of this most precious *achar*, the word *prachar* ends up merely as *pr* or, more specifically, P.R.: *public relationships*, or a mere political campaign.[24]

Ministering to other people not only depends on our internal inreach, but is something deeply personal, ultimately transpersonal, but, especially in our present stage, interpersonal. We communicate sacred revelation by our words and inner example, but also through our living presence. In other words, we have to reside as close as possible to the hearts of those we are trying to serve. Preaching is deeply intertwined with sacred healing, and it is this combination which brings forth any possible conversion. While the printed word may be somewhat effective in this regard, it will remain impersonal by comparison. Without giving ourselves away, without letting others encounter us through some genuine form of interaction, without an actual *experience*, each of our words will remain halfway believable at best, at least in terms of inner impact. We can distribute thousands of spiritual books, but we may not necessarily be giving people the experience of unconditional love that everyone so much needs. Most of us know only conditional love and get repeatedly trapped into its loop, since we may have never experienced an alternative to it. This alternative is unconditional love, which is not about *what* we give but *how we give ourselves*. We thus give others the opportunity to taste and then voluntarily choose this second and most sacred option. People need to be put in touch with other people for real magic to happen. In fact, person-to-person was the way our ancient doctrine was originally spread—person-in-love-with-person, person-respecting-person, person-forgiving-person, person-crying-with-person. Radical Personalism.[25]

Radical Contemplation

> *The proper appreciation and role of prayer remains underestimated in many Gaudiya circles, being reduced to mere repetition instead of heartfelt invocation, to counting instead of chanting—to quantity instead of quality. Daily established periods of focused prayer and contemplative introspection could add deeper layers of insight and experience in the lives of many. We call this Radical Contemplation.*

For many, prayer is almost synonymous with a toxic system of God-domestication. In other words, we often resort to prayer when we want God to do our bidding instead of us doing his. Or we simply pray with a shallow confidence that we are doing God's bidding by merely completing our daily number of chanted rounds or prayers. Or we simply do not pray at all. While Conventional Dogmatism will surely reduce sacred prayer to these unwanted possibilities, Radical Personalism will promote a different, and basically opposite, understanding of prayer. It will promote prayer as an open reception of reality beyond our current needs, ideas, and understanding, with a deep trust in the active agency of reciprocal disclosure. Praying is not limited to a mere recital of prayers, but includes *doing whatever we may happen to be doing in a prayerful mood*. This is the very meaning of leading a contemplative lifestyle, where every act can become prayer. Without embracing this spirit, we run the risk of losing the ethos of prayer even during those moments when we are officially praying. Radical Contemplation is thus a life trade, a career that one chooses. Like any other well-chosen vocation, it consumes us to such an extent that eventually it ceases to become a trade in our life and becomes the very life of our life. Prayer is a *way of life* to be thoroughly assimilated through dedication and practice. It is not an occasional weekend ritual but something with the potential of becoming second nature in us and a genuine source of shelter and divine revelation.

As Gaudiya Vaishnavas, one of the main ways we are encouraged to pray is through the daily recitation of God's sacred names. However, recitation can also become a mechanistic, formulaic, and superficial performance if not accompanied by a sincere prayerful spirit. The very goal of prayer is to offer our hearts through our daily recitation, and not to finish a certain number of beads on our *mala*, or rosary. As someone who writes becomes a writer, and someone who plays becomes a player, *someone who prays becomes a prayer*. Prayer does not constitute meritocracy or a moral worthiness contest, through which we will be rewarded in the future for having attained the proper quantity of tokens, without any consideration of the internal quality of the presentation. Prayer is not an effort-based endeavor, a calculated interaction with the Sweet Absolute, but the most genuine way we can possibly submit ourselves unto the Divine. It's not about deserving, but humbly begging for the undeserved grace we so much require. Furthermore, since the Supreme Lord loves to reside in and reveal his secrets through silence,[26] some daily moments of silent contemplative prayer can be added to our daily prayer engagements, to bestow powerful impressions that may be then carried throughout the rest of our days and lives.

Due to its meaningful significance, this particular face of Radical Personalism will have its own chapter in the third part of this book.

Radical Counseling

> *Considering the ever-unfolding nature of reality and our spiritual journey, we Gaudiyas require a detailed direction and*

> *individualized guidance about how to relate with our surroundings as well as the specifics of our inner expedition and its different chapters. To label and accommodate everyone according to generic stages that do not necessarily correspond with each specific individual may be helpful as a starting point, but more personalized direction will become crucial as the practitioner begins to develop their own identity within the group. We call this Radical Counseling.*

No single journey is traveled exactly the same way by two people. Spiritual life, being a whole journey unto itself—actually, *the* journey—holds this truth in its ultimate form. Such a pilgrimage is personally customized not only due to specifics of each unique individual, but also because no individual will ever experience the same point of the journey exactly like any other traveler. In fact, to properly establish at every step where we are in our journey is one of the most important aspects of our spiritual culture. When we stop doing so, we start to relate to ourselves and others as abstract nonindividual beings, something which dangerously starts to resemble Radical Personalism's main nemesis, impersonalism. While the voice of Conventional Dogmatism may tempt us to go into this unsafe direction of compliance, we should know that *to remain a person* is the very crux and essence of our life expedition.

There are universal principles for all of us to follow, and there is specific advice necessary for each practitioner to receive. Thus, in conjunction with general guidelines for universal application, it is imperative to organize our lives and communities in such a way that Radical Counseling is provided so each of us can be better equipped to confront the unknown and complex landscapes that inner progress will bring forth. While sacred scripture clearly describes various stages and symptoms that most of us will eventually go through, not every person will *experience* them in exactly the same way. Likewise, our shadow work will reveal obstacles that may seem to disappear, while they are actually adopting a new, more subtle shape. We will need to deal with all these intricacies while remaining ourselves—that is, in an individualized way. And hopefully we do so not alone, but with the affectionate guidance and Radical Counseling of elders and fellow pilgrims.

Radical Education

> *A Vaishnava lectionary is always desirable for each Gaudiya community, through which the study of sacred texts can be organized around daily, weekly, monthly, and even yearly cycles of readings that aim at grounding and guiding us in our scriptural legacy. But even above this external structure of study, the inner spirit of our learning should be open to revision as well as new methods that may facilitate a more ruminative approach to divine revelation. We call this Radical Education.*

The word *education* comes from the Latin verbal root *educare,* which means "to bring out of" or "to lead forth." In other words, real education is not an act but a *process*, positive and empowering, that continues after the official lessons are finished. Education is not information but transformation. Stages in Vaishnava education would be those of initial hearing, learning, and study, then to be upgraded by further understanding and insights acquired through sincere reflection. Eventually we will properly assimilate and internalize our subject, having acquired new skills that have become second nature for us, through which we end up effortlessly living and breathing our subject.[27] Only then can we think about comprehensively sharing that fruit with others. Radical Education thus prompts the progress of scriptural study through this gradual and sequential methodology, such that we can take the necessary time and effort to grasp the very essence of revealed knowledge. In fact, according to Gaudiya Vaishnavism, one of the potential offenses to the sacred message is *neglecting the required endeavor* to understand it properly. Instead of jumping ahead and asking what books we should read, first we should have enough integrity to ask if we should read, and if so, then the necessary sequel is how should we read. Naturally, *what* to read will become self-evident in due course of time. And the fruit of that process will naturally overflow from our hearts to the hearts of others.

In the Gaudiya tradition, *sastra*, or sacred revelation, is expected to be properly complemented with *guru* and *sadhu*, or the example and teaching of one's divine preceptor and saintly people, respectively. That said, virtues like common sense and critical thinking need to be added as a significant fourth pillar to this original triad. These additional assets will help us realize how in many cases "taking scripture seriously" will not equate with *taking it literally, but transformationally*. In fact, the sacred message is possessed of—and thus can be read through—endless layers of meaning, summarized as the literal, the archetypal, and the esoteric. In this connection Gaudiyas will say that scripture may speak at times as a king (giving orders/literally), as a friend (telling stories/archetypically), or as a lover (in secret/esoterically), and we need to properly decipher each of these usages.

Another example of critical thinking in the context of exegesis could be the acceptance that absolute scriptural inerrancy, as well as the saints' sheer infallibility, is not something we actually *need* to believe for us to attain spiritual consummation. In this connection, we should add to our syllabus the understanding that some statements in scripture are not absolute, but relative to time, place, and circumstance, and thus we are not expected to necessarily follow them. This crucial discernment is called for in *Srimad Bhagavatam* 11.8.10, where it is stated, "Just as the honey bee takes nectar from all flowers, big and small, an intelligent human being should only take the essence from scripture." If intelligent people are instructed to extract the essence of the sacred texts, then it logically follows that scripture also includes nonessential and relative content that is destined for the nonintelligent. A classic example of this would be the advocacy of slavery in some sections of the Bible,[28] or in the Vaishnava-related texts, some sections in the *Manu-samhita* which are significantly misogynistic.[29] The acceptance of nonessential content in the scriptures is further confirmed in *Srimad Bhagavatam* 12.3.14, which describes how certain stories found in this work "do not in themselves constitute the ultimate aspect of knowledge." Sri Jiva Goswami comments on this verse concluding, "These stories do not contain absolute truth." In connection with this, studying scripture through the lenses of diverse yet complementary fields, such as cultural anthropology (studying the development of human culture and societies), may be just as important as the texts themselves. We can make a similar statement about learning classical scriptural languages, such as Sanskrit. These various disciplines will allow us to respectfully yet critically study the work of our ancestors in their specific historical and social contexts. This multidimensional approach to understanding scripture sheds light on the necessary context, both longitudinally across time and presently, within which the understanding of scripture is to be seen. While the voice of Conventional Dogmatism may cry out and impose a copy-paste relationship with revelation, Radical Education will take a step further and emphasize the freedom—or dare we say, moral obligation—that each of us has in relation to properly examining both the essentials and the accidentals included in sacred texts.

As mentioned above, part of this educational project could take the form of an organized Vaishnava lectionary, through which students engage with seasonal and daily studies, and which can and should take different forms according to the individual and local situation in one's community. Apart from existing certificate programs that may be compelling for a few practitioners, here we mostly refer to a laid-out curriculum and path for everyone. Needless to say, projects like this may take years—or probably decades, centuries, and even millennia—to be thoroughly developed and established, but we can always begin from a modest and realistic space. This could mean setting up some specific order of the main Gaudiya texts to be ideally studied by every aspirant, setting clear periods of time to engage with those texts throughout yearly or monthly cycles, selecting certain sections from the scriptures to be meditated upon daily, establishing special readings for Vaishnava festivities of different types, and so on. Eventually, a committee could be formed to continue developing this original lectionary into a more sophisticated form. Once this lectionary is stabilized, books can be published which may include the readings of each month and season. An extension of this same principle could take place by sharing daily, weekly, or monthly vows and/or meditations, where one is invited to reflect with others upon some particular teaching, text, or virtue, or even journalize about it.

Finally, beyond the above suggestions of how to implement Radical Education in our scriptural reading, we would like to conclude by emphasizing that the study of divine revelation is ultimately not about merely accumulating information but cultivating *transformation*. Thus, ideally, our approach to scripture should be as transformative as we can allow. As part of the cross-pollinated nature of Radical Personalism, for this we turn to the Christian method of *Lectio Divina*, or "divine reading," which could be easily applied to our own Gaudiya approach to scriptural study. This method consists of four simple steps: (1) Read some section of scripture ("What does this say?"); (2) meditate and ruminate on its significance ("What does this say *to me*?"); (3) pray to the Sweet Absolute for grace and further understanding ("What does this say *to him*?"); and (4) contemplate, using contemplation as a pure gift where God replies to our prayer ("What does *he* say to me?"). A fifth stage sometimes added to this equation is "action," or engaging in a concrete activity that may embody the fruit of this precious fourth-step process. This lingering practice, which can be effortlessly applied to our own tradition, basically intends to make the word of revelation *become flesh* in us through our going beyond a mere intellectual apprehension of the text while entering the deep contemplative space of Radical Education.

Radical Speech

> *In the context of Gaudiya mystical theology and the concern of how to properly convey its essence, another significant consideration would be to determine whether longer lectures could be replaced with shorter presentations followed by dialogue, or whether classes could sometimes be replaced with dynamic conversations. We call this Radical Speech.*

To speak and hear about the unending glories of Ultimate Reality, and to do it for its own sake, is one of the favorite daily exercises of Gaudiya Vaishnavas: when you are in love, you can talk about your sweetheart forever and ever. But as we have said earlier, *the more sublime the gift, the more delicate the container*. In this case, this principle takes the shape of considering alternative necessities and new vessels in order to communicate a particular idea to specific audiences. While Conventional Dogmatism may perpetually opt for traditional modes of delivery that are often still effective, Radical Speech proposes a new methodology capable of complementing the routine procedures.

In this particular case, when appropriate, the alternative orthodoxy leans in favor of dialogue rather than monologue, of conversation rather than one-way sermons. This system often sets the stage for thrilling brainstorming, full of dynamism and inspiration, which may not manifest if a lecture is delivered by only one person. While monologues can be exciting and dynamic if both audience and speaker are equally invested and actively participating in both hearing and speaking, this same format can lead to monotony and stagnation if the involved parties participate simply from a place of protocol and formality—from a place of Conventional Dogmatism. Radical Speech, however, is characterized by dialogue, whether through actual discussion or a full communion between orator and listener. Such communion manifests a deep and active interest that goes beyond simply hearing the words another person speaks; it also seeks to understand the meaning, intent, and implications behind the words, and how such perspective can nourish, augment, and upgrade progress toward the ideal. Since without this active communication we have no real dialogue and no possibility of meaningful relationships, then what we have is again impersonalism. Conversely, Radical Speech will continuously attempt to seek ongoing ways of transmitting reality to one another.

Radical Embodiment

> *Although we are not the physical/psychic body, this doesn't mean we shouldn't take care of it and learn to properly integrate the bodily dimension into all the other layers of being. In fact, if properly linked with transcendence, our present body can become fully spiritualized and potentially accompany us for eternity. Therefore, all the more, it deserves to be properly honored and attended in the context of sacred service. We call this Radical Embodiment.*

While we have repeatedly heard that we are not this body, in a deeper sense we could come full circle and say that we actually are this body. The process of transfiguration first begins with a *sadhaka-deha*, or the practitioner's body Gaudiya Vaishnavas receive during spiritual initiation, and culminates with a *siddha-deha*, or that moment when our *sadhaka-deha* becomes fully spiritualized and accomplished through the gift of divine grace. Considering this, we have the right to say that we are this body, since we are this *sadhaka-deha*, which has the potential of attaining full consummation and "becoming us" for eternity. Since this practitioner's body is a gift bestowed upon us during the initiation rite, our present body is thus a gift which does not belong to us but to the Divine, and which we should therefore take care of—*even venerate*.

In stark contrast with this view, Conventional Dogmatism disparages the bodily dimension as a temporary material distraction and even moral temptation to our anti-material souls. This view is nothing but a toxic notion that puts us at odds with our bodies—as strangers to them—those same bodies that deserve our respect and care. This dangerous proposal allows for neglect and dismissal of those venerable elements that deserve our attention, starting with our present physicality. By discounting our own bodies, we deprive ourselves of the grounding necessary to function in a holistic way. Radical Embodiment thus calls us to get off our theological elevators that take us up into an abstract sky of over-idealized ideas of transcendence, and instead ground ourselves in immediate reality. A tall and expansive tree can only be such by its deeply rooted grounding. In this connection, Carl Jung is said to have quoted from a rabbi, "Modern man cannot see God because he doesn't look low enough."[30] We don't need a *climbing* religion, but rather a *descending* one. In brief, we need to give permission to the word *health* to come onto the stage, and lead the way. We need deeper health care in the form of proper exercise, rest, and food, none of which are necessarily material attachments, but aspects of our own life and practice. We may also need proper psychic concern in the form of whatever psychological therapy may be required. In fact, we could say that the physical body is the visible part of our mind, while the mind is the invisible part of the body. As our physical body can get damaged and require the help of professionals, the same criterion applies to our psychic or subtle body. In fact, we could say that most of our problems are psychological in their manifestation but spiritual in their solution. While our Gaudiya predecessors more easily trusted the spiritual solution than we probably do, they seldom had the vocabulary we have today to describe the psychological manifestations, a vocabulary we need to employ in the service of our spiritual ideal.[31] As mundane as this may seem to the untrained eye, each of these engagements can constitute another glorious side of being a Radical Personalist.

In our premature sense of transcendence, we generally engage in what we may call *disembodied spirituality*. We usually do not inhabit our body with intimacy and depth, but spend most of our time in its uppermost chamber—the *head*quarters—relegating our physical existence from the neck down to an "it." From this *heady* place of psychoemotional decapitation and schizoid detachment, we conceive the body not as a whole but as an assemblage of poorly connected parts, since going deeper into our body may uncover some unpleasant feelings and unresolved issues embedded in our cellular constitution. Thus, disembodied spirituality (another way of invoking the voice of Conventional Dogmatism) will view the body as a mere karmic burden and the price to pay for incarnating, rather than something we can value and that can become fully spiritualized and assist us in the pursuit of our highest ideals. In fact, "the flesh" has received negative press for millennia, being associated with sin, carnality, moral weakness, and disease. In contrast, Radical Embodiment chooses to define matter, and thereby our body, in positive terms, as *something that can become extremely gross, but also (and especially) extremely spiritualized.* And on top of that we could say that since everything is connected to God, then our body is also connected to him. Thus, by connecting with our bodies we are connecting in one sense with God, since we are connected with something intrinsically connected to him. Cutting through spiritual disembodiment is a journey into and through the very pain that first drove us to disown and dissociate from our body, a journey through which the bodily dimension is explored and appreciated for what it is. It is not some*thing* that belongs to us, but sentient energy on the move, in concert with Ultimate Reality. This journey implies a meta-movement, not from here to there, but *from here to a deeper here*. The more we dismiss our body, the more we become a no-body. Radical Embodiment *is* in itself relationship. It means consciously and responsibly embracing every layer of our present experience in connection to our source. It means bringing us into a more integral wholeness until we clearly are in body what we are in spirit.[32]

Radical Correlation

> *A big neglect of and erosion in the social fabric of the Gaudiya community has become more and more apparent throughout the last decades. This is evident from parenting to caring for elders and everything in between, including toxic ways of relating to earning and spending. Each of these domains needs to be dealt with for what they are—potential sacred ingredients of our spiritual project. We call this Radical Correlation.*

Bhakti is the Gaudiya term for devotional service, another way of referring to our loving attempt to connect with the Sweet Absolute and everything related to him. And absolutely everything, *without exception*, is related to him. If everything has an intrinsic connection with our common source, we can acknowledge it as worshipable. Thus our main task will be to become aware of that inherent relation that every thing has with its center. In this "every thing," we thus include things our Conventional Dogmatic voice has unfortunately deemed unbecoming. This judgment quite often dares to speak in representation of the Gaudiya tradition and refers to things like family life, parenting, money, and so on.

Beginning with the supposed inferiority of the family unit, this underestimation is tightly connected with the overestimated monastic superhero archetype and its corresponding bubble of immunity, as well as a misrepresented emphasis on renunciation of the world as something necessarily superior. At least from a strict Gaudiya perspective, whether married or renounced one will belong to an *ashram*, or shelter. A family person will find himself in what we Gaudiyas call the *grihasta-ashram*, while the renounced will find himself in the monastic *ashram*. Whatever the case, these are *ashrams*, or shelters, and the person embracing a particular shelter won't be necessarily higher than one who chooses a different refuge. Since the goal of Gaudiya Vaishnavism is *bhakti*, or devotion, if *bhakti* stops being the priority and *ashram* considerations become paramount, an *ashram* stops being an *ashram*, since it will no longer facilitate the attainment of the goal of divine love. A well-known example of how family life is not an obstacle in itself is presented in *Srimad Bhagavatam* 10.14.36, where Brahma says to the Sweet Absolute, "Until people become your devotees, their material attachments and desires remain thieves, their homes remain prisons, and their affectionate feelings for their family members remain foot-shackles." This verse indirectly but clearly points to how, if properly centered in God, family life, home, and even desires can all act in a redeeming way. This is clearly mentioned in Srila Prabhupada's commentary on this verse, where he says that "if we engage our family in the loving service of the Lord, our endeavors to maintain our family become part and parcel of our progressive spiritual duties." Even more clearly, Visvanatha Chakravarti comments, "In that way, the same home, which was formerly a prison cell created by favorable and unfavorable karmic reactions, becomes for the devotee a place filled with service to God by hearing and chanting his glories, and a host of other activities meant to please the Absolute. These activities carry one to God's eternal abode." Similarly, *Srimad Bhagavatam* 7.15 describes the duties for a married person. The conclusive verse of that chapter (7.15.67) states, "If a person worships the Lord with devotion, though he remains in the home, he can attain the Supreme." Visvanatha Chakravarti comments on this verse declaring even more emphatically, "The subject is concluded. If one is a householder and worships the Lord, he can attain the Supreme." Interestingly enough, family life will be the eternal prospect in both Vraja and Nadiya for all Gaudiya Vaishnavas. In other words, no Gaudiya will be a renunciant in eternity.

If a particular doctrine is renunciation-centric, it will naturally be inclined in a pessimistic way toward family and social dealings. Even persons in family life will come to see their present situation as something to get rid of as soon as possible. As a result of this, neglect and spiritual bypassing in the name of religion occur. Although we are concerned about the so-called negative influences of the world on ourselves and our children, we may be less concerned about the negative ethos coming from our own religion or our misunderstandings of it. Thus we create involuntary abuse of our own children by imposing upon them a whole series of undigestible dogmas that result in eventual trauma. We may impose pressure and an over-idealized projection about how they should behave spiritually in the future. Although each of us wields a certain amount of power, parents are especially loaded weapons with tremendous potential to inflict both light and darkness upon their children.

The erosion of our social fabric has proven to create deficiencies in our ability to give our children a positive and holistic approach to life. These deficiencies fail to satisfy the needs of individuals throughout their life. From the moment of conception up to the moment of death there is a dearth of holistic care in education, psychological and social counseling, and physical and financial support for the ill and aged. Similarly, a very important aspect of Radical Correlation will be to assist each practitioner in transitioning from one *ashram* into another. This applies not only to persons moving from monastic life into married life after an anticipated span as a monastic has come to an end, but also to longtime monks who come to recognize their unexpected need to have a family. Our assistance will be to include and accommodate them without shame or stigmatization from their communities; this is vital. In this connection, the classical Hindu epic called *Mahabharata* refers to an intermediate stage called the *snataka-ashram*, which refers to those transitional periods that are *as important* as the permanent stages.[33] Finally, Radical Personalism promotes a healthy approach to spending and earning. For example, most ex-monks, and even current monks, may require further education about how to make a living and be prepared to deal with the world's financial challenges. Seeing how each of these neglected areas may affect the other in a snowball effect, Radical Correlation tries to bring healthy awareness to the various threads of our social fabric, like health, housing, employment, marriage, vocational guidance, financial assistance, and spiritual counselors who may guide us through each of these natural chapters of our lives.

Radical Sexuality

> *Nowadays Gaudiya Vaishnavism is possessed with a serious case of erotophobia. We need to make peace with this reality and stop fearing sexual expression, attacking it, and stigmatizing its practice and implications. We need to understand sexuality more organically, not only by establishing its purposes and boundaries, but especially by avoiding shallow denial and detrimental repression. We call this Radical Sexuality.*

Among his endless contributions, the prominent Gaudiya saint Sri Rupa Goswami presented the important notion of *niyamagraha*. This Sanskrit term has different meanings, one of them referring to how we should first *understand properly what we are rejecting* before rejecting it. After understanding whatever we planned to reject, we may realize that we don't have to reject it, but rather only recalibrate our approach to it in a more nuanced way. When anything is properly understood, it will create unlimited possibilities for spiritual advancement. However, when that same thing is grossly misinterpreted, it will invoke more and more varieties of guilt, shame, and toxic lifestyles. Regarding sex, if you start with a theology of sin management administered by a too-often elite clergy, you will for sure end up with a schizophrenic religion.[34] Arguably, the place of sexual expression in the life of spiritual aspirants is one of the main topics that begs for a comprehensive treatment. Sex in itself is not something bad; there would be neither a writer nor readers of this book without it. But our approach to it may need to be reviewed. The Gaudiya theologian Sri Jiva Goswami presents the idea of *sanga-siddha-bhakti*, which basically means that everything can potentially be included as part of our spiritual project if connected with a proper understanding and conception. Following this line of thought, we could then make the case for sex potentially being an aspect of *bhakti*.[35]

At this point, Conventional Dogmatism will raise multiple red flags and insist on its promotion of shame-based sexual understandings through so-called "purity culture." But if we study a little bit of history, we will find how the ancient Vedic culture from which Gaudiya Vaishnavism has historically sprung was free from erotophobic narratives. Eros-friendly *Kama-sutra* promotes throughout its texts the notion of *kama* (sensual delight) as one of the four human goals of life. Denying these facts and instead encouraging a suppression and even demonization of natural human eros has deep damaging consequences for people of all ages. No wonder research has shown that socially forced repression contributes to exploitation and manipulation, especially in religious settings. As already mentioned, transcendence is not about indifference but integration, so not only lay people but even monastics will have to deal with their sexual dimension successfully. A good way to approach this could be to conceive of sexual interaction in broader terms as (a) creative energy, (b) intimacy, and (c) connection. Needless to say, creativity can and should be expressed in multiple forms apart from physical procreation, and both intimacy and connection can also be experienced not only on the bodily platform, but also psychically and spiritually. Interestingly, the Sanskrit term *sanga* indicates both sexual activity and intimate fellowship with kindred spirits.

In the contemporary Gaudiya dynamics, it is often proclaimed that sexual union can be invoked only for bringing a child into this world. Otherwise, it falls into the category of sin or "illicit sex." This restricted understanding of the role of sexuality has had terrible consequences in the past decades throughout many Gaudiya communities, and urgently needs to be revised. As an alternative, Radical Sexuality suggests a more realistic and detoxified approach to this department: sexual activity outside of procreation in a committed relationship is not something that necessarily goes against one's spiritual goals. Instead, it can represent a very laudable attempt to sincerely acknowledge one's need for intimacy and trying to satisfy that in a controlled way, as part of balancing one's needs as a human being. In fact, Thakura Bhaktivinoda mentions in his *Bhaktyaloka* that the term *brahmacharya* can be understood as continence but also as "proper use of one's semen," and he then further qualifies his idea by explaining that this form of *brahmacharya* refers to "not indulging in sex with women other than one's own wife."[36] He doesn't further qualify sex as limited to procreation. Thus, there is a place for sexuality outside of procreation in the context of a committed and mature relationship. In other words, between the two extremes of procreative sex and selfish carnal exploitation, we should be able to find some in-between point, where sexual interaction can promote a healthy development of our personality as well as the necessary intimacy in our human relationships. On the basis of these wider considerations, we will be able to embrace spirituality much more comprehensively than by being traumatized by guilt and shame due to having sex for some reason other than procreation. In fact, one could be a married person who only engages in sex for conceiving a hoped-for exemplary, saintly child but at the same time becomes arrogant due to having attained such "purity." Although technically speaking that person has done things "legally," in a deeper sense he may be in a worse position than a humble practitioner who acknowledges his limitations and sincerely struggles to continue growing in his spiritual practice. Another scenario to consider is if one man has sex exclusively for procreating but is not fully responsible as a father and neglects his parenthood, while a second man has sex without the purpose of procreating, and his wife becomes unexpectedly pregnant, but he then takes full responsibility for the child. What would be a greater expression of *bhakti* here: having sex only for procreation or taking full responsibility for the result of one's sexual activity?

As strange as it may sound to some, relational intimacy can become a very powerful path to inner healing and awakening. However, by saying this we are not proposing a cheap and superficial experience of sexual fantasies, but actually a deep awareness of the underlying motivations behind our sexual drive. In other words, we may think that our sexual arousal in response to a particular person is no more than an expression of our natural sexuality when it may actually be an eroticizing of our conditioning or of some nonsexual need we have. We can give the example of a woman who, having had an emotionally unavailable father, is attracted to a man who is also emotionally unavailable, or that of a man who feels attracted to sadomasochistic porn and practices because, as a boy, he was severely beaten almost daily by his mother and that was the only touch he got from her. As we learn, unresolved violence can lead to eroticized trauma. In fact, we can eroticize just about anything from our undigested past and merely employ sexual pleasure as a release valve, a fast-fix depressurizer, with our partner being little more than the outlet for this. In contrast to this toxic template, Radical Sexuality invites what we may call *sexual integrity*, a de-eroticizing of our needs and wounds by seeing them in their rawness, so we can turn toward what we *really* need. However, we cannot have sexual maturity without a corresponding emotional, moral, mental, psychological, and spiritual maturity. A healthy integration of all these layers will naturally result in sexual expression not as a symptom of unresolved trauma, but as a natural expression of trust, affection, and uncensored loving intimacy with one's partner.[37]

To put it bluntly, we are to be honest and sincere with our present situation and capacities, and from there we should proceed accordingly. This is known in Sanskrit as *adhikara*, or establishing our nature, potential, and vocation by first acknowledging our present limits and abilities to engage in a particular activity. In other words, *adhikara* does not mean to do what we cannot yet do, but to do what we can actually do (but may not be doing). It means not rushing toward something too high or evading something with the excuse that we are too low. If we act above or below our present abilities, we will be evading whatever challenges we need to embrace in the present moment. Thus, being irresponsible not only means doing what we should not do, but also *not doing what we should be doing. Adhikara* implies taking full responsibility for who we are at present and fully acknowledging whatever happened in our past to bring about such a result. Only then can progress take place. Sacred scripture considers such sincere recognition to be real beauty.[38] Radical Sexuality calls exactly for this: an honest assessment of ourselves in the context of one of the most powerful energies in existence, so we can properly honor its strength and function.

Radical Monasticism

> *The way monastic life is currently conceived, over-idealized, and implemented in many Gaudiya communities needs to be rigorously reviewed and properly adjusted to the needs of the present time. We call this Radical Monasticism.*

Among other things, a monk is someone who engages his creative energy in inventively expressing his own nature and vocation in the context of intimate fellowship. In the context of monasticism this creative energy, known in Sanskrit as *kriya-shakti*, needs to be expressed and never repressed, unless we desire to witness a dangerous case of perversion. In fact, to have repressed energy while embracing a lifestyle that does not fit our nature is one of the main problems with current Gaudiya monasticism, and especially with the *sannyasa-ashram*, a lifelong vow of renunciation. Every vocation has its professional risks, especially in a technocratic hypersexual world,[39] and the *sannyasi* who loses sight of the meaning of his monastic vocation may very well lose his life in a sterile preoccupation with himself. And this is especially the case where the very environment over-idealizes—and therefore dehumanizes—the monastics, seeing them as inherently superior to the lay practitioners, and projecting unto them some form of superhero archetype which leads to an unnatural level of expectation and social pressure to reciprocate accordingly. The monk receives the message that his duty in his profession is to be perfect and immaculate, or at least appear that way to the community. This is *big* pressure. However, we want to be devotional human beings, not devotional superheroes. A *sannyasi* is not necessarily a superhero, nor does he need to be. Nor is a monk necessarily more advanced than any other person.[40] In fact, the essential teachings of Gaudiya Vaishnavism do not consider monasticism the goal of life or even a limb of *bhakti*. Additionally, we Gaudiya Vaishnavas have a very specific and clear projection in eternity, and in those identities of service none of us will be a monastic. Thus, a Gaudiya monk should deal with his present monasticism in such a way that it does not get in the way of the ultimate nonmonastic identity he wants to attain in the spiritual world.

Essentially, to be a monk has to do with embracing what lies outside of the comfort zone, and that's why one of the main qualities of a monastic will be *abhayatva*, or fearlessness in the face of uncertainty. Interestingly, this attribute is intimately tied to the virtue of creativity, since to be creative means to go where other people have not gone—to explore the unknown and uncertain without fear. Embraced for the wrong reasons, however, monasticism can be employed to foster its exact opposite: a toxic sense of security, superiority, and complacency through attachment to position, followers, and other superfluous perks.[41] This façadelike presentation is typical of the Conventional Dogmatic inner voice. It will make the whole renunciation project less than what it should be. Or in some cases, it will render it obsolete by keeping a false sense of monasticism and engaging in it for further wrong reasons. Some so-called monks may embrace this order as their security system and lifelong employer. For others, monastic life may be like joining a male club to get the male energy they never got as sons. As Thomas Merton has wisely said, "Only God can make monks, and human expedients to increase the number of monastic vocations would only end with the ruin of the order."[42]

Since external renunciation can easily be employed to attract and attain its actual opposite, the spirit of *inner poverty* is to be equally embraced in Radical Monasticism to prevent this from happening. In Sanskrit, this is referred to by the term *yukta-vairagya*, or "proper renunciation"—one of the most abused ideas in Gaudiya Vaishnavism. Why? Because in the name of engaging everything in divine service, more often than not we end up exploiting those same resources with hidden selfish purposes. *Vairagya*, or renunciation, means "a special type (*vi*) of attachment (*raga*)." In other words, renunciation is a mere byproduct of passionate sacred love and divine attachment. On the surface, this understanding of renunciation may be quite confusing for some. Why? For most, material enjoyment is located on one end of the spectrum and renunciation is generally considered its exact opposite, and thus overtly identified with spiritual advancement. A good litmus test for this is to put the Sanskrit term *sadhu* (saint) in Google Search and check the result. Each reference points to a renunciant, indicating the preconceived notion that "renunciant" equals "saint." Interestingly enough, due to the nondual nature of the Sweet Absolute, the Gaudiya idea of sacred dedication harmonizes the dualistic divide of exploitation and renunciation, giving room for absolutely everything to be engaged in the service of Divinity. The material world needn't be renounced; consciousness, however, must be reoriented—the field of absorption must change. Due to its nuanced nature, this stance can be not only difficult to understand for outsiders, but difficult to grasp by insiders as well.

Beyond all that has been discussed so far, monasticism is not something necessarily limited to a religious order while living in a monastery and practicing full-fledged celibacy. We can expand the essence of this term and speak about the possibility of a "universal monastic archetype," as it has been famously put by Raimon Panikkar.[43] This proposal intimates that all of us have what we may call a "monastic side," which only needs to be activated for it to fully express its main defining feature:[44] a particular level of commitment with the development and maturation of one's spiritual life as something fully integrated and not separable from one's daily endeavors. This is a new way of conceiving the monastic order and practice—a New Monasticism.[45] Even if we choose to live in a remote monastery and follow all of its expected mandates, we will be actual monks if we choose to *embrace the lifestyle* that corresponds with such an ideal. Or even more accurately, as much as we choose the monastic approach, no matter where we live and who we are, we are living the monastic experience. Radical Personalism considers this kind of vision the very future of the monastic order. It is a vision and an opportunity available for everyone. By definition, a monk is someone who "goes into himself," who embraces introspection, depth of thought, and commitment with the spiritual discipline as his all-in-all. This is the type of Radical Monasticism we choose to encourage, whether in the form of actual monks, communities centered on such principles, or experiences all of us search for as a way to remain sober and focused in our modern life.

Radical Egalitarianism

> *Gender-based myths, such as women being intrinsically less intelligent and less qualified than men to engage in mystical life*

> *or serve as gurus, or practitioners from transgender designations being less eligible for devotion, are outdated conceptions and are no more than folk tales of inequality that need to be rightly dispelled. We call this Radical Egalitarianism.*

As femininity can surely express its toxic side through venues such as victim consciousness, masculinity is widely (in)famous for its own toxic catharsis in the form of chauvinism, authoritarianism, and tyrannical patriarchal systems which discriminate, underrate, and disempower everything that is not male in its constitution. This all-pervading fraud has affected religion to unimaginable degrees, and Gaudiya Vaishnavism has been no exception to this rule. Ironically, in almost all cases, the more patriarchal a culture, the greater its devotion to the Goddess in one form or another. Maybe unconsciously, and often not very successfully, these traditions are actually trying to balance themselves out.[46] Correspondingly, despite being members of a tradition which is female-oriented at its core, with its enormous emphasis on *shakti*, or the principle of the Divine Feminine, we Gaudiyas have exhibited throughout history a large amount of toxic masculinity in more than one form. We have done this not only by overemphasizing males above females, but by excessively indulging in masculine qualities like authority, honor, and worship, to the point of abuse and oppression. Needless to say, abuse can happen not only to women or children, but to adults of any gender designation in varieties of forms, such as shunning, ostracizing, scapegoating, character assassination, and so on. Therefore, we first need to frame and name every form of abuse possible and then proceed accordingly. Radical Egalitarianism fully validates this procedure while opposing those so-called refuges where predators may still hide.

As absurd and primitive as it may sound, some Gaudiya organizations still consider that only men are capable of serving as gurus, or even occupying certain posts and services in their communities. Instead of considering the individual's eligibility for any of these activities (regardless of gender, race, and social standing), these archaic ideas portray what we may call Regressive Vaishnavism, not Progressive Vaishnavism. The voice of Conventional Dogmatism will of course insist on retrogressive action, one of its highly-attuned skills. Taking the opportunity to enter one of its favorite departments, androcentrism, Conventional Dogmatism will cry out things like, "Women need a different set of rules than men; other gender designations need a different set of rules than men; in fact, everybody else needs a different set of rules than men!" Radical Personalism will simply shout back louder and deeper, with a kind but resounding "no," *re-minding* our inner Conventional Dogmatic that twisting the structure of reality to fit our whims—while thinking there won't be a price for that—may not only be the highest form of arrogance, but the highest stupidity as well. Even if we have never been abused, let's nonetheless remain empathic and compassionate with those who have. Let's profoundly identify with the despised ones and thus enter the disfigured state where much of humanity now lies. *Let's never seek to be undespised.* That's Radical Egalitarianism at its best.

Radical Contemporaneity

> *Gaudiya Vaishnavism needs to include in its conversations contemporary themes that remain unaddressed in the classical literature, such as ecological and racial awareness, abortion, social injustice, substance addiction, postmodern psychic scars, economic inequality, dysfunctional families, gender issues, and even the possibility of nuclear catastrophe, among other pressing predicaments. We call this Radical Contemporaneity.*

While each of these issues ideally requires a separate chapter and even book unto itself, it is of paramount importance that Emerging Gaudiya Vaishnavism rises to the occasion and successfully engages with emerging situations of our modern era. While ancient theology and philosophy have their corresponding domains of reach and influence, these noble disciplines can and should embrace unto their fold the notion of Radical Contemporaneity, as one of the ways not only to remain relevant to the world, but to make the world relevant for us in the context of our practice and interaction with it. For example, at times theocentric doctrines like Christianity have expressed an unrestrained anthropomorphism that led to exploiting the world and its resources because of seeing the world as disconnected from a divine source. This, in part, led to our present ecological crisis: we gained God but lost the world. Above this we may find proposals like ecocentrism, which invites us to fully identify with the world and protect it as if it were God through some kind of pantheistic approach. Here we regain the world but lose God. An ideal synthesis of these two would be panentheism (literally "all-in-God"), through which both the world and the Divine are preserved, the former being seen as a venerable energy of the latter. We thus move from theism, to pantheism, to panentheism or, even better, from egocentrism, to ecocentrism, to theocentrism.

Religion and spirituality profoundly affect the way we see nature, the world, and its multiple challenges. Therefore, the way we conceive all of these will be a byproduct of how we conceive our own faith and beliefs. If our relationship with theology and philosophy is toxic and only processed through the voice of Conventional Dogmatism, then probably our way of relating to the environment and its contemporary issues will be so as well. Finally, as intricate and complex as many of these issues may be, we shouldn't feel the urge to establish conclusive universal opinions as soon as possible about any of them, since sometimes there may not be one unique correct answer. But at least we must inaugurate an open and abundant dialogue about subjects which have been utterly neglected in many of our current conversations as a community. With proper dialogue in place, proper conclusions may arrive in time, even when we may not fully agree with each other on everything. This brings us to another point in the discussion: conclusions don't have to be universal. We can leave room to coexist with paradox and differences of opinion in the same group. First we need to talk with and not shout at each other, and then learn to agree to disagree in a loving and mature way. While most people prefer to judge instead of think, let's instead embrace Radical Contemporaneity and belong to the thinking party that essential Gaudiya Vaishnavism is all about.

Radical Activism

> *In connection to the above point, social action and involvement should be encouraged in the Gaudiya community for those so*

> *inclined, and they should be properly educated by the elders as to how to engage in compassionate social action. We call this Radical Activism.*

Action is good, compassion is good, and this world is also good. Combined into a synergistic whole, they become compassionate action in the world. This is exponentially greater than complete components that remain independent of each other. There is no genuine reason that the Gaudiya tradition should not activate its social side as have other mystical traditions, creating in the world authentic steps toward truth, justice, and mercy. Informed by a proper internal conception and a committed inner life, our actions can be balanced by prayer and introspection—and vice versa—rather than born out of the rage and resentment which fuels much of current social activism. As Andrew Harvey has wisely stated, "A spirituality that is only private and self-absorbed, one devoid of an authentic political and social consciousness, does little to halt the suicidal juggernaut of history. On the other hand, an activism that is not purified by profound spiritual and psychological self-awareness and rooted in divine truth, wisdom, and compassion, will only perpetuate the problem it is trying to solve, however righteous its intentions."[47] Properly executed and complemented, *every action can become prayer and every prayer can become action that influences the world in ways beyond our imagination.*

According to their corresponding natures, each member of the Gaudiya community is invited to find their place in the equation of sacred activism, which is a deep fusion of knowledge, courage, passion, and wise action in a world that begs for systemic change, peace, and sustainability and not merely individual conversion. As you may expect, those who possess the gift of Radical Activism will be loudly opposed by a campaign of Conventional Dogmatism that conveniently insists on a spiritual journey of exclusive privacy and non-involvement with any form of sociopolitical dynamics. Conventional Dogmatism will consider all types of sociopolitical dynamics mere expressions of worldliness and illusion, a "playing out of karma" in which we should not involve ourselves. This twisted voice will insist that the only valid form of compassion is directly sharing spiritual knowledge with others.[48] In reply, Radical Personalism will emphasize the importance of each individual wholly—each living entity completely—in all of their dimensions and with all of their needs, an integrated aspect of our spiritual project. To embrace the fullness of our humanity in context of our spirituality, there are unending ways to express care and concern in today's world as an aspect of our inner practice. Those inspired to do so should be encouraged and facilitated in the service of our highest ideals. Thus, Radical Activism is indeed about sharing spiritual knowledge, but in ways that go far beyond the binding of books: in the shape of spiritual compassion responding to human needs.

Radical Conversation

> *Real holistic dialogue is one of the most fundamental key features of any healthy community and relationship, and it is profoundly lacking in our present-day interactions among ourselves and with other communities. As a solution to this, we Gaudiyas should be open to learn not only from members of our own lineage but also from other traditions, appreciating their contributions in ways that complement our own school rather than compete with it. We call this Radical Conversation.*

As mentioned above, Gaudiya Vaishnavism fully revolves around the idea of love. However, while love is an all-pervading reality that is to be expressed through each of our actions, an uncanny disconnect can be seen today in the Gaudiya community between talking about love and *showing love in motion*. While we can engage in the former relatively easily, the latter demands much more from us, since love in motion is something to be demonstrated at all times, beginning with dialogue, or how we relate with each other on one of the most basic levels. Considering that what matters above what we say is what we *embody*, as Gaudiyas we do not seem able or equipped to talk to one another, to agree to disagree, to respect each other's differences without trying to impose dogma on one another. We do not even need to talk about attacking other creeds to see examples of discord, sectarianism, and divisiveness. We need simply to reflect on how we, as a community, have perpetrated abuse of Gaudiyas *by* Gaudiyas. Attempting to distract our attention from these important facts, Conventional Dogmatism will belittle any form of Gaudiya excess by comparing it with that found in other traditions, such as Christianity's horrendous Inquisitions and Crusades. While fortunately we don't have those horrors to count among our misconducts, we have nonetheless launched our own parallel versions of them. Among other forms of nonconversation, we have our unending online inquisitions of sorts and brutal philosophical crusades, often aimed simply at annihilating the "opponent" for no other reasons than those born of imperialistic pursuits. To counteract these tendencies, an essential virtue of Radical Conversation is its humility to accept others for who they are. That means going beyond whatever differences we may have with others, instead of judging them based on our own insecurities. And as Gaudiyas, humble we must be.

Three forms of conversation have been described in our tradition with the terms *vada*, *jalpa*, and *vitanda*. Respectively, in the first case both parties seek to sincerely find the truth, whatever it is and wherever it exists; in the second, both seem to hear each other but are convinced of their own version of reality; in the last category, each participant wants to win at all costs, even to the point of not allowing the other party to speak. Real dialogue does not end at only hearing each other, but rather goes far beyond that to being *willing to change* and, even further, to *allowing others to change* as well. For example, a practitioner may be accused of something, and many of us may jump to a conclusion and consider that person guilty (or innocent) without knowing the details. When a person has engaged in misbehavior, we may hold it against him even decades later, never considering the possibility of sincere repentance and atonement through divine grace. However, the Sweet Absolute always looks upon us not on the basis of our past, or even our present, but of our bright potential waiting in the future. If we want to perceive this most generous glance upon us, then we must first be willing to extend it to others as much as we can.

As Gaudiyas, we are quick to accept that God's residence is in Goloka. But despite knowing there is nothing outside of God, we are less inclined, and sometimes resistant, to accept that *God's address is everywhere*, and not limited to the Gaudiya address book. In other words, our niche does not make us superior, and knowledge gifted to us does not provide an exclusive backstage pass. Therefore, we should not only be open enough to dialogue with our own faith siblings, but also to rediscover our own teachings in other wisdom traditions. Sri Gaurahari himself taught this valuable principle by engaging in interreligious dialogue with Muslims, Sikhs, various Vaishnava *sampradayas*, and Hindus of other designations.[49] Similarly, Gaudiya stalwarts such as Thakura Bhaktivinoda are well known for their interaction with Christianity and Western philosophy, through which they nourished their own Vaishnava journey. The opposite of this basic God consciousness is a toxic over-identification with our own tradition to the point of not being able to appreciate anything beyond it, terrified to look beyond the self-created wall of bias and, out of fear, quickly labeling, judging, and hiding from so-called outsiders and enemies. In this connection, it is important to note that the very first book of the Gaudiya tradition (called *Brihad-bhagavatamrita*) depicts the spiritual love journey of Gopa-kumara, a devotee of Sri Krishna who, on his way to attain his ultimate desired goal, meets with countless devotees of different faiths and moods. Each time Gopa-kumara hears one of them glorify the Lord of their heart, his own faith in his Lord is nourished. Needless to say, *their* Lord and *his* Lord are *the* Lord.

The voice of Conventional Dogmatism may argue that by allowing ourselves to be inspired and thus influenced by different traditions we may acquire *samskaras* (impressions) that may divert our faith in Gaudiya Vaishnavism, or at least confuse it on some level. Radical Conversation will quickly reply that although others might create *samskaras* in us, more influential and defining is *how we choose to receive and process* those influences. Correspondingly, we can properly associate with, for example, a mystical Jew in a way that beautifully nourishes our own Vaishnava faith, while we may associate with another Gaudiya in such a way that it may interfere with our inspiration as Gaudiyas. We have not been commanded to love our religion; we have been commanded to love God and our neighbors—even if they happen to be in another religion. As one of the many facets of this Gaudiya diamond, Radical Conversation lovingly insists on finding God in the faith of others and thus nourishing our own path through those intimate foundational patterns that every mystical tradition shares in common. This is a crucial exercise of "holy envy."[50]

Let us finish this section with a beautiful set of verses from our own Gaudiya canon first, and then with some wise words from a contemporary Christian mystic, both of which *re-mind* us of the ideal spirit with which to engage in this Radical Conversation:

> *Dear father, the Supreme Lord is one for all living entities. The difference between the Muslim God and the Hindu God is in name only. All scriptures, whether the Koran or the Puranas, state that there is only one Supreme Lord. He is the nondual, eternal, transcendental Absolute Truth, infallible and perfectly complete and, in that capacity, he resides in everyone's heart. The Supreme Lord's transcendental name and qualities are glorified throughout the world by various scriptures. The Lord accepts each individual's mood of surrender. When you are violent to others, you are being violent to the Lord himself.*[51]

> *You can take my word for it too that Greece, Egypt, ancient India and ancient China, the beauty of the world, the pure and authentic reflections of this beauty in art and science, what I have seen of the inner recesses of the human hearts where religious belief is unknown—all these things have done as much as the visibly Christian ones to deliver me into Christ's hands as his captive.*[52]

Radical Unknowing

> *In general, present-day Gaudiya Vaishnavism seems to be stuck in what we may call an overdose of confidence, or a profound inability to deal with uncertainty, liminality, and paradox, all of which create a necessary displacement from our comfort zone. Instead of discarding mystery by claiming a perfect understanding, we are invited to harmonize and include all contradictions*

> *and dilemmas in a higher synthesis, as part of our inner project. We call this Radical Unknowing.*

In Hindu aesthetics, there is no possibility of the experience of *rasa* (the highest refinement of sacred emotion) without first having passed through the holy tunnel of *chamatkara*, or holy bewilderment. Since we cannot be astonished by the familiar, we are exposed to realities that are totally unknown to us—*we must not know some things in order for them to capture us.* In fact, rather than being repelled by the unknown, we should learn to relate to this dimension to the point where it becomes truly venerable. Following his own example in this connection, genuine followers of Sri Gaurahari remain humble and teachable. They not only know that they don't know everything; they even know that they don't know how much they don't know. And they are okay with it. In fact, in the absence of ease and certainty, amazing things can happen. Our very life can happen, filled with wonder, hope, love, and renewed strength to thrive in difficulty and uncertainty. A new humanity can be reborn—and we as a tradition along with it.[53]

At this point our inner character of Conventional Dogmatism will explode and regurgitate heavily unprocessed dogma, vomiting claims of absolute perfect knowledge one after another, as if trying to secure its own existence by proving itself right. Why is this so? Insecure people long for excessive security and certainty because of not having learned to be humbly confident regarding their own being, especially in the midst of uncertainty. *Conventional Dogmatism is a voice addicted to certainty.* Constantly on watch for things that keep us from being the best version of ourselves, Radical Unknowing responds like a divine clarion call and encourages us to embrace and coexist with the paradoxical and mysterious, to value unlearning at times even above learning, and to be willing to sit with the unknown long enough to be provided the key to move forward in sync with Ultimate Reality.

Due to its significant function, Radical Unknowing will be further unpacked in its own chapter in the third part of this book.

Radical Freedom

> *Shame, guilt, and fear are not the way to conceive of and relate to reality, especially to Ultimate Reality, the Sweet Absolute. Ours is a positive-oriented tradition, and we adore a loving and most merciful God. Although most Gaudiyas know this in theory, we still need to actualize our own potential by the way we embody each of these core values. We call this Radical Freedom.*

Presently, we Gaudiyas live in an honor/shame culture, whose influence pervades our lives and communities more than we may think. This unique form of social entrapment sometimes takes the form of exaggerated praise and over-idealization, and then quickly invokes its counterpart in the form of extreme shame and blame for things that are never as grave as we choose to see them. Because of not being fully aware of our intrinsic connection with Ultimate Reality, many of us lack the inner dignity that comes only from awareness of such a fact. Unfortunately, many times we try to attain dignity through external attainments like authority, honor, respect, and assets. Instead of giving inner dignity to ourselves by *allowing reality to happen*, we sometimes choose the honor/shame culture that so much inhibits our inner liberty. A positive orientation is thus required for a sustainable life and practice, and this is the very task of Radical Freedom.

When the voice of Conventional Dogmatism expects others to act toward us in certain ways, we unknowingly steal others' ability to act freely from the heart, thus crushing any chance for organic spirituality to be expressed. Instead, our expectations promote fear of alienation, fear of rejection or failure, or fear of losing benefits or a post within the community. If spiritual leaders knowingly or unknowingly use negative motivating tactics, they will be hindering the tender creeper of devotion from growing and will be thus committing violence to those under their care. Of course, subordinates do not have to submit to coercive behavior. They may instinctively feel that there's something amiss, but if they are new to the world of devotion, blind submission may be imposed upon them in the name of humility. And since some of these subtle forms of intimidation can occur en masse, they may seem acceptable to many of us just because everyone else seems to be accepting them. To give a crude example, if a criminal points a pistol at us and demands that we love him, he may get many of his captives to utter the words "I love you," but what is the value of those words even if said by many people? Similarly, whenever there is fear, group pressure, alienation, psychological intimidation, or any other negative motivating factor, a similar phenomenon is in effect.[54] Thus, insufficient freedom ends up nourishing and assisting impersonalism, the very nemesis of Radical Personalism.

Srila Prabhupada, the famous Vaishnava world ambassador, has repeatedly established the Gaudiya teaching of Radical Freedom through his own example and words, stating that his movement is meant to make people who are "independently thoughtful,"[55] that "in all spheres of devotional service freedom is the main pivot,"[56] and that "without freedom there is no execution of devotional service."[57] In fact, Sri Krishna himself concludes his immortal *Bhagavad-gita* by inviting his friend and student Arjuna to fully deliberate on the teaching he has just received and then "do as you please."[58] Spiritual life is to be performed out of our own volition, not out of fear or under oppression or intimidation, since the lotus flower of devotion will never grow in the lake of coercion but only in the crystalline waters of freedom.[59] Radical Freedom, to be more precise.

Radical Earthliness

> *The world is not bad—it is one of the sacred energies of God. In fact, when properly conceived of and approached, the realm of matter can beautifully reveal the Sweet Absolute's presence in the here and now. Thus, there is no need to reject the temporary (or anything, for that matter) in the pursuit of the eternal, since reality is nondual and, by its very constitution, everything is a potential portal to infinity—even the material domain. We call this Radical Earthliness.*

As we reminded ourselves in the previous point, essential spiritual life is always something positive—something that seeks to embrace reality on every occasion, and never to reject it. However, it seems practically to be the "duty" of immature representatives to constantly shape new dichotomies in order to keep dualistic thinking on track, a favorite dichotomy being "material life vs. spiritual life." This problematic outlook, which we can invest our own choice in or not, carries the taxing implication of seeing matter and the world made of it as diametrically opposed to the transcendent. Nothing is further from the truth. This Earth that so generously hosts each of us is not the creation of Satan, or something disconnected from the Divine that is merely to be transcended as soon as possible. Similarly, the Gaudiya notion of *maya* (material energy) has nothing to do with an evil, ill-motived, and perverse potency that wants to see us falling into her grip. *Maya* is a sacred energy that we need to understand and honor. We need to take more responsibility about how we choose to see things and relate to them. *If there is a wrong conception, there will be a wrong relationship.*

Conventional Dogmatism will shout back its predictable jargon, labeling the world as necessarily bad and insisting that we try to distance from it in every possible way through so-called spiritual discipline. But it's not that religion is holy and the world is profane. Both religion and the secular can be holy, *and both can be profane.* When our Gaudiya texts describe this world as a perverted reflection of the spiritual realm, it basically indicates an upside-down perception of reality. In other words, the perversion of such reflection *is in us* and not in the world itself, and for it to change we require a 180-degree inner revolution in our own point of view—from I-centeredness to God-centeredness. Therefore, "this world" and "that world" are not as much geographical places as they are states of consciousness, and we are the ones to choose where to stay. If proper awareness is in place, then we don't need to go anywhere, since *this world*, if properly approached, can be a privileged portal into depth and truth—a privileged portal to *the other world.* Heaven or hell can be experienced immediately, depending on our choice of consciousness.

Radical Personalism emphasizes not only God's transcendence and presence in a transcendent abode, but his immanence and immediate presence in every single aspect of creation, localized *and* universal. In fact, Gaudiya Vaishnava theology teaches that, in one of his expansions, the Sweet Absolute is present not only in every heart but even in every atom! How inert can matter be if inhabited by the most living of all entities? Through the lens of Radical Earthliness, *the presence of the Sweet Absolute is oozing from each pore of creation*, with every single atom being an embassy of the Divine. We are distracted beings who have enormous capacity to ignore the extraordinary, but let's not lose sight of the constant miracle of God's indivisible presence in everything we see, feel, hear, taste, and smell, as well as those things that the senses do not touch—and all of the space in between—and thus learn to rediscover infinity through the gateway of matter. Our actual salvation especially starts during the most ordinary moments of our daily lives. It starts by realizing how nothing is ordinary, since the will of the Absolute reveals itself constantly through everything, this world included.

As with many other topics, this particular face of Radical Personalism will have its own chapter (in conjunction with the next point of the manifesto) in the third part of this book.

Radical Involvement

> *Participation in God's lila, or divine play, is not limited to the beyond. It is a state of consciousness and therefore begins and continues wherever we may be physically. In other words, Gaudiya Vaishnavas can realize the most extraordinary form of ultimate existence in the most ordinary moments of their daily life. Correspondingly, this divine lila is to be approached as something always participatory and fully relevant to our present situation. We call this Radical Involvement.*

In Gaudiya Vaishnavism, the Sweet Absolute fully validates this world by repeatedly coming to it and revealing his transcendent abode and *lila*. And through his *lila*, he shows us that participation in divine life depends on inner considerations and not on mere physical location. While Conventional Dogmatism may keep evading the world in the name of some fantastic post-liberated prospect, we are still here—and the possibility of being part of God's life is also still here, waiting for us. Radical Involvement is not about distancing from the secular, but about always bringing it closer as a portal through which Ultimate Reality chooses to convey itself to us. In fact, the closer the secular, the more ordinary things and moments become epiphanies of the Supreme Lord's presence.[60]

The divine play of Ultimate Reality descends and manifests among us to vindicate our humanity. Thus, in whatever stage we may be at present we should be able to make this *lila* relatable to us. We should see it not as something we can participate in *someday somewhere*, but as something that *comes to us here and in this moment*, inviting us to participate in it from wherever we may be. In other words, instead of reading the *lila* literally or trying to jump into its most esoteric conclusion without proper qualification, we can learn to extract from it relevant teachings, values, and messages that may be crucially applicable to our present chapter as practitioners. We can appreciate the faith, sacrifice, and surrender of the direct participants in the divine play while learning to relate to those qualities in our local situation. This will be a very concrete and realistic way of feeling that we belong to the domain of *lila*, that we are part of it, and that we can participate in it. Participation comes by feeling that we are *a part* of something, and not *apart* from it. In other words, we should learn to behold how this domain of *lila* unfolds in our daily life, connecting the missing dots between divine existence and daily experience through the lens of Radical Involvement.[61]

Radical Resolution

> *We need to remember that we won't get all of the above points right in our first attempt, or even in a short time. We are embarking on a long-term growth process, so each of these steps and suggestions are merely a beginning—but a necessary one. Locally, each of us can plan a celebration whenever we succeed in any of these first steps. Then, we should learn from our mistakes and continue unfolding the process with courage and determination. We call this Radical Resolution.*

While the above conceived vision is not an easy one to implement in our lives, it's not impossible either. As individuals and as a collective, we Gaudiyas should be strict and demanding with ourselves, but also patient and forgiving. This especially applies to projects that can be developed infinitely (like this manifesto) and which, by their very nature, can easily create discouragement or even neurosis if we expect sudden results in magical ways. This manifesto invites us to embrace Radical Resolution, which includes additional virtues like Radical Patience and Radical Realism. We should gradually change those things that can be changed, step by step. In fact, incremental progress is more powerful than we can imagine, but is often underestimated or totally neglected by excessive unripe restlessness. Let's engage responsibly in whatever way we can today, trusting that any genuine commitment to do something will always pay off, no matter what the result may be. We have to begin—or better put, continue—somewhere. And that starts here, now, and today.

Life is certainly complex, and this complexity often shifts in the most unpredictable ways. As a matter of fact, we could say that complexity beyond comprehension is the very pattern of reality. On top of that, we may possess a limited-resource capacity to deal with emerging complexity. But there is mercy, if we are sincere. Acceptance of our brokenness will attract experiential salvation—the touch of causeless grace—to come to our rescue. However, this rescue may take unimaginable forms. What if many of the structures that are now failing *need to fail*? Are we willing to admit this is a possible part of the Absolute's plan, after first having fought against such an option? After all, entropy is a vital aspect of any evolving system. This principle applies not only in terms of lack of order and predictability, but as a constant cycling of loss and renewal and, therefore, a gradual *descent into disorder*. But God likes disorder—he is especially found there!—and so shall we. While disorder implies a previous order, it also invites for future *reorder*. Subsequently, after committing ourselves to this heroic task, we should get together as many times as necessary to celebrate and learn from our attempts to put the present external state of Gaudiya Vaishnavism into reorder, which both includes and transcends the order and disorder stages. Through this Radical Resolution, we can further align ourselves with the pristine and ever-evolving inner essence of our blessed tradition.

FURTHER REFLECTIONS

Radical Personalism is nothing but another way of referring to Gaudiya Vaishnavism and, more precisely, to what we have identified as Emerging Gaudiya Vaishnavism—a collective of souls aligned with the ideals presented and unraveled in this Revival Manifesto for Proactive Devotion. At the same time, what has been shared in this chapter is just one list and one manifesto, based on the initial points shared in the Introduction to this work. Despite the possibility that many of you may have felt partially or fully represented by it (or not), in any case I encourage each of you to make your own list—your own manifesto—and then *manifest* its content by embodying it through your daily behavior, values, and principles, in sacred service to the Gaudiya tradition. *Please do it.*

It is in this spirit of sacred service that the above manifesto has been shared, hoping to present it in a way that the reader would neither be held captive by rigid ideology nor addiction to mere novelty. Intentions were also invoked to make this offering free from either the pointless accusations of a ruthless witch-hunt—over-dramatizing certain specific circumstances—or a one-size-fits-all type of generic abstraction. In other words, the above list has been presented in the spirit of Gaudiya common sense, a virtue that all of us need to be deeply trained in. At the same time, Radical Personalism is totally aware that actions based on misconceptions will no doubt continue to happen in one form or another, since there will be always people with different levels of consciousness, maturity, and sincerity. But this doesn't mean that we should be silent or passive about those things that require attention and active involvement. Hypocrisy and pretense should not be tolerated, even if they present themselves on official letterhead or wrapped in sacred robes. Also, please remain aware that the distorted character of Conventional Dogmatism will generally speak inside of us first, and only then somewhere else, probably as an inner projection. In other words, we are not here to cheaply accuse others, but to remain attentive to our own internal landscape and embrace the full weight of personal accountability. Before going back home, we should start working at home by doing our inner homework.

In chemistry, a *free radical* constitutes a unit that attacks important macromolecules, leading to homeostatic disruption and ill health. In our tradition, a Radical Personalist is someone who also embraces freedom (and is thus also a *free radical*) and similarly attempts to create "sacred disturbance," by pointing at those areas where excessive balance, such as complacency, laxity, and status quo, require update and challenge. This transformation is not about modifying the spotless quintessence of Gaudiya Vaishnavism and its divine revelation, but about how such essence can at times be misrepresented in this world throughout time and space. And this certainly happens. Sri Krishna confirms this fact in *Bhagavad-gita* 4.2 by declaring that from time to time divine wisdom becomes obscured and is thus in need of resurrection through *parampara*, the system of disciplic succession that conforms to a lineage and tradition, but whose spirit is that of nonconformity in sincere service to the Supreme Nonconformist, God himself. In this same reforming spirit and as we have already mentioned, the Gaudiya saint Thakura Bhaktivinoda has said that those who have been entrusted with the responsibility of being leaders in Gaudiya Vaishnavism should "try to remove all *anarthas* [contaminations] from the lineage."[62] Sri Bhaktivinoda also often spoke about various possible *apasampradayas*, or heterodox deviations (*apa*) from the original living school of prophets (*sampradaya*). However, while we may belong to an authorized *sampradaya*, there is every chance to conceive and represent it in an *apasampradayic* way, whether by complying or complaining as an evasive device. However, what Gaudiya Vaishnavism needs is renovators, not mere renegades.

Thought-provoking conversations need to be brought to our table and even daily meals, through which we step forward to humbly but courageously question, object, and seek healing while trying to overcome present impasses and grow up as servants of the Sweet Absolute. While these exchanges should be welcomed and encouraged, however, we should be equally concerned that sacred hope is duly protected and preserved in the midst of those clamoring voices that surely need to reverberate. We should speak—and even shout—only to nourish proper faith and understanding, and never as an excuse to dismiss these two. There is a price to pay for speaking, and there is also a price to pay for remaining silent. Radical Personalism chooses the former, the latter being far more expensive. Sri Gaurahari himself taught this same principle in his famous *samvada* (conversation) with Raya Ramananda,[63] through which he repeatedly requested "*augment that truth*!" driving them deeper in their dialogue. In fact, any sincere dialogue is nothing but an ongoing unpacking of reality. And this is also the role of any revival manifesto. Although silence may be enjoyable at times, it must often be broken *for a higher purpose*. Thus, by promoting holy dialogue, we allow ourselves to come out, announce, and invite others to make a similar choice of their own: to acquiesce to the stagnation of carelessness or to embrace renewal and ultimate redemption.

The spiritual journey is a *constant* purification of our motives, and spiritual perfection is a horizon that always recedes, since there is no limit to how much progress we can make through eternity. Likewise, there is no limit to how much this Revival Manifesto could be developed, which means there is no limit to how much Gaudiya Vaishnavism can evolve and expand in unlimited new levels. However, we need to let go of Gaudiya Vaishnavism on one level before we can accept it on its emerging level—*die to live*. In order to flourish, the Gaudiya tradition in its present state may need to go through some serious changes. While those changes are ultimately determined and engineered by the Supreme Lord, we have to remain open and honor them *as they may be revealed within our own inspired hearts*. Let's rediscover our own tradition. We don't need permission for doing so. Being active participants automatically gives us that right and duty.

This Revival Manifesto for Proactive Devotion has been mainly conceptual, since, as one of my main teachers would say, "All of our problems arise due to our lack of proper conception."[64] Once the right ideas are in place, pragmatics will follow gradually and accordingly. In saying this, I do not presume to have presented the highest possible recommendations. But as a steady patient on the road to recovery and having some ability to understand the process of rehabilitation and healing, I've attempted to share a few musings for each of us to evaluate and reevaluate—each on its own merit. At the end of the day, this manifesto and its various proposals all boil down to this simple query:

To what degree can I actually make things better? A proper awareness of the answer to this question can rewire us on every level—physical, neurological, emotional, and spiritual. Unless this happens, Radical Personalism and this Revival Manifesto for Proactive Devotion will remain another irrelevant and lifeless ideology. *Let's instead augment these truths and continue dynamic living.*

In one sense, our Revival Manifesto has finished here. While many of you may choose to close the book at this point and engage in deep proactive action, we are only halfway through this presentation. As clarified throughout the manifesto, the third part of this book will further unravel some of the most significant points from our list in the very spirit of Radical Personalism by playing out the implications of things to their furthest reach. This section will include not only the voice and spirit of a Radical Personalist, but also the inner voice and narcotic promises of Spiritual Bypassing, the most well-disguised enemy of Radical Personalism, ranking as an adversary even greater than Conventional Dogmatism due to its keen ability to camouflage the sacred, and conjure a dream not to fulfill but to awaken from.

For the adventuresome contemplatives, let's meet next in such a dramatic arena.

Part Three
A DEEPER DIVE

8 Vulnerability & Empowerment

Vulnerability is not winning or losing; it's having the courage to show up and be seen when we have no control over the outcome.

– Brené Brown

AMONG A WHOLE MULTITUDE OF HOLY SHIFTS and transformations that we may need to embrace as humans and spiritual practitioners, vulnerability will always be the very first one to invoke. Why? Because without the preliminary presence of vulnerability, we won't be able to admit our own faults, neediness, and brokenness, and as a consequence of that, we won't be open enough to embrace the corresponding upgrade, renovation, and empowerment. As Gaudiya Vaishnavas, we deeply need all these things, both individually and collectively. Thus, before attempting to delve into whatever other qualities we may need to integrate as members of this tradition, let's first begin Part Three by discovering the beautiful power of vulnerability, a theme that will pervade the balance of this book and through which every remaining page is to be ideally apprehended.

WE CANNOT PRACTICE VULNERABILITY—WE ARE VULNERABLE

As happens with every other virtue, a comprehensive definition of vulnerability also entails a clear demarcation of what vulnerability is *not*, so let's begin there. Vulnerability is not something we choose to engage in or not; vulnerability is something *we are*, whether we admit it or not. *We don't do vulnerability, we are vulnerable*—we are personified vulnerability at every moment. Thus, our only option is, so to say, to embody vulnerability maturely or immaturely. We can do vulnerability knowingly, or *it will do us*. We want to maturely embody vulnerability because empowerment comes only from an accurate assessment and conscious embrace of our vulnerable nature.

As paradoxical and counterintuitive as it may sound, the way to stay strong is by embracing our weakness—by embracing vulnerability we become empowered. Unfortunately, more often than not we fail at coexisting with paradox and therefore lose sight of vulnerability's empowering prospect. Misreading this virtue as being no virtue at all, we try to reject it as much as we can. However, we cannot get rid of vulnerability since it's part of our very ontological makeup. But we can make things even more difficult for ourselves if we become experts in concealing it, especially from ourselves, and even resorting to evasive spirituality as an armor to protect us from our own vulnerable DNA. Ideally, we should happily acknowledge who we actually are, vulnerability included. Genuine self-esteem involves acknowledging our nature, which in this case would imply being healthily vulnerable. In Sanskrit, our very composition is described by the term *tatastha*, which basically speaks about how vulnerable we are to the influence of our environment, but also how that same vulnerability, if properly expressed, constitutes our greatest prospect and empowerment. We are *tatastha*, vulnerable, and it's more than okay to be so. To acknowledge who we are can be one of our greatest virtues, and to express our nature in a nurturing milieu will open the door to our brightest future. In other words, we need to develop a deep sense of worthiness and self-esteem, not from self-centered arrogance, but in the context of vulnerability and the gift of our potential.

Experiencing vulnerability is not an option but our inescapable condition as living beings. As a result, we could say that we are not only vulnerable but, even more precisely, we are *the very form of vulnerability*. Whether we know it or not, as infinitesimal beings we are facing Infinity on a 24/7 basis. That's pretty vulnerable—and it can be quite intimidating. However, if we properly understand the loving nature of Infinity, as well as the empowering prospect of vulnerability, our vulnerable position will turn out to be our most valuable treasure by showing the ultimate beauty and charm of who we are *in* vulnerability. For some Gaudiya Vaishnavas, however, this may seem foreign, unheard of, or even heretical. Therefore, next we will further define vulnerability by showing how this attribute is not only allowed in Gaudiya Vaishnavism, but actually represents a virtue around which the whole tradition perpetually revolves.

GAUDIYA VAISHNAVISM IS SYNONYMOUS WITH VULNERABILITY

Among other definitions, vulnerability could be defined as uncertainty, risk, and emotional exposure.[1] As already clarified, whether we admit having these experiences or not, they are always there as part of our daily lives. Thus, being vulnerable will entail a brave willingness to acknowledge our moments of risk, uncertainty, and emotional exposure, and allow ourselves to ultimately be empowered by them. Do you remember the height of Covid-19, and how humanity had to forcefully face its own vulnerability in ways that were unthinkable before? In this most unexpected period, we each had to contend with our own frailty, uncertainty, and smallness. For some, the experience was diminishing, while for others it was an opportunity to grow in and through vulnerability. Although the height of our exposure has seemingly passed, we still remain as vulnerable as we have always been. Let us now look a little deeper into what vulnerability brings to and springs from our tradition. This investigation will thereby inform us of what is to be done with this crucial side of ourselves.

As we have tried to show in Part Two of this book, one of our main challenges as Gaudiyas is that quite often we misunderstand and thus misrepresent our own lineage. Because we don't fully understand who we are as Gaudiyas, we misrepresent the tradition to ourselves to begin with, and then to others as an extended byproduct. One shape of such a misconception is the aversion and denial that many Gaudiyas experience in regard to vulnerability, although the Gaudiya tradition *is all about vulnerability*. It finds itself in a particularly vulnerable moment historically, and also, in its pristine essence, it is a tradition that fully revolves around the principle of vulnerability and empowerment. Gaudiya Vaishnavism is mainly concerned with the notion of divine love, and this love has been described as *moving in a crooked way*.[2] In other words, love's movements are unpredictable, unexpected, and uncertain. Divine love also represents the ultimate form of emotional exposure, as do those who express this highest love in the Gaudiya tradition, the cowherd girls of Vraja, who leave everything behind to meet with their beloved Krishna, taking full risk and being totally uncertain whether their love will finally be consummated or not. Such risk, uncertainty, and emotional exposure results in the highest remuneration, or empowerment: the attainment of the highest form of divine affection. Considering that the highest divine love arises from a well of uncertainty, emotional exposure, and risk—the very definition of vulnerability—and that Gaudiya Vaishnavism is synonymous with that divine love, we can then conclude that Gaudiya Vaishnavism is also essentially tied to vulnerability.

Further examples of how vulnerability plays itself out in the sacred texts of the Gaudiyas can be seen in the immortal *Bhagavad-gita*, which begins with Arjuna, the greatest warrior on Earth, being totally dejected and vulnerable on the battlefield—not only physically, but emotionally. However, by his acknowledging his brokenness and opening himself to further empowerment by Sri Krishna's grace and teachings, the most terrible fratricidal war ends up giving rise to the highest good: the *Gita*'s message of love. Similarly, the main character of the Gaudiyas' central scripture, the *Srimad Bhagavatam*, is the saintly king Parikshit, who has been cursed to die in seven days. Parikshit fully embraces vulnerability by fully embracing his imminent death, that factor of life that makes us the most vulnerable. Parikshit's being the most vulnerable brought about the appearance of his guru, Sukadeva, and the whole unfolding of the *Srimad Bhagavatam*, which itself is a story of empowerment from beginning to end. Similarly, in the eyes of Christianity, what is manifest on the cross is *the internal structure* of God himself. Thus, the crucifixion of Jesus will be simultaneously conceived as both vulnerability and empowerment: the worst possible thing in human history but also the best possible thing, since his archetypal death exists as an example of how to heroically accept finitude, betrayal, and tyranny heroically, or, better put, how to accept vulnerability in an empowered *and empowering* way. In more contemporary Gaudiya history, the glorious example of how Srila Prabhupada did what he did shines like a self-effulgent example in this regard. He was totally vulnerable while emptying himself fully, crossing the ocean and fervently praying to Sri Krishna to empower him so he could deliver the Lord's teachings to the Western world. Another contemporary narrative can be found in the concentration camps of Auschwitz and similar places, where the worst of the worst horrors took place, but the best of the best was able to be drawn from it, as we see in Viktor Frankl's moving testimony and so many other empowering narratives. The list is unending, showing us repeatedly how the vulnerability-empowerment template is not only a Gaudiya landmark, but a fully embedded pattern in reality itself.

For the more skeptical Gaudiyas who may still harbor suspicion about how our own lineage is synonymous with vulnerability, let's conclude this section by reminding ourselves of something mentioned at the very beginning of this work: how Radical Personalism is translated for Gaudiyas as Radhikal Personalism, since the very Deity of the Gaudiya tradition is Sri Gaurahari, none other than Sri Krishna himself relishing the heart of Sri Radhika in the most radical way. And it is exactly because of this that Sri Gaurahari deserves to be portrayed by Gaudiyas as the ultimate embodiment of both vulnerability and empowerment. How is this so? If vulnerability revolves around uncertainty, risk, and emotional exposure, as it certainly does, then these three qualities make our venerable God a vulnerable one like no other. How does this happen? In connection with uncertainty, we should remember that Gaurahari is Sri Krishna being totally uncertain about Sri Radhika's experience, and it is that very uncertainty and curiosity which impels him to appear as he does. As to the risk element, Radhika herself wonders what will happen to her beloved Krishna when he tastes her bottomless heart. He is similarly aware of the risks involved, and therefore he is always accompanied by Svarupa Damodara and Ramananda Raya. Finally, Sri Krishna as Gaurahari indulges in the deepest possible form of emotional exposure by eternally subjecting himself to the love of Sri Radhika. And since her love possesses an ever-increasing nature, these three qualities of uncertainty, risk, and emotional exposure unfold and evolve perpetually in the heart of not only Sri Radhika, but Gaurahari himself. For these reasons, Sri Gaurahari symbolizes for Gaudiya Vaishnavas the most robust and climactic moment in the life of the Absolute: he eternally remains not only as the most fragile and needy face of the Divine, but also as the Divine's most explosive and volcanic expression—combined vulnerability and empowerment in the context of Radhikal Personalism. Thus, for Gaudiya Vaishnavas God is both All Mighty *and* All Vulnerable, in equal measure. Those who have failed to include God's vulnerability in the equation have largely been dealing with half of God.[3] Therefore, the life and precepts of Sri Gaurahari teach us a most valuable lesson: *our most empowered prospect lies in the land of vulnerability*. This is our open secret as Gaudiyas, and this is the God we worship—an all vulnerable and empowering one.

VULNERABILITY AND EMPOWERMENT IN GAURAHARI'S GOLDEN RULE

Since we invoked the figure of Sri Gaurahari, let's turn for a moment to what is arguably his most famous and important instruction: the third verse of his renowned *Siksastakam*. There he mentions that "he who is humble like a blade of grass and more tolerant than a tree, and who expects no recognition but shows respect to all, can constantly glorify Hari." This poem describes the spiritual stage of *nistha*, or devotional fixation, this being especially expressed in its last line, where a constant praise of the Sweet Absolute is alluded to. However, this form of fixity and empowerment begins with the verse's three initial lines, all of which are deeply tied with the idea of vulnerability, since in this verse humility, tolerance, unassertiveness, and respect are first described. Initial openness and acceptance bring forth renewed strength.

The humility that Gaurahari speaks of is intimately connected with realizing our infinitesimal situation and our need for the shelter of and connection with our affectionate source. As insignificant as we may be, we are deeply significant in the eyes of God. To realize this truth is probably more humbling than any other notion of humility we may have had, but it is precisely this vulnerability—where we admit our imperfection and, despite that, know that we are loved unconditionally—that allows us to be fully empowered. In other words, vulnerability implies allowing the moment, the person, the idea, or the situation to influence us *and even change us*.[4] This change is synonymous with empowerment, and true humility will be synonymous with vulnerability, the exact opposite of egocentricity. In fact, in the verse previous to this third one, Gaurahari further prepares the ground by lamenting about his *durdaiva*, or misfortune. He does so by confessing his lack of taste for God's name, while taking full responsibility, admitting that this is because of his *anarthas*, or false set of values. In other words, he shows us how to fully embrace our present imperfection with genuine honesty and repentance (vulnerability) and how this will take us to a deeper expression of ourselves (empowerment) which eventually will invoke a still higher form of vulnerability and then a more empowered empowerment, ad infinitum.

Interestingly, this third verse of *Siksastakam* is traditionally connected with the attitude through which the devotional aspirant will attain the platform of *prema*, or divine love, thus setting the template even clearer—vulnerability/humility is the path, empowerment/*prema* is the goal. Therefore, if both vulnerability and empowerment are present in the intermediate stage of *nistha* depicted in this verse, they will be even more present in the ultimate converging point of the spiritual journey—divine love. As Freud has said, *we are never so vulnerable as when we love.*[5] Apply this to fully consummated spirituality and you will then have the quintessential expression of vulnerability as well as the topmost expression of empowerment, since *prema* is nothing but an inexhaustible dose of energy to be offered in sacred service. And such transfiguring power can become manifest only by first taking shelter on the altar of vulnerability.

In this way, Gaurahari's life and only written legacy could be seen as an ongoing journey through deeper and deeper layers of vulnerability and empowerment. In fact, since each of the eight verses of his *Siksastakam* basically portray each of the different stages of our *bhakti* project, we are also invited to conceive our whole spiritual journey—as individuals and as a collective—in terms of vulnerability and empowerment, each stage of the journey showing a particular face of these two sacred and inseparable twins.

Having established how Gaudiya Vaishnavism and reality itself revolve around the axis of vulnerability and its corresponding empowerment, let's continue delving into what constitutes the very experience of vulnerability, examining not only some of its main symptoms but also possible obstacles that may get in the way of its expression.

COURAGE AND INNER NAKEDNESS

A deeply accurate way of depicting the inside experience of vulnerability would be through the term *inner nakedness*. As intimidating as it may sound, this expression clearly conveys the courage that is foundational and is an intrinsic part of our involvement with vulnerability. How is courage related to vulnerability? Let's just think for a moment about any life situation in which we had to be courageous but without the need to embrace vulnerability, or risk, uncertainty, and emotional exposure. Very quickly (hopefully!) we will realize that such a condition is not possible. For courage to be there, there must be some form of vulnerability as a prelude. In other words, if we think we are being brave but our action does not involve risk and uncertainty, then we are not being brave at all.

While a toxic masculinity archetype may choose to relate courage with strength and vulnerability with weakness, it is not willing to expose itself to risk and uncertainty. Instead, it invokes a false sense of bravery, which is nothing more than an attempted escape from inner nakedness and the much-needed embrace of vulnerability. In fact, by showing immoderate assertiveness or an excess of similar qualities, many of us in our Gaudiya tradition do embrace this template of toxic masculinity, while dismissing healthy vulnerability (a feminine virtue) and thus preventing any form of inner nakedness to show up, and as a consequence of that, any form of real empowerment. The greatest shame for most men is to be seen as weak, and toxic masculinity creates a superficial sense of strength through a thorough denial of all forms of potential weakness. Therefore, as much as our tradition and its members are affected by this pattern of avoidance, we will be deprived and disempowered. This is due to our inability to embrace sacred vulnerability and the courage we so much need, courage that comes only after allowing ourselves to be utterly vulnerable—*utterly surrendered*. Whether we know it or not, longing for full surrender is nothing but longing for full vulnerability.

Courage can be easily related with allowing ourselves to be seen as imperfect and, through such authenticity, enabling ourselves and others to experience real compassion and connection, or empowerment. Such courage is the landmark of any real hero who, by the way, is depicted in traditional Indian drama as someone necessarily vulnerable. Vulnerability is an indispensable requirement in the perfect Indian dramatic hero, or *nayaka*, in both secular and transcendental lore. And for Gaudiya Vaishnavas reality itself is ultimately conceived as a drama. Krishna *lila* and Gaurahari *lila* are the ultimate representations of reality and thus the greatest drama of all—God immersed in eternal love play, forgetful of his own Godhood due to the extreme measure of devotional sweetness and intimacy. Krishna *lila* and Gaurahari *lila* are the greatest dramas ever told, and their great heroes must be fully vulnerable for the dramas to succeed eternally. In this way, vulnerability is not to be seen as weakness but as the greatest measure of courage and heroism.

This inner nakedness that is synonymous with vulnerability also speaks of its necessity for proper boundaries, since *vulnerability without boundaries is not vulnerability but abuse*. While all of us need to expose ourselves in full rawness, we need to do so in front of someone who will be able to understand and appreciate such nakedness, turning a situation that could easily end up in abuse into a sacred moment of deep empowerment. Therefore, a healthy vessel for our vulnerability should be someone who is, first of all, willing to fully empathize with our present situation. It should be someone who is ready to enter the arena of our life to accompany us in whatever battle we may be fighting at present. That person should be inclined to taste the particular flow of blood, sweat, and tears we may be experiencing in our battle. If, on the other hand, the so-called vessel chooses to remain in the coziness of a spectator's seat, not entering the arena, then that person is not actually being empathic. Our boundaries will tell us not to pay attention to whatever words may be coming from that comfort zone, since they won't come from a place of empathy and appreciation of our vulnerability. If it doesn't feel vulnerable, the sharing is probably not constructive.

If we want to grow as individuals and as a community, we then need to have unsettling conversations instead of resorting to prejudice and cowardice. If we escape from something merely because it feels uncomfortable, then that's the very definition of privilege. Our personal comfort must never be at the center of the discussion. Inner nakedness thus mandates a healthy and "boundaried" exposure, where we will have the courage to talk to people instead of talking *about* people, the latter being gossip. Our duty is to excavate the unsaid, to hear about what is not being pronounced, and then talk about it.[6] Without vulnerability, courage, heroism, and inner nakedness, this is not possible. But it is urgent.

In Gaudiya terms, sometimes we call this process of courageous inner nakedness "revealing one's mind in confidence." That means being naked in front of at least one person who can appreciate our wounds and then empower us through them. If we want to access the heart of a saintly person, as Gaudiyas aspire to, this principle teaches us that we must let that person access our heart, after having established that person's trustworthiness. We grant this access by emptying our heart without the fear of having someone else witnessing our deepest fragility. We trust the principle of unconditional love and allow ourselves to be emptied, or vulnerable, and then filled and fulfilled, or empowered. While for some this interaction may feel like a form of psychological breakdown, it is actually a *breakthrough*. In fact, Sri Rupa Goswami describes this act as a *priti-laksana*, or "loving exchange." To illustrate this kind of reciprocity, Gaudiya Vaishnavas invoke the sacred example of Draupadi, who upon being partially disrobed by aggressors in a public assembly, used one hand to call out for Krishna while holding her sari with the other. She was thus expressing only half-vulnerability, as if still able to control the situation. At this point, Krishna did not appear as Draupadi required. Some moments later, she fully acknowledged her vulnerability and raised her two hands to the Sweet Absolute, revealing her condition and mind. Only then did Krishna appear and empower her by providing an unlimited sari and his shelter. Another famous example in this connection is Krishna's flute playing. Through his renowned bamboo flute, he fully expresses his heart's desire—his clarion call—to each soul. However, for us to hear the flute song, Krishna's full breath has to first pass through his flute without any obstacles. The flute has to be hollow, as we should be as well, by emptying ourselves so that only God's breath, or his mercy, fills us and empowers our ultimate prospect.

One further story that depicts this inner nakedness, literally and allegorically, is the *gopi-vastra-harana-lila*, or divine nondual play in which Sri Krishna steals the garments of the *gopis*, the cowherd girls of Vraja. These young maidens were bathing naked in the sacred river Yamuna to celebrate their success of completing a one-month sacrifice to (secretly) obtain Krishna as their husband. Seeing the *gopis* from the branch of a nearby tree, Krishna took their clothes and told them to come one by one to him to recover their garments. The *gopis* lovingly obeyed and approached Krishna fully naked but covering their intimate parts. Sri Krishna, however, wishing to contemplate the full beauty of their inner nakedness (since the *gopis'* surrender is such that their inside and outside are one transparent reality), requested the *gopis* to beg pardon from the Yamuna for bathing there naked, by putting their two hands above their heads. Krishna wanted to appreciate the full beauty of the young girls, which in this case was synonymous with their full inner nakedness. In other words, inner nakedness has to be in place first for full empowerment or beauty to happen—for Krishna to be fully attracted to us and see us like he did the *gopis*. In this charming *lila*, the *gopis'* vulnerability, nakedness, is the very thing which ends up empowering them. Their original desire was to have Sri Krishna as their husband, and that happened only as an immediate consequence of their nakedness. Since according to the Indian tradition only a husband can see his wife naked, by seeing the *gopis* naked, Krishna was fulfilling their desire and accepting them as his wives. In other words, their very act of vulnerability/nakedness immediately created its corresponding empowerment—Krishna's accepting them fully. In this way we can only offer ourselves to God completely by first allowing ourselves to be seen and showing up with full vulnerability, in complete nakedness.

THE BEAUTY (AND TERROR) OF BEING SEEN AND LOVED FOR WHO WE ARE

In the Gaudiya tradition another way of conceiving inner nakedness and vulnerability is through *darshan*, which literally means "to be seen" and, more precisely, "to be seen by *God*." This term entails two considerations: how we should present ourselves in front of the Sweet Absolute, and how he will gaze upon us. Our part to play, as already described, is to approach the Supreme Lord as naked as we can while not pretending to see him or even attempting to, but seeking to be seen by him in all our frailty and nakedness. God's role—or, more precisely, natural reaction—will be to look upon us unconditionally, loving us despite all of our imperfections and flaws through the lens of his tender and redeeming grace. In fact, because of his infinite compassion, our brokenness and weakness seem to be especially attractive to the Divine. And *darshan* verily implies such sacred exposure; it implies the ultimate vulnerability. We can't have love in our life if we don't allow ourselves to be seen first, and we must be vulnerable to be *seen completely*. This is what real love is about, and this is what actual *darshan* is about. It is not so much about seeing God and admiring his daily outfits (as we Gaudiyas may do while viewing our temple Deities), but about standing naked in front of Infinity and allowing ourselves to be gazed upon and loved for what we are in God's eyes. *Darshan* is about learning to see ourselves according to how we are being looked at from above.

The admired Christian mystic John of the Cross often said, "Love what God sees in you." Due to his unconditional love and despite our own messiness, the Sweet Absolute always manages to successfully find something lovable even in the worst of hearts. Thus, instead of judging ourselves according to how we, society, or any other person chooses to see us conditionally, we are invited to rediscover ourselves through the unconditional gaze of the Divine, through which he loves us unrestrictedly in our nothingness, *not in our somethingness*. Loving what God sees in us also implies loving the causeless grace through which God sees in us something worthy of being loved. It implies loving the unconditional love through which he contemplates everything. And since loving someone implies loving the things loved by our beloved, if God loves something in us, we should learn to love that as well. We do this not because of self-centeredness, but because we want to fully identify and love the things our beloved Lord is passionate about. As usual, this incredibly empowering method requires full vulnerability from our side.

The Sweet Absolute looks at us in a gentle, intimate, tender, and personal way. During God's presence in our lives (and that is always), everything in our life is transparent. His seeing is *darshan*. He knows everything about us—all our weakness, brokenness, sinfulness—and still he loves us infinitely! To become aware of such divine presence is healing, strengthening, refreshing. And that's what *sadhana*, or spiritual practice, is basically about: to train and discipline our minds not to be distracted from this extraordinary daily miracle. Actual *sadhana* is not a worthiness contest or meritocracy of any type, but rather our attempt to reciprocate with a Sweet Absolute who is *addicted to mercy*, obsessed with showering unconditional love. This has been beautifully and paradoxically expressed by Paul in the Bible: "The Law was given to multiply the opportunities for failing, so that where sin abounds, *grace abounds even more*."[7] As counterintuitive as this may sound, it is equally true: God's glance upon us is so infinitely gracious that he even uses our sin for our own redemption.[8] God does not *decide* to love: *he is Love itself*. Therefore, the Sweet Absolute cannot *not* love, since love is his blueprint and the nature of his very being. In this way God's love can never be determined by the worthiness or unworthiness of the object—it has always been unconditional.[9] In fact, every time Sri Krishna says in scripture to always think of him (and that's a lot of times!) he does not necessarily mean to do that only in a literal way (to visualize his flute, peacock feather, etc.), but to also meditate on this unique feature: his constant presence and gaze of unconditional love upon each of us and everything else. If the Sweet Absolute can receive us that fully, who are we to not receive ourselves in the same way? Ironically, many of us never entertain these notions, because to be loved in this way is to live in the naked now, and it is indeed a quite naked moment.[10]

God is in total solidarity with each of us at every stage of our inner journey. Without first accepting how radically the Sweet Absolute is accepting every pore of our being, we won't be able to fully accept ourselves either. This is exactly why it is crucial to allow the Supreme Lord, and hopefully at least one other person, to see us in our imperfection and even our nakedness, as we are rather than as we would wish to be seen. Not "fake it till you make it," but *naked till you make it*! The more we go through this process, the more we can and should offer to others the experience of being lovingly looked upon in *their* imperfection; otherwise, they may never know the essential and utterly transformative mystery of causeless mercy, the actual key to real conversion. It means not merely riding on a float, having purchased a ticket to be part of the parade. Rather they will go through a genuine experience of being truly gazed upon, accepted, and loved despite (or even because of) their woundedness. To put it another way, that very thing that we let God see and accept in us also becomes what we can then see and accept in ourselves. And even more, the process of unconditional acceptance becomes that through which we see everything and everyone else. Since the Sweet Absolute is always the one who kickstarts this exercise, taking the initial step toward us, it is crucial to understand where he is coming from, so we can reciprocate accordingly. If we misread the intent of his initial approach, although we may try to reciprocate "accordingly," our aim and resulting conception will be off the mark. As we described, God's initial approach (and not limited to one time, but *continually initial*) is through the eyes of unconditional love. So the more we remain aware of this fact, the more our reciprocation will be informed and contextualized by it, and the more our service attitude toward God and everything else will be defined by how we conceive this unconditional loving gaze.

As beautiful as all this is, it can be as equally terrifying for some. Members of AA (Alcoholics Anonymous) are very well acquainted with this, as they recognize that the very first, daunting step in their healing process is admitting their powerlessness (vulnerability). Only then can they openly and voluntarily put themselves under the shelter of the Divine (empowerment), which is the much-needed transition from personal effort to spiritual receptivity.

But to deeply acknowledge our powerlessness is always easier said than done. We could say in this connection that *real aliveness is to be affected by everything*. While that's precisely what we need the most (aliveness, love, empowerment), this level of exposure (vulnerability) may be what we fear the most as well. Although we Gaudiyas may not be struggling with the same form of substance abuse as those in AA, we may simply be experiencing more subtle forms of substance abuse: cognitive rigidity, emotional apathy, institutionalism, elitism, authoritarianism, fundamentalism, and a whole parade of other toxic and terrifying "isms." As with AA, the way to be cured from our current intoxicated condition is to first acknowledge our powerlessness and then open ourselves to divine intervention. In other words, we as a community may need to humbly admit how unmanageable some situations have become, pray for sacred mercy to descend upon us, and decide which changes need to be engineered. Remember the formula: first vulnerability, *only then* empowerment.

STILL AFRAID OF BEING VULNERABLE?

Despite having accepted and understood all of the above points in principle, we probably still dislike the word *vulnerability* and are paralyzed by its prospect. Why may this be so? One possible reason is that we may unconsciously link vulnerability with excruciating shame, fear, and disconnection, while our life purpose is its exact opposite; it is *yoga*, or realizing our connectiveness with everything. Acknowledging our vulnerability may be difficult, but never impossible. *Difficult is the middle point between the two extremes of easy and impossible*. Of course, being vulnerable is sometimes made more difficult by the environment we are living in. In some cultures there is zero tolerance for vulnerability. Perfectionism and armor are rewarded and necessary, while conversations about our woundedness may be seen as totally unproductive. But again, it's never impossible to be vulnerable.

In our challenge to find the middle point of healthy vulnerability, we may end up in some of its classical extremes. We may either stop caring at all what people think about us and fall into universal apathy and indifference, or we may allow ourselves to be excessively defined by others' judgements. In either of these scenarios, we lose our capacity to be vulnerable. At this point we can again invoke two terms shared at the beginning of this work: belonging and fitting in. As we have discussed, vulnerability is related to being seen and thus allowing for deep belonging, while fitting in is its exact opposite. It is an avoidance of being seen at all costs while constantly discerning what should and should not be done and said in order to match the expectations of the audience—how to hide in plain sight. That's not us, but rather an acculturated sense of self. In contrast, deep belonging implies belonging to yourself *first*. It means never *ever* betraying yourself for other people, because betraying yourself is the most painful and dreadful thing you can do. True belonging doesn't require us to change who we are. It requires us to *be who we are*. And, one more time, that's what vulnerability is about: to be who we are. *And we are vulnerable.*

The more we dare to insist on vulnerability, the more afraid we may become. Ironically, we tend to fear and even hate the very things that will save us. As mentioned above, vulnerability may be especially terrifying to us because of shame. We feel too embarrassed to allow others to witness our woundedness as humans. In fact, our inner critic generally clings to shame and cancels every possibility to express genuine vulnerability. In a famous poll where people were asked about their greatest fear, dying came in third or fourth place, while making a fool of oneself when speaking before a crowd (shame) topped the list. In its most toxic forms, shame simply grinds us down, making us wish we could disappear or even kill ourselves; hence, people often describe feeling *mortified* in relation to shame.[11] Therefore, although we may think that we are afraid of vulnerability, we are actually afraid of shame.

In the Christian tradition, the shame pattern is clearly present and depicted from the very earliest times. After biting the primeval apple (representing the dualistic mind, which creates self-consciousness), the first thing that happens to Adam and Eve is that they become aware of themselves and notice their nakedness. They feel vulnerable and easily damaged. They then immediately make themselves loincloths to cover up their fragile bodies, or protect their egos. They quickly hide, feeling unworthy and ashamed to stand before God. Unsettled by their vulnerability, most people fear to walk along with the Divine, embarrassed by the contrast between godly potential and who they may be at present. This embarrassment may not only be too difficult to acknowledge, but extremely difficult and painful as well. To embrace his vulnerability was so painful for Adam that he invoked a toxic version of it, victim consciousness, by immediately blaming Eve for inviting him to bite the forbidden fruit. If this was not enough scapegoating, on top of that Adam even blamed God for giving him Eve! Surely, she was the cause of his failings. This powerfully symbolic story clearly depicts how vulnerability and shame have been tied together and weaponized for millennia, thus representing one of the most basic and difficult challenges for most of us to integrate from time immemorial.

But still there is hope. Like any other quality, shame can be expressed in a healthy way that redeems us from its distorted articulation and allows us to express our so-needed vulnerability. While unhealthy shame is generally personified by a ruthlessly relentless inner critic who makes us shrink into disempowered states, healthy shame activates our conscience and leads us toward clear, empowering amends. In other words, the moral hub of healthy shame is responsibility, while the moral hub of guilt, which is unhealthy shame or shame polluted with fear, is blame.[12] Knowing their difference will help us deal with shame properly, so we won't hinder the expression and experience of vulnerability.

TOXIC EXPRESSIONS OF VULNERABILITY: VICTIM CONSCIOUSNESS

While unhealthy shame may terrify and paralyze us in relation to being vulnerable, there is another, probably more subtle way of not only avoiding vulnerability, but actually exploiting it. It is known as *victim consciousness*. As toxic masculinity promotes a false sense of courage devoid of vulnerability, its counterpart of toxic femininity exhibits a false sense of vulnerability in the form of victim consciousness. Through this deceptive pattern we may be convinced about our own vulnerability and even convince others to think the same about us as well; however, by doing so we will be acting as actual abusers by imposing tragedy on others instead of carrying our own cross with dignity and honor. Victim consciousness can be performed not only by playing the victim ourselves, but even by overidentifying with other victims in an attempt to somehow transfer their innocence to us. In this case, we often vaguely assume the victim to be a noble target of unfair circumstances, thus depriving that person of any agency and personal responsibility not only in the past, but in the present and future as well. And with this type of thinking we replicate that debilitating pattern in ourselves, even without noticing it. In any of its many forms, this victim consciousness is the exact opposite of Krishna consciousness, another name for Gaudiya Vaishnavism. And Gaudiya Vaishnavism is also another name for Radical Personalism, a path in which we are to become victors, not victims.

In a nutshell, victim consciousness is about denying personal responsibility (response-ability) for what happens in our lives while placing all the blame on some so-called outside enemy. Conversely, genuine vulnerability is about being fully committed to who we are and all that we can be, as well as not pointing outside ourselves in an attempt to justify our actions. In fact, the latter tendency could be called "the Satanic impulse," the ever-present urge to accuse others, and never ourselves. In fact, the very word "Satan" means *the accuser*. This toxic expression of vulnerability is deeply disempowering, creating the false necessity to prove ourselves right by proving someone else wrong. That said, if we find ourselves accused by someone steeped in victim consciousness, we should invoke compassion and patience with them, knowing that on some deep level, they feel so excessively guilty that they cannot bare to admit their actual involvement, even to themselves. And we, who are not yet totally free from this pernicious impulse to accuse others, should recognize that "we" are the "they."

We live in special times. Gaudiya Vaishnavas refer to the present age as Kali-yuga, "the age of quarrel and hypocrisy" or, in its more updated translation, *the age of victim consciousness*. We live in times where the more victimized we are, the more moral superiority we achieve. The more labels of oppression and victimhood we have accrued, the more our view of reality is deemed authoritative and the more we are considered to have moral worth. Thus, with such a validation from our present environment, we should be especially careful of this fake mask of vulnerability, because buying into it and creating a self-justifying story line will make our emotional entrapment within that story quadruple, to say the least. Thus, to get rid of victim consciousness we need to invoke its genuine healthy expression in the form of not only vulnerability, but Radical Vulnerability, which is a crucial facet of Radical Personalism. Without it, whatever current brokenness we may have as individuals and a community will prove unseen, dismissed, or, even worse, transferred to the outside through the deceptive guise of victim consciousness.

Radical Vulnerability proposes a comprehensive embrace of our messiness and flawed side, understanding the urgent need to get rid of the ego folktale that keeps insisting that we have to be perfect, or at least that we must present ourselves as such. An actual perfect person can consciously forgive and include imperfection, in both himself and others. As has been said, *we grow spiritually much more by doing it wrong than by doing it right.*[13] It is in this wrongness and imperfection that the Sweet Absolute has hidden the secret of holiness, so only those willing to look in that unusual direction will find it. Radical Vulnerability thus invites us to find God, and ourselves in him, *in disorder and imperfection.* This is how wisdom is usually disclosed to us. Instead of evading reality through the toxic template of victim consciousness, we are invited to fully embrace life and things, *as vulnerable as they may be,* with acceptance, gratitude, and responsibility.

THE CHARM OF RADICAL VULNERABILITY

No matter how hard it may be to acknowledge our vulnerable side, hopefully at this point we have realized that vulnerability is not only necessary and a part of our very makeup as humans, but also one of the most charming and empowering portals even in the life of God himself. We have begun this chapter by pointing to some examples in this connection, and we will conclude it by going full circle and sharing some further testimonies from the Gaudiya tradition and other sources, all of which point to this foundational principle of the charm of Radical Vulnerability.

We already talked about the connection between vulnerability, courage, and heroism. So let's reach our conclusion by sharing the example of Superman, one of the main popular heroes of Western culture. When this comic was initially published, Superman was, for all intents and purposes, invulnerable and omnipotent. Nothing could ever kill or even harm him, and he was triumphant in any situation. There was no risk, no uncertainty, no emotional exposure—he was *not* vulnerable. After some time, and to the dismay of its publishers, the readers of this initially successful series eventually started to become bored: Superman was too powerful, too removed from the readers' own experience and reality, too unrelatable. Thus, in order to retain their audience, the publishers made Superman vulnerable. For one, they added green kryptonite, which under certain levels of exposure could not only weaken Superman, but even kill him. The result of this? Sales sky-rocketed again, since readers could again relate with their hero. He was again relevant to them *since he was vulnerable like them*, or at least vulnerable on some level. As we already said, for a hero to be a hero, he has to be vulnerable. Conversely, a superhero who can do anything turns out to be no hero at all. He has nothing to strive against, so he can't be admirable.[14] In other words, *fragility is a precondition for heroism*—and God himself enters this equation.

Vulnerability is not only a desirable quality in the Supreme Lord, but an ontological necessity of his. Among other places, such unique intimation is hinted at in the beginning of an old Jewish koanlike story which asks us to imagine a being who is omniscient, omnipresent, and omnipotent. Then we're asked what such a being lacks. It seems he lacks nothing, and yet still something is missing. The answer? *Limitation*. If such a being is already everything and everywhere, always, then there is nowhere to go, nothing to do, and even *nothing to be*. Everything that could be already is, and everything that could happen already has happened. It is precisely for this reason, at least according to the Jewish tradition, that God created man, because without limitation there is no story.[15] Of course, Gaudiya Vaishnavas have their own creation narrative, one without the need to invoke the creation of humans for God to be "limited." Gaudiya Vaishnavas have the unique concept of God's *nara-lila*, the sacred eternal play in which the Sweet Absolute is humanlike or, better put, both fully human and fully divine. This is not only the most charming of all *lilas*, but also the most vulnerable. God's fully human *lila* takes us to his fully divine, eternal play.

There is a very intimate correlation between vulnerability and beauty. For example, a newborn baby is especially attractive due to her extremely fragile condition. It seems the more vulnerable someone is, the more drawn we feel toward them. In this connection, the Gaudiya lore describes Sri Krishna as the Supremely Attractive One, that is, the Supremely Vulnerable. Being viscerally affected by the love of his nearest and dearest, Krishna will typically be found in a permanent state of vulnerability. He is wounded and defeated in wrestling with his friends, pierced by the sharp arrows of separation from his beloved, and chastised by his divine parents while crying and imploring mercy. On top of this, as already mentioned, God's own vulnerability then takes a whole other dimension when Sri Krishna manifests as Gaurahari and displays the crowning point of God's vulnerability, beauty, and empowerment. In other words, for the Absolute to be absolute, every possibility has to be there in him in its most perfect expression, including the possibility of eternal vulnerability. So yes, God can be wounded and vulnerable and not be affected in his Godhood. In fact, through the display of vulnerability and apparent limitation the charm of his humanlike divinity only increases. As has been accurately put by Jordan B. Peterson,

> *Being of any reasonable sort appears to require limitation. Perhaps this is because Being requires Becoming, as well as mere static existence—and to become is to become something more, or at least something different. That is only possible for something limited.*[16]

Or, we may add to the above quote, in relation to the Unlimited "becoming something more": *Such a thing is possible only for someone who remains eternally vulnerable and open to further evolution*—an eternally vulnerable God open to further evolution. The Gaudiya tradition not only presents but perpetually worships such a face of divinity, gifting a perspective of divine mystery that takes *all* patterns to new levels. Thus, the natural question that follows may be: How much are we embodying this prospect of continual evolution through our own conduct and disposition toward the virtue of vulnerability, so our own eternal becoming can perpetually unfold?

CONCLUDING REMARKS

As we have seen, vulnerability is synonymous with the courage to be seen in our inner nakedness and with the prospect of overarching empowerment, all this ultimately converging in the reality of divine love. Without the willingness to be vulnerable and without admitting our woundedness as individuals and a tradition, how can we hope to receive the necessary empowerment to transform whatever may need to be transformed? And by contrast allowing ourselves to be thoroughly vulnerable, Gaudiya Vaishnavism can experience its highest reach and required revival.

When speaking about Gaudiya Vaishnavism's ultimate prospect and empowerment in the context of Radical Vulnerability, we must remember the sequence to get there: potential is related to potency, potency to the possibility of empowerment, empowerment to vulnerability. And to become empowered, we may find some uncomfortable and unsettling experiences that we may need to embrace and go through, at least in the very beginnings. It is no wonder that most of the things that unsettle us ultimately seek to empower and take us to our full potential.

There is no absolute separation between working on our vulnerability as humans and how this virtue plays itself out in the divine realm. Of course, being merely vulnerable as a human won't necessarily take us to transcendental consciousness. But if vulnerability is integrated with spiritual practice, there will be a correlation between how we cultivate vulnerability as *sadhakas* (practitioners) and how vulnerability expresses itself in the ultimate realm of *lila*, or divine nondual play. In this connection we have Visvanatha Chakravarti's commentary on *Srimad Bhagavatam* 10.29.11. He describes how, in the beginning of one's practice, the body of a *sadhaka* will be a combination of material and spiritual influences but, as the *sadhaka* is further infused by divine grace, his physical and psychic bodies become more and more spiritualized, proportionately to how much he has received God's causeless mercy. Ultimately, in the consummate stage of divine love, no material portion remains in the physical and psychic dimensions of a *sadhaka's* body. While our humanity can thus become perfectly integrated with our final divine prospect, that integration begins wherever we may be at present. If we don't integrate these two experiences, we may be creating an unnecessary dichotomy between material and spiritual, which healthy vulnerability seeks to dissolve and then consolidate into a higher synthesis.

Gaudiya Vaishnavism fully revolves around the sacred virtue of vulnerability, a virtue which, properly appreciated, can allow us to learn from life's most valuable lessons. Those lessons will always be there, but *we need to learn how to learn from them.* As T. S. Eliot put it, "We had the experience but missed the meaning, and approach to the meaning restores the experience."[17] And by orienting our attention toward meaning within any given circumstance we can make it a *learned lesson.* Those learned lessons could be compared to bright pearls, or "pearls of wisdom," as it is said. In fact, Sri Krishna says in the *Bhagavad-gita* 7.7 that everything rests upon him "as pearls are strung on a thread." What kind of pearls are strung on that thread? Pearls of wisdom. What kind of wisdom? Layered wisdom. Just as pearls form inside a mollusk, pearls of wisdom are deeply reflective lessons. They are *learned* lessons, layered one upon another and formed around the broken pieces of our own inner shell. In fact, this is how pearls are actually formed: the nucleus of a pearl is a broken piece of the oyster's own shell, which the animal considers an irritant and coats with a secretion that ends up forming a pearl. In a similar way, from our own brokenness and vulnerability we can grow beautiful pearls of empowering wisdom to be strung on the thread of purpose that runs through our life's lessons. Everything rests upon the black velvet mystery of our Sweet Absolute, as pearls are strung on a thread.

9 Individuation: Carving Out Our Full Humanity in Divine Service

The privilege of a lifetime is to become who you truly are.

– Carl Jung

RADICAL PERSONALISM IS SYNONYMOUS with being as personal as we can be. This refers not only to the fact that behind every aspect of existence there is ultimately a personalized expression, or to being as personal as we can in our relationships, or to attaining our ultimate spiritual identity in eternity. While all these aspects of Radical Personalism are certainly true and a crucial part of this equation, in the stage where most of us find ourselves there will be another facet of Radical Personalism, probably the most important to embrace as current practitioners. That is the facet of carving out our full humanity in a way that fosters a unique and divine sense of being, which we'll call *sacred transhumanism*. General transhumanism is a philosophical and cultural movement that seeks to enhance or perfect human beings beyond our biological limits. Sacred transhumanism, or individuation, also has to do with enhancing our humanity beyond its biological limits, but it attempts to do so by extracting our ultimate potential as humans in connection to our divine prospect in transcendence.

At this point, a doubt may come concerning the great emphasis on the role of humanity in connection to our spiritual nature as souls. Although according to Gaudiyas the soul is not ontologically human, humanness is a very crucial portal through which we can realize who we are as souls. Without our humanity we cannot realize our ultimate spiritual constitution. As mentioned in the previous chapter, our *sadhaka-deha*, or practitioner's physical and psychic bodies (our humanity), can become fully spiritualized to the point of accompanying us in eternity. Visvanatha Chakravarti confirms this spiritualization in the conclusion of his commentary on *Srimad Bhagavatam* 10.29.11: "When one reaches the stage of *prema* [divine love], one's body is *completely* spiritualized, *and no mundane portion remains*."[1] A famous example in this regard is that of Dhruva, who is described in *Srimad Bhagavatam* as entering the spiritual world in his selfsame human body. In *Chaitanya-charitamrita* 3.4.191–193, Gaurahari himself confirms this same point by saying, "The body of a devotee is never material. It is considered to be transcendental, full of spiritual bliss. At the time of initiation, when a devotee fully surrenders unto the service of the Lord, Krishna makes him as spiritual as himself. When the devotee's body is thus transformed into spiritual existence, the devotee, in that transcendental body, renders service to the lotus feet of the Lord." This is why a saintly devotee's body, when the devotee has passed away, is entombed and not cremated, because it is considered that in that same spiritualized body he is eternally serving Sri Gaurahari in his abode. Therefore, we can start to grasp how our humanity is not antagonistic to spirituality, but perfectly compatible. We can refer to the body as a vehicle, but when the body is fully spiritualized and thus fully human and fully divine, it becomes part of our eternal identity. As Krishna's humanlike body in his *nara-lila* is nondifferent from his own essential identity, the same thing happens with those who serve him in a humanlike body. In other words, if Sri Krishna's body is not only fully divine but also fully human, then his very essence is also not only fully divine but fully human as well, since *he is his body*. Similarly, although a soul is not ontologically human, it will be fully human (and fully divine) in *lila*, where the soul attains its final and highest potential. Thus, we need to become fully human, not by only ceasing to be inhuman in our present situation, but rather by positively developing our humanity, since our final identity as Gaudiyas will be both fully human and fully divine. And that identity is to be developed as practitioners in our present human condition, in the context of our spiritual practice.

We can develop this proposal even further. The human condition is the only way for a soul to experience itself. For Gaudiyas, there are only two instances where a soul can be disconnected from the possibilities offered by a human body: (1) when experiencing *brahma-sayujya*, or eternal absorption in the undifferentiated Absolute, known as Brahman, and (2) when inhabiting a nonhuman body, like that of an animal or a plant. While in the first of these two cases the soul won't have any experience of its own individuality due to the nature of undifferentiated absorption, in the second case the soul will have an individualized experience but it won't be conscious of itself—we need self-consciousness to understand ourselves as souls. In each case the soul is not experiencing a human condition and is not aware of itself as a soul. Awareness of ourselves as souls can occur only in human experience. In other words, the only vehicle by which we can become aware of our own existence as individual souls is the human form of life. And when that awareness attains its perfection, the same humanity which facilitated that possibility "joins" the soul for eternity in the *nara-lila*. In other words, *nara-lila* is eternal perfection playing itself out in humanlike form. The human form is the only place where we can become aware of the soul that we actually are, and this explains exactly why the Gaudiya scriptures repeatedly praise the human form in this connection.[2] Considering all this, how much can we separate the human experience from the soul's potential and ultimate prospect? In fact, the human vehicle and its corresponding humanity is the perfect *and only* vehicle through which we can not only experience ourselves as souls, but attain all that we can be as such. That means all our potential as conscious beings in our humanlike, fully human/fully divine existence in *lila*. So, it's all about humanity—all the way up to our eternal goal.

The goal of Radical Personalism is not a naive personalization but, in the classic expression of Pierre Teilhard de Chardin, a "super-personalization." It is about how to become completely unique as human spiritual beings, and how to retain and upgrade our uniqueness in the self-forgetfulness of divine love where, paradoxically, we seem to disappear due to our selfless surrender. But that's exactly the place where ultimate uniqueness will be found in its fullest form—lost and found, that is—in a sea of specified sweetness and affection. As usual, the exact opposite of this proposal is impersonalism, a force which possibly lurks in every corner of our psyche, adopting different garbs according to how we choose to depersonalize ourselves in our spiritual pursuit. While some people hide by merging into an ontological void, others conceal themselves by merging into an institution and becoming just another blank face in the crowd while considering this to be spiritual participation. Others may be afraid of the social implications of their own opinions, thus numbing themselves into varieties of emotional atrophy. At this point we may rightly ask what is left of a human being.[3] In his commentary on *Bhagavad-gita* 4.10, Srila Prabhupada portrays this scenario as follows:

> *Retaining the personality after liberation from matter frightens them. When they are informed that spiritual life is also individual and personal, they become afraid of becoming persons again, and so they naturally prefer a kind of merging into the impersonal void.*

The way to be cured from all these different layers of impersonalism is by practicing being a person, a practice which will gradually bring us to the point of being not only persons, personal, and personalists, but Radical Personalists. Therefore, Radical Personalism could be seen as both the means and the end, since we aspire to remain as individuals and to become *as personal as we can even in eternity*. But it all begins wherever we are now, with a proper integration of all the elements of our current personality. Another name for this process is *individuation*.

ON BECOMING INDIVIDUATED

As with the notions of the subconscious and the shadow, the term *individuation* was also coined by Carl Jung. In fact, he considered individuation the central and most important concept in his view of human development. According to his perspective, individuation could basically be described as a process of deep transformation, whereby both the personal and collective unconscious are brought into consciousness to be assimilated into the whole personality—a deep fine-tuning of our aligned physical, mental, emotional, and spiritual dimensions. In fact, Jung's notion of individuation points to the very essence of the word "person," which refers to "sounding (*sonare*) through (*per*)"; we are relational beings whose various dimensions can be perfectly aligned with and thus *sound through* other beings. This meaning is almost the exact opposite of the meaning of "person" that many of us hold today: an autonomous, independent, and self-contained unit. In our present era, the rise of postmodernity signaled an end to all forms of fundamental metanarratives: our unifying stories that provided shared meaning in our human community. In their stead—right in the center of ultra-relative ambivalence and fragmentation—was placed the individual whose autonomy must not be disturbed or challenged. To put it in one word, *individualism.*[4] By contrast, individuation points to the deepest possible reach of individual *integration* which, by definition, includes our interrelatedness with everything.

The idea of individuation can also be tied to the shadow work presented in the first part of this book. It is an idea which finds its Sanskrit correspondence in the form of *anartha-nivritti* ("getting rid of false values"), a process which basically revolves around the principle of creativity. It means turning what may at present be your worst enemy into your best friend. In *Bhagavad-gita* 6.6, Sri Krishna described the mind's potential both as a friend and as an enemy, depending on how we deal with it. Sri Gaurahari himself established how glorious are those engaged in the individuation process by garlanding and decorating those followers of his who were about to clean the Gundicha temple. That famous occurrence symbolizes the heroic task of *anartha-nivritti*, through which our heart is to become a shrine of divine presence.

Individuation involves incorporating, blending, and consolidating whatever messiness may still accompany our present humanity, very much like the ancient Japanese *kintsugi*. In this unique form of art, the cracked areas of broken pottery are mended and highlighted with powdered gold and other valuable substances. By this method, a very crucial point is made: scars and brokenness not only have their value but are a crucial part of our history. They are never meant to be disguised, but rather underscored. In fact, while Gaudiya Vaishnavism fully blooms and converges in the idea of divine love of full-fledged heart openness, to keep our heart space open we almost always first need emotional healing in regard to past hurts.[5] Therefore, for Gaudiyas individuation entails what we may call *integration of complexity*, an alchemical process through which we become more and more wholesome in our humanity by completing our present personality and identity as humans and *sadhakas*, or spiritual aspirants. For Gaudiya Vaishnavism, such wholeness allows for the eventual attainment of the wholeness (and holiness) which is to be found in the *siddha-deha*, or our eternal identity of divine service.

But before reaching this consummate stage, we have to first deal with our human nature and its different components, and all of that in service to our divine ideal. This is Radical Individuation, another facet of Radical Personalism. And since Radical Personalism is nothing but another term for Gaudiya Vaishnavism, the Jungian notion of individuation can become an organic aspect of *bhakti* for Gaudiyas, if properly linked and conceived. How can this be so? Jiva Goswami's *Bhakti Sandarbha* (Anuccheda 225) presents the concept of *sanga-siddha-bhakti*, a notion that implies that although some activities are not in and of themselves inherently devotional (*svarupa-siddha-bhakti*), they can nonetheless become such by association, or *sanga*. In other words, while having a shower or mowing the grass (or engaging in individuation) may not be transcendental endeavors per se, they can nonetheless become such by being properly conceived in service to the Sweet Absolute, since ultimately everything is the energy of God and, therefore, everything can be consecrated in his sacred service. Jiva Goswami makes it clear that *sanga-siddha-bhakti* is not necessarily *misra-bhakti* (devotion mixed with ulterior motives) but has the potential to be *suddha-bhakti* (devotion free of ulterior motives). Accordingly, individuation can fully become a crucial aspect of our spiritual practice. In this way, by learning to be fully integrated humans in the context of spiritual practice, we will naturally be prompted to the fully human individual uniqueness that similarly waits for us in relation to the Divine—*divine humanism.*

DIVINE HUMANISM AND THE GAUDIYA TRADITION

Due to its theologically precise details concerning unending possibilities for penetration into transcendence, Gaudiya Vaishnavism could naturally be defined as "the path of specificity." The phrase "pure love of God" represents for Gaudiyas a rough and generic way of referring to their highest spiritual attainment, with an abundance of details still to unfold throughout their journey. These details include varieties and intensities of divine love, different faces of the Sweet Absolute that will constitute the object of that love, different abodes corresponding to each mood, groups and subgroups of divine service, and so on. This degree of specificity, however, is not to be restricted to the transcendental realm. A parallel level of detail should ideally complement and inform our present situation as human practitioners. Thus, in this University of Specificity that Radical Personalism is synonymous with, we should be able to detect our present needs for human individuation in the context of the ultimate specificity of divine humanism found in the eternal domain.

For Gaudiya Vaishnavas, the notion of divine humanism refers to a twofold prospect which allows God and the soul to remain both fully human and fully divine *for eternity*, and relate to each other correspondingly. This is a unique theological contribution, where the Sweet Absolute himself eternally embraces humanity so we can fully embrace divinity. Interestingly, a difficulty we often experience while trying to conceive of God as fully human is closely tied to our own difficulty in fully embracing our own humanity. It's not so much that we are human beings trying to be spiritual; *we are already spiritual beings, now trying to be fully human.* No matter how refined our conception of the Godhead, if our humanity is not in place, it will be more than difficult to relate to the Divine in any realistic sense. Even a good theology will have a hard time making up for a bad anthropology.[6] Thus, *the place for humanity in our life has to be such that it puts in context our spirituality*, while the role of spirituality will similarly contextualize our humanity. The ultimate converging of these two is what Gaudiyas call *nara-lila*.

Nara-lila translates as "humanlike divine play." The "like" in *humanlike* refers not to some dysfunctional half-baked humanity expressed in this *lila*, but to the fact that full humanity coexists in total harmony with full divinity in one person: God, or even us. Thus, the "like" part of this compound mostly indicates the divine aspect of this equation, that aspect being fully divine. And the word "human" similarly points to the complete presence of humanity *despite divinity*. Gaudiyas thus consider *nara-lila as* the highest expression of all *lilas*. It is where humanity and divinity meet, embrace, and are perfectly integrated.[7] Apart from Gaurahari's own *lila*, *nara-lila* is typically performed by Sri Krishna in the idyllic village of Vraja. For Gaudiyas, it is in this place that the full potential of humanity can be discovered. It is where God retains every feature of his humanness in a way that fully nourishes his own divine schedule. We are warned that if we desire to live forever in such a place, we must become godlike. That means we must attain the same humanlike status that the Supreme Lord expresses in his *nara-lila*, along with its fully divine expression. What ancient Greeks called *theosis*, or divinization, here we call *divine humanism*. It is a transformative process whose aim is likeness to or union with the Sweet Absolute in humanlike terms.

The power of *bhakti* is such that our present humanity, with its own unique attributes, will accompany us when it is fully spiritualized in the perfected state. In other words, when *bhakti* fills the heart, it does not change the structure of the devotee's empiric character. This is confirmed in *Bhakti-rasamrita-sindhu* 1.3.4, where it is said that "while *bhakti* in the form of *bhava-bhakti* [devotion in ecstasy] is totally independent of all mental functions, still it manifests in a person's empiric character and in his mental functions and becomes one with his mind, his character, and his individuality." A classic example of this is the demon Vritrasura, who even after being redeemed retained his demon empiric character instead of becoming a pious sage. Similarly, among the companions of Sri Gaurahari, we find devotees with very different dispositions, all of whom show this same principle. For example, the eccentric Pundarika

Vidyanidhi completely concealed his identity as a devotee by pretending to be a rich person dedicated to mundane pleasures. Despite being immensely rich, Pundarika did not do anything for the poor, because he never came to think of the suffering of the world, as he was always absorbed in Krishna and his *lila*. By contrast, Vasudeva Datta represented the extreme of compassion for all living beings. As we can see, each of Gaurahari's associates had particular characteristic features, exemplifying the limitless range of devotees' personalities. In this way, the conclusion is that each practitioner has his own individuality and empiric character, and this will be retained after the complete spiritualization of one's physical and psychic dimensions.[8]

As Krishna and his *lila* are both fully human, we should also allow our full humanity for both Krishna and his *lila* to happen in our lives. If we do not allow the frailty and vulnerability of our human condition, then most probably we are not allowing Krishna's *nara-lila* to happen in us. And we are not allowing humanlike Krishna to exist in our lives. *By not allowing ourselves to be who we actually are, we are not allowing our conception of Krishna to be like he actually is.* Needless to say, as Gaudiyas we want to be who we actually are, but for that to happen we need to *inhabit our concepts* and not merely parrot them; we need to act out our beliefs accordingly and not simply proclaim them; we have to play out the implications of our ideals to their maximum possible degree and see if, after doing so, they still unfold and converge organically in the goal we have set theoretically for ourselves. If this does not happen, we may be indulging in one of the most unpalatable forms of misrepresentation: speaking about the highest theological peaks while simultaneously remaining dysfunctional in our humanity.

ASCEND, TRANSCEND ... BUT FIRST DESCEND

Ironically, "practicing spiritual life" can become one of the best excuses *not to practice spiritual life*. We can easily dismiss individuation and integration of complexity by invoking fancy doctrines and metaphysical elitist narratives, thus indulging in varieties of spiritual bypassing while abusing the integrity of the most noble spiritual ideals. If we don't invoke integration, we will then have its opposite—*disintegration*. To prevent this from happening, we need to realistically acknowledge not only where we want to arrive, but first and especially where we are at present. As with any navigation systems, these locations are interdependent in our journey. So, where are we? Probably here and now, in our humanity. Thus, before attempting to be devotional superheroes and leap beyond our present condition in a single bound, we may find it more sustainable and progressive to try to become *devotional human beings*. That means trying to be good devotee and not a great devotee, a natural person and not a supernatural one.

Unfortunately, our humanity, with its physical, mental, and emotional dimensions, is sometimes presented in Gaudiya circles as an obstacle to be "transcended," that is, *rejected*. But we should be reminded from our previous chapter on vulnerability how the limitations and imperfections ascribed to humanness, if properly dealt with, can add charm and beauty not only to ourselves, but even to God himself. And we can offer such humanness in divine service now. When fully spiritualized, our humanness can express itself in *lila* for the rest of forever. Considering such a prospect, *our human dimension is not negotiable*, and it is certainly not an ontological global obstacle. Of course, humanity, like everything, has a very dark potential if improperly handled, but a very bright one as well. Thus, we need to be anthropologically astute and very smart in how we choose to coexist with our humanity while integrating each layer of complexity. While this does not mean that we need to perfectly individuate every pore of our being before attaining the spiritual realm, it doesn't imply its opposite either. Just as we should not overemphasize preliminary psychic perfection as an obligatory prerequisite to devotional accomplishment, we should neither totally dismiss our human dimension as irrelevant, but do the needful as we perceive the need to do so.

One way of misusing our human dimension is to misread what we are supposed to do with it, especially in the context of spirituality. We may think that our practice is only about ascending and transcending, but never descending. Not only this, but we may (mis)conceive ascending as being some form of meritocracy, where all results depend exclusively on our personal effort; misconceive transcending as rejecting all that is supposedly "not holy enough"; and misconceive descending as some form of falling down that should be totally avoided. This distorted yet commonly envisioned scenario characterizes the exact opposite of what each of these terms actually represent. Ascending is the dependence on grace, transcending is the rejection of nothing but the integration of everything, and descending is not something to prevent but rather something totally necessary, even before the two other stages. First descend, and only then ascend and transcend. This describes not a climbing religion, but *a descending one*.

As noted above, the ultimate spiritual ideal of Gaudiya Vaishnavas is extremely specified and, we should add, intimate and exclusive in nature. However, before attaining such a level of divine exclusivity we need an initial form of inclusivity. We need proper human grounding to accommodate everything before we get too specific about the details of post-liberated life. Without this inclusivity, the only exclusivity that we will be able to express is fundamentalism—exclusivity separate from inclusivity. Conversely, Gaudiyas only cherish the exclusivity that arises *out of* inclusivity, which is the intimate service in sacred *lila*. However, this inclusivity includes and integrates our human dimension as part of our devotional project, since human development is not an adversary of spiritual development but an ideal complement and friend to it. In our search for the Divine, we should not rush from the personal to the transpersonal, since the price to pay in that case may be in the currency of depersonalization. However, if we do our homework and become wholesome, grounded human beings, we can then humbly reclaim our rights (so to say) to the specifics of our ideal. The path to such fruit will be littered with pits, but do not worry, since our inner progress could be defined as *the process of making deeper and deeper mistakes*. It entails ascending *through* the excavation of descent.

Part of our human grounding and personal individuation has to do with acknowledging our present nature and personality, and working in a suitable vocation. This is what Krishna himself advised at the onset of the *Bhagavad-gita* by recommending to Arjuna to act according to his *dharma*, or duty, in the ancient social system of India known as *varnashram*. Similarly, when Sri Gaurahari inquired from Ramananda Raya about the ultimate goal of life, Ramananda began by promoting the performance of one's role in *varnashram*. While Gaurahari rejected this proposal *as representing the ultimate goal of life*, it is nonetheless worthy to notice that an organic balance of one's psycho-social dimension was proposed at the very beginning by Sri Ramananda and, although Gaurahari rejected it in terms of its being the highest point of transcendence, he nonetheless accepted it as a crucial preliminary foundation, as human balance is an ideal precondition to the attainment of divine love. Although the *varnashram* system is nonoperative in our times, its very essence remains present. We need to ascertain what our *adhikara* (eligibility) is in order to engage in any activity, considering our abilities and limitations, and to do so will be real virtue and beauty.[9] The balance and satisfaction that comes from this exercise is known in Sanskrit as *sattva*, or "beingness." It is an inner state of consciousness where we glimpse who we are as both human and spirit, as well as the accompanying combined potential. In *Bhagavad-gita* 6.17, Sri Krishna advocates the domain of material composure by recommending that whatever one does should always be done in a well-balanced and levelheaded way. This integration of our humanity could be described as arrival at our departure airport. Although we have not yet boarded our flight to transcendence, getting to the airport is a necessary preliminary step. *No descending into our humanity means no ascending into transcendence.* And paradoxically, the more we ascend into transcendence, the more human we'll naturally become.

While we may have reached the airport of individuation, we should be careful not to instruct others in ways that may only be applicable to ourselves, not to compare our own human needs to those of others, and not to force ourselves or others to act in ways that do not fit one's nature. This is an ultra-personalized journey, and each individual experience is unique. As Radical Personalists we are to always keep this important notion in mind. Individuation is not something to perform globally and in a generic sense, but always in very specific and personal terms—attending our own case while not imitating another's path. Sri Krishna emphatically presented this important point in what could arguably be described as *the* verse on individuation in the *Bhagavad-gita* (3.35):

> *Acting in accordance with one's own nature, even if somehow done deficiently, is superior to taking up another's duty, even if performed well. Even death occurring in the discharge of one's own duty is superior to the execution of another's duty, since following another's path is dangerous.*

In other words, no matter how poorly we may be executing our individuation process, that will never be as bad as trying to be someone else. Individuation—or better put, Radical Individuation—requires that we operate with intentionality. That means *justifying our very existence by accepting responsibility for having our own experience.* Let's repeat this last line and allow it to soak in: Radical Individuation is all about justifying our very existence by accepting *response-ability* for having our own experience. That should be both normal and normalized. It entails holding ourselves accountable not only to others, but first and foremost to ourselves. Life is a responsible affair.

We need to give ourselves permission to be different. In fact, *to be who we are means to be different from everyone else* (at least on some level). If we were all to be the same, we would fall into another variant of impersonalism. However, each of us is a unique being with the potential of being loved by the Sweet Absolute in a unique and unrepeatable way. So we must honor that specificity. Our individual self is nothing but the personification of a unique relationship with God. But that self can individuate only in the eternal present, or not at all.[10] "Be yourself—no one else will do it," says an ancient Judaic proverb. While there are thousands of ways to be *almost* yourself, there is *only one way* to be all that you can be. That way is individuation, never imitation. For Gaudiyas, this process of individuation remains perpetually in the service of their ideal of divine love, since for them God himself is the topmost individuated being. In fact, Gaudiya Vaishnavas call Sri Krishna "the Supreme Personality of Godhead," which is another way of referring to the supremely individuated form of the Absolute. That form is the Sweet Absolute expressing the supreme side of his personality. Gaudiyas believe that this is possible only because of how much space God allows for humanlike emotionality in the transcendence of his *nara-lila*, where we find the Divine allowing himself to be *as human as he can be.* However, to allow the Supreme Personality of Godhead to exist in our lives we should similarly attain the most personalized version of ourselves through proper individuation.

THE SUPREME PERSONALITY OF GODHEAD AND THE SUPREME PERSONALITY OF OURSELVES

Being an individual implies allowing the Sweet Absolute to be an individual and exercise his individuality in our life. It means his being an individual in the context of our being individuals. And God is not only an individual, but the most individuated entity we could possibly imagine. To put it indirectly, *God is neither a psychopath nor a terrorist,* as many of us still think, consciously or unconsciously. As it is popularly said, *God is love,* and love is constantly transcending itself toward greater union and greater individuation in a fractal-like, never-ending pattern. So, what's our role as individuals to facilitate such an individuated God to be an individual in our life? As basic as it may sound, we should begin by acknowledging that both God and us are actual individuals, and then we should contemplate the prospect of these two individuals meeting together in the only form that is actually possible, the form of divine love and sacred service to that very love. But again, such a divine prospect will eventually be attained only by first embracing our human personality in our present condition, at each step of the way. If we deny our personality, we may immediately become neurotic due to still lacking a deep spiritual sense of self. In fact, the only way to find objective truth (and super-subjective truth) is to clarify our own subjectivity first: we should primarily work on the receiver, and not only on what is being received. Therefore, the more we allow for this Supreme Personality of Ourselves to arise through proper integration, the more the Supreme Personality of Godhead will become alive in us. The Sweet Absolute will become more a verb than a noun, more a process than a conclusion, more an experience than a dogma, more a personal relationship than a theological idea.[11] *Reality is a person*—and so should we be.

A very interesting point in this connection is found in the notion of *pramana* (epistemological evidence) and how Sri Sanatana Goswami refers to it in his *Brihad-bhagavatamrita*, the very first book of the Gaudiya tradition. Although we normally hear that Gaudiyas ascertain reality mainly through the triad of guru, *sastra*, and *sadhu* (teacher, scripture, and saints), according to Sanatana Goswami one's personal experience is the strongest form of evidence. He says that "of all forms of evidence [*pramana*] for establishing the truth, personal experience is the best."[12] What he means by this is that despite the indisputable role and influence of guru, *sastra*, and *sadhu*, we nonetheless always filter these three through our own experience. In other words, our experience provides the criterion for us to accept them (or not) as authoritative in our lives. Before the *Brihad-bhagavatamrita*, this notion was similarly portrayed in numerous verses in which *Srimad Bhagavatam* describes *pratyaksha* (direct experience) as a form of *pramana* through which God can be perceived and becomes knowable.[13] Another similar example is found in *Bhagavad-gita* 9.2, where it is mentioned that the most confidential knowledge of *bhakti* is understood through *pratyaksha*. Likewise, *Srimad Bhagavatam* 10.48.19 invokes the term *sruta-pratyaksha-gocharam*, which refers to how God can be experienced by hearing scripture and by *pratyaksha*, or direct experience. If there is no personal experience, then there is no possibility of accepting the other three forms of evidence—or anything at all, for that matter. Of course, our experience is based not on *what* we experience (its content) as much as *how* we experience what we experience (at which level of significance are we taking in the experience). For this, the assistance of scripture and tradition proves to be crucial. But even if we choose to emphasize scripture as our main *pramana*, as most Gaudiyas do, we should understand that the scriptures are not just words, but actually someone's direct experience and thus a form of *pratyaksha*. Therefore, we could say that the ultimate *pramana* is direct perception only. But in the case of scriptural revelation it will be a perception of a different type, generally known as *vaidusha-pratyaksha*, or divine perception by a realized, transegoic perceiver. Therefore, when someone like Brahma speaks, he is not just speaking a particular scripture, but what he has realized and internalized. He first has direct experience, and then he speaks. This is the whole idea of *parampara* (disciplic succession). *Parampara* transfers not just the word, but the experience. Thus, sacred scripture is ultimately *pratyaksha pramana*. While for a beginner, evidence is found through revealed sound, *shabda pramana*, for a perfected being ultimate evidence is a matter of perception.[14] In this sense, if we want to conceive of life as a journey (as we should) and *pramana* as our vehicle, we could then envision a tricycle whose back two wheels are scripture (*sastra*) and tradition (guru and *sadhu*) and whose front wheel is our experience, processed and held accountable by the other two wheels. Every wheel must be in place for us to thrive and blossom on the journey.[15]

To do what others do in order to fit in is conformism. To do what others want us to do because they are forcing us to do so is totalitarianism. To do what we *should* do according to our nature, capacities, and prospect is called individuation. To be motivated by the crucial aspects of individuation, one must first understand that respect for our own individuality is not only *not* wrong, but is a prerequisite for individuation. In fact, the Sweet Absolute himself validates and even begs for us to approach him with full individuation. He tells Uddhava, "Whatever is most desired *by one* within this material world, and whatever is most dear *to oneself*—one should offer that very thing to me. *Such an offering qualifies one for eternal life.*"[16]

As members of what we have called Emerging Gaudiya Vaishnavism, we need to understand that the evolution of the present structure of our tradition will largely depend on the extent to which we humbly accept that *our individuality must be kept intact for any significant change to occur*. To allow ourselves to be stifled and stagnant would be tantamount to denying our duty to become fully actualized individuals in the service of the tradition. While the need to be an individual is one thing, the need to respect one's individuality is something different, yet connected—equally necessary and important. One of the ways to accomplish this healthy self-respect is by realizing how each of us is a living tabernacle of the Sweet Absolute. This realization gives us a tremendous respect for ourselves, but in a deeply humbling way. It acknowledges that this sacred tent we embody is a totally free gift from the Supreme Lord.[17] While many of us can be individuals in not unique ways, this healthy and humble respect for our own individuality (and that of others) constitutes a defining factor that pushes us into being individuals in a respectable, unique, and truly individuated way. In fact, our present place in the Gaudiya landscape represents quite a calling in this connection. Our situation is like the healthy struggle of a caterpillar becoming a butterfly within its cocoon. Respect for our individuality implies the sacred space in which our wings can fully stretch wide. We can create connections between the inner and outer worlds, between time and space, *between yes and yes*—a win-win scenario for all involved.

THE ROLE OF HUMAN EMOTIONS IN THE LIFE OF A PRACTITIONER

For Gaudiyas, merely addressing our material needs without cultivating the spirit is clearly unhealthy. We call it material life. However, cultivating spirituality without addressing our material needs could be equally undesirable. Should we also call that material life? Or perhaps something even more self-denying? Among their various expressions, material needs include emotional needs, but the word "material" is not necessarily profane. Unfortunately, this term has historically been equated with negative connotations of the word "mundane," so that "material" converges with "bad," axiomatically accepting two things which are equal to the same thing as being equal to one another. As a result of this sequence from material to mundane to bad, our material emotions are more often than not (even unconsciously) labeled and dismissed as being bad, inferior, and unworthy of even our acknowledgement. Although the sequence may be logical, because of an initial misconception of "material" as being something limited in its potential to the mundane, our conclusion misses the mark of the wholesomeness of reality. Physical and psychic matter are not ontologically bad. It all depends *how we choose* to relate to them. Instead of defining matter as being limited to the mundane and substandard, let's redefine it in a much more realistic way: matter is *something with the potential to become either extremely gross, or extremely spiritualized.* Remember, every single thing is to be defined in consideration of its potential. That means not only what it is, but *all that it can be* as well.

In Gaudiya Vaishnavism we believe in what Christians refer to as *transubstantiation*, or the possibility that a material substance can be infused with the spiritual to the point of morphing into spiritual substance. In this line of thought, for Gaudiyas our present physical body has the potential to become spiritualized to the point of expressing itself in an everlasting version and accompanying us eternally in *lila*. Therefore, if physical matter can be fully pervaded and reshaped by the spirit, why not apply this same criterion to psychic matter? In other words, why not conceive of our human emotionality as capable of being fully transfigured, to the point of attaining divine status? Furthermore, the Gaudiya tradition entertains the notion of *tadiya-seva*, a unique term which mandates that we should render service to the paraphernalia that is to be offered for the pleasure of the Lord. In fact, many Gaudiya authorities even consider this service to be higher than serving God directly. This proposal is immortalized in the famous *damodara-lila*. In that *lila*, Krishna's mother, Yasoda, interrupts Krishna's breastfeeding to attend to the milk boiling on the stove. The milk was destined to be used in the service of her divine son. If serving those items through which God is served is deemed as paramount, then we should deeply consider how to relate with our *sadhaka-deha* (body of a practitioner), which for a devotee is technically considered part of the paraphernalia to be offered in sacred service. Our *sadhaka-deha* is composed of both a physical dimension and a psychic one, emotions included—all in the process of gradual spiritualization. If properly conceived, service to our own body (which is not actually ours, but God's) can be thus seen as one of the highest forms of worship, or *tadiya-seva*. For Gaudiyas, such a proposal does not reduce the glory of *bhakti* but highlights its potency, reach, and glory. It shows how the spiritual energy of the Sweet Absolute can penetrate, spiritualize, and integrate everything to the point that each of these things can accompany us into eternity.

Ours is a religion that is not afraid of emotions, and certainly not a crusade for emotional apathy. Gaudiya Vaishnavism is synonymous with heartfelt realness, a sacred path where emotions are not to be rejected but integrated. We are expected to cultivate as much intimacy as possible with all of those disowned aspects of our human personality that can nourish our *bhakti* project. In fact, for a full transformation of our heart to take place, we have to (properly) allow ourselves to *feel it all*, emotions included. The Gaudiyas' conception of God is thus depicted in ultrapersonalized terms to encourage us in our quest for "feeling it all" from a proper place. *Chandogya Upanishad* 7.14.4 describes the Absolute as *sarvakarma sarvakamah sarvagandhah sarvarasah*—performing all activities and possessing all desires, all fragrance, and all aesthetic relish. In other words, Ultimate Reality is not only qualified, but qualified in endless ways. Not only is he an individual, but he is the supremely individuated entity. Therefore, the Supreme Lord himself grants permission through his own example for us to embrace each of our dimensions.

Although we are not the body in the way a materialistic person will consider himself to be his body, in another sense we do need to get more embodied—more grounded—and not only on the physical level, but also on the emotional one. This is to be done by spiritual practitioners making deeper and deeper contact with what we are feeling and by cultivating significant intimacy with our human emotions. We need to sit *with* our emotions, not sit *on* them. Most people know that their IQ represents a dimension that affects their experiences, and they correlate higher IQs with a higher quality of life. But not as many people are aware of their EQ, or *emotional intelligence*. This is especially true in our modern culture, where, at least in the West, there has been a historical devaluing of emotion relative to cognition, resulting in a diminished capacity to acknowledge, experience, and express our emotions in positive ways. Thus, we need to integrate our male-side rationality with our female-side emotionality, and then act out with our body what we think, feel, and will. Head and heart can and should be deeply integrated—*reason is meant to support emotions, not suffocate them*.

THERE IS NO SUCH A THING AS "BAD EMOTIONS"

As already explained, emotions in themselves are not bad or ontologically mundane. But what about the so-called bad emotions, those feelings which seem to be inherently negative under any circumstance? The answer to this question is still the same: in themselves, no emotion is negative. In fact, there is no such thing as a negative emotion. *There are negative things that we do with our emotions*, but our emotions in themselves are neither negative nor positive; they simply are. All weather of the heart is welcome.

A classic example in this regard could be anger. Anger as an emotion is not bad per se, but we can express it badly. While healthy anger is expressed without aggression, blaming, and shaming, toxic anger is expressed with all of those things in the form of hostility. And this hostility is not an emotion in itself, but rather a negative framing and expression of an emotion, namely anger. Conversely, if an abuse in a relationship makes us angry but we express that anger in the form of establishing healthy boundaries that protect and nourish us, then what we have is a positive expression of that same emotion. Of course, another equally damaging "expression" of toxic anger is not to express it at all, but to repress it. Whatever the cause, we don't need to exclude the angry "I," but be sufficiently mature to include it and allow it to be expressed without letting it overcome us. We need to possess an emotion, rather than *be possessed* by it, as if "possessed by a demon." Whichever scenario we play out, we are doing something with our anger—choosing to express it either negatively or positively. Let's now extend this consideration to other emotions we may still judge as inherently negative. Let's introspect about whether they are actually negative emotions or rather negative expressions of them.

One such commonly misjudged emotion is fear. More often than not, we are quite fearful of our fear. However, we can open ourselves to that emotion. We can be present with it and cultivate intimacy with its message. We can decide not to fall into its grip, or we can try to quickly get rid of it through some spiritual discipline. Then we will gradually lose our fear of fear. While choosing to stay outside of an emotion, we will be trapped by its distant appearance and distorted image. When we get to its inside and cultivate some intimacy with it, we are then no longer a prisoner of its potential negative expression. Therefore, whatever we feel as negative is not to be immediately numbed or rejected. That response is a template for a psycho-emotional flatland. We rather need to harmonize and reconcile what we feel as negative. We don't need to transcend our negativity but to reclaim and embody it—to integrate it as part of our being, as part of our individuation.

That said, harmonization is to be done with gravity, honesty, and realism. We are not meant to enter a superficial zone of exaggerated gentleness and niceness that we invoke only to avoid integrating our own shadow and dealing with our raw emotions. This form of evasiveness would reduce us to *harmony junkies*, people who only look for a shallow sense of balance and who employ such masks to avoid any real inner work. In contrast, when the process of individuation is healthy, what has been transcended is not excluded from our being but rather *repositioned* and related to in ways that serve our well-being and spiritual prospect. When transcendence is unhealthy, what we "transcend" has actually been excluded from our being, resulting in escapism and disconnection. Conversely, healthy transcendence is integration of complexity. It turns whatever has been transcended into another aspect of our true self. It doesn't disown that thing, but recognizes it as part of a reclaimed "I." By contrast, unhealthy transcendence turns whatever has been transcended into a disowned object, an "it."[18] While the former is a pivotal facet of Radical Personalism, the latter is nothing but the archenemy of Radical Personalism—impersonalism. And one of its symptoms is not only emotional denial, but emotional repression.

HUMAN EMOTIONS ARE NOT TO BE REPRESSED BUT EXPRESSED

Emotional expression in the context of individuation is a gradual and sometimes even tedious process. It will take different shapes according to each person and the stage of evolution one may be in. However, as already mentioned, it begins with acknowledging that emotions are not bad in themselves and that there is not even such a thing as a bad emotion. Even with all this preliminary understanding, an important question may remain: What are we to do with our emotions? As usual, we can begin by describing what *not* to do with them: do not repress your emotions, but *express* them.

In *Bhagavad-gita* 3.33, Sri Krishna clearly advocates sense control, which is healthy emotional expression, and he condemns repression with the rhetorical question "*What can repression accomplish?"* The implied reply to the question is "nothing." In this connection we should also note the difference between repression and suppression. Suppression implies consciously pushing away a feeling, and not allowing emotion to be experienced. Repression refers to an unconscious inhibition of emotional expression, where feelings are pushed down into the subconscious regions of our psyche without us knowing what is actually taking place. As the role of our immune system is to protect our physical body from invasion by setting proper defense boundaries, when we repress our emotions, our emotional immune system kicks in and protects our subtle body from "invasion" or more accurately "evasion" in the form of depression. The result of this? It turns against us, since we turned against it to begin with. It is easy to see why repression and depression are tied together by more than mere semantics.

We can indulge in repression when we are especially immature in our conception of life and reality. For example, a novice spiritual aspirant may imitate lofty stages of transcendence without even knowing he is doing so. However, this initial confusion may become even worse if he imitates a false conception of transcendence because he misunderstands "being transcendental" as being the least emotional as possible. This, again, is impersonalism, a doctrine that proclaims that God has no senses. By extension, this proclamation includes emotions. If we subscribe to this narrative and attempt to become emotionless, we will then be promoting Radical Nondualism instead of the Radical Personalism we are supposed to embody as Gaudiyas. Moreover, this distorted promotion of impersonalism will be embedded in our actions and detected by outsiders. Also, and especially, this impersonalism will be expressed in how we relate (or fail to relate) with each other as practitioners. It will result in insufficient fellowship, lack of fraternity, and many other varieties of impersonalism that may "inspire" some members to even leave their tradition altogether. However, this is not what Gaudiya Vaishnavism is about at all, as Srila Prabhupada clearly points to:

> *Depending on our level of spiritual advancement or consciousness, we can control emotions, but we should not deny them. Anger will continue even in the liberated stage. ... Dhruva Maharaja's becoming angry, overwhelmed with*

> *grief, and envious of the enemies was not incompatible with his position as a great devotee. It is a misunderstanding that a devotee should not be angry, envious or overwhelmed by lamentation.*[19]

A similar example is found in *Srimad Bhagavatam* 5.13.24, where the topmost saint Jada Bharata is described as experiencing some "waves of dissatisfaction in his mind" due to the insulting words of King Rahugana. Despite his disturbance, we are told that he "neglected" those emotions and his heart became calm and quiet again. In other words, Bharata acknowledged his emotions but was not overcome by them and, only in that sense, he neglected them. In this and the above example of the famous saintly child Dhruva we can see that even exalted souls acknowledge and experience their emotions. While the anger of a liberated being may be different than that of a conditioned soul, still both are anger—an emotion—and both are to be properly expressed and integrated.

At this point we may think of verses like *Bhagavad-gita* 4.10, in which Sri Krishna describes those who attain him as being, among other things, "devoid of anger." While this is in fact the case, we should analyze these statements in the context of the quotes shared above, since scripture is never meant to be understood from an isolated perspective. As a result of this exercise, we will conclude that anger will be present in conditioned souls, but also in general practitioners (like us), in advanced practitioners (like Dhruva), and even in perfected practitioners (like Jada Bharata). In fact, in the eternal *lila* of Vraja, Sri Radhika will show anger to Krishna daily as a loving expression of her ecstatic affection for him. Thus, it is no wonder that Sri Rupa Goswami considers anger one of the seven secondary *rasas*, or devotional mellows, that will play out in eternity as something that nourishes the loving interaction between God and his devotees. So, putting all these considerations on the scale, we should then go back to *Gita* 4.10 and understand "devoid of anger" as not being necessarily free from *every* form of it, but of the toxic expressions of it we already described.

Going back to our previous topic, another possible reason for the emotional atrophy we sometimes experience in our current Gaudiya community could be related to clear sociohistorical circumstances, including how Gaudiya Vaishnavism was transplanted to Western soil in the 1960s. By this we don't merely refer to the when's of it on a calendar, but more precisely to the how's of its development. It was an extreme sociological phenomenon, probably never seen in history. Thousands joined a newly formed and underdeveloped society, totally shunning their entire culture of origin almost overnight. The result of this was an inadvertent form of cultural deprivation, which is but another way for impersonalism to take root. In fact, from this cultural deprivation we can then have cultural appropriation and eventually cultural imposition. Thus, it's important to study our own history as a movement to better grasp possible influences that may be defining whatever needs to be addressed in the present moment and whatever may be getting in the way of it.[20]

Emotional expression is pivotal to the process of individuation. Our initial vulnerability needs to be there to allow any real feelings to be expressed. Similarly, emotional expression needs to be performed in a healthy context and perimeter—with protected boundaries. However, if we develop a blunt apathy toward our own human emotionality, we may be depriving ourselves of the very goal of our Gaudiya tradition, which is all about emotion. We seek a world of ecstasy in which we serve perpetually. As has been said, emotions are not themselves bad, but it's what we do with them that determines our emotional health. Therefore, if properly engaged, emotions can show their ultimate face in the realm of divine love, but for that to happen, we have to begin wherever we are at present and honestly engage in a proper integration of our human complexity. This is unambiguously expressed by Swami Sadananda (the most well-known European disciple of Bhaktisiddhanta Saraswati) in one of his letters to Vamandas:

> *A complete acceptance of oneself, be it as a righteous, orderly citizen, a criminal, or a saint—with all consequences—is the sole prerequisite for a man to be able to lead a life as himself and then really be able to dedicate his life to God. ... One can only wish to be, what one really is—and to have the courage to do so—that's very rare. It all starts with being who and what one is, only then one*

> *can be and become joyful. To force oneself into wearing a spiritual uniform ... cannot be anything but an attitude Krishna strongly rejects in* Bhagavatam XI. ... *If one believes one has to be something special and demands too much of oneself, it will lead to self-inflicted stress, violence against oneself and despair, because one has not attained one's "goal" and has gotten into a pointless fight of the one "self" against the other "self." ... One can help one's fellow being to be himself, not in a metaphysical, transcendent way, but simply in a human way, with all virtues and vices. No one should try to jump over his own shadow or make others do this. One must always leave room for the other to be (able to be) who he is. Freedom always means freedom for the other, otherwise it is no freedom. Why? God wants us to be just as free as he is; he does not want any slaves.*[21]

As mentioned earlier in this chapter, the perfect integration of humanity and divinity is found by Gaudiyas in the concept of *nara-lila*, the humanlike, divine, and nondual play of the Sweet Absolute. There he is both fully human and fully divine, and there we can be so as well. In fact, any religion that dares to call itself such should teach and permit being both fully human and fully divine. Of the two, it may be harder to be fully human. God is humanlike because he is not only fully human but also fully divine, and the "like" pertains to that aspect of him. On the other hand, we are also humanlike but for a very different reason: in most cases we are *like* humans, but not yet even fully human. We are in the process of becoming fully human and fully divine. That's the *humanlikeness* we desire to attain. As mentioned, we are not human beings trying to become spiritual but spiritual beings trying to become fully human, with the prospect of *nara-lila* in mind. However, the holiness of this *lila* won't come to us if we do not develop the corresponding wholeness pertaining to our humanity. We need to wake up (holiness) and also to grow up (wholeness). Holiness without wholeness results in *holeness*—a deep hole in our life and character. We need a comprehensive integration of both holiness and wholeness. We need *wholyness*. Or, as this chapter has shown, individuation.

10 Nondual Thinking: Everything is One, but Never Impersonal

In the Vedas it is said that only the Lord alone exists, and all others' existences depend on him. He is the generating reservoir for everyone's existential capacity. He is the Supreme Truth of all other categorical truths.

– Srila Prabhupada

IN THE FIRST CHAPTER OF THIS THIRD PART, we talked about the importance of vulnerability as a preliminary, crucial virtue in our progress toward Radical Personalism. It is a virtue that allows whatever openness we require in order to acknowledge our current predicaments as both practitioners and community. Then, in the second chapter, we delved into the principle of individuation, or addressing those predicaments while integrating our uniqueness as humans in the context of our spiritual project. In the present chapter, we will attempt to balance the element of diversity, brought about by the notion of individuation, by talking about unity and nonduality or, more specifically, *nondual thinking*. Nondual thinking is the sacred awareness of what makes every single thing universally connected as part of one unit and common source. In other words, we all share and are part of an underlying nondual foundation. As we have already talked about how variegated and specific each of us is, let's now tip the scale by addressing our collective nondual DNA. We can all be one in a way that is not impersonal. In fact, this oneness is essential and undeniable.

NONDUAL THINKING: THE BASIS FOR BOTH REALITY AND OUR EXPERIENCE AS INDIVIDUALS

While nonduality is a well-known trademark of Radical Nondualism and its impersonal narrative, Radical Personalism has its own version of it. This will prove pivotal in allowing for an involvement with individualized experience and interaction. In other words, it is the nondual nature of reality that makes personal relationships possible at all. Without this unifying principle of being, we would remain not as uniquely individuated persons but as isolated, separated, and divided individualists—an island unto oneself. But no man is an island.

The unifying principle of nondual reality affords us the opportunity to have a direct relationship not only among us, but especially with the Sweet Absolute. It allows us to experience the presence of divinity not just in some other place or time, but right here and right now: in every atom and in the heart of the person we are sitting next to. How can this be possible? Because reality is nondual and we are part of it. This unifying principle, the nonduality of reality, is the foundation and support for a penetrating reach into specificity, or individuality. In the Gaudiya lore, this is portrayed in the story of the materialistic demon Hiranyakashipu, who wanted a world where nothing in it was based on a relationship with God; he wanted everything to be in relation to him. He thought he could accomplish that by going beyond all duality. But when he arrived there—where there was no longer any day or night, inside or outside, earth or sky, human or beast—he did not find himself as an isolated entity against which everything else was defined, but rather he found himself in the very lap of the Absolute, consumed in the immediacy of relationship.

There cannot be personality without nonduality. Why? Because that is the nature of the Divine. He is the *nondual* Supreme Person. He is the inside, the outside, and everywhere in between. He is all of the past, all of the future, *and all of the present.* In fact, we cannot be separated from him for even one moment. Appreciating at least theoretically this simple but most mysterious fact can change our entire orientation to life. It can change how we conceive of ourselves, the world around us, divinity, and the relationships between each of them. Nonduality is the "ship" in relation-ship that makes it possible for us to navigate and relate to one another. And that means relating not only intimately but unlimitedly, because the nondual is nothing but unlimited presence.

The Gaudiya's main sacred canon, *Srimad Bhagavatam*, is said to have been composed by Vyasa in the language of *samadhi*, or the trance of nondual awareness. Correspondingly, a work revealed through *samadhi* will be fully understood only in *samadhi*. In a similar way, reality may be nondual and we may be a part of it, but for us to internalize these astonishing facts we need to *become aware* of nondual reality by adopting nondual *thinking*. While reality is always ultimately nondual, it will be understood as such only from a nondual perspective. Therefore, we need to train our minds in nondual thinking. That training is in itself *a way of thinking* because it involves a nondual lifestyle, and not a mere theological stance.

Whereas Gaudiya Vaishnavism officially proposes a nondual doctrine, we may still not have the nondual mind required to understand it. We need a vision of reality that is integrative and not fragmented. It is a vision where diversity is permitted and even necessary, but it rests on a nondual and totally unified foundation. Nondual thinking teaches that the inseparability of all that exists is not a concept or an experience or even something to attain, but our very nature and the nature of reality itself. These are not just nice words to repeat, but a reality to become aware of—a way of thinking we must be trained in. This crucial rewiring is what Gaudiya *sadhana* (spiritual discipline) is basically about. It involves putting our fragmented realities back together (relinking, *re-ligion*, *yoga*), fully aligned with the nondual substratum of reality.

THE NUANCED NONDUALITY OF GAUDIYA VAISHNAVISM

While some Gaudiyas may be accustomed to relate nonduality exclusively with Radical Nondualism, it is important to bear in mind that Gaudiya Vaishnavism is in fact a nondual school of thought. As a matter of fact, every tradition of Hindu mystical theology (and every other non-Hindu mystical tradition as well) must be nondual for it to convey an actual mystical proposal, since nonduality and mysticism are basically synonymous. In other words, if we do not embrace some form of nondualism then dualism will be the only remaining option. And as long as dualism is present, it will eliminate the mystical side of any equation. However, Vedantic texts insist that all reality is in the end indivisible. And Gaudiya Vedanta is no exception to this rule.

Arguably, the most famous Gaudiya dictum that defines reality as nondual is found in *Srimad Bhagavatam* 1.2.11. It is a crucial verse upon which Sri Jiva Goswami, the main theologian of the tradition, based his monumental treatise, *Sat-sandarbha*. While describing the Supreme Lord and his variegated expressions and levels of conception, this verse defines God as reality (*tattva*), which is nondual (*advaya*) consciousness (*jnana*): *advaya-jnana-tattva*. In other words, the most fundamental aspects of Ultimate Reality are two: it is conscious and nondual. Interestingly, the term *advaya* (nondual) here implies that *dvaya*, or duality, is also part of reality. But it's not a separate existence. Self-existent reality is only one, not two, and is therefore, nondual. That Ultimate Reality is nondual, however, does not mean that no individual being exists apart from one single homogeneous substance, as the impersonalists think. They refer to it as Brahman. The word "nondual" in this verse basically indicates two things: (1) Absolute Reality is self-existent and self-contained (it is grounded in itself and depends on no external support); (2) nothing else can exist independent of the support of this nondual Ultimate Reality. Gaudiya wisdom refers to this by saying that the "Absolute Reality is one without a second." Echoing this teaching is *Srimad Bhagavatam* 5.12.11 where it continues to explain that the ultimate truth "is nondual knowledge." And the ultimate reality that is one without a second, expresses itself in different degrees of realization such as Brahman, Paramatma, and Bhagavan. Although there are multiple expressions of that same Absolute, it never stops being the one nondual reality. Each expression of Absolute Reality, has a corresponding perceiver of that expression depending on their angle of vision. This means that if a worshiper has a nonpersonal concept of reality, then reality will manifest to that person as impersonal Brahman. However, if a worshiper has a personal conception, then that same absolute reality will manifest in one of its various personal forms, such as Bhagavan. Every face of Ultimate Reality is a different facet of the same jewellike Absolute. According to Gaudiyas, the only difference between Bhagavan and Brahman is that of perception: Bhagavan is the qualified expression of Ultimate Reality, while Brahman is its unqualified expression. But reality is only one nondual existence.

In fact, the opening verse of *Srimad Bhagavatam* entices the reader to engage in the sacred exercise of nondual thinking. It invites her to think or meditate (*dhimahi*) on the nondual Supreme Truth (*satyam param*). This foundational Gaudiya contemplation, *satyam param dhimahi*, is essentially synonymous with nondual thinking. Additionally, not only is reality referred to as *advaya/advitiyam*, or nondual, from the very inception of the *Srimad Bhagavatam*, but we find numerous examples throughout the work.[1] For example, one of its last verses (12.13.12) invokes the term *vastu advitiyam*, which is synonymous with the above *advaya-jnana*. This verse not only speaks about nonduality, but declares that *the whole subject* of the *Srimad Bhagavatam* is nondual reality. Thus, what we find is that from beginning to end this most significant Gaudiya masterpiece revolves around the principle of nondual thinking. Logically, we can conclude that since the Gaudiya tradition revolves around this central work, and this central work revolves around nonduality, then Gaudiya Vaishnavism similarly revolves around nondual thinking.

However, the nondualism of Gaudiya Vaishnavas is a nuanced one. It conveys the notion that the only thing that exists is the Sweet Absolute and his potencies, all of which are nondifferent (*abheda*) from him, but are also simultaneously different (*bheda*). In other words, between God and his energies there is neither absolute *bheda* or *abheda*. In fact, all branches of Vaishnavism (including the Dvaita school, a tradition which proposes mystical dualism) accept this simultaneous presence of difference and nondifference. Just as fire itself and the heat of fire are one but at the same time not absolutely one, the "fire of God" and the "heat of his potencies" are simultaneously one and different. This perspective is neither Radical

Nondualism nor Radical Dualism. It stands between the two and harmonizes them. We can call it Nonradical Nondualism, Nuanced Nondualism, Unity in Diversity, or as traditionally stated by Gaudiyas, *achintya-bheda-abheda-tattva*, or inconceivable and simultaneous bipolarity. This idea is not exclusively applicable to the realm of metaphysics, but it can apply to all dimensions of human experience. If a philosophical system doesn't do that, it can only be a partial treatment of reality.[2]

Things are not totally one, but they are not two either. If everything were one in every sense, there would literally be no-body, no-thing to do, and no interactions of any kind—sheer boredom. If there were only difference and exclusivity, we would then have division and conflict with no sense of unity. However, if we establish nonduality as the foundation from which difference arises, then diversity becomes complementary to oneness, enhancing the beauty and harmony of reality. The musical principle of harmony includes and integrates different notes to create one whole and single sound. Similarly, for Gaudiyas reality in itself *is* music and harmony. It is the unifying diversity of individuals on the ground of their shared nondual bedrock.

GAUDIYA EXAMPLES OF PANENTHEISM

A Western term that closely resembles the Gaudiya doctrine of *achintya-bheda-abheda-tattva* is *panentheism*. It basically refers to the idea of everything-in-God (*pan-en-theos*) or, in other words, how God exists in everything and everything similarly rests in him.[3] A well-known example of this is found in *Bhagavad-gita* 6.30, where Sri Krishna says, "For one who sees me in everything and sees everything in me, I'm never lost to him and he is never lost to me." Similarly, *Srimad Bhagavatam* 11.2.45 describes the topmost devotee in these same terms, as someone who sees everything in relation to God and understands everything to be eternally situated in him. These are obvious examples of nondual thinking, where God is everything and everything is God, or, even more precisely, where God is in everything and everything is in God. To deeply contemplate these points constitutes a crucial aspect of Gaudiya daily meditation. And while the above verses depict the realization of the highest devotee, we should at least theoretically appreciate that state and strive to gradually attain its corresponding vision. In fact, *sadhana-bhakti,* or the stage of practice, is constituted of a theoretical appreciation of the higher stages of divine love. It involves a realistic longing for those peaks and a progressive arrival in our spiritual journey. Spiritual practice is not about remaining in a primitive stage for eons and then suddenly arriving at our final goal. Rather, it is about making gradual and steady movement toward the ultimate object of our aspirations.

Another classic example of panentheism/nondual thinking is the notion that God's presence is basically everywhere, omnipresence being one of the defining features of Ultimate Reality. Gaudiya Vaishnavas refer to this face of the divine as Paramatma, a form of God residing in every heart and even in every single atom. As poetic as it may sound for some, each atom is *literally* an embassy of God—every pore of creation oozing with the sacred presence of the Sweet Absolute. To help us gain a better grasp of this intricate topic, the example of the sun has been given throughout the Gaudiya tradition, as in the prayers of Bhisma:

> *Being free from the delusion of duality, I have come to understand that Krishna, who is situated before me, is one. Though he is unborn, he appears in the hearts of all embodied beings, who have been manifested from within him, just as the sun is one, though appearing differently to everyone.*[4]

In this verse the example of the sun is given specifically to illustrate the oneness of all of God's forms. However, the metaphor should not be misunderstood to indicate that God is situated in only one place, as is the sun. A similar idea comes from Jiva Goswami's *Bhagavat Sandarbha* (Anuccheda 31). There he describes that the body of Bhagavan is all-pervasive. He concludes that since Bhagavan's divine body is nondifferent from him and he is omnipresent, then his body is as well. It is important to note that this section does not speak about Paramatma, whose pervasiveness is readily acknowledged, but about Bhagavan, who is often mistakenly seen as someone separate and distant. But, again, they are two expressions of the same Absolute. Thus, for Gaudiyas, Bhagavan Sri Krishna—and not only his partial expansion, Paramatma—is everywhere. Being nondual awareness, he exists everywhere at all times. From a different but complementary perspective, *Srimad Bhagavatam* 10.14.17 describes how the entire universe resides within the belly of God and therefore "All that appears here is in you." Or as stated in verse 10.42.22, "The creation is situated in God." Similarly, this panentheistic view is also closely tied to the notion of all-pervasiveness. In different sections in his *Sandarbhas*, Jiva Gosvami uses the Sanskrit word *vibhutva* for all-pervasiveness. This word literally means "greatness" or "prowess," but in philosophy it conveys the meaning of *sarva-gatatva*, or "going everywhere." Through use of this specific term, he wants to show that the Lord exists everywhere in his personal form, and not simply through his energy.[5] Likewise, in his *Laghu-bhagavatamrita* 1.21, Rupa Goswami defines this aspect of panentheism thus: "The appearance of a single form in many places at the same time, but which is, in all respects, the same essential form of the Lord, is called *prakash*." Needless to say, without a foundation of nondual thinking, many of the teachings coming from our Gaudiya revelation will remain incomprehensible for us.

POTENTIAL DANGERS OF BELONGING TO AN EXTREMELY SPECIFIED TRADITION

As described in previous sections, Gaudiya Vaishnavism possesses a very sophisticated and detailed way of expressing the nuanced nature of nondual reality. This surely has its pros, but it can also involve some cons if unproperly dealt with—if dealt with a lack of nondual thinking. Our Gaudiya theology entertains unlimited expressions of the Absolute, and while there are surely differences between them, it will be equally important to keep their ontological unity in mind. If improperly handled, the blessing of theological diversity can create a fragmented perception of God, or dualism.

A classic example could be the one shared above: we Gaudiyas may think that Paramatma is in every heart and atom but that Krishna is "somewhere else," absorbed in his pastoral *lila*—nondual play—of Vraja. By saying so we have created a dualistic division in our minds about the Supreme Lord, in spite of the fact that the

Sweet Absolute remains nondual in nature and is all-present, everywhere and always. Once we over-localize God's action or presence in one place—or one mission, ritual, Deity, or any isolated event—we can easily conclude that he is *not* in any other place. Or even worse, *that he is not available everywhere and at all times*. While Gaudiyas officially accept that Ultimate Reality is both immanent and transcendent, sometimes too much emphasis on the transcendental side makes us lose sight of the reality of God's presence in every heart and atom, and we may end up conceiving him as being somewhere "upstairs" in heaven, or the spiritual realm. An initial nondual foundation will prove crucial before entering into the details of Gaudiya post-liberated life in *lila*. Likewise, to have the immanent side of God in place first will be equally beneficial for us before we address and understand his transcendent expression. In fact, the more these two aspects are properly conceived of, the more they will become integrated, to the point that God's transcendence can be fully perceived here on Earth. God is not dualistically "out there." At the end of the day, "here" and "there" are not mere geographical locations, but *levels of awareness*.

Gaudiya Vaishnavism promotes not polytheism, but what we may call *polymorphic monotheism* (literally, "one God with different forms"). This is established in *Srimad Bhagavatam* 10.40.7, where Akrura refers to the Sweet Absolute as *bahu-murty-eka-murtikam*, or "the one Supreme Lord, who manifests in multiple forms." Ultimate Reality is always one, but expresses itself in unlimited faces, such as the three Vishnus; the three main expressions of Krishna in the abodes of Vraja, Mathura, and Dvaraka; the Pancha-tattva, or quintuple expression of Divinity; and the Dasavatara, the well-known descent of God in ten forms. With such a diversified pantheon, if nondual thinking is not emphasized enough, we Gaudiyas may not be able to fully navigate the abundant variegation of our tradition. We may get lost in a sea of diversity—or even polytheism. If we add the strong historical opposition that Gaudiya Vaishnavism has expressed toward Radical Nondualism, we may end up in very unusual landscapes. On one side we may wrongly think that all forms of nondualism "have to be attacked," and on the other side we may immaturely take part in an extremely diversified tradition. Without the required basis of nondualism, we Gaudiyas can therefore become dualistic, or even polytheistic. In other words, trying to breathe the full air of Gaudiya Vaishnavism through only the lung of diversity will leave us with a very impoverished or even distorted vision of who we are as a nondual tradition.

There is diversity in life, but too much diversification means too much emphasis on the *bheda* side. And that can make us dualistic. Similarly, too much opposition to any form of nonduality means too much rejection of the *abheda* side. That can foster a dualistic pattern that makes us reject all expressions of nondualism, including the one we are supposed to represent. If we leave reality's nondual foundation *out of our own conceptual foundation*, we may become polytheistic, seeing many separate gods instead of one undivided nondual reality. To put it bluntly, forms of God like Vishnu, Krishna, Narasimha, and Gaurahari *are not different people*. This is surely a very basic point, but have we thought about this in any real depth? How much are we contemplating these truths as individuals and as a community? Do we internally relate to these ideas and faces of the Absolute in nondual terms or in a dualistic way? How do all of these concepts work in our minds and play themselves out in our lives? While any of us can say, "They are all one," we may still lack the inner vision and realization to support our claims. In fact, we may be monotheistic Gaudiyas at a lip level, but we may remain polytheistic in terms of deeper wisdom and understanding.

In other ways as well, we may further limit our potential to understand and experience the presence of the Absolute. For example, we may present through a heavily dualistic framework the wondrously extreme level of theological specificity offered in Gaudiya Vaishnavism. We will then basically be dragging the whole spiritual realm down to worldly/dualistic terms. Conversely, on a foundation of nonduality the diversified expression of spiritual life (*lila*, or nondual play) can actually happen. Without a proper foundation, there is no *lila* and no sustainable spiritual project. Thus, it is crucial to become aware of how nondualism plays itself out in Radical Personalism/Gaudiya Vaishnavism, and to properly embody such a principle through each of our actions.

It is said that *what mystics often intuit and live, scientists later prove to be true*. Interestingly enough, contemporary science is recognizing that there is no solitary *anything* in the universe. Maybe they are reminding Gaudiya Vaishnavas of their own mystical heritage.

FURTHER CONSEQUENCES OF DUALISTIC THINKING

As much as we have praised nondual thinking, this should not be at the cost of stigmatizing duality in all of its forms. As we mentioned, the term *advaya* (nondual) includes in itself the notion of *dvaya* (dual). In fact, the basic skills of our beginning chapters in life are mostly based on binary templates and dual thinking, through which we divide the world in different dual categories—good/bad, happy/sad, us/them—to obtain a basic container or point of reference for our initial relationship with existence. Thus, binary or dual thinking is not bad in itself, but is actually central to most situations in life. However, this tendency to divide up the realities of the world will prove deeply insufficient when attempting to address life's bigger questions and quandaries, such as infinity, grace, love, death, God, and the soul. Dualistic thinking cannot operate in relation to these realities.

In other words, *the very foundation of reality* is to be approached through a nondual perspective because that very foundation is itself nondual. Paradoxically, to bridge the apparent gap from dual thinking to nondual thinking requires critical thinking, a specific kind of dual thinking. Ironically, it is the clashing of oppositional elements found in dual thought that sharpens our critical thinking into the tool that can free us of its own grip. If we insist on reading life as if it is *ontologically* dual, that amounts to a dualistic worldview, or a philosophical dualism. This philosophical dualism does not refer to those times when dual thought, grounded in a nondual bedrock, is needed to navigate our relationship with existence. Rather, philosophical dualism speaks of a denial of the existence of a nondual foundation, and, therefore, the need to examine its own sense of being in relation to the nondual doesn't even come up, what to speak of a need to integrate itself within Nondual Reality. This dualistic approach to reality is one thing when embraced by a radical dualist, but if in the name of Gaudiya Vaishnavism one verbally promotes nondual thought—since that *is* the Gaudiya philosophy—while acting as if nonduality does not even exist, then that is an unfortunate missing of the mark and a misuse of an opportunity to enact a cornerstone of Radical Personalism.

As the *Srimad Bhagavatam* extols the glories of nondual thinking and fully revolves around it, it similarly shows how dualistic thinking (and its lacking when required) is the underlying source of our primary problems. In verse 11.2.37, the *Bhagavatam* speaks about how absorption in dualistic thinking (*dvitiya-abhinivesh*) is the cause of all fear and is even what makes us turn away from God and forget our constitutional position in relation to him. In other words, the *Srimad Bhagavatam* teaches that difficulty arises when we see something as being other than or separate from the Sweet Absolute, creating what one could call a separate interest. As Srila Sridhara Deva Goswami accurately pointed out, "The first deviation from *advaya-jnana* [nonduality] is the conception of separate interest."[6] Likewise, the first verse of the *Bhagavad-gita* portrays Dhritarastra's dualistic psychology, implying how this pattern was the cause of the Kurukshetra war—dualism behind the cause of every avoidable conflict. Of course, this pattern is not limited to Gaudiya theology but is a universal one. In Genesis 2:17, we find the declaration that "by eating of the tree of knowledge of good and evil [dualistic thinking] you will die."

A proper understanding of Gaudiya nondualism will nourish our prospect tremendously. This applies in theological terms and in how we relate with reality itself, which is nondual. Failing to adopt such a perspective can force every aspect of our existence through the filter of a dualistic lens that will be unfavorable and diametrically opposed to our school's foundational viewpoint. We can officially be Radical Personalists but convey impersonalism through our own lifestyle, and we can similarly embrace a nondual doctrine but misrepresent it through a dualistic way of life and its natural overflowing and overwhelming byproducts. These include tribal thinking, narrowmindedness, fanaticism, rationalism, secularism, and so on. In other words, the potential price for rejecting all forms of nondualism is that we end up becoming a dualistic tradition ourselves. And probably even worse, we may end up (mis)representing a nondual tradition in extremely dualistic ways. We may do this philosophically and through a whole dualistic lifestyle and set of attitudes. Richard Rohr describes with detailed precision how this dualistic mindset expresses itself:

> *Dualistic or divided people live in a split and fragmented world. They cannot accept or forgive certain parts of themselves. They cannot accept that God objectively dwells within them. ... This lack of forgiveness takes the forms of a tortured mind, a closed heart, or an inability to live calmly and proudly inside your own body. The fragmented mind sees parts, not wholes, in itself and others, and invariably it creates antagonism, reaction, fear, and resistance. ... Here is the normal sequencing of the dualistic mind: it compares, it competes, it conflicts, it conspires, it condemns, it cancels out any contrary evidence, and it then crucifies with impunity. You can call it the seven C's of delusion, and the source of most violence.*[7]

As we can see, the dualism we may have in our conception of reality will be expressed in how we may be conceiving God in fragmented terms and especially in how we relate with each other and everything else. If to begin with we are dual to the core in how we see God, then how we will relate with one of God's energies, by which we mean each other? As usual, most of this dualism will be totally unconscious. For example, we may be speaking about diversity in terms of our theological ideal, but we may not have much diversity of opinion when it comes to appreciating different Vaishnava groups or other traditions. Nonduality is a crucial ingredient in relating to each other, and should not be used as an excuse to avoid proper individuation. Each needs to be present to keep the other in check and maintain a healthy balance. In fact, it is quite easy to intellectually appropriate nondual teachings and use them to justify or rationalize the impersonal ways by which some of us may still conduct ourselves. *But easy is never the way out.*

By our remaining dualistic, another unfortunate outcome is that we end up creating an unnecessary divide between this world and the next. This will deeply affect our relationship with the whole of creation, with its creatures, our own body, and the suffering of the world at large. All of them are energies of our beloved Lord and thus potentially venerable. With a proper nondual framework, this world doesn't need to be seen as "a horrible illusory place to escape from as soon as possible." It can be seen as a potency of God that if addressed properly can act as a portal of transcendence. This is not a portal to step through as if going from one place to another. Rather, it can be *a medium to enter into* through transformative sacred practice that shifts our angle of vision. It can do this to such a degree that we can experience the "transcendent" that is already here, right now. This world is not an illusion; the illusion is in *how* we see the world. In fact, for Gaudiyas, God repeatedly descends to this world as multiple *avataras* to validate the existence and importance of every aspect of creation. If proper nonduality is thus in place, then there is no need to dissociate from phenomena, no need to withdraw from life, no need for any form of bypassing, since all is deeply integrated. However, this is not the premise that informs much of our behavior in our contemporary Gaudiya community. Rather, we Gaudiyas often (mis)represent our own teachings in terms of dualistic splits. Thus, a healthy nondual approach to our philosophy would mend this current deeply problematic dualistic split. Upon close scrutiny, it can be justifiably attributed with many of the major problems in the present state of the Gaudiya community.

Dualistic thinking means fragmented consciousness. Maybe this is a good way to understand why any community may be fragmented at any point of its unfolding. In our particular situation as Gaudiyas, the current fragmentation in our community may be at least partly caused by how fragmented many of us still are in our own dualistic approach to God himself and, by extension, to everything else, which is his energies. We can have a hyper-personalized tradition and theological conception, but a total depersonalized—or even impersonal—way of conceiving and relating to those very ideas and to one another. All of this is a reflection of how we are relating to the Divine. This delicate condition we are in should lead us to realize the need to emphasize the unity and foundation that nondual thinking provides. This is not a sentimental sense of being united, but a grounded and ontological one in which the principle of individuality is properly honored. Remember, *everything is one but never impersonal.*

LEARNING AND COMPLEMENTING FROM OTHER NONDUAL TRADITIONS

If reality is nondual by nature, then other mystical traditions should share the same philosophical foundation as Gaudiyas. And that is the case. Therefore we Gaudiyas should be able to discover that same underlying bedrock found in other nondual schools, and even learn from them in order to nourish our own practices. The willingness to do so is another vital aspect of both nondual thinking and Radical Personalism, to which we will turn next for the balance of this chapter.

How we see anything is how we see everything. In other words, there's a correlation between how we do anything and how we do *everything else.* Understanding this and remembering it makes us take the moment in front of us much more seriously and respectfully.[8] As much as life is full of nuance and embedded in what we may call "the grace of grays," there is also a place for both black and white, and this is one of those places. Either we see the divine image in all created things and all mystical traditions, *or we don't see it at all.*[9] As it is said, *God's address is everywhere.* It is not limited to the Gaudiya address book. To put it bluntly, our niche doesn't make us superior. The Sweet Absolute honors each unique journey and mystical tradition, since he is not threatened by differences—it is we who feel so. Therefore, as shown in this chapter, nondual thinking is to be properly conceived and expressed not only in terms of our own Gaudiya practice, but also in how we relate with everything else, including other mystical traditions.

Like any other monotheistic tradition, Gaudiya Vaishnavism should be the first to recognize that truth is one. There is one God, one nondual reality. If we Gaudiyas really believe in our own tenets, then we would not have difficulty recognizing that our tent is pitched in the same camp as the rest of the monotheistic traditions. This doesn't mean, however, that every tradition is the same in every sense of the term. If we were to accept such extreme sameness, each tradition would lose their own specific flavor and identity: practitioners would be left with an impoverished choice of expression and society would be deprived of rich diversity born from uniqueness. Distinct tastes, identities, and expressions are all core values of Radical Personalism. As different as each mystical school may be, they nonetheless share enough common ground from the perspective of nonduality, each of them representing one of unlimited approaches to the same Ultimate Reality. In fact, before we enter into the specific details of any spiritual tradition—including ours—we should first learn to appreciate the universal foundation of nonduality shared by all of them. With that footing and substratum in place, we can then analyze the specifics of each mystical school. Without this grounded basis, we will be tempted to invoke a forced and sentimental sense of unity, which may appeal to our longing for human togetherness but which, on close inspection, will prove to be one of the trickiest positions of all if not handled with maturity and sincerity: we must be able to ascertain what's essential and what's negotiable in terms of religious differences.

Immature practitioners have always existed and will always exist. In an ordinary sense, the goal of human life could be seen in terms of becoming humble but appreciated elders, but it is equally important to note that to attain such a status we must first go through childhood, adolescence, and so on. Similarly, the mature fruit of spiritual elderhood first involves the experience and symptoms of immaturity. These are normal and acceptable, unless it's already our time to have made some further journey. In the immature stages of spiritual practice, we may, among other things, fanatically think that ours is the only possible conception of God or, at least, the best. This is nicely portrayed in the ancient Sufi poem "The Blind Men and the Elephant," where six blind men approach an elephant from different sides, each touching a different part of his body. One person touches the tail, another the tusk, someone else the trunk, another the ear, and so on. Each person concludes that to experience an elephant is tantamount to touching a rope, a wall, a snake, and so on, and they defend their perspective and fight with one another about it. While each of them was partially right in their assessment, from the Bigger Picture *all of them were totally wrong.*

While Radical Personalism promotes appreciating and even learning from other traditions, this does not mean that every single Gaudiya must do so to be genuine members of their lineage. It is perfectly fine if someone does not feel the need to inquire into other traditions, but they should be able to acknowledge that others can and that such appreciation is authentic. The prospect of those who find interaction with other traditions inspiring and even necessary should be allowed and encouraged. That said, such interaction is to be done in a committed way. We should learn from diversity with sober maturity of vision. We should be able to acknowledge how "our God" is being worshiped in many legitimate ways. In other words, there is a place for appreciating other traditions in a way that is not threatening to our Gaudiya faith, but rather nourishes it.

A neophyte practitioner, however, may need to be first properly grounded in his own tradition before attempting to deal with the diversity present in other schools. First have your *muladhara-chakra*, your roots, in place and then reach for the remaining *chakras*. Giving a set of absolutes to a novice is like giving a gun to a five-year-old child. Similarly, a neophyte with a broad theory but poor realization of it can be a danger to himself and others. Before addressing other traditions, we should have our own theological foundation in place, and we should learn from and be sobered by the shortcomings of our own tradition. With this healthy and realistic background, we will be better equipped to eventually appreciate the intrinsic commonality within other schools, and even the ups and downs of those traditions. By following this sequence, we are sure to arrive at an experience of deep and renewed re-cognition, coming full circle to eventually nourish our participation in our own tradition. Some call this exemplary dynamics *perennialism*.

PERENNIALISM IN THE GAUDIYA TRADITION

The perennial philosophy, also referred to as *perennialism* or *perennial wisdom*, is a perspective in philosophy and spirituality that views all of the world's religious traditions as sharing a single metaphysical truth or origin from which all esoteric and exoteric knowledge and doctrine has grown. In other words, it recognizes a common foundation of nondual reality. That said, it is important to differentiate at this point between what we may call *popular perennialism* and the mature version of it. In popular perennialism, the accommodation of different traditions is more of a forced homogenization. It is a sentimental sense of unity but not a comprehensive one. In popular perennialism the common foundation has not yet been deeply ascertained, and therefore the differences among traditions cannot be properly appreciated. Conversely, mature perennialism acknowledges both the commonalities and the differences among mystical traditions in a sober, respectful, and committed way. A classic Gaudiya example of mature perennialism is exhibited in the famous *Bhagavata* speech by Bhaktivinoda Thakura:

> *Our* sastras, *or in other words, books of thought, do not contain all that we could get from the infinite Father. ... The great reformers will always assert that they have come out not to destroy the old law but to fulfill it: Valmiki, Vyasa, Plato, Jesus, Mohamed, Confucius and Chaitanya Mahaprabhu assert the fact either expressly or by their conduct. ... It may be, that both the Christian and the Vaishnava will utter the same sentiment, but they will never stop their fight with each other only because they have arrived at their common conclusion by different ways of thought.*[10]

While Thakura Bhaktivinoda wrote the above at the beginning of his devotional career and his general presentation shifted to something more exclusive in time, he nonetheless sets the precedent that the perennialist perspective is not only allowed in Gaudiya Vaishnavism, but probably necessary for most of its adherents at some point of their journey. And it is probably necessary for many others until their very end of their spiritual sojourn. In this connection, even after the above speech Bhaktivinoda Thakura continued to express himself in terms of perennialism until the very end of his life. He did so with more precise terminology, promoting the concept of *sanatana-dharma*. This well-known Sanskrit expression, which basically translates as "the eternal function of the soul," clearly points to how Gaudiya Vaishnavas approach other traditions. Since the soul and its function are ontologically the same cross-culturally, then for Gaudiyas the vision of differences is only *sanatana-dharma* expressed in different degrees or, to be more precise, *with different nuances*. Let's share next a few scriptural examples of how the Gaudiya tradition proposes this perennialist *sanatana-dharma* in terms of the nondual nature of reality.

To begin with, we can refer to the famous Vedic one-liner from the *Maha Upanishad* (6.73) which says *vasudhaiva-kutumbakam*, "The world is one family." This is totally in line with *Bhagavad-gita* 14.4, wherein Sri Krishna similarly mentions how he is the universal seed-giving father through whom, therefore, all of us share a common nondual source, which makes us one family. Another well-known verse from the *Gita* (4.24) in this connection says, "*This ritual is one; the food is one; we who offer the food are one; the fire of hunger is also one; all action is one; we who understand this are one.*"[11] This points to how not only every mystical tradition shares a common nondual bedrock, but every aspect of existence can be seen and related to as part of *one single project*: full alignment with our nondual source.

In more recent times, Gaurahari himself met with members of different traditions throughout his life and his travels across India. He taught others, but on many occasions he was deeply moved by them. Apart from documented meetings with Muslims, Sikhs, Buddhists, and Advaitins, Sri Gaurahari also interacted with different Vaishnava denominations, especially *rama-bhakti*. In fact, many of his own students, such as Murari Gupta and Anupama, were inclined to worship Sri Ramachandra and did so with the full support and blessings of Gaurahari. Not only this, but when he met Ramadasa Vipra in his South Indian journey, Gaurahari was so moved by his love for Ramachandra that he later returned to Ramadasa's aid, bringing an important verse from the scriptures to give him solace and support in his disturbed faith.[12] Another significant example of Gaudiya perennialism is the entire *Brihad-bhagavatamrita*. As the first literary work of the Gaudiya tradition, it therefore sets a very clear precedent for the tradition in the future. The main character of *Brihad-bhagavatamrita* is the young Gopa-kumara, a devotee of Krishna who travels to different planets, which represent diverse layers of religious conceptions. He is nourished by each conception in his own specific search and attainment. For example, when he meets Hanuman, the saintly monkey devoted to Ramachandra, Gopa-kumara requests Hanuman to sing the glories of his Lord. While hearing Hanuman glorify Ramachandra, Gopa-kumara shouts, "Hail to Sri Krishna!" Thereafter, Hanuman requests the same from Gopa-kumara and, while hearing praise of Krishna, Hanuman cries out "Hail to Sri Rama!"[13] Arguably, this constitutes *the perfection of interreligious dialogue*. By witnessing the devotion of someone belonging to another tradition, we are nourished in our own faith and spiritual prospect. Needless to say, this was possible because both Gopa-kumara's Lord and Hanuman's Lord are one and the same Supreme Lord.

Another interesting case of perennialism in the very formation of the Gaudiya lineage is found throughout the writings of the school's original authors. For example, in his magnum opus known as *Bhakti-rasamrita-sindhu*, Sri Rupa Goswami acknowledges Vallabhacharya, with whom he had a friendly relationship, and demonstrates his familiarity with Vallabhacharya's school of thought by referring to their terms *maryada* and *pushti* as being parallel to the Gaudiya concepts of *vaidhi* and *raganuga*.[14] Even more impressive is Jiva Goswami's extensive quoting of Ramanuja, Madhva, and even the Advaitin Sankara, all of them technically members of other religions, in his *Sandarbhas*. Jiva Goswami also allowed the Gaudiya theology, which he was developing and establishing through the *Sandarbhas*, to be *informed and formed* by contributions coming from other traditions. One final and impressive example connects to the way different Gaudiya stalwarts such as Baladeva Vidyabhusana, Thakura Bhaktivinoda, and all of his successors portray their *parampara*, or disciplic succession. They include not only their own Gaudiya teachers but also personalities such as Ramanuja and Madhva. They are not Gaudiyas per se, but members of other mystical traditions who happen to enrich our school.

At this point some of us may legitimately wonder what might happen if we as Gaudiyas allow ourselves to be inspired and thus influenced by different traditions. Will we acquire *samskaras* (impressions) that may divert our faith in Gaudiya Vaishnavism and its ultimate specific goal? Or will we at least be confused on some level?

While this possibility may be true for neophytes, or unprepared practitioners, there is a place for interreligious experience in the context of mature perennialism.[15] It's important to bear in mind that while *samskaras* are impressions that others create in us, their effect depends on *how we choose to receive and process* them. Our choices are the most defining aspect. Thus, there is a place for integrating impressions coming from other traditions in a way that informs and stimulates our own journey.

As the above examples have clearly shown, the main Gaudiya teachers were familiar with other traditions and not necessarily in the spirit of refuting them, but appreciating the underlying common foundation. Further, they allowed themselves to be maturely influenced by other traditions, that influence eventually leading to certain things becoming part of the Gaudiya tradition. With this premise in mind, we could then venerate and learn from, for example, Christian mystics like Thomas Merton or Teresa of Ávila in a way that beautifully nourishes our own Vaishnava faith. Similarly, we should not force ourselves to honor someone from our Gaudiya tradition who interferes with our inspiration as Gaudiyas by mutilating or distorting its teachings. We have not been commanded to love our religion. *We have been commanded to love God as well as our neighbor* even if they happen to be in another religion.

THEOLOGICAL CROSSPOLLINATION

Each mystical tradition has its own goal, and each goal is an ontological possibility unto itself. Gaudiya Vaishnavism has a very distinctive goal and prospect in transcendence, but as we wrote above, there is a place for nourishing that prospect in relation to other traditions. We've called this possibility perennialism. Now we will address going beyond appreciating other traditions to being positively affected by them, under the notion of *theological crosspollination.* Crosspollination happens biologically when the pollen of one flower is applied to the pistils of another with the help of insects and wind. Similarly, a healthy experience of theological crosspollination will happen when nondual traditions share with one another through the sacred winds of their mature representatives. This crosspollination is not to be mistaken for syncretism, the amalgamation and merging of religious traditions. In the words of Huston Smith, it will be more like embracing our own tradition as our main meal while also remaining a strong believer in vitamin supplements (the contribution of other traditions) that will add strength and relish but won't replace one's main meal.[16] As a matter of fact, one of the clearly perceived needs of Emerging Gaudiya Vaishnavism is exactly this: to become mature enough to engage in this holy exercise without losing the tradition's defining features while enriching and expanding them by proper integration.

Theological crosspollination can lead us to a rediscovery of our tradition. That can occur by our being inspired by what other traditions say and then returning to our tradition and finding those same elements there, or by enriching our practice with elements not present in our tradition but naturally adaptable to it. One example is Christianity's *Lectio Divina*, a contemplative method of studying scripture. Another possibility of crosspollination could be appreciating that Native Americans do not have any word for "art," since *everything is art* for them. While Gaudiyas may have their corresponding Sanskrit term for "art," we can nonetheless be inspired by this important contribution coming from the Native Americans. It does not contradict any Gaudiya premise. In other words, we should be able to go to other wisdom traditions and come back to our own tradition and rediscover it with the help (*by the grace*) of other traditions, instead of seeing them as competitors. An inspiring example of how this is possible is cited below in the words of Thakura Bhaktivinoda:

> *If one goes to someone else's place of worship, one should think, "These people are worshiping my Lord, but in a different way. Because of my different training, I cannot quite comprehend this system of worship. However, through this experience I can deepen my appreciation for my own system of worship. The Lord is only one, not two. I offer respect to the form I see here, and pray to the Lord in this new form that he increases my love for the Lord in his accustomed form." Those who do not follow this procedure, but instead criticize other systems of worship and show hatred, violence, and envy, are worthless and foolish.*

> *The more they indulge in useless quarreling, the more they betray the very goal of their religion.*[17]

Another interesting contribution to the field of theological crosspollination comes from Spanish scholar Raimon Panikkar, who coined the notion of "homeomorphic equivalents between traditions." Homeomorphism is a math term which refers to a continuous stretching and bending of an object into a new shape. More specifically, it speaks about the possibility of two objects being bent or molded into one another. Thus, the notion of homeomorphic equivalents between mystical traditions refers to how one similar situation is handled differently by two different schools. For example, Buddhists handle with the problem of ego aggrandizement through the concept of *anatma*, or no-self, whereas the Gaudiya tradition deals with it by emphasizing how each soul is utterly dependent on God. Needless to say, not every single thing in every tradition has its homeomorphic equivalent with every other tradition. In other words, each school is not necessarily doing the same thing but just using different languages and frameworks.[18] Then again, they nonetheless share enough common ground as to allow themselves to meet with one another and collectively bless the world as a result of that. In light of this, Raimon Panikkar also shared an interesting analogy of three of the world's main rivers—the Jordan, the Tiber, and the Ganges. They nourish the lives of those who live along their banks while flowing respectively through Israel, Rome, and India. Though they are connected to three of the main world religions, they never meet on Earth. But, Panikkar said, they do meet in the heavens, where their water condenses into clouds that rain down on all of us on Earth. In the same way, he said, the religions of the world remain distinct and "unmixed" on Earth, but "they meet once transformed into vapor, once metamorphosized into Spirit, which then is poured down in innumerable tongues."[19] So despite our many differences, every mystical tradition points to one same nondual reality as their goal and foundation. Therefore, *we are already meeting in the clouds.*

INTERFAITH AND INTRAFAITH DIALOGUE

Another way to speak about perennialism and theological crosspollination is to do so through the notion of interfaith dialogue. As we already described, this is not synonymous with superficially talking to other traditions while remaining sectarian and dualistic inside. We may even be trying to convince them about the so-called superiority of our tribe. Fruitful interfaith dialogue involves remaining committed to our tradition while also becoming committed to what we may be receiving from other traditions. In this experience we will embrace the wonder of deeply rediscovering the essence of our own lineage expressed in other schools and thus "returning" to our own school with a refreshed sense of commitment and participation. If we allow ourselves to be inspired by other traditions, then part of the challenge and accountability for our tradition will be to ask ourselves: How do I rediscover this unique aspect in my tradition? How do I integrate it or at least learn from it? In fact, if other traditions help us with our tradition and nourish our understanding and practice of it, then at least on some level *they are not different from our tradition,* at least not radically different.

Interfaith dialogue offers an undeniably charming prospect. However, to be successful it has to be prefaced by what we can call *intrafaith* dialogue. Interfaith implies sharing with other traditions; intrafaith involves a dialogue with our own tradition and among ourselves as its members. So first intrafaith, then interfaith, and then a further intrafaith dialogue. What do we mean by this? Before having a dialogue with other traditions (interfaith) we need to have a dialogue with our own tradition (intrafaith). That means we have to understand our tradition properly. We do this to avoid becoming confused when we speak with others. And we do it to avoid seeing other traditions and ours in a dualistic way. We find our common essence in all of them while being open and respectful. A natural byproduct of this first dialogue will be a second one: a deep and committed interfaith dialogue. Then, after having heard and learned from other traditions, we will be ready for our second intrafaith dialogue. This involves "returning" to our own school in a renewed way, being able now to rediscover it by the grace and contributions of "other" traditions.

For this to happen, however, both our interfaith and intrafaith dialogues must contain the genuine possibility of transformation, with subsequent consequences for the trajectory of our life. Conversely, if we enter into this dialogue on excessively rigid ground—knowing and adhering to our beliefs as nonchanging and static—then we won't be able to enter what we may call a *dialogical dialogue.* Implicit in that rigid view is a subtle ego game. It basically says that the revelations of others are not revelations for us and cannot affect our journey. But the "us" in this case is not actually us, but rather our self-centered ego. Through nondual thinking, we'll realize that the true "us" has a part which is one with others, not separate. As already mentioned, the authentic revelations of the other are not separate from one's own self. "Other" traditions are closer to ours than we may think. Therefore, we are to engage in such a dialogue not only looking above, toward a transcendent reality, or behind, toward an original tradition, but also *horizontally,* toward the world of other people who have found other paths leading to the realization of human destiny.[20] In fact, globally speaking we are at such a tipping point, where avoiding potential self-destruction as a species will require solidarity across all our mystical traditions. We are after divine union, not private salvation.

Intrafaith dialogue refers to speaking within our tradition and grounding ourselves in it as a prelude to engaging with other schools. Therefore we must learn to communicate with other members of our own tradition, and agree to disagree. As with other forms of diversity, differences of opinion test our affection. However, as siblings, we can have differences without the need to stop loving each other. If our relationships change because of a disagreement, then this should make us question how much of a relationship was there to begin with. In fact, real love, which is our goal, has little to do with agreeing on everything. It's about harmonizing differences. *That very act* will increase our love for each other. As mentioned above, Gaudiya nondual philosophy is *bheda-abheda.* There is a place for both *abheda* (nondifference/agreement) and *bheda* (difference/disagreement). As it is said, "Variety is the spice of life." However, too much spice (hostile opposition) may spoil the *masala,* but too little spice (too much agreement) will make the recipe tasteless and boring. Thus, as Gaudiyas we are always interested in the middle menu of unity in diversity, or *agreement in disagreement.*

AGREEING TO DISAGREE THROUGH NONDUAL REALITY

The Gaudiya landscape is dotted by endless *parivaras* (families) as well as groups and subdivisions of those groups. As a result of that, we may find different ways of doing almost everything. While we may disagree considerably among one another, we should bear in mind that our differences are often about details and not principles. In a substantial sense, we are still part of the same family. This is sometimes described as the "Gaurahari tree," which has many branches, each representing one facet of Gaudiya affiliation. Ideally, each branch is sustained by the same trunk, the main Deity of our lineage, Sri Gaurahari. As branches from one tree all get along and are equally nourished from the same trunk, we are invited to relate to each other in that same harmonious way. Tree branches do not usually fight with one another. In fact, no tree in nature has ever been observed where its branches were at war with each other. While we may be one sad exception to this universal rule, through dialogue we can still reclaim our own heritage and participation in it and thereby strengthen Gaudiya Vaishnavism.

We should know that disagreements exist even in eternity. Worshipers of Narayana in Vaikuntha will consider Krishna an *avatara* of Narayana, while Krishna's servants in Vraja will think the opposite. *These differences of thought are happening in the spiritual world,* not just here. Even within the same school of thought there will be eternal differences of opinion. When Sri Krishna goes to his bedroom at night, his mother, Yasoda, prays intensely that he will sleep soundly after a full day of pasturing. On the other hand, his lover Srimati Radhika prays that Krishna may join her for the entire night, which means he won't sleep at all. Yasoda and Radhika differ eternally in this regard, but they love one another eternally. Therefore, if we are to sustain that tension as *siddhas* (perfected beings) first we need to harmonize similar differences now as *sadhakas* (spiritual practitioners). If there is a way to disagree even in transcendence, it must be possible now as well. Therefore, an intrafaith dialogue in the context of nondual thinking among Gaudiyas entails not so much proving our siblings wrong as knowing how to explain to ourselves, our beliefs, and decisions. Only when we can explain our theology to ourselves in a way that holds true and valid for us will we be able to allow a humble but confident interaction with the differences of others, including members of our own tradition. In fact, fruitful disagreement entails knowing why and how to disagree, *while increasing our affection for those we disagree with.*

A person will be known differently in diverse environments, such as work, society, and home, and perhaps even called by different names unknown in the other circles. Similarly, the Sweet Absolute will appear and be approached differently in various schools, and even in the diversification within one's own tradition. If we are open to learn from this in the context of nondual thinking, each of these differences will shed light on previously unknown aspects of reality. If our coworkers, family, friends, and partners would get together and swap stories about us, they would probably get a fuller, more comprehensive understanding of who we are. That would further nourish their own relationship with us. Someone's love for us as a friend would be deeper once she knows another side of us as experienced by a coworker, boss, or daughter. And that won't make that friend want to stop being our friend and become a coworker, because she loves us as a friend. And now that she knows more about us, there is more to love, share, and experience. Our common source possesses this same nature. His nature is nondual and indivisible, yet expressed in unlimited ways and forms. And we, being inherently linked with such a nondual foundation, are to relate to each other likewise. Arguably, this is the ultimate perfection of nondual thinking.

Issues & Tissues Between Guru and Disciple | 11

I did not come to make disciples: I want to be a friend of those very few who desire to get a glimpse of a path and goal which is possible to reach. One should know each other very well and such understanding may take a long time.

– Swami Sadananda

If there is one primary aspect that characterizes India as an ancient culture and civilization, that may be the emblematic relationship between guru and disciple. This sacred bond is one of the most glorified throughout Hinduism in general and Gaudiya Vaishnavism in particular. This distinctive interaction creates a unique level of emphasis and significance that needs to be addressed with a corresponding level of understanding. With things that are highlighted or even absolutized, there is the potential danger of misrepresentation, inaccurate expectations, and over-idealization. In the guru-disciple relationship these dangers are posed not only by the student but sometimes even by the teachers themselves. Since a crucial aspect of Radical Personalism is addressing what's not being addressed but needs to be, in this chapter we will unearth some important but often unexplored issues—and *tissues*—involved in this unique relationship. Our hope is that as Gaudiyas we can address, conceive, and embrace this divine principle in the healthiest and most committed way. Although this topic deserves a book of its own, at least we will try to start doing justice to it here in this chapter.

THE INTRICATE IDENTITY OF THE GURU PRINCIPLE

As our last two chapters spoke about individuation and nondual thinking, emphasizing the principles of diversity and unity, respectively, in this chapter we will combine these two topics while speaking about the guru, who according to Gaudiya Vaishnavism represents a department that is simultaneously constituted of unity and diversity. On the unity side of the equation, Gaudiyas say that guru is always one and never two. This stems from the nondual foundation we already talked about, through which the original guru is God himself, the Ultimate Nondual Reality whose sweet will is expressed through and represented by a multiplicity of individual agents. The diversity side of the equation refers to the guru being not one, but different and many. Each guru is a different representative of the one nondual God, the original guru. In Sanskrit, these two aspects of guru are called *samasti-guru-tattva* and *vyasti-guru-tattva*. The first refers to the agency and the second to the agent—the macrocosmic and microcosmic sides of this distinctive equation. We will discuss these two aspects further below. As reality is to be understood as nondual before we attempt to understand its abundant diversity, similarly, the guru is first understood as being one and indivisible before we attempt to grasp its many individualized representations. In other words, God is the original guru and very source of the disciplic succession. *Srimad Bhagavatam* confirms this, referring to the Sweet Absolute as the supreme guru (*paramo gurur*, 8.24.46) and the supreme guru of all other gurus (*paramo guror guruh*, 8.24.48).

Before proceeding, it will be helpful to clarify a few terms and premises. First, although guru in a female body is technically called *gurvi*, we will always use the term "guru," since it's more well-known. Second, we will often refer to "guru" by the pronouns *she* and *her*. The time is ripe to normalize the reality of female gurus and dispense with the current misconception that ladies are not "allowed" to serve in the capacity of guru, being somehow disqualified as a population. Lastly, we will refer to the *vyasti*, or individual, guru as "guru" (with small "g"), and to the *samasti*, or conglomerate/universal, guru as Sri Guru (with capital letters). Now, on to the subject at hand.

To unfold the intricate topic of guru, Sri Guru, and their relationship, let's consider the notion that guru is not limited to one person but is a whole nondual agency which reveals itself through many specific individuals. In proportion to how much an individual guru (*vyasti-guru*) is truly surrendered, the universal principle of *samasti-guru* will flow through her. Thus, we should bear in mind that there are always two sides to the guru equation: (1) the individual (*vyasti*) who occupies the guru post and serves in that capacity, and (2) the foundational side (*samasti*), which is nondifferent from God himself and is represented through different individuals who have varying hosting capacities. Whether that capacity is total or partial, when the term Sri Guru is applied to the individual guru it always refers to the capacity filled by Sri Guru and not the individual guru herself divorced from such representation.

As you may have sensed, this is a complex topic. In fact, *guru-tattva*, or "the reality of the guru principle," is said to be one of the most difficult *tattvas*/realities to understand, and therefore *one of the easiest to misunderstand.* That being the case, let's pay close attention.

WORSHIP OF THE GURU VS. IDOLATRY OF THE GURU

An individual guru who perfectly represents her function will be deeply valued by her sincere followers. In the superlative words of Srila Sridhara Deva Goswami, such a guru personifies our *own potential appearing in front of us.* That is to say, the guru is not different from all that we can become. She represents our bright spiritual prospect. This will be exemplified by the guru through her teachings and example (which disciples will follow), and through her inner world of loving realizations (which disciples will worship as the goal). That said, in some cases the relationship may not be as idyllic as just portrayed. For some disciples, to have someone in their lives constantly reminding them of all they can be may result in an overwhelming and even neurotic experience, since the guru's example reminds us of all we have not yet become. It is the guru's responsibility to guide and support her disciples in a way that they do not become intimidated by a constant confrontation with their own potential appearing in the form of their guru. If this guidance and support are not present, then different unconscious defense mechanisms may surface, through which a disciple may try to avoid this challenging situation. Let's consider a few of them next.

The guru's example is to be followed (as long as it's commendable), and the inner ideal she represents is to be worshiped. *We worship the ideal; we follow the person.* In fact, even worshipping the person of the guru will be done only in connection to the worshipable ideal the person represents. That said, it's generally easier to externally worship the guru than internally follow her example. To embrace the guru's ideal example is demanding. Therefore, disciples may end up resorting to so-called worship as an unconscious, evasive device in the name of internally following the example. While this may appear as surrender and devotion, it is actually a form of idolatry. We can worship the wrong person, or we can *worship the right person for the wrong reasons.* Worshiping for the wrong reasons is not worship.

For Gaudiya Vaishnavas, *the guru is God in a representational sense.* Ideally, she represents the will of the Sweet Absolute in a very condensed and specific way, and by seeing her example and hearing instructions one will gradually be able to perceive the divine not only in that individual guru, but in every person and place. One will enter "the land of gurus."[1] But it all begins with one guru who points to that land. And a disciple is to learn how to coexist with the prospect such a guru brings to his life. A guru will never ask the disciple to worship her as guru. But, provided she is a proper role model, she will expect her students to follow her example while helping them deal with their potential. In fact, the role of the guru could be defined as a "*facilitator of potential,*" since she enables and empowers the disciple to actualize his ultimate prospect. This is a big task for the guru. And to allow the enablement and empowerment offered by the guru is a big task for the disciple.

If all these elements are in place, the guru's example and inner gifts will naturally become worshipable for the disciple. This approach has nothing to do with idolatry, but represents the worship of the guru principle *for the right reasons.* In other words, the guru should not be worshiped independent of her inner world of devotion and insight. If we take this out of the equation, then the guru is no different from anyone else. The guru is not to be worshiped merely because she is *my* guru or due to some mental projection I imposed on her. She is to be worshiped because she represents the Sweet Absolute in my life. And this divine representation won't play itself out in black and white terms—there are degrees to the relationship that need to be considered.

WE SHOULD SURRENDER PROPORTIONATE TO HOW MUCH A GURU REPRESENTS GOD

The guru is God in a representational sense. Therefore, when we worship the guru, we worship the *degree to which she represents God in our lives*. Different people will represent God's will on many different levels, and the sacred Gaudiya texts mandate worship of that specific degree of divine manifestation alone—not more, not less. Thus, before speaking of how and how much a disciple should surrender to his guru, first we need to clearly know what qualities are expected from a genuine guru. Then we can examine *how fully* those qualities are being exhibited by a particular guru. Since the degree of a disciple's surrender should be proportionate and reciprocal to the degree of the guru's surrender, we must properly assess and corroborate how fully guru represents the divine. Otherwise, in the name of full surrender we may be opening the door for different forms of personality cults and even abuse. Thus, the guru should be scrutinized so the demand for surrender from a disciple is appropriate and healthy. Both guru and disciple are to be equally examined by the other.

For example, if a guru requests her disciples to compromise their integrity and sacrifice their values and principles through different forms of spiritual bypassing, then we will be instructed *not to surrender* in that direction because that won't be the agency of Sri Guru acting through that individual agent. In other words, the main point in one's surrendering proportionately to the level of representation in the guru is that one should *not surrender* to something that does not represent the principle of Sri Guru. That said, it's naturally necessary for anyone to be able to give his heart completely to at least one person. For the disciple, that person is generally represented in the figure of the guru. Therefore, when we say that one should surrender to a guru proportionate to the guru's own surrender, we don't imply that only the most advanced gurus deserve full surrender. If a guru is not situated in the highest stage but is fully sincere and transparent and fully surrendered in her present capacity and stage, this will allow for the necessary dose of divine representation the disciple needs to receive from his teacher. Then a disciple can and should fully surrender according to his own capacity and stage. At this point we should remember that full surrender is not a one-act performance but an ongoing process that in one sense will never end. *We will always be able to surrender a little bit more.* Thus, "full surrender" is not so much a state limited to something only superlative devotees have attained and others have not, but a disposition to fully give ourselves to, according to our present situation and capacities. At each stage there will be a corresponding way of being fully surrendered, and both guru and disciple should ideally be fully surrendered in this sense.

As it's not healthy for a disciple to blindly surrender to someone who does not fully represent God's will, it is similarly damaging for the guru to accept disproportionate surrender from the disciple. A disciple should be surrendering to someone who is at least as surrendered as him, although ideally much more. If this is not the case, the guru will not be able to properly reciprocate and deal with her disciple's surrender. *A guru who receives a level of dedication that she herself isn't able to process will have her own standing and function as guru compromised.* Each of these important considerations is to be equally applied to both guru and disciple, without any partiality to one side or the other, since both parties need to be properly honored and cared for.

It is imperative to keep in mind that *a disciple surrenders not to a person, but to a principle.* That principle is the principle of divine revelation, which generally comes to our life through a particular individual. That being the case, the surrender is not to someone, but to *something that flows through someone.* We surrender to a principle, to an ideal, and to a commitment in service to that ideal. As much as that ideal is not represented in a person, then there is no need to surrender to and worship that particular *lack* of representation.

An ordinary example of this is a policeman. A person who serves as a policeman does so only to the extent that he represents the principles of the law. If he deviates from the principles he was meant to embody, then the officer is not fully representing the agency. The extent of his deviation indicates how separate he is from the department he is supposed to represent. Historically, we have seen that when a police officer wasn't accountable to the office, there were riots in the street properly protesting the abuse of power. "Surrendering" to a policeman is not surrendering to that person divorced from the police department, but rather to the department and the fullness in which that person represents it. We surrender to the principles and ideals that constitute that department, and ultimately to the people who carry those ideals. In this same way, we do not surrender to the person who serves as guru but to the principles the guru represents and the fullness with which she embodies them. Ultimately, we surrender to the heart of the Absolute Truth who is carried in those principles and that agency.

There are many different gurus on many different levels. While some fully represent the Divine and the agency of Sri Guru, others represent it partially in a multiplicity of degrees. Therefore, we are to address the reality of *guru-tattva* with a nuanced conception in mind. While it may not be easy for everyone to establish how much an individual guru (*vyasti*) is representing the universal guru agency (*samasti*), at least we should begin by acknowledging that such a nuanced scenario not only exists but needs to be addressed with both deep sincerity and subtle discernment.

THE SACRED SCRIPTURES MOSTLY SPEAK OF GURU IN IDEALISTIC TERMS

In response to the nuanced scenario depicted above, some Gaudiyas may point out that each time the Gaudiya scriptural canon refers to Sri Guru, it almost always praises such a principle in absolute terms, and calls for an absolute submission by the disciple to such a divine personality. This seems to suggest that whoever is serving as guru will always be situated in the highest possible level of spiritual realization. And while there is surely a place and need for those paramount examples, there is also the possibility of various shades and overtones in this intricate template. In order to grasp this apparent contradiction, we need to first understand from which place scripture speaks about guru.

In general, every time scripture invokes the term "guru" and proceeds to chant her unlimited glories, it does so *while assuming the guru to be fully qualified to execute that function*. It is only from this perspective that scripture says what it says in absolute terms. In other words, the sacred Gaudiya texts speak of the ideal guru. That means one who is synonymous with Sri Guru, or one who is a *vyasti* agent perfectly representing the *samasti* agency. In fact, this is but one example of the typical way in which Gaudiya scriptures tend to refer to sacred practices or personalities in absolute terms. For example, *Srimad Bhagavatam* 9.4.63–68 and similar sections speak of devotees as being absolutely uninterested in material affairs and even liberation, and as controlling God by the strength of their love. While we know these are the symptoms of the topmost devotee, Gaudiya scriptures usually don't make this clarification so when they speak in these idealistic terms their application can easily be mistaken to describe any devotee regardless of their level of progress. This same idealistic spirit is invoked when speaking about the virtues of *sadhu-sanga* (saintly company). The scriptures say that by one nanosecond of such association one can attain all perfection.[2] Similarly, the glories of God's names are repeatedly extolled to the point of proclaiming that by merely saying even half a syllable of the Name one can transcend material influence.[3] After reading these statements some may conclude that they are either exaggerations and can't be true or they are absolutely true regardless of any condition. Neither of these dualistic conclusions are fully accurate. The idealistic statements of scriptures, like those mentioned above, depict something that *in potential* could happen if all the ideal conditions are in place—starting with the purity of our own hearts. Similarly, almost every time the scriptures speak about guru, they do so from this "idealistic" perspective. They take for granted that the most ideal type of personality is serving in that capacity and do not even entertain the idea of a partial level of representation.

Taking the ideal situation of a guru for granted, scripture then proceeds to speak about how a disciple should reciprocate with such an ideal guru: with full surrender. In this connection, it is important to consider that scripture not only assumes that the guru is an ideal representative every time it refers to such a person, but it also takes for granted that the reader is aware that scripture is speaking from such an idealistic viewpoint. It also assumes that the reader won't apply this absolute criterion to every single person serving in the capacity of guru, but rather will use the ideal as a standard of expected character and behavior. An ordinary example is a description of something, let's say, an apple, given in an encyclopedia. It is taken for granted that the description is of an *ideal* apple and that each apple, to some degree or another, will approximate the ideal. In the same way, scriptures speak of the ideal guru. It is one thing to speak generally about the guru principle in its ideal expression and how we as disciples should also reciprocate ideally, but it is something different—*very* different in some cases—to deal with a localized individual expression of this same principle when ideal features portrayed in scripture are not exhibited. It is with this crucial detail in mind that we speak of the expectation of a disciple to surrender proportionately to a guru's representation of the ideal.

God does not descend as the guru, but rather *through* the guru. Therefore, Gaudiyas say that the guru is the *prakash,* or manifestation, of God.[4] Guru and God are one in glory—*not in person.* The guru reflects a light she has received, and the disciple, the receiver of that light, should know that and reciprocate accordingly. If we forget this fact and absolutize the guru's position, skipping the macrocosmic original fountainhead of *guru-tattva* and jumping directly to the person serving in that capacity without a clear distinction between the two, we risk engaging in idolatry rather than divine worship and sacred following.

THE ABSOLUTE AND RELATIVE SIDES OF THE GURU

Another way we can refer to the above aspects of *vyasti* and *samasti* is to describe them as *the relative and absolute sides of the guru,* respectively. Some people interpret the relative side as referring to the humanity of the guru (and the potential for some mild mistakes on her part), and the absolute side as referring to the guru's transcendental side (which is never affected by the relative side). These two terms, originally invoked by Srila Sridhara Deva Goswami throughout his book *Sri Guru and His Grace*, refer to the *vyasti* and *samasti* sides of *guru-tattva*. By "absolute" he referred to Sri Guru (God, the *samasti* principle), while by "relative" he referred to the *vyasti-guru*, the human individual and devotee of God who represents the *samasti* agency to one degree or another. We can also refer to these two sides of the guru in relation to the potential relativity of the guru's human nature, as well as the divine representation she ideally embodies. We'll turn to this next.

Although the relative and absolute sides of a guru are not the same, they are not entirely different either. On some level one side speaks of the other, at least in the sense that the relative side of the guru (her human character) may reflect her absolute side (her inner spiritual realization and identity). As different as these may be, there is no need to absolutely divorce the guru's relative side from her absolute side. Our humanness can and should be integrated in our spirituality even to the point of accompanying us in eternity. We previously wrote about individuation, and the qualities of an individuated person should be applied to the guru. The guru's humanity cannot be totally divorced from her side as a devotee. In fact, if the guru is fully representing Sri Guru, then her humanity will somehow reflect her own spirituality, and thus they won't be as separate as we may think. Conversely, if we make these two sides totally unrelated, this can lend itself to various forms of abuse. For example, a "guru" may end up being a sexual predator but the guru's disciples may "harmonize" that by saying, "That behavior is his relative side only, but on his absolute side he remains untouched by this." Therefore, the guru's relative and absolute sides do not run on divergent tracks, but in fact they are closely related.

Transcendence of the relative side occurs in our integrated embrace of it, not in its avoidance. Considering the guru's humanity can also give rise to a charming prospect: if the guru is a fully transparent representative of God's will, then even some apparent imperfections (not grave faults) in her character may result in a sweetly endearing scenario. For example, a guru may be a little grumpy, a quality of her personality even before becoming a saint. However, in the context of her current purity and saintliness, this grumpiness will play itself out in a totally different way—in a way that does not compromise her inner standing. A different case occurs when the guru's relative side creates an interference that clearly affects her inner standing, especially if both guru and disciple try to over-justify it and dismiss such a deviation in the name of "the relative side." In some of these unfortunate cases, we may even end up saying things like "Even the relative side of the guru is absolute." This characterization opens an ample door for abuse and raises more suspicion than relief. Also, by absolutizing the relative side one *relativizes the absolute side* of the very guru principle.

In the main Gaudiya verses which describe the guru's qualities, the chief symptoms are always depicted in terms of deep knowledge of scripture and inner realization of God.[5] These facts are somewhat reflected externally in the fact that a genuine guru "has taken shelter in tranquility" (*upasama-ashrayam*). Her senses are controlled. In other words, she has *balanced her humanity.* While the human side of a guru may within reason remain unintegrated on some level, it should at least be integrated to a point where the guru can teach others and her unbalanced humanity does not carry her away from exemplary behavior or get in the way of her teaching. If, for whatever reason, disciples choose to dismiss this possibility of unintegrated humanness and instead indulge in over-idealization of the guru regardless of the circumstance, that may lead to excessive expectations. And if the guru and disciple sign such a contract, both may embark upon a fantasy journey where they over-idealize each other, over-expect certain exchanges with each other, and basically end up cheating each other in order to make the journey "sustainable"—and to ignore the journey's imminent demise. While the guru-disciple relationship has the greatest potential to personify the most mature form of relationship, we see here how it often remains crippled by a neophyte understanding of what to expect from each other. The disciple's over-idealization of the guru circles back to the guru's over-idealization of what she expects from the disciple. A vicious circle indeed.

It's important to note that gurus are not absolute in their relative opinions either. Whether we refer to political views or social issues, a guru *does not need* to be perfect in every area of knowledge and, as a consequence, be expected to act as our psychologist, financial counselor, or romantic advisor. If a disciple expects advice of this nature from his guru and the guru offers it, then very confusing scenarios may develop. If I have absolutized the relative side of my guru and then he advises me wrongly on some relative issue, then (a) my over-absolutizing faith will collapse, or (b) since "the guru must always be right," then I will blame myself, experience absolute failure, and enter an endless trip of brutal feelings of shame and guilt. This scenario can even lead gurus to promote such toxic patterns and react to whoever does not comply with their relative advice by ostracizing, shunning, defaming, scapegoating, and similar forms of abuse. For a guru who expects such unrestricted treatment from students, Srila Prabhupada would say things like "If a man who does not factually possess the attributes of a great personality engages his followers in praising him, with the expectation that such attributes will develop in the future, that sort of praise is actually an insult."[6]

As much as the relative side of the guru can speak of his absolute side, in some unique cases we find extremely saintly personalities who seem to be somewhat dysfunctional on a social/psychic level. In those exceptional cases, we should be careful not to judge their inner spiritual standing by the external shape of their current humanity. That said, it is one thing to recognize such exceptions as saintly, yet it is another to extend that exceptional circumstance to someone who is serving in the capacity of guru. Despite being equally as saintly as our first example above, the latter example needs to also be qualified on a human level, since she will be dealing with her disciples and guiding them in the integration of their own humanity. Therefore, to serve in the capacity of guru, two types of *adhikara* (eligibility) are required. One has to be qualified on a spiritual level as well as wholesome and intact on a human level. Without the latter, the guru may not be able to deeply interact with her students in all of the human dimensions they still need to address and integrate. As we have already said, part of the Gaudiya project is to have our humanity in place as a crucial aspect of our spiritual advancement.

CAN THE GURU BE FALLIBLE OR IS SHE ALWAYS INFALLIBLE?

One of the Gaudiyas' favorite names for the Sweet Absolute is Achyuta, "the Infallible One." Bearing this in mind, some may naturally conclude that since the guru is known as a representative of God, then the guru should exhibit all of the exact same qualities of the agency she is supposed to represent. If God is infallible and omniscient, then the guru must be so as well. While this conclusion may be applicable in some ways, it is not an appropriate criterion for all considerations. We will contemplate this next as we explore the concept of mild mistakes written about by Radhamadhav das in his work *Perfect Imperfection*.[7]

Let's begin by establishing that the guru does not possess blanket infallibility and, as we saw in previous sections, may indulge in what can be called "mild mistakes" which, in contrast to grave mistakes, won't challenge inner purity. As should be expected, even if an individual *vyasti-guru* commits a grave mistake which compromises her inner standing, this doesn't mean that the universal agency of *samasti-guru* has become affected. On the other hand, even if a guru is a perfect representative of God and thus infallible in terms of devotional purity, such a guru may at times lack complete infallibility in terms of her external conduct (which, again, won't compromise her devotional infallibility).

An example of grave mistakes committed by a guru could be that of repeated sexual abuse, dehumanizing mistreatment of other Vaishnavas, or different forms of conscious manipulation, such as persistent hypocrisy, exploitation, and evasiveness. An example of a mild mistake could be not remembering a particular verse from scripture, misspelling a word when writing, or celebrating a particular Gaudiya festival on the wrong day. In any case of mild mistakes, widely mentioned throughout scripture, integrity has not been compromised. In fact, we Gaudiyas are invited to recall how our entire lineage revolves around the message of *Srimad Bhagavatam*. Therefore, in one sense it could be said that our entire Gaudiya tradition *is* based on *mature correction of imperfection* since the *Srimad Bhagavatam* is a critique of Vyasa's own previous works, which he himself found lacking. Also, in the *Srimad Bhagavatam*, Vyasa famously extends his mature spirit of self-correction when he admits in verse 1.5.11 that while the work may possess some mild mistakes, its content is worshipable despite that. Or in a deeper sense, we might say that *because* of those errors the work is *even more* worshipable, since imperfection can add its charm as long as it is rooted within the context of purity, sincerity, and divinity.[8] In fact, *Srimad Bhagavatam* demonstrates this principle like no other Gaudiya work by presenting Krishna *lila* and its apparent limitation and imperfection. There we are shown that imperfections are present not only in us humans and even the guru, but in God himself!

Limitation does not necessarily compromise freedom, but it can allow for and even facilitate it. For example, when Krishna was tied by his mother, Yasoda, he appeared externally limited, but that "imperfect" moment allowed him to taste a deeper type of love than he would if he were not tied. Increased affection means *increased freedom*. Therefore, if God's limitation can facilitate a deeper experience of love, how limited and imperfect is that so-called imperfection? It is popularly said that *errare humanum est*, "To err is human." Astonishingly, in a transcendental sense, *errare divinum est*—"to err is divine"—also applies! In fact, one of the sweetest aspects of God's apparent defects is that they give his devotees the opportunity to prove their unconditional love for him. And the opposite is also true. Our own mistakes give the Sweet Absolute the chance to express his unconditional love for us. Therefore, just as Krishna's apparent mistakes make his *lila* all the sweeter, so it is with the apparent mild shortcomings of the guru—provided we are endowed with the proper vision. This will allow for a less stigmatized and more harmonious and integrative perspective on mistakes in our spiritual life.

In a way similar to a truly genuine guru being infallible in terms of her loving representation of God but not necessarily infallible in terms of mild mistakes, a guru doesn't possess blanket omniscience like the Sweet Absolute, but exhibits a particular aspect of this attribute by being intimately connected with the Supreme Lord in the heart. In other words, when the scriptures refer to the guru as *sarvajna* or all-knowing, this implies that God reveals in the guru's pure heart as much as she will require to know. In other words, the guru's so-called omniscience refers to her knowing *everything she wants and needs to know*, which means that she knows everything she needs to know about *bhakti*, or loving devotion. In fact, one aspect of the *samasti-guru* is the *chaitya-guru*, the localized form of God residing in each heart. This form is fully omniscient and will inspire a sincere guru accordingly. Or we could say that since a pure guru loves God perfectly, she then knows the Sweet Absolute fully, and since knowing God fully means knowing everything—at least *everything one needs to know*—then in that sense we could say that the guru is omniscient. When the scriptures refer to a guru being omniscient, it thus refers to these types of examples, since as we have already explained, the guru is nondifferent from God in a representational sense. To equate the guru as being one with God in every sense of the term, including attributes like blanket infallibility and omniscience, is tantamount to the opposite of Radical Personalism, or impersonalism.

IF A GURU COMMITS A MISTAKE, IT SHOULD BE ACKNOWLEDGED TO SENIORS, PEERS, AND EVEN STUDENTS

As we have seen, a guru can commit mild mistakes which do not necessarily compromise her integrity. However, if the guru commits grave mistakes, they should be properly acknowledged. Unfortunately, we find in the Gaudiya community a common landscape of stigmatizing anyone who points out a guru's mistake, labeling such people as offenders (*aparadhis*), thereby weaponizing this term and paralyzing critical thinking and honest speech. At the same time, this pattern promotes complacency in others who may feel that, since they don't criticize anyone (although they may have to in some cases), then they are free from all *aparadha*, or offense. However, being a passive witness to misbehavior is known as a "sin of omission," and this is similarly labeled as such in our own Gaudiya school. In this regard, *Chaitanya-charitamrita* 2.5.90 declares, "A person who knows things as they are and still does not bear witness becomes involved in sinful activities." Thus, while some think that any form of criticism is an *aparadha*, it should be known that remaining silent may also fall into that category. The notion of *aparadha* points to ill-motivated criticism. But healthy and friendly critique is not offensive and is a crucial way of showing loving care and concern. In his essay *Vaishnava Ninda*, Thakura Bhaktivinoda highlights this point thus:

> *Provided one has the right motive, the scriptures have not condemned a careful analysis of someone's faults. Proper motive is of three types: desiring the welfare of the other person, desiring the welfare of the world, and desiring one's own welfare.*

In other words, *aparadha* is fundamentally about intention. If a Vaishnava behaves in an exemplary way, then it is offensive to criticize that person out of envy. However, if a Vaishnava behaves in a non-Vaishnava way and someone points that out in a constructive spirit, that isn't *aparadha*. It is a loving expression of concern. Finding faults is one thing; seeing faults is a very different thing. While the former can become a deadly addiction, the latter can expand our heart enormously.

Having "unstigmatized" the possibility of perceiving faults in the guru, let's analyze how a guru should hold herself accountable for whatever mistakes she has committed. Unfortunately, these days we often find that those who hold the position of guru try to escape criticism, apology, and even rectification. However, this is not the behavior of a genuine guru, who will apologize even if she unintentionally hurts others, what to speak of making intentional mistakes! In fact, genuine gurus have often allowed the public to witness their own correction in order to promote education and healing on the societal level. Therefore, to protect the dignity of the infallible *samasti-guru*, whenever needed we must be ready to correct the fallible *vyasti-gurus*, who are the representatives of the universal guru agency. If we do not do so, doubts will arise regarding the purity and infallibility of the guru principle as a whole.

We find many examples in our Gaudiya tradition of gurus correcting themselves or acknowledging the mistakes others see in them. As already mentioned, our most foundational Gaudiya scripture, *Srimad Bhagavatam*, is the outcome of a genuine guru, Vyasa, correcting himself. Similarly, when Advaita Acharya was corrected by his son Achyutananda, he humbly begged his son for forgiveness. Likewise, when Sri Gaurahari himself was corrected by the little boy

Gopala, he accepted the correction. He glorified the boy and even considered him his own guru! A genuine guru will never claim a holier-than-thou status and duplicitously downplay his mistakes. Following in the footsteps of these mature devotees, who never think they are exempt from fault and accountability, we should add our own example to the list when need be, remaining open to admit our mistakes and in doing so inspire others to give themselves permission to do the same. Thus, correcting ourselves shouldn't represent a form of threat, but rather something that confirms we are heading in the right direction.

Accepting one's mistakes as a guru is a noble act to be performed, shared, and accepted in intimacy and confidence with different people. Depending on the specific circumstance and nature of the mistake, a guru may have to hold himself accountable in front of seniors, peers, or even students. Gurus who do not have seniors with whom to express accountability or peers who will lovingly confront them as equals will most likely be much less willing to admit shortcoming to their students. In those cases, the guru is in a very dangerous position. With nobody available or allowed to offer constructive feedback, the guru will remain in that precarious situation, very often until her mistakes, having taken on a life of their own, reveal themselves in a louder way. Ideally, a guru is an elder—a mature, integrated individual. *And mature individuals do not resent correction*; they identify more with their long-range selves and with the profit from such correction than they do with the momentary self that is being advised.

While the Gaudiya tradition has historically recognized hierarchical or vertical accountability, it sometimes lacks enough emphasis on lateral accountability, by which gurus are lovingly corrected by peers and equals. Similarly, the possibility of a student, in service to his guru, lovingly pointing to some mistake is not generally entertained as something with the potential of nourishing the relationship between guru and disciple. But a genuine guru will be humble enough to think of herself as a "student forever," and she will therefore hold herself accountable even to her disciple if that's necessary for their mutual growth. The exchange between guru and disciple is based on a free flow of faith and an open-hearted back-and-forth, with both parties equally committed to each other in service to their common goal. If both guru and disciple are sincere, *it doesn't matter who corrects whom*. Both sides will feel equally blessed and humbled by the care and affection shown by the other.

ON LEAVING ONE'S GURU

If the guru misbehaves considerably, disciples may find themselves in unexpected or even inconceivable predicaments. One of these less-than-ideal templates, which unfortunately is becoming more and more prevalent, is the "emergency case," where the disciple is basically forced to abandon his guru. In this connection, Gaudiya scriptures present general rules and emergency rules (*apad-dharma*). In an emergency, the predicament is so out of the norm that general rules do not apply. Therefore, if a guru is engaged in immoral behavior so aberrant that "normal" is not equipped to deal with the situation, then all of the scriptural statements which speak about the greatness of the guru do not apply, since they do not take into account a guru of immoral behavior. As we previously said, one surrenders to the guru because she represents the Sweet Absolute. Or, more accurately, one should surrender to a guru proportionately to how much that person represents God.

Before speaking about why a guru should be rejected, we should first ask ourselves why a guru should be accepted. We are to ask ourselves not only what to expect from a guru but *why we are looking for a guru*. In fact, this is one of the main symptoms of any true disciple, who must be concerned with *jijnasu-sreyah-uttamam*, or comprehensive inquiry into the ultimate good. This spirit is beautifully depicted in *Srimad Bhagavatam* 2.9.36, where the Sweet Absolute describes how a person sincerely searching for God must conduct his inquiry "in all circumstances, in all space and time, and both directly and indirectly." If this inquiry is not there to begin with, then we may be accepting a guru for the wrong reasons. In that case, even if we never reject her, we have never actually accepted our guru in any real depth. To prevent this, Sanatana Goswami emphatically indicates that guru and disciple should live together for at least one year so they get acquainted.[9] The disciple's responsibility is to have his own motivations in place, and the role of the guru is, among other things, to make sure the disciple is looking for a guru for the right reasons. After establishing that we are somehow sincere in our disciple project, we should know what qualities are to be exhibited by a genuine guru. When we understand this clearly, it will become indirectly evident what the valid reasons are for potentially rejecting a guru.

As already mentioned, the main attributes of a genuine guru speak of her knowledge of scripture and how much that knowledge has been realized internally through practice and exemplary character. Therefore, considering these qualities, a guru who repeatedly and consciously, and not merely accidentally, deviates from them is fit to be rejected. Some of the main Gaudiya quotes in this regard say:

> *It is ordained that a guru who is arrogant and self-conceited, who does not know what is to be done and what is to be avoided, and who has stumbled down the wrong path, is to be given up.* (Mahabharata, Udyoga-parva 179.25)

> *One should give up a guru who does not have knowledge of scripture, does not speak the truth, and is a showman. Since he does not know the means to liberation for himself, then how can he guide others?* (Skanda Purana, Guru-gita 198)

As we can see, the qualities for which to reject a guru are intimately connected to the qualities that qualify a guru. An absence of the required qualities makes the guru "fit" to be rejected. One should reject a guru (a) who does not know scripture and (b) who takes the wrong path. If we pay close attention, we'll notice that these two are the exact opposite of the main qualities of a genuine guru: being proficient in scripture and deeply realized and well-behaved.

If one's guru falters in some way, it is recommended that the disciple not reject the guru immediately but first take some respectful distance, pray sincerely, and, if required, even approach the guru and point these things out in the spirit of service. It is said in *Krishna-bhajanamrita* 1.59: "If the guru commits inappropriate acts, then one should privately confront him and reprimand him using logical conclusions—but one is not to give him up." However, this instruction applies to the beginning of a particular deviation. If the guru remains in denial of his own situation and continues deviating, after a long and painful insistence and period of deep prayer the disciple is advised to abandon him. Since every particular situation is unique and radically personal, a more nuanced situation might be when, due to some nonpermanent misbehavior on the part of the guru, a disciple may feel the need to take some respectful distance from him, not rejecting him, but complementing that connection with the guidance and shelter of an instructing guru.

As mentioned above, a guru is not the owner of his disciples. While the disciple may feel that his guru owns him, the guru should not feel that way herself. Instead, a guru is a *servant* of his disciples—a servant of the disciples' faith. Therefore, if the student's faith is not fructifying as it should, the guru should arrange for his student to renew his faith, either under his guidance or that of another qualified Vaishnava. However, if the guru grossly misrepresents the divine agency of Sri Guru and does not allow her disciple to obtain guidance from someone else, then the disciple is advised to abandon her. A famous scriptural example in this connection is that of Bali Maharaja. He abandoned his guru Sukracharya, who instructed Bali not to serve the Sweet Absolute in his form as Vamana. Despite rejecting his guru, Bali is one of the famous twelve *mahajanas*, or "great personalities." He acquired this title not merely by rejecting his guru, but by his unconditional adhesion to truth, which, in part, took the form of rejecting his guru. This unconditionality is the actual principle never to be compromised, as Srila Sridhara Deva Goswami indicated:

> *In the beginning, we may neglect some occasional problems; some instances of these kinds of deviations may be ignored. But if we find that they are becoming more prevalent, then we must inspect the situation carefully. ... When we find that what appeared to us first in a small way is real, injurious, and of a big magnitude, and that our spiritual master is going down, then we must act to save ourselves. We must try to take steps which may save us from that epidemic contamination. We must try to save ourselves. And we must also try to save others who might fall prey to the same exploitation as us. That must be done in all sincerity. There is the possibility. ... So, we*

must not make progress in a slumber, but we must go forward with our eyes always opened.[10]

Sincerity of the heart is our real capital, and according to the dictation of our heart, we will go on. Some might question, "If we were sincere, why were we afforded a guru who eventually failed in her representation of God?" As there are different cases, there will also be different ways to answer such a question. But in brief, we could say that if our prayer as disciples was sincere, then the Supreme Lord put us in contact with a guru who, at that moment, was the exact person we needed to meet at our particular stage. And although that person eventually failed, we should nonetheless appreciate whatever we have received from her and not be ungrateful. If at the present moment, however, that person is no longer acting as a guru, then we are invited to deepen our sincerity and fully trust that our prayers won't go unnoticed by God, who is eternally present in our heart. In fact, our willingness to trust that guidance is still available allows it to show up as guidance.[11] God's reply is according to our present stage and need. While we may not necessarily receive the most advanced personality on Earth as a second guru (since we may not be able to properly benefit from such a high example), we should be able to accept with trust and gratitude whatever the Sweet Absolute has considered best for that moment. Just as we should remain discerning but not fall into cynicism, we should also be trustful without falling into excessive naiveté.

ON BEING REJECTED BY ONE'S GURU

As unexpected as abandoning one's guru may be, being disowned or rejected by one's guru is something even more improbable. While in the above section we declared how a considerable absence of the expected qualities in a guru make her rejectable, we may similarly wonder if the same criterion applies to a disciple. If he does not exhibit the sincere inquiry for truth, proper surrender, humility, and service attitude expected from him, is a disciple then fit to be rejected by his guru? Needless to say, if a disciple does not exhibit submission or surrender because the guru is not behaving as she should be, then the disciple's attitude falls into the category of emergency. Such an attitude may be pointing to the sincerity and integrity of the student, who is not willing to submit to any form of deviation, imposed untruth, or blind faith.

Some may wonder, what about a situation in which the guru has not deviated, yet a disciple fails to show the exemplary qualities expected of him? In that case, the failure of the student is not to be judged to the same degree as the teacher's. In other words, if we assume that the guru is ideally situated on a higher platform than her student, then it is expected that a disciple will fail more often and in ways that a teacher is not expected to fail—the closer we come to the truth, the more responsibility we have to avoid error. This is like expecting a child to fall down while learning to walk. It is expected that the child will make considerable mistakes that his father is no longer supposed to commit. If a father fails as a father, and in doing so becomes abusive, then the child may eventually need to distance himself from his father. But if a child makes childish mistakes, the father will naturally forgive him and continue assisting his growth. This reality is not to over-justify any extreme bad behavior from a disciple toward a guru, but to establish the typical framework of a guru-disciple relationship. The guru is like a loving parent toward the childlike disciple, since the guru represents the very personification of God's *kripa-shakti* (mercy-giving potency) in the life of the student. This clearly speaks about the guru's generous and merciful disposition, and in turn hints at her capacity to overlook various mistakes of her student. All of this fills the disciple with shelter, hope, and gratitude.

Considering the above scenario, it is then natural to discover that in the ancient Gaudiya scriptures there is *not one single verse* where the qualities of an accepted disciple are described as making him fit to be rejected by his guru. The spirit of this notion is that the principle of Sri Guru is such a merciful agency that its genuine representative will never reject a disciple who has been accepted within its fold, no matter how mistaken the student may be. This is not meant to invite disciples to become lazy and complacent, but to highlight the glory and mercy of *guru-tattva* and remain humbled by those glories. In this regard, a series of verses from the *Hari-bhakti-vilasa* may be quoted:

> *Although a spiritual master may accept a surrendered soul who has faith and devotion as his disciple, even though he may not have the other good qualities that were mentioned, he should avoid making disciples with the faults that are now being described: One should not accept as a disciple a person who is lazy, impure, proud, a miser, wretched, diseased, angry, attached to sense gratification, greedy, envious, jealous, a cheater, or harsh. He should not accept a person who over-endeavors for material gains, earns money through improper means, enjoys another's wife, is inimical to intelligent persons, falsely claims to be learned, does not follow any vow, earns his livelihood with great difficulty, finds fault with others, or gives distress to others. He should not accept as a disciple one who is a voracious eater, cruel, sinful, evil-minded, crooked, or the lowest among human beings. Those who cannot be restrained from performing activities that should not be performed, and those who are unable to follow the teachings of a spiritual master are also unfit to become disciples. A spiritual master should unhesitatingly reject such people; they should not be made disciples.*[12]

The above verses do not speak about *accepted disciples* who should be rejected, but *prospective candidates* who are not to be accepted by the guru. In fact, if we examine the context in which the above verses appear, we will see that they are spoken while describing *the preliminary qualifications* to be judged by a guru. It is only after this that the *Hari-bhakti-vilasa* speaks about receiving initiation and whatever else follows. The difference between rejecting an accepted disciple and rejecting a candidate is a subtle but crucial one that indicates that once a guru accepts disciples she will never reject them. The difference between these two cases could be compared to the difference between choosing not to get pregnant or choosing to abort the fetus. The result is objectively the same: there will be no child. But they are very different acts. In one case, the child is not conceived, not born of one's seed. In relation to the disciple and guru, this seed is tantamount to the seed of devotion, or *bhakti,* and placing it (or not) within the heart of the disciple. If one choses to abort what has been created, there is violence against the soul, forcing it from the womb of shelter, just as there is in disowning an accepted, "conceived," disciple. The fact that ancient Gaudiya scriptures do not say anything about when to reject an accepted disciple speaks strongly about the nature and dynamics of the guru-disciple relationship and especially about the extremely merciful nature of the guru. In fact, after the above verses, *Hari-bhakti-vilasa* 1.77 mentions that having accepted the prospective candidate, the guru has to "accept the accumulated sins of his disciple." This level of responsibility represents the exact opposite of the notion of a guru rejecting a student that she has already accepted. Srila Prabhupada clearly depicts this spirit in a letter written to his disciple Umapati, where he said that "any good soul who approaches me once for spiritual enlightenment is supposed to be depending on my responsibility to get him back to Krishna. ... A bona fide spiritual master *never lets go of a devotee once accepted.* When a disciple misunderstands a bona fide spiritual master, the master regrets for his inability to protect the disciple and sometimes he cries with tears in the eyes."[13] The mercy of Sri Guru is categorical—*it's irreversible grace.*

Although there are no scriptural statements to support the disowning of an accepted disciple, there is a section in the *Srimad Bhagavatam* which seems to do so. In verses 9.2.3–14 we hear about the story of Prishadhra, who was once appointed to protect a cow, but he killed it by accident. When hearing about this, his *kula-guru* (family priest) Vasistha became enraged and cursed Prishadhra to attain a lower birth in his next life. Prishadhra accepted the curse, deeply engaged in spiritual culture, and in the next lifetime attained God's supreme abode. While this section may seem to be an example of a guru rejecting a disciple, a few important points are to be considered: (a) Vasistha was Prishadhra's *family* guru, which does not bear the same level of commitment to the disciple's progress as does one's initiating or instructing gurus; (b) while Vasistha certainly cursed his disciple, it is not said that he rejected him; (c) even if we disregard the above two reasons and accept this as an example of rejection, Vasistha's curse was an exaggerated response and out of order, since Prishadhra's killing was unintentional. In fact, in his commentary on verse 9.2.9 Srila Prabhupada points out that since Vasistha was Prishadhra's guru, he should not have cursed his disciple but rather given him relief. Instead, he acted in an opposite manner and against his role as guru. Similarly, Visvanatha Chakravarti comments on this verse by pointing to how Vasistha's curse was "because his intelligence had disappeared, being subject to great ignorance." In this way, Visvanatha Chakravarti highlights how Vasistha cursed Prishadhra for the wrong reasons. Finally, (d) the fact that Prishadhra attained the ultimate goal of life despite being cursed/rejected by his guru shows that, if abandoned for the wrong reasons, a sincere disciple nonetheless continues to receive God's full shelter and mercy. His guru's misbehavior will not adversely affect him, and he will eventually be promoted to the supreme abode. It is noteworthy that in connection to this topic, the Gaudiya's main book shares only one example of a guru cursing his disciple, and that curse was for the wrong reasons. Therefore, the guru acted against what's expected from a teacher, and despite that (and even if that rejection is seen as valid), the rejected disciple attained the highest possible spiritual goal, which shows he was not rejected in any substantial sense. Therefore, the message is clear: *Srimad Bhagavatam* does not entertain the possibility of a guru disowning any of his own students.

In his *Harinama-chintamani* 6.43–47, Bhaktivinoda Thakura (according to some translations) seems to indicate that if the disciple becomes unqualified, then the guru must reject him and, if he does not do so, the guru will fall down. However, we should go to the original Bengali of Sri Bhaktivinoda's verses. When we do, we discover that he doesn't use the word *rejection* but rather the Bengali word *danda*, which translates as "chastisement." If the disciple is unqualified, then the guru will chastise him *lovingly*. This is very different from the inaccurate translations which basically depict the guru as being forced to reject his disciples so he himself does not fall down.

We also have the well-known instance of Madhavendra Puri dismissing Ramachandra Puri, who advised his guru to focus his mind on the impersonal Brahman as his guru was about to die while lamenting in divine separation. Disturbed, Madhavendra Puri asked Ramachandra Puri to leave his sight.[14] Although this exchange is often accepted as illustrating the rejection of a disciple, and is sometimes even offered as a precedent by which to judge more contemporary situations, it is interesting to note that the *Chaitanya-charitamrita* does not clearly speak of such as a rejection, and as the story unfolds it indicates that had there been a rejection it was only temporary. After this incident it is described that Sri Gaurahari showed respect to Ramachandra Puri by washing his feet and even considering him his guru, since he was a disciple of Madhavendra Puri. This implies that Gaurahari still considered Ramachandra to be Madhavendra's disciple. If some people maintain the opinion that Madhavendra Puri rejected his disciple, it should be concluded, nonetheless, that this was an exceptional and rare case: a disciple advising his Vaishnava guru to meditate on Brahman while dying! Due to the atypical grounds of the situation, it does not serve well as a generalized example of rejection, even if temporary, not to mention that it does not represent a case of the guru disowning and thus permanently disconnecting from his disciple. Such a disconnection is implausible due to the extremely merciful disposition of the guru. But even if we consider some slight prospect for a guru disowning his disciple, then the only possible conclusion is that in those cases the disciple must have done something horrific, or he must be a very evil person. And in that case, due to the extreme *guru-aparadha,* or offense to the guru, such a so-called disciple will most probably abandon the practice altogether, or will behave in horrible ways from that moment on, as a reaction coming from his dreadful misdeeds.[15] Although in these cases the guru may keep such wretched disciples at a healthy distance to avoid further disturbance in her community and followers, it would be surprising to hear that the guru, the very embodiment of the unconditional grace of the Sweet Absolute, fully abandoned those disciples.

Consequently, if for some reason a guru rejects or disowns a disciple, this does not mean that the disciple is guilty. Scrutiny should be applied to both sides to understand how justified the rejection was. The guru may have failed to act as a guru and rejected the disciple without cause. Then it is the guru who behaved improperly and committed a mistake. And if a guru rejects a disciple for the wrong reasons, then the guru could be rejected, though for the right reasons.

We may wonder about the position of the rejected disciple. If he was wrongly rejected, is he still connected with the mercy of

God and the Gaudiya disciplic succession? If the *vyasti* representative of the *samasti* agency rejects a disciple for the wrong reasons, then that in and of itself shows that the rejection did not come from the agency of *guru-tattva*, but from an individual who did not properly represent that agency, at least not when unjustly rejecting the disciple. Thus, the conclusion is that Sri Guru as a principle has not rejected the disciple, and therefore the disciple has not lost the shelter and guidance of Sri Guru, the fountainhead of the guru agency. This conclusion applies not only to a disciple who has been unjustly rejected, but also to a disciple who has abandoned his guru for the right reasons.

Despite the fact that the disciple may be temporarily without a guru in these cases, Sri Guru as a principle remains always present, so those disciples have not become bereft of a guru. From the moment anyone accepts God as the Ultimate Reality and sincerely seeks him, the Sweet Absolute will take the role of guru actively within that person's heart and inspire him where to seek. Thus this inner guru will eventually reveal the "outer" guru, who will appear in the form of one or more saintly personalities whenever that has to happen, *if that has to happen.* Why "if that has to happen"? Because in some cases God himself will take the main role as one's spiritual master, as the *Srimad Bhagavatam* confirms in some of its sections. One of those passages presents the sage Markandeya praying and addressing the Sweet Absolute as "the guru of the soul" (*atma-guroh*) in verse 12.8.44, as "the guru of all beings" (*akhila-guroh*) in verse 12.8.48, and as "the guru of all" (*gurave*) in verse 12.10.32. Similarly, in *Srimad Bhagavatam* 6.16.33 and 6.16.65, Sukadeva Goswami refers to the Supreme Lord as *jagad-guru*, "the spiritual master of the whole universe." Likewise, the seventh volume of this work refers to God as *loka guruna* or "the guru of all the universes" (7.4.29), as *akhila-guro* or "guru of all beings" (7.9.42 and 7.10.4), as *sarva-loka-gurum* or "guru of all the planets" (7.10.16). Even more emphatic are Satyavrata Muni's prayers in *Srimad Bhagavatam* 8.24.46–53. In most of these verses he addresses the Sweet Absolute not only as his guru, but as his supreme guru (*paramo gurur*, 8.24.46) and even as the supreme guru of all other gurus (*paramo guror guruh*, 8.24.48).[16] The unusual but plausible case of someone accepting God as his main guru is further confirmed by Srila Prabhupada in his commentary to these verses, where he says that "*either the Supreme Lord* or his representative can become guru" (8.24.50) and "the Lord, being situated in everyone's heart, can give one *complete instructions* on going back to Godhead" (8.24.52). In his commentary on the very last verse of this section, Srila Prabhupada further elaborates on this possibility:

> *Sometimes it is argued that people do not know who is a spiritual master and that finding a spiritual master from whom to get enlightenment in regard to the destination of life is very difficult. To answer all these questions, King Satyavrata shows us the way to accept the Supreme Personality of Godhead as the real spiritual master. The Supreme Lord has given full directions in* Bhagavad-gītā *about how to deal with everything in this material world and how to return home, back to Godhead. Therefore, one should not be misled by so-called gurus who are rascals and fools. Rather, one should directly see the Supreme Personality of Godhead as the guru or instructor.*[17]

The above points are not meant to cancel or diminish the principle and importance of the disciplic succession, but to highlight that some scenarios necessitate nuanced consideration, especially in unusual circumstances like the ones addressed in this section. Generally, a foundational point is clear: before considering an individual as our guru, we must first accept God himself as our guru. From that moment on, there will only be new manifestations of the same Supreme Guru coming to our lives. That same inexhaustible principle always is, was, and will be a single indivisible Absolute Truth (*akhanda-guru-tattva*) and not two, three, or four, and will appear in our lives according to the need of the moment. Despite the difficulty for those going through disorienting situations involving a guru, they must remember that Sri Guru continues to exist in his original and irrepressible form, and such agency will continue to make arrangements for every sincere aspirant so they continue advancing toward their goal. *The inner guru will not allow anyone to stop moving toward the goal, and the genuine seeker will not allow anything to stop him in his progress toward that goal.*

CODEPENDENCY VS. HEALTHY SURRENDER

Having addressed the possibility of abandoning one's guru or being rejected by her, we will address a different but equally damaging scenario: guru and disciple accept each other externally, but on an internal level they reject the very essence of their mutual relationship. While the natural currency of the guru-disciple relationship is healthy surrender, at times this may be replaced by unnatural codependency and similar dysfunctions that need to be ascertained so this sacred mutual bond can grow into all that it is meant to be. But before delving into *what it should not be*, let's share a few words about the ideal relationship between guru and disciple.

In brief, the guru-disciple relationship is one of trust, affection, and mutual service to an ideal that eternally lies above the heads of both: divine love. In one sense, *both guru and disciple are disciples.* Not only are they disciples of their own respective gurus, but also servants of one ideal. In this sense, *to be a guru means to remain a disciple but from a different seat.* A genuine guru is so fully a disciple that even in some cases she won't hesitate to hear and learn from her own disciples, as exemplified by Vyasa, who was absorbed in receiving Sukadeva's discourse of the *Srimad Bhagavatam.* While it was Vyasa who originally taught the *Srimad Bhagavatam* to Sukadeva, the guru was humble enough to acknowledge that now it was his turn to relearn that book from his disciple. Since the nature of sacred scripture is that it's "never the same," Vyasa is thus setting the ideal example and official blueprint of how a guru should remain in a perpetual teachable moment.

For Gaudiya Vaishnavas and Hindus in general, Vyasa is the very prototype of the guru figure. Guru Purnima, the famous "guru day" on the Hindu calendar, is the celebration of Vyasa's appearance day. As the original archetype of the spiritual teacher, Vyasa sets a clear precedent of how an ideal guru should behave: (a) not only being humble enough to acknowledge his shortcomings and remaining open to further education and upgrade (as he did when feeling dissatisfied with his authoring various scriptures before the final version of

Srimad Bhagavatam), but also (b) being willing to learn from his own disciple Sukadeva, thus showing that the guru-disciple relationship is not one in which only the disciple needs the guru, but the guru also needs the disciple. It is a mutual exchange where they need and support each other in order to perform their respective functions.

Without a disciple, one cannot officiate as a guru. In an even deeper sense, the guru needs the disciple in order to learn from him, just as the disciple needs and learns from his guru in his own way. They learn from each other and *need* each other. Therefore, the ideal guru-disciple relationship is not so much a hierarchical, monarchical, or pyramidal relationship, but the result of a circular (or even spiral) collaboration, where the sharing and nourishing are always mutual and never unidirectional, flowing in every possible direction. In the highest sense and ideal situation, *both guru and disciple will be guru, and both will remain as disciples* simultaneously. The words *guru* and *disciple* merge into each other till they become synonymous. Just as we souls cannot and *do not* exist outside of a mutually informing relationship with our environment, the guru and the disciple *exist within each other* in their relationship and thereby mutually inform the presence of the other.

In the words of Rupa Goswami, the ideal mood to be cultivated once a relationship with one's guru has been formalized through initiation is that of *visrambhena guroh seva*, or serving one's guru with friendly confidence.[18] As the relationship with one's father ideally develops into a unique type of friendship (while he nonetheless remains one's father), the bond with one's guru should progress similarly, with each part serving the development of the relationship and reciprocating accordingly. There ought to be a 50-50 equation, in the sense that both sides should be investing one hundred percent of themselves. They will spend considerable time together to get to know each other. The disciple's duty is to be utterly raw and vulnerable in front of his guru, willing to open his heart and surrender. The duty of a genuine guru is to acknowledge, honor, and nourish such vulnerability, filling that open heart with shelter, clarity, and abundant affection and learning from such a process. In fact, not only will both guru and disciple be learning from each other, but if the guru is more advanced than her disciple, as she should be, then by the strength of her greater advancement *she will be learning more from the disciple than the disciple is from her*. The more advanced you are, the greater capacity you have to learn from everyone, including your disciples. As we already mentioned, proper vulnerability opens the door for deep empowerment, and this pattern won't be an exception in the guru-disciple relationship. When they are vulnerably open to each other, each is enthused by the other in corresponding forms of empowerment.

As Sri Krishna shows in *Bhagavad-gita* 18.72, the guru should be prepared to explain the spiritual reality to her disciple until he has fully understood, even if this involves repeating her instructions again and again. Correspondingly, the disciple has the right and duty to vulnerably expose himself with all his doubts and reasonable needs, and the guru has the duty to nourish and guide him in that process. In fact, a few verses earlier (18.63), the *Gita* employs the word *asesena* ("endlessly") to depict how comprehensive the disciple's inquiry and corresponding vulnerability should be. Ideally, the guru is to recognize what stage (or state) her disciple is operating from. From there she will reflect back to them an understanding of this, and then help her students relate in a healthy way to that unfolding of their hearts. In fact, a guru is someone who listens *with* her students to *what God is asking them to do*, and not someone who merely tells them what to do. A guru should not usurp her disciples' destiny by making their problems her own, but should ideally hear, accompany, and nourish her disciples. However, if a guru cannot appreciate the disciple's vulnerability and therefore does not know what to do with it, that same portal to empowerment can suddenly turn into a portal for abuse and exploitation, even without the guru's intention to do so. Just not knowing what to do with another's vulnerability can be dreadful. Sometimes observable patterns can be detected. Gurus who have not allowed themselves to have deep, close relationships and intimate friendships are often the same people who may end up trampling one's vulnerability, something that can be rightfully deemed abuse of power. To put it bluntly, if a guru does not know how to deal with her student's vulnerability, she should probably not be serving as a guru.

While the duty of a disciple is to surrender and be vulnerable, for this template to be healthy requires autonomy, voluntary acceptance, and freedom. Without these, the disciple may artificially force surrender or enter patterns of codependency, rather than give one's heart naturally. In the codependent template, we give ourselves to someone else but only with the intention that such a person fills a void we want them to fill. Externally it seems like surrender, but internally we are actually exploiting that person. This template often includes the idea "I need you to need me." While a guru can easily fall prey to this, a disciple can also become toxically codependent on his guru in a similar way. One classical example in this connection is unacknowledged parent/child transference issues, in which a disciple still endeavors to appease a guru who may be punitive and even violent. This is especially possible if the disciple had an angry or abusive parent. As shocking as it may seem to some, many of us submit to this kind of template because it fits our own story line.[19] Therefore, whether it is this or any other form of unresolved trauma, both guru and disciple should remain on guard against these fake versions of actual surrender.

Codependency usually disguises itself behind the mask of obedience. While *obedience* is not by definition harmful, we may embrace it through a codependent template. We may not know why we should be obedient in a particular situation, but, having the need to perhaps feel different and special, we try to satisfy this need through obedience to our guru. Also, being social creatures and deeply concerned about the tribe's opinion of us, we may be extremely vigilant for any sign of social rejection or disapproval from our tribe, and be willing to sacrifice everything—even our integrity—to fit in. Conversely, Srila Prabhupada said that he wanted his disciples to become "independently thoughtful people." That's the quality of surrender and obedience we Gaudiyas want to gradually attain. While a novice may understandably use a codependent template in the beginning, the guru, who ideally should not be a novice herself, should detect this pattern and know how to deal with the disciple's initial codependency, guiding him into full-fledged maturity and freedom. However, if a guru allows or even promotes codependency in her students, then she herself is a victim of codependency. This creates a dangerous pattern where guru and disciple will be cheating and exploiting each other. Although externally it may all look like spotless surrender, they will knowingly or unknowingly be using the form of surrender to avoid the substance of surrender.

Another display of codependency occurs when gurus have an emotional dependency on some disciples. The emotionally dependent person does not take full responsibility for their own feelings, especially those considered negative. Although they have emotions like sadness, anger, fear, disgust, happiness, they don't accept or nurture these feelings. Denying their emotions makes it impossible to embrace their own emotional fulfillment so they turn to others for the fulfillment of their emotional needs. They often feel isolated and develop a strong need for approval from others. Because this pattern of behavior does not describe the ideal behavior of a guru, oftentimes a guru is not willing to admit their condition but rather try to hide their codependency from others (as well as themselves) by criticizing others' emotions and even emotional expressions altogether. Or we find disciples who "surrender" as a way of not taking responsibility for themselves. "I have surrendered myself, and my guru is taking full responsibility for me." Therefore, if the disciple happens to do something wrong, his reply will be, "I just did what my guru told me!" In other words, if I "surrendered" to my guru, then my failure is no longer mine but belongs to my authority; I am not the one who needs to change. Unfortunately, many of us are still terrified of freedom, desperately wanting authority figures to tell us what to do, so we don't have to hold ourselves accountable for our actions. But this is codependency and not healthy discipleship. Any guru system built on and fostered by codependency is destined to collapse because *every codependent relationship is destined to collapse.*

SPIRITUAL BYPASSING IN THE GURU-DISCIPLE RELATIONSHIP

The most sacred bond between teacher and student runs the risk of not only becoming a codependent one, but also of showing endless distorted alternatives. This goes deeply against the very substance of Radical Personalism, which promotes transparent and committed interactions, especially between the guru and disciple. If not properly taken care of, this most crucial aspect of Krishna consciousness (another name for Gaudiya Vaishnavism) can easily devolve into what we may call "celebrity consciousness." This spiritual bypassing happens when followers focus more on the external features of a spiritual leader than on his spirituality. These external features may include reputation, charisma, nationality, opulence, material talents, a large following, material education, or institutional position. Such spiritual leaders become more like pop stars than saints to their acolytes, who are usually starry-eyed neophytes. Focusing on externals in this way tends not only to keep our faith nourished for the wrong reasons, but also breeds neglect of and disregard for practitioners who are noncelebrities. Another negative result is that a celebrity leader cares little for anyone other than his own followers or potential followers, and the followers care little for anyone other than their celebrity leader—a situation that gets closer and closer to a cult scenario.[20] And these are just a few of the harmful aspects of this template.

What do you call it when a guru (or anyone) needs people for his own ego and advantage, and the people need the leader for their own ego and advantage? The best word we may find to describe such interactions is *narcissist*, a word that can describe the phenomenon of celebrity consciousness. In fact, every guru should be aware that many codependent people will probably approach him, and if he doesn't deal with them properly, he may end up becoming a narcissistic person, which is the "perfect" fit for the codependent model. Even if a guru is advanced on some level and has followers who serve him due to his inner standing, these very gifts that attract people to him and to his teachings may subtly and insidiously incline the guru toward a glamorous self-image. In fact, it is precisely because of his spiritual attainments that the temptation arises to identify with the role of wonderworker, enlightened teacher, martyr, or charismatic leader—in short, as God's gift to humanity.

Another related drawback is that a guru can become addicted to the adoration of his followers. He may even see that adoration as a sign of his own spiritual advancement and even promote it as the standard. Trapped in this pattern of spiritual bypassing, such a guru ends up seeing no reason to strive and dive deeper in spiritual life, and he becomes proud, complacent, and even over-demanding. At this point we should be reminded that guru is not a position, but a *seva* (service) one is offering to others. As the Sweet Absolute never assumes to own anybody, although he has all the right to claim so, in the same way the guru, God's representative, should relate to his disciples from a position of serving them, *not owning them*. He must not demand or even expect them to worship him or have faith in him, but to have faith *in the ideal* the guru should be representing. In this way a genuine guru will command respect by his example but will never *demand* respect. If both guru and disciple are not attentive to these important features of their relationship, the celebrity consciousness template can easily degrade further into something cultish, and then into something authoritarian.

Members of a cult are always self-referring. For them, there is no need to learn anything from anyone outside of the group's boundaries. Everything is contained there with the most perfect revelation in every single aspect one could conceive. Interestingly, almost every cult starts out innocent and genuine, but ends up cultish as spiritual potential is bypassed again and again in favor of exploitation. Similarly, while Gaudiya Vaishnavism is not a cult, it can be represented and conceived in extremely cultish ways. In Gaudiya terms, these deviations are generally called *apasampradayic*. They are not only doctrinal deviations, but *deviations from the ideal character* expressed in the doctrine as well. In fact, one cultish *apasampradayic* expression of the Gaudiya tradition is the above-mentioned self-referent adherence. This is a toxic over-identification with one's own tradition to the point of not being able to appreciate anything beyond it. This cultism over-separates the tradition, embodying a tightly encapsulated and self-obsessed *us*, with the rest of the world becoming a rather distant *them*. Followers of any cult, however benign it may seem, tend to dissolve too much of their identity into group-think without maintaining a robust sense of discerning individuality, while the hierarchical side of the group grows exponentially. The range of this cultic behavior is enormous. Our own false ego can arguably be seen as a cult of one, plenty of couples function as cults of two (including a toxic guru-disciple relationship), and various religious and political movements are cults of the many.[21] Where do we in our Gaudiya community stand today in relation to this?

From this slippery slope of cultish mentality, it is a short descent to a different but related scenario—authoritarianism or, more specifically, "authoritarian religion."[22] In authoritarian religion, the subjective experience of the participants is that of subordinating themselves to a higher power in obedience, reverence, and worship. This surrender is not in response to the moral quality of the authority or the love and justice the authority displays, but rather is due to the simple reason that the authority holds power over them. In this system, *the foremost sin is disobedience.* In authoritarian religious systems, the position of the leader is over-emphasized and the individuals diminish themselves, becoming deprived, empty, and poor, qualities that lead to further alienation from themselves. They naturally intensify their supplication and "surrender" to their leader and thus feel more deprived, empty, and poor. In other words, a cycle is set in motion. Fear and despair are followed by worship and supplication, back and forth, round and round, leading to nothing more than a variety of neurotic symptoms. In fact, this is why after undergoing disciplines like psychoanalysis, many people who experienced authoritarian dynamics in their religion quit the religion. That was not because psychoanalysis set them at odds with religion, but because they came to realize that authoritarian religion had an unhealthy grip on them. Instead of empowering them to deal with the world, the unhealthy system reduced them to fear and trembling, causing them to shrink away from the world and themselves.

This vicious circle of celebrity consciousness, cultism, and authoritarianism will continue until checked by the healthy skepticism of spiritual and critical faculties beneficially coexisting in what Erich Fromm calls "humanitarian religion," or, in our own terms, Radical Personalism. It is a stance where we become unexploitable and empowered, instead of disempowered and abused. While the various forms of spiritual bypassing are different faces of impersonalism, Radical Personalism seeks to instill individuation and the attainment of one's full sense of being, both as gurus and disciples. As the disciple endures, the guru is also expected to endure and reciprocate accordingly. Considering that Sri Krishna, the Gaudiya's Sweet

Absolute, unconditionally adapts himself to each of his devotees, so does Sri Guru—Krishna's direct representative—willingly adapt himself to the necessities of the disciple. Ideally, guru-disciple is a bond made of the deepest love, and love transforms both parties. Therefore, both guru and disciple are expected to embrace this sacred transformation that love is all about. *For the rest of forever.*

12 Divine Ignorance: Knowing through Darkness, Doubt, and Paradox

God does not offer himself to our finite beings as a thing all complete and ready to be embraced. For us, he is eternal discovery and eternal growth. The more we think we understand him, the more he reveals himself as otherwise. The more we think we hold him, the further he withdraws, drawing us into the depths of himself.

—Pierre Teilhard de Chardin

WE HAVE BEEN DISCUSSING the ideas of vulnerability, individuation, nondual thinking, and the relationship between guru and disciple, all of which intertwine with one another and will continue to interface with the subsequent facets of Radical Personalism as we come to learn the essential aspects of our Radical Syllabus. Let's now allow these different facets of Radical Personalism to overflow and converge in the present chapter and express themselves from the perspective of "divine ignorance," or the capacity to embrace uncertainty, coexist with mystery, and be nourished by what we don't know. For us to embrace such an experience, we surely require a deep recognition of our vulnerability (which goes hand in hand with uncertainty). Similarly, any mature individuation process will blossom and thrive only after we allow doubt and paradox to shape it. Likewise, nondual thinking will prove a foundational bedrock while we face these two intrinsic features of nondual reality and then properly integrate them. Finally, while the guru is the personified emblem of sacred knowledge, a crucial aspect of imparting knowledge will involve the principle of knowing through unknowing, another trait of divine ignorance. Therefore, we turn to this pivotal feature of spiritual life by addressing it with a variety of terms and perspectives. We do this with the aim that we can be accurately stricken and deeply affected by at least one of these different approaches. *Hopefully by all.*

THE REAL GOAL IS SACRED UNCERTAINTY, NOT SHALLOW CERTITUDE

As mentioned in the previous chapter, the role of a guru is to remain considerably outside of his comfort zone. From there, he will be expected to gradually make his disciples inhabitants of such a land, through both precept and example. In fact, a crucial aspect of the guru's instruction will consist of teaching his students how to embrace darkness, mystery, and uncertainty, so they can balance whatever they have received and learned from their teacher. While the guru typically gives clear, authoritative answers, sometimes he will also have to invoke new "higher" doubts in the minds of his disciples. We could call this *holy uncertainty*. The guru will do so not by giving predictable answers but by offering *newly discovered questions* to create a "sacred disturbance." Through that, he will show his students that the nature of the spiritual odyssey is unlimited and thus something they should be very careful not to take for granted. In this connection, we need to be utterly clear about a very important point: *what may disturb someone's faith will nourish someone else's*. Is the disturbed (or disturbing) one wrong? Not necessarily. Is the inspired (or inspiring) one wrong then? Not necessarily. It is what it is. That said, while each of us can (and should) be inspired (and even disturbed!) for the right reasons, there is also the chance of being equally affected for the wrong reasons. And we should be careful about this latter possibility.

When our current beliefs are challenged (even for the right reasons), many of us may react in a defensive mode, through the lens of what's generally known as *cognitive dissonance*. This is basically a mental conflict which occurs when new information contradicts one's beliefs. The conflict activates areas of our brain involved in personal identity and emotional response to threats. When we feel threatened, our brain's alarms go off, causing us to shut down and disregard any rational evidence that contradicts what we previously regarded as truth. The possibility of this challenge occurring is why the relationship between guru and disciple must be based on deep trust and affection. Without this, we could feel that the guru's sacred disturbance may be about to kill us. However, with proper trust in place, this disturbance will be understood for what it is: a nourishing of our faith through the creation of new layers of uncertainty. This keeps the disciple in a permanent state of wonder, humility, and sincere ongoing inquiry. Since reality is a never-ending pattern of constant unfolding and evolution, we should never be too sure about what we already know and understand. Probably more importantly, we should never consider what we know as fixed, frozen, and static. *What in the morning was true will at evening have become a lie.*[1]

In opposition to this ideal template of ongoing epiphany and intimation, many of us choose to worship workability and predictability. As disciples, we probably love to receive answers *but not questions.* Similarly some spiritual teachers may like to share their opinions instead of loving the questions. Unfortunately, they sometimes get used to giving "perfect" answers to every single question. This takes away the natural humility all of us should retain in the presence of an infinite subject. In fact, more often than not we end up creating unnatural circumstances where we believe we have an absolute right to certitude, or *circumstances where there is no vulnerability left.* But a faith without vulnerability becomes basically useless. In fact, such so-called faith will be just another way of keeping the false ego in control, but now in the disguise of being anointed. Those who indulge in such scenarios are mostly obsessed with the idea of "closure"—even in the name of disclosure—while thinking they are people of faith. In those pitiful cases, "I have faith" will be another way of saying "I am right." Accordingly, we need to clearly distinguish between a shallow believer and a person of actual faith, as Alan W. Watts did in *The Wisdom of Insecurity*:

> *The believer will open his mind to the truth on the condition that it fits in with his preconceived ideas and wishes. Faith, on the other hand, is an unreserved opening of the mind to the truth, whatever it may turn out to be. Faith has no preconceptions; it is a plunge into the unknown. Belief clings, but faith lets go. In this sense of the word, faith is the essential virtue of science, and likewise of any religion that is not self-deception.*[2]

In the spirit of the above quote, true faith and genuine wisdom could be defined as *a constant openness to different layers of uncertainty.* The more perfect faith is, the darker it becomes.[3] Actual wisdom and faith are not satisfied with merely citing traditional explanations from a place of certainty and excessive security, *but actively distill ultimate meaning from unknown lands.*[4] By contrast, a shallow believer will quickly run away from all forms of uncertainty. In our Gaudiya tradition, that means taking Gaudiya Vaishnavism for granted. Someone can go through an initial spiritual honeymoon of awe and wonder but gradually get accustomed to the extraordinary. Such a person ends up becoming stagnated in the status quo of predictable formulas instead of cultivating a permanent sense of *chamatkara*, or sacred astonishment, which will keep us in a constant state of transformation and evolution. Actually, not only Gaudiya Vaishnavism, but every relationship we have requires the above dynamics to thrive *and even survive.* And our relationship with the Sweet Absolute is not an exception to this rule. There is a richness and a complexity in reality that is completely inexhaustible. Again, Gaudiya Vaishnavism is not an exception to this rule. In fact, for us Gaudiyas the nature of our tradition *is the very essence* of that rule. To put it in other words, *that rule is the essence of our tradition.* Instead of an overdose of certainty and toxic assertiveness, we should remain aware of an inexhaustible excavation of essential truths. The first is utopia, the second is reality.

Generally, utopian visions of reality are profoundly inhuman. Unfortunately, we may adopt a utopian view to conceive of our spiritual goals and practice so that we have a one-hundred-percent static certitude instead of an optimal amount of uncertainty. However, essential Gaudiya Vaishnavism has nothing to do with any form of utopia. There is no place where everything is absolutely perfect and certain and everything runs on schedule with no interferences. As a matter of fact, a utopia, by its very definition, can never exist.

The ultimate goal for Gaudiyas is something real and existent and also in a constant state of eternal becoming. In addition, such eternal becoming and ultimate goal allows for imperfection and, on top of that, is deeply nourished by it! All of this is utterly possible, since the ultimate goal of the Gaudiyas is totally ruled by love's crooked movement,[5] which by its very unpredictable nature requires sacred uncertainty daily and eternally. In other words, our final destiny as Gaudiya Vaishnavas involves being comfortable with *not* knowing (eternally!), rather than being certain about everything. *To imagine that our ultimate destiny is fully conceivable constitutes our final ignorance.*

Sad to say, many of us have erected an understanding of our tradition solely on the principle of certainty. With such a detailed description of transcendence and our charming post-liberated prospect, we have sometimes ended up feeling very sure *about almost everything*, with little place left for uncertainty and mystery. If, in time, holy doubt doesn't refine our mulish certitudes, we tend to become arrogant, rigid, and finally fundamentalistic—we end up loving our explanations and ideas of God rather than *falling in love with God*. But we should remember that knowing *about* God is not the same as knowing God. The former belongs to the realm of mere theory, while the latter implies actual loving and personal conversion. It is reality that converts us, not ideas. And a further conversion should always be welcome. In Latin this ideal state is known as *in statu nascendi*. Instead of boxing things into concepts within a fixed philosophical system, this ideal favors an open attitude that lets things appear upon the horizon of one's perception in relation to an ever-evolving *living* Absolute. Conversely, one may convincingly speak about reality (even Ultimate Reality) as "so and so." But most of those words, even if unknowingly, will be conceptual entrapment for both the person who utters the words as well as for those who choose to believe in them. As Mark Twain once said, "It ain't what you don't know that gets you into trouble. *It's what you know for sure that just ain't so.*"[6]

FIRST LEARN IGNORANCE, THEN ATTAIN WISDOM

Without a doubt, the Sweet Absolute is both loving and beautiful, but he is also equally unknown and unknowable. And while the "Gaudiya certainty side" may be confident enough to declare that God is never an old man with a white beard on a cloud, but a young blue boy playing a bamboo flute, that blue boy we Gaudiyas know in so much detail still remains, for the most part, unknown and unknowable. While our bluish Absolute appears as a sweet flute-player, he is not *only* that—he is not only what we may think he is. That same bluish Absolute, Sri Krishna, establishes his own inscrutability in verses like *Bhagavad-gita* 7.26, where he describes how he knows everyone and everything (past, present, and future) "but me no one knows." Similarly, in *Bhagavad-gita* 10.15 Arjuna tells the Sweet Absolute, "Only you can know yourself, by your own divine potency."[7] Furthermore, the wise Bhisma soundly declared, "No one can know the plan of the Lord. Even though great philosophers inquire exhaustively, they are bewildered."[8] Additionally, one of the Sweet Absolute's names, Adhoksaja, also bears witness that he is unknowable as this means, *that which transcends the limits of sense perception or sensual experience.*

Essential Gaudiya Vaishnavism agrees with this premise, but despite that, the abundance of revelation about God's intimate life can prove not only an obvious blessing but also a serious curse. How? Well, we may easily convince ourselves that we already know the Infinite, while we will always be ignoring much more than what we can possibly know about him (remember, our subject is Infinity itself!). This statement does not constitute any type of anti-knowledge campaign, but its opposite. By properly embracing uncertainty, *only then* are we able to know unlimitedly. By remaining addicted to certainty, however, our span of knowing becomes more and more restricted. The very nature of Ultimate Reality is both undeniable and inconceivable—*too self-evident to doubt, too deep to comprehend.* While we cannot deny the obvious presence of the Absolute, neither can we ever fully apprehend that presence. Far from being a problem, this should be our greatest of hopes, since such a state of constant incomprehensibleness will indefinitely keep us in a perpetual mood of astonishment and rediscovery. We will be *students forever*.

This so-called ignorance is an absolute precondition for wisdom. *First we must learn to be fools, and then we can become wise.*[9] Or, in Socratic terminology, "All I know is that I know nothing." In fact, it takes a lot of learning to finally "learn ignorance."[10] This is known in Latin as *docta ignorantia*, or that moment when learning understands its own limit, especially when facing Infinity. Since absolute uncertainty may lead to paranoia, we certainly need some degree of certitude and knowledge. We similarly need to remind ourselves that in relation to Ultimate Reality there is never a limit to how much progress we can make. We should therefore always remain open to further evolution, allowing uncertainty to put our certitudes in their proper place—to humble them one after another. Infinity and its corresponding uncertainty exist not only in the religious realm, but even in the secular domain. In connection to the latter, ever since 1927, when the German physicist Werner Heisenberg formulated the principle of uncertainty, the existence and implications of uncertainty have been studied in the fields of quantum and classical physics as well as mathematics. An article published by CalTech explains, "A common misconception about the uncertainty principle in quantum physics is that it implies our measurements are uncertain or inaccurate. In fact, uncertainty is an inherent aspect of anything with wave-like behavior."[11] And since the Sweet Absolute is always expanding, wave after wave, we will never be able to be fully certain of his glories. It is not merely the instruments of knowing that create uncertainty, but the inherent nature of what we think is knowable. Looking at uncertainty and the unknowable from the lens of cognitive and social psychology, Jamie Holmes writes in *Nonsense: The Power of Not Knowing*, "In an increasingly unpredictable, complex world, it turns out that what matters most isn't IQ, willpower, or confidence in what we know. It's how we deal with what we don't understand."[12] For most, the capacity to deal with the unknown will verily represent a new layer of our "survival of the fittest" paradigm. And it is a type of fitness we may urgently need to invoke.

As enticing as the above proposal may sound to some, for most of us it may feel threatening and terrifying. Why? If knowledge is power, then certainty practically makes us a god. We generally love to be in full control of our lives, thinking that the more control we have then the more likely we will get what we want. And anything that can secure our control over the various aspects of our lives is considered an ally. Take a quick mental inventory of the numerous companies that are in the business of securing our control over the data and private resources in our lives. By definition, there is no certainty in mystery; we are totally out of control of the elements. And for most of us, that lack of security is terrifying. So how do we deal with that? In the wise words of Martin Luther King Jr., "Most people's loyalties are with security, public image, and the comforts of the status quo." We seek tribe validation, tribe narrative, and tribalism—but not in a healthy tribe. Instead of a deeply committed faith, we have an absolute fear of losing these so-called perks. While we may externally show an apparent strong faith and absolute certainty, the underlying foundation of that "faith" is total unwillingness to leave behind our explored territory and comfort zone. This abundance of inner fear adopts the guise of extreme certainty, which *is supposed* to be its opposite. In practice, however, certainty and fear are synonymous. They are both a façade of strong faith, usually invoked to conceal our lack of courage. Therefore, if this inner fear is closely tied to the expression of certainty, and if fear is generally understood as the very opposite of faith, we could then conclude that *the opposite of faith is certainty*. Let's next unpack this paradox.

CERTAINTY AS THE ANTITHESIS OF FAITH

The opposite of faith is certainty. Why? To excessively insist on being certain about everything has little or nothing to do with the sacred realm of faith. That realm is deeply tied to and nourished by mystery, darkness, and, yes, uncertainty. As a matter of fact, doubt, uncertainty, and unknowing are all crucial rooms to visit in our inner faith journey. Only a person truly blessed by Sraddha Devi (the very Deity of faith) will be able to follow the traces of doubt. *Deep doubts and complete faith always belong together*. In fact, one thing we can be absolutely sure of in our faith pilgrimage is that whatever we are expecting to happen *will not happen*—at least not exactly like we expect. If we think things are going to proceed according to our understanding (our certainty), then for our benefit the Sweet Absolute will reverse the normal order through uncertainty. Therefore, since a deep mature faith is destined to progress through the winds of sacred doubt and uncertainty, it is no exaggeration to conclude that doubt and faith are correlative terms. We cannot have one without the other.

In *Bhagavad-gita* 4.40, however, Sri Krishna seems to contradict the above notion by saying, "For those who doubt, there is no happiness either in this world or in the next." This apparent clash is quickly resolved by understanding the context of this statement. There, Sri Krishna is talking about those who doubt the content of revealed scripture and, by extension, express unhealthy and skeptical doubting. They doubt for the sake of doubting. Krishna's words here are directed only to them. His words are not for those in whom uncertainty plays a sacred role of nourishing one's *abhisara*, or love journey, toward the Absolute. As we will see in the last chapter of this third part, the *gopis* (cowherd girls of Vraja) are a perfect example of how *abhisara* expresses itself in the context of abundant uncertainty. While the *gopis* are certain they love Krishna, it is not fully clear to them if they will meet him in the dead of night despite being called by his divine flute. Regardless, these young girls not only risk everything for the sake of their ideal but also *integrate* everything as a part of their love journey, even allowing uncertainty to nourish their passionate longing. The *gopis* did not want to understand Krishna, but to simply love him. We want to love God so much that the very idea of him being God could not enter our hearts! As these divine maidens show, knowing God requires loving God. There is no other way to know him. As stated in *The Cloud of Unknowing*, "I'm willing to abandon everything I know, to love the one thing I cannot think [God]. He can be loved, but not thought."[13]

Among other qualities, the Vraja *gopis* exemplify the perfection of what's known as *jnana-sunya-bhakti*, literally "love devoid of knowledge." It is a love so enthralling that the very idea of knowing God as God will be left behind, so we can know him for *who he actually is in sacred intimacy*. The opposite of this is our narrow tribal narratives, unending fears, and insecurities (all of them usually taking the shape of certainty). In those cases, we undo our spiritual project by a total unwillingness to be exposed to any form of uncertainty and unknowing. *But it is there that the majority of the mystery of God lies*. This most valuable lesson is given by the *gopis'* running into the darkness and fully embracing uncertainty. They rush into that mystery without thinking twice (or even once!) about it. As a result, they attain the highest form of knowing, divine love. As counterintuitive and paradoxical as this may sound, we shouldn't forget that uncertainty and doubt, which inform and illuminate our faith journey, are how sacred things are understood. In fact, if we find the path before us totally clear and certain, then we are probably on someone else's path. Watch out for the sandpit of certitude.

ADDICTION TO CERTITUDE = COMPETITION WITH GOD

Unfortunately, due to practitioners' misplaced fears, one of the major heresies played out in our Gaudiya community (and every other tradition as well) is that we have largely turned the very meaning of faith into its exact opposite—an obsessed quest for absolute certainty and security. True faith, however, involves not knowing and even not needing to know. But so often we turn faith into a demanding to know and an insisting that we do know! Especially for us Westerners, this addiction to certitude can be traced back to the Enlightenment. Despite giving us important contributions such as science and medicine, it also apparently gave us a right we don't and can't deserve: the right to know it all. But from a more universal perspective, we could say that this goes back in time even before the Enlightenment. Christianity locates this classic temptation to replace faith with knowledge at the very genesis of their creation myth and as the source of original sin. In this well-known scenario, Adam and Eve are both warned about the allurement and seduction of knowing, as well as its concomitant factors, which are certitude and a potential addiction to it. Religion is not meant to give us certitude, but rather patience with mystery.

Addiction to certainty is tantamount to competing with God, because it means that the underlying principle of our quest for certitude is not so much a sincere inquiry for truth and love, but a desire for control and power. This desire runs closer and closer to the desire for omniscience and omnipotence. While we offer lip-service to our spirituality and present ourselves as devotees of God, behind our lip-curtain we may be indulging in a poor form of God-playing. The modern educator Parker Palmer named this *functional atheism*. To put it bluntly, it is where we pretend-play theism while exhibiting a practical daily atheism by our example. We do this by trying to replace God by aspiring for absolute certitude. If truth be told, many of us are still control freaks (even in relation to the Supreme Controller!). Hence part of our Gaudiya notion of surrender should be directed at allowing sacred uncertainty to nourish our faith, and not insisting upon perfect and absolute answers. We should be willing to coexist with unresolved questions, being patient toward what is still unresolved in our hearts. In other words, we should seek to love the questions themselves, to *fall in love* with them (a bona fide "falling" for Gaudiyas). Perhaps we will then gradually, without even noticing it, live into the required answers.[14] In other words, *we get our answers by first loving our questions*. However, questions are typically seen as mere bridges to the answers we so much cherish—bridges to be crossed as soon as possible. But why not see this relationship otherwise? Why not see answers as *bridges which take us to further questions*? In fact, we get a deeper certainty by loving uncertainty. In this regard Richard Feynman once said, "I'd rather have questions that can't be answered than answers that can't be questioned." While the first is healthy faith, the second borders on totalitarianism. *A question is always more interesting than an opinion*, right?

The journey of doubt through uncertainty and perplexity involves questioning not so much specific beliefs, but the whole belief system's approach to faith at certain stages. In other words, *how* do we believe in what we believe? By questioning like this we won't be doubting the realness of our tradition, but rather questioning how realistic our current approach to it is, and how much our process may need to be upgraded by holy uncertainty. This will allow us to go from a two-dimensional faith to one that is much more nuanced, vibrant, textured, and sustainable.[15] By contrast, the totalitarian inner (or outer) voice may retort, "You must rely on faith in what you already know." But the point is that this is not what saves us. *What saves is the willingness to learn from what we don't know.* That is faith in the possibility of human transformation; that is faith in the sacrifice of our current self for the self that we could be.[16] While we are already something, we can become something else in terms of our potential, and we shouldn't sacrifice all that we can be for who we are. But as we will see, the very idea of potential, which is the realm of possibility, is always tied to the domain of the unknown and the principle of uncertainty. So it is up to us to learn how to embrace it with courage. *Uncertainty is never a torture chamber but always a breakthrough portal.*

KNOWING THROUGH UNKNOWING

Another way to speak about divine ignorance, holy uncertainty, and sacred doubt is through the notion of unknowing in order to know, or unlearning in order to learn. A classic Gaudiya example of the latter comes from Bhaktisiddhanta Saraswati Thakura, who once wrote to his disciple Sadananda Swami, "The first thing you have to do is to collect all what you learned, read, excerpted, felt, know. Put it in a big bag and throw it into the sea where the sea is deepest, and start anew."[17] This learning through unlearning is similar to the method of *epoché* found in Hellenistic philosophy and generally translated as "suspension of judgment" or "withholding of assent." We should not be so sure about what we know. And especially in relation to the Sweet Absolute, we should first unlearn and set aside what we assume to know in order to achieve a radical openness to receive not more of the same, but something *radically* new.

While our list of certitudes may still prove useful in the relative realm, we should understand that the Divine does not necessarily respond to those same laws and to how we think everything works. To talk about the Absolute implies entering a whole different category and space, one that requires a whole new language and method. Therefore, to know God we have to first *unknow* God. We need to again and again shed our neat conceptions of the Divine as if they were old snakeskins, and then emerge into the world bare, vulnerable, and new. God and love's true nature *remain forever beyond the grasp of all our faculties.* A proper Gaudiya humility should be expressed accordingly in this regard. In early Christianity, St. Augustine expressed this same thing in his own words: "*If you understand it, then it is not God.*" In regard to Infinity, this is the basic stance to adopt. If you can fully explain it, then it's not true. The idea here is that ultimately *reality is not figurable*. It's prejudice to think it is. Descartes said, "I think, therefore I am." But when we consider the Sweet Absolute and the principle of divine ignorance, we will say, "I think, therefore I am *not*." So let's try to be okay with not knowing everything and not being in control. At the same time, we can know that someone else is doing that job perfectly.

In Western terms, knowing-by-not-knowing is also known as *apophasis* (or *via negativa*). An apophatic approach to God literally means "to not say" or "to un-say" God. In complement to this, the cataphatic method (also known as *via positiva*) is employed to positively express God's identity. Since we Gaudiyas possess a lot of "cataphatic content" in the form of abundant details about who God is, we should therefore be very careful about balancing it with a proportionate dose of the "apophatic trinity" of humility, darkness, and silence.[18] The Sweet Absolute is not only "that" (whatever "that" may be for us) but always much more. And this applies not only to the Divine but even to us in relation to our own potential. When describing the attributes of the soul in the *Bhagavad-gita*, Sri Krishna first resorts to the apophatic method by repeatedly saying what the soul is *not*. After this, when the time comes for the Sweet Absolute to say something about who we actually *are*, he can only use the same word three times: *ascharya*, or "amazing."[19] The fact that Krishna is practically speechless when trying to find sufficient words to describe the soul speaks loudly to our inability to grasp all that even we can be, what to speak then of our inability to grasp the Sweet Absolute! If we don't *unknow* God (or ourselves, or anything), we won't be able to know him in further detail and thus love him as much as we can. Remember, it's not the same to know *about* God as it is to actually know him in the only way possible—in love. In this way, all saying must be balanced by unsaying, and all knowing must be humbled by unknowing. Without this balance, religion invariably becomes arrogant, exclusionary, and even violent.[20] By contrast, a sober balance of light and darkness, of knowing and unknowing, invokes the higher nondual consciousness we usually refer to as *faith*. This sacred expression of nondual thinking doesn't need to eliminate the mysterious and the unknowable; it just needs to integrate them.

Zen Buddhism would refer to what we've been talking about through the term *shoshin*, or "beginner's mind," which indicates an empty state that remains open and always ready to be filled with reality as it unfolds. This template never allows one to consider that one has attained something fully, and thus it invokes a healthy sense of both humility and ongoing wonder and discovery. A related Buddhist example through which we can attempt to describe knowing through unknowing could be that of the cryptic Zen koans. Basically, a koan is a story, dialogue, or question that forms a riddle that one cannot resolve by normal means of logic. (A famous koan example is "What's the sound of one hand clapping?"). On first impression, a koan appears illogical because our reason proceeds within structured parameters. However, outside those parameters a koan is not inconsistent. It has its own logic. This unique method tries to drive the mind to a state of agitation wherein it hurls itself against its logical cage with the desperation of a cornered rat. This provokes, excites, exasperates, and eventually exhausts the mind until it sees that thinking is never more than *thinking about*, that feeling is never more than *feeling for*. Then, having reduced the rational mind to an impasse, we often find a flash of sudden insight moving from the realm of narrative to that of post-narrative. Accordingly, every time we approach the unbounded nature of reality, we should remain koanlike or, as Jesus said, *childlike* (not childish!). We should allow the realm of the paradoxical to inform our new set of movements.

COEXISTING WITH HOLY PARADOX

Another way to speak about unknowing, unlearning, and unsettling koanlike structures is to do so through the notion of paradox. A paradox appears absurd and contradictory, but upon closer scrutiny it proves to be not only profoundly true and well-founded, but capable of hosting and combining contradictory features. This we surely need to develop if we are to tread the path of loving devotion, as I've mentioned in my first book:

> *"Unless and until we are duly introduced into the realm of paradox and gain some universal grounding in such 'grey areas'... greater inclusivity will not be attained, and thus we will lack the 'hosting capacity' in relation to the highest prospect of spiritual exclusivity ... something that moves in a zigzag way because it acknowledges, embraces, and harmonizes everything in its wake. ... Christian scholars have termed this form of epiphany which so much characterizes wise love as* coincidentia oppositorum, *or that moment where, after duly undergoing the perplexing rite of passage to maturity, things normally seen opposed coincide to reveal an underlying unity."*[21]

Most of life's main epiphanies belong to the realm of the counterintuitive and the paradoxical. Therefore, any prospective spiritualist should learn to coexist with these features, and even love them. Simply put, we can call this coexisting *patience*, since the virtue of patience is exactly that: *the willingness to coexist with what you cannot control*, while deeply trusting it. That's basically the price to pay to live in the Bigger Picture. We must hold onto a bit of doubt and anxiety about the exact how, if, when, where, and who of it all, but never the that.[22] This will deeply endear us to our Beloved, as has been beautifully said in *The Cloud of Unknowing*: "Your patience in sickness and in dealing with different kinds of problems pleases God even more than the keenest devotion in times of good health."[23]

The pattern of paradox constantly replicates in the religious realm, since God himself is the very seat of hundreds of mutually conflicting potencies. But paradox can also be easily discovered in various systems of our natural world. For example, water displays anomalous behavior compared to other liquids. When cooling, liquids consistently contract in volume, but at 4° C, instead of contracting, water starts to expand until it reaches 0° C. Though this is outside the normal bounds of logic, to consider it illusion would be foolish.[24] It's just a paradox. Similarly, we have the classic example of light's being simultaneously and paradoxically both particle *and* wave. As we can see, the principle of paradox arises not only from what we don't know (God as an eternal mystery), but also from what we do know (the natural world). We could thus conclude that whatever phenomenon remains inconceivable to our rational mind is not necessarily illusory. *It's just paradoxical.*

If these paradoxes are naturally possible in water and light, then we should ponder how much this is true of the Light of Lights and the source of every element in creation. Considering how undeniable the experience of paradox is in both the religious and secular realms, we could then conclude that, correspondingly, both faith and science have the potential to meet and deeply coexist. However, this meeting can only happen in humility, awe, and wonder. In other words, in the realm of paradox. As science can clearly point to the mystery of physical reality through dark holes and black matter, faith will similarly point to the Ultimate Mystery. Both are mystery, both are paradoxical, but both are *undeniable.* Therefore, we need to welcome enigma and hold the reality of holy paradox close to our hearts and minds. We shouldn't "plunder the Mystery with concepts," as Buddhist Zen masters would typically say. In a similar way, we shouldn't be afraid that this unknowing will be something "less." In fact, we could say that to know anything fully is always to hold that part of it which is still mysterious and unknowable.[25] In other words, *by paradox and unknowing we'll get to know those things that we would never know otherwise.*

CHAOS AND ORDER

Up to this point we have portrayed the principle of divine ignorance through a myriad of perspectives such as paradox, uncertainty, doubt, and unknowing. Before turning to similar notions such as darkness, mystery, and secrecy, we will first address this most simple, but supremely elusive topic, from the standpoint of *chaos and order*. In this case, "order" will relate to a masculine archetype which here parallels our previous notions of certainty and knowing, while "chaos" will refer to the feminine principle, characterized by the unknown, the mysterious, and the paradoxical. Another word for this chaos would be openness, a template that is clearly observable in nature. Apart from an obvious universal order, we also find an openness, or an ever-evolving and unpredictable pattern, where things not only are but *can become*. In the realms of both faith and science, there is no order without openness, and no openness without order. *Symmetry and surprise are closely bound together in the fabric of reality.*

An excess of either of these two will be undesirable and even dangerous. An overdose of order can manifest as terribly destructive and oppressive qualities displayed in a totalitarian regime or something like concentration camps. Similarly, too much chaos, disorder, and unpredictability and too many out-of-control scenarios may result in neurosis and paranoia if not counterbalanced by order. But order by itself is not enough. We need uncertainty and chaos so we can venture into new layers of learning and growing. However, if chaos overwhelms us beyond our present capacities, it won't allow us to learn what we need to learn. Thus, we are expected to stand with one foot on what we have already learnt, and the other foot on what must be explored and discovered. We need to locate ourselves between knowing and unknowing, fact and possibility, chaos and order. Since most of us may be over-familiarized with the principle of order, let's unfold the implications of a healthy dose of chaos in our attempt to balance our life equation.

In its positive guise, chaos is possibility, the source of ideas, the mysterious realm of gestation and birth.[26] It is in that unknown that our brightest, intermingled potential lies like a Pandora's box. Ironically, we may be terrified of our brightest prospect because it lies in a place unknown to us. In other words, we may not be terrified of our brilliant future per se, but of whatever lies in the lands of the unknown, and since our potential is partially unknown to us, we are generally terrified of it. The potential that chaos represents could be further depicted as a most valuable treasure, and the unknown darkness that surrounds it as the dragons that guard such riches. In fact, medieval maps showed uncharted territory at the edges and included the warning, "Here be dragons." We confront these dragons when we approach the edge of our comfort area[27] and embrace chaos. In other words, chaos is all that exists outside of our comfort zone or "order zone," but is what we need to go through to become all that we can be. *If you want peace, prepare for war.*

While chaos has mostly to do with the realm of the unknown and provides an exile from our habitual patterns where we can renew our plans and prospect, order is explored territory that involves "inhabiting the homeland." It is where the behavior of the world matches our expectations and desires, and where all things turn out the way we want them to. We also need that on some level. But as we already mentioned, order can become tyranny and stultification when the demand for certainty and uniformity becomes too one-sided[28]—*too unrefined by chaos*. Thus, in our spiritual journey we must coexist with these two forces in creative tension while we create proper balance and harmony. This harmony, however, has little to do with things being always nice and ordered, but with an ongoing effort to *harmonize* chaos and order. This is a perpetual affair that will take us to deeper and broader levels of ongoing harmony. This creative process has been accurately described as follows:

> *When things fall apart, and chaos re-emerges, we can give structure to it and re-establish order. ... In other words, we need to confront chaos and turn it into productive order, or, in the case of an order that has become too restrictive, then we should know when to reduce it to chaos, and render such order productive once again. ... When you voluntarily confront the unknown, you gather information and build your renewed self out of that information. ... We eternally inhabit order, surrounded by chaos. We eternally occupy known territory, surrounded by the unknown. We experience meaningful engagement when we mediate appropriately between the two of them ... one foot firmly planted in order and security, and the other in chaos, possibility, growth, and adventure.*[29]

As a community, we Gaudiyas currently need to become more adventuresome. Instead of an overdose of certainty, order, and explored territory—which do away with our creativity, possibilities, and bright potential—we need to embrace a healthy dose of chaos and allow it to nourish and refine our current order of things so we can visualize more clearly the brilliant prospect that awaits us in the uncharted land of the unknown. Let's try to de-numb ourselves and become more and more comfortable with our discomfort. Let's find that deep peace that surpasses mere understanding. It is a treasure-like peace which, despite being surrounded by unknown dragons, still waits for us to be heroically reclaimed.

GOD IS ESPECIALLY FOUND IN (AND FOND OF) DARKNESS

From the above chaos, uncertainty, and unknowing, let's now turn to the principle of *bright darkness*, and how this is beautifully found in the Sweet Absolute. By *darkness* we do not refer to something bad or undesirable, but merely to a situation in which we don't know (don't see) what's going on, although *something is clearly going on.* God works mostly in the dark, and we should be willing to coexist with something that is ultimately synonymous with him. While also being known as the Light of lights, the Sweet Absolute can justifiably be defined in terms of darkness; both light and dark find their perfect balance in him. And while we may already be accustomed to conceive of the Divine himself as light, we may need to be further introduced to his dark side. In other words, we need a *theology of darkness*—and we have it. But before turning to our own Gaudiya version of such a theology, let's briefly touch upon how other mystical traditions approach this same principle.

For most mystics, God as the Beloved is always an endless mystery. And we agree. Therefore, we are expected to be humbled by the mysteries of faith and by the very mystery that God himself is. Such an epiphany will never allow us to demand the right for absolute certainty about Infinity or any form of copyrights of him, but rather the exact opposite. When we say that the Divine is mystery personified, please bear in mind that mystery is not something we *cannot* understand, but is something we can *endlessly* understand![30] Similarly fashioned, *Vedanta-sutra* 1.1.5 says, *iksater nasabdam*: the Absolute is inexpressible. In other words, *we can never say enough about him.* No matter how much we try to say, we can never fully *say* this Sweet Absolute. *Srimad Bhagavatam* 1.18.20 further confirms this fact by declaring that, since God is unlimited and no one is equal to him, "no one can speak of him adequately." In fact, it's ironic that the topic we most want to discuss leaves us speechless. It is a topic that gives us a boundless joy but which also teaches us a humble economy of words.[31] To maintain this foundational humility toward Infinity is to change our perception of God for good. In fact, changing our perception of God has the potential to change *everything*. Correspondingly, not changing our perspective of God has the potential to change *nothing*.

We have to keep in mind the Absolute's quality of unforeseeability—his surprise party—and allow ourselves to allow him in our lives with all that entails, including unpredictability, shock, perplexity, and infinite astonishment. Unfortunately, most of us have a hard time dealing with unforeseeability, especially if it's infinite. Our human mind cannot comprehend the notion of infinite because we have no frame of reference. However, this is *not* a problem, but a veritable source of the most necessary substance we are starving for: sacred wonder. In connection to this astonishment, awe, and wonder—whose very source *is* mystery and darkness—Albert Einstein said:

> *The most beautiful thing that we can experience is the mysterious. It is the source of all true art and all science. He to whom this emotion is a stranger, who can no longer pause to wonder and stand rapt in awe, is as good as dead.*[32]

Since we want to be as alive as we can be, we ought to embrace the mystery that God is in our lives, in all the ways he chooses to be so. One of the endless expressions of his sacred darkness is related to how we need him to heal us beyond our current awareness. In other words, we need the Sweet Absolute to act in the darkness for our own benefit. He has to undo our illusions secretly, when we are not watching and not in "perfect" control.[33] In this underground stage of what we may call *participatory mystery*, the Sweet Absolute will perform miracles that aboveground we may still resist. Therefore, instead of plundering the mystery that God is, and through which God redeems us, we should learn to *preserve* such mystery, as Dietrich Bonhoeffer once wisely expressed:

> *How we fail to understand when we think that the task of theology is to solve the mystery of God, to drag it down to the flat, ordinary wisdom of human experience and reason! Its sole office is to preserve the miracle as miracle, to comprehend, defend, and glorify God's mystery precisely as mystery.*[34]

Preserving the mystery that God is also has to do with allowing him to be more in us than what we think he already is. Since the life motion of the Absolute is an ongoing crescendo of eternal becoming, we should be careful with expressing overconfidence in relation to someone who has no limits. And interestingly, this does not apply only to the Sweet Absolute but also to our unlimited potential for transformation under the shelter of God's infinite mercy. Therefore, we still don't know all that we can be, nor do we fully know the very source of our own potential, the Sweet Absolute. In this sense only, we could say that we profess a "theistic agnosticism." We are theists, since we believe in God (we know he exists), but at the same time we are agnostics, since *we don't know*. We don't dare to affirm that we already know God—at least not perfectly. Or, much less, we don't dare to affirm that we already have full and perfect faith in him. An interesting example in this regard comes from Jordan B. Peterson, who upon being asked if he believed in God would repeatedly answer, "I try to act as if God exists." When asked to elaborate on his peculiar reply, he said:

> *Who would have the audacity to claim that they believe in God, if they would examine the way they live? ... To claim that you believe in God means that you live out such belief fully. To believe in God doesn't mean to state it, but to fully act out what you believe in. Unless you act it out, you should be very careful about claiming it. God only knows what you would be if you truly believed. If you would truly believe, it would be a transfiguring event, and although we may have experienced some of that to one degree or another, we don't have an idea of the limit of that.*[35]

Again, here we have a clear example of theistic agnosticism, expressing itself not only in relation to God but in every possible direction. We not only do not have a clue about who God is, but we similarly ignore all that we could be if we truly believed in him—if we fully dedicated ourselves to his sweet will. Remember, *belief without struggle is not the same as faith.*

God is always bigger than the boxes we build for him, so we should not waste too much time protecting the boxes.[36] These boxes are our mental structures that keep us in the comfort zone, and that often give us a distorted picture of the Sweet Absolute. In relation to remaining free from inaccurate and partial ideas about the Divine, the medieval mystic Meister Eckhart was famous for repeatedly praying, "God, rid me of God!" In other words, we need to experience *the God who will rid us of the God we need to get rid of.* This teaching is echoed in the Zen Buddhist story attributed to the Buddhist sage Lin Chi who told a monk, "If you meet the Buddha on the road, kill him!" There are many lessons that can be drawn from this koan. One lesson is offered by George Draffan who was an executive director of the Northwest Dharma Association. He said, "Buddhists are not trying to be free of thoughts and emotions, but not to be ensnared by the error of giving them more substance than they actually have. Not to believe my ideas of Buddha are actually Buddha. The 'Buddha' I would kill is only my idolized projection."[37] Ironically, while the God many atheistic people cannot believe in actually constitutes an unbelievable idea of the Divine, many so-called believers justify their faith by embracing such an implausible notion of the Absolute.

Before turning to our Gaudiya canon, let's conclude this section by repeating what may still be a challenge to grasp: *the Sweet Absolute can never be fully known.* Judaism makes this point in its own way by emphasizing God's name as YHWH, or "I am who I am." It does so to preserve God's final unknowability, and to keep religion and believers humble about their ability to know who God is.[38] Similarly, mystical Christianity portrays God's unknowability by describing him as being situated in "thick darkness"[39] or even literally dwelling in it.[40] While Gaudiya Vaishnavism not only agrees that God resides in darkness and even refers to him as Syamasundara ("the Beautiful Dark One") or even Ghana-shyam ("Dark Cloud"), still some Gaudiya members may argue that although God may not be fully knowable, he can certainly be fully loved. And since for Gaudiyas love is the king of knowledge,[41] we could say that, by being fully loved, God can then also be fully known. That said, we should remember that the nature of divine love is ongoing expansion and exponential growth. Therefore we conclude that we can always love God more, despite loving him fully already. As God is unlimited, so is our potential to love him eternally. This is confirmed in *Chaitanya-charitamrita* 3.20.28: "Wherever there is a relationship of divine love, its natural symptom is that the devotee does not think himself a devotee. Instead, he always thinks that he has not even a drop of love for God." The devotee doesn't feel this lack of love because he or she does not actually have divine love. Rather, the ever-evolving nature of love makes them realize *how much more love* one can have, "a more" without end. In this way, we are once again back to our original proposal: God can never be fully loved, and therefore he can never be fully known. But he can always be more loved and therefore more known, endlessly. *Full circle.*

MYSTERY AND SECRECY IN THE GAUDIYA TRADITION

Science and mystical Christianity conceive of God and reality itself as an eternal mystery. We Gaudiyas do so as well. Before sharing a few classic examples from the Gaudiya canon, let's reflect for a minute on the word *mystery*. While we may immediately connect it with something unknown (and that's accurate), more specifically the term is etymologically related to the notion of *mystic presence*. In other words, what we find here is some deep connection between mystery and mystical. In fact, when this notion of mystery is applied to the mystical Divine, we find expressions such as him being *mysterium tremendum*,[42] a tremendous mystery or, more precisely, *the overwhelming mystery*. God is an inscrutable mystery that cannot be penetrated. Thus, accomplished mystics mainly experience the Sweet Absolute as deeply mysterious, utterly fascinating, and totally urgent. This is how the cowherd girls of Vraja experienced Sri Krishna when running to his sacred flute call in the dead of night.

So yes, Gaudiya Vaishnavism also conceives of Ultimate Reality in terms of mystery and secrecy. For example, before the presentation of the four main verses of the *Srimad Bhagavatam*, the essential content of this section is described in verse 2.9.31 with the words *rahasya*, "mysterious," and *parama-guhya*, "supremely secret." Similarly, the *Bhagavad-gita* (verses 9.1–2, 15.20, 18.63–64, and 18.68, among others) refers to its message in terms of different degrees of *guhya*, or secrecy. Another classic Gaudiya example and reminder showing that what we are approaching is *infinitely knowable*, and that every moment of knowing simply opens up another possibility to know more, are the different stories of Krishna and his mother, Yasoda. She tries to bind her child, but is never able to do so, despite Krishna remaining medium-size and never expanding. She looks inside Krishna's mouth, trying to confirm if her son ate dirt, only to witness a spiral of endless portals, like nested *matrushka* dolls, where she, Krishna, and the whole universe appear inside her child's "little" mouth.

Another way to conceive of the Sweet Absolute as mystery is to understand that regardless of our efforts, we can only know him, see him, or love him by his own will and grace. A well-known example is King Uparichara, who performed a sacrifice for the pleasure of the Lord. When God appeared at the sacrifice to accept the oblations, only the king could see him. Brihaspati, the chief priest, became enraged at this and threw the sacrificial ladle into the air in frustration while shouting, "Why can't I see him?" The assembled devotees tried to pacify Brihaspati, telling him, "Neither you nor we can see the Lord at our will. *Only those he favors can see him*."[43] Likewise, Brahma wanted to see Sri Krishna again after having seen him for a first time, but he was unable to do so, though he searched for him for many years. Similarly, as a young boy in his previous lifetime, Narada had a vision of the Lord, but despite trying to see him again after losing sight of him, he was not able to regain that vision. As a matter of fact, even when the Sweet Absolute does disclose his mysterious form to us, we are advised to deal with that revelation in secrecy. This is confirmed in *Srimad Bhagavatam* 8.17.20, where the Supreme Lord tells Aditi, "That which is very confidential is successful if kept secret." Similarly, in *Bhagavad-gita* 10.38, Sri Krishna tells Arjuna, "Among all secret things, I am silence." Therefore, mystery and secrecy constitute the veritable essence of the Gaudiya's Absolute. Those who aspire to serve such a mystery should remain perpetually humbled by it. This is clearly expressed by Sri Brahma. After exhibiting excessive certitude and confidence about his knowledge of Krishna's identity, he was eventually overwhelmed and humbled by the Absolute to the point of sacred unknowing. In the spirit of divine ignorance and theistic agnosticism, he then prayed as follows:

> *Those who say that they know, let them know. As far as I am concerned, I do not wish to speak very much about this matter. O my Lord, let me say this much: as far as your opulences are concerned, they are all beyond the reach of my mind, body, and words.*[44]

An interesting related practice in line with Brahma's prayer is what has been known in mystical Christianity as Centering Prayer.[45] As long as this silent contemplation lasts, the practitioners do not try to *think* about God in any way. They simply maintain their intention to remain present and consent to God, just as he is, without demanding to know what that is, or who he is. *They remain open to allow God to further introduce himself to them.* To not have any specific idea about God during prayer may sound strange and even shocking for some Gaudiyas, who very quickly will visualize Krishna's bluish form, flute, peacock feather, and so on. However, Centering Prayer is not about doing away with a personal God, but about *not being too attached to whatever idea we may have of God at present.* We should not conclude that our notions about the Divine are definitive, that we already know him perfectly, and we don't need to upgrade our sense of who God is. That would be equivalent to saying that *we don't need to develop our relationship with him.* It has little or nothing to do with the actual Gaudiya stance, exemplified by Brahma in the above quoted prayer. Since the Sweet Absolute is the very personification of Infinity, we should remain open to him further introducing himself to us *over and over again,* since he is always much more than what we may think he is. In other words, our relationship with God needs to remain in a constant state of upgrade through the principle of participatory mystery.

Another way to conceive of this upgrade through the principle of mystery is seen in the idea of divine separation. Since without separation there cannot be reunion, the very purpose of this momentary distancing, subjectively experienced as eons for the advanced devotee, is to further renew and condense the intensity of love. Among other places, this is confirmed in *Srimad Bhagavatam* 10.47.34, where the Sweet Absolute tells the Vraja *gopis* that the actual reason why he stayed far away from them was that he wanted to intensify their meditation upon him and thus draw their minds closer to him. This sacred experience, through which further knowing and revelation take place, is basically synonymous with the above notions of darkness, uncertainty, and unknowing. A classic Gaudiya example of divine separation can be found in the eighth verse of the *Sad-gosvamy-astakam*. Its author describes how the famous Six Goswamis of Vraja would cry their hearts out while looking for their beloved Lord, intensely inquiring about his whereabouts in every nook and corner of Vraja. While each of these Goswamis already possessed pure love for Krishna, they continued to increase their love for him through, in this case, the principle of divine separation.

Although we may not experience these exact emotions in our amateur stage, we can still experience separation by realizing how, despite knowing the Sweet Absolute on some level, we can still know him—love him—much more. In other words, the level of our unknowing of God will be the level of our separation from him. In fact, we could say that even the divine separation experienced by exalted saints is connected to this principle. Since the Divine is always evolving and expanding his loving capacity, the saints' loving capacity equally evolves in correspondence to that. This is confirmed in *Srimad Bhagavatam* 10.44.14, where the term *anusava-abhinavam*, or "constantly new at every moment," is invoked to describe the nature of the Sweet Absolute's form. Therefore, the separation felt by saints like the Six Goswamis implies that because they are now meeting a "new Krishna"—an upgraded version of the Absolute—they were initially experiencing him as unknown and unprecedented. Divinely confused by meeting their Beloved in that newly fresh facet, these pure devotees may not immediately recognize him. Thus they experience sacred separation and conclude that their Lord has disappeared from their vision, while their Beloved is actually getting closer to their hearts than ever, *but in a new form*. In other words, the devotee will experience the hyper-presence of the Sweet Absolute as a type of absence. In whatever stage we may be in, every Gaudiya Vaishnava is advised to gradually imbibe this unique mood of sacred unknowing to rediscover one's Deity through uncertainty and mystery. *Perpetually.*

This perpetual rediscovery of one's Beloved is possible and indispensable because the very nature of reality is impermanence, or, more specifically, a state of constant change and perpetual becoming—starting with God himself. While the Sweet Absolute is famous for being immutable and unchanging, his less famous (but more intimate) side entails an ongoing crescendo of his loving capacity, giving rise to loving experience. If there is any constant in God, it's that he keeps changing. *He keeps loving*, more and more. Hence what doesn't change about the Sweet Absolute is that he is always changing. That's why God is not just a noun, but also *a verb*: a very active one, since *he is always happening*. A famous example in this regard is found in *Srimad Bhagavatam* 7.9.2, where Lakshmi, the eternal consort of the Supreme Lord, becomes bewildered after seeing him appearing in his form of Sri Narasimha, a form Lakshmi never saw before (*adrista*) nor heard of (*asruta*), and which was wondrous (*adbhutam*) and thus totally unprecedented for her, the eternal companion of the Sweet Absolute. Therefore, we should adapt accordingly to the permanent unfolding and mystery that God is, and never be absolutely sure that we own the full conception of the Supreme Lord. As it is said, *God can most easily be lost by being thought found.*[46] Or, in the words of *Kena Upanishad* 2.3, "One who claims not to know the Absolute, knows; but one who claims to know the Absolute, does not know."

We must add to the above that the Sweet Absolute is a mystery not only for us tiny souls, but even to himself! In *Srimad Bhagavatam* 10.87.41, the personified Vedas praise Sri Krishna with deep taste and accuracy. They tell him, "Because you are unlimited, neither the lords of heaven *nor even you yourself* can ever reach the end of your glories."[47] As one cannot know something that does not exist, and since the very limit of God's glories does not exist, God himself cannot know his limit, *since it does not exist. Srimad Bhagavatam* 2.7.41 establishes this same point by describing how Shesha, an aspect of the Sweet Absolute, has not been able to reach the limit of those glories despite being exclusively dedicated to singing about them with thousands of mouths. As shocking as this may sound, *even*

God does not know everything. If God is actually unlimited—as he is—then he cannot be omniscient in every sense of the term, because anything unlimited can never be known completely. No one fully knows the Sweet Absolute, *not even himself*. However, he knows everything he wants to know. And that is the true meaning of him being omniscient. On the basis of this unique insight, unable to contain himself, a Gaudiya Vaishnava will then proceed to apply this principle to its ultimate consequences. Sri Krishna doesn't know the extent of his own glories and personal beauty, and he doesn't know the extent of Radha's love. But in his ultimate and most consummate form of Sri Gaurahari, he desires to taste all that is unknown to him. While Gaudiya Vaishnavas will practically be unable to contain themselves at this volcanic peak of the Sweet Absolute known as Gaurahari, we nonetheless need to do so since a whole separate book—*zillions of them*—would be required for a thorough and rigorous elaboration on this divine unfolding.

THE DARK NIGHT OF THE SOUL

God is mystery and secret, to the point of being called Ghanashyam, "Dark Cloud." If the Sweet Absolute is described as a sacred dark cloud of unknowing, we are invited to *embrace the Dark Lord by embracing our own darkness*. That said, in scripture Sri Krishna has also been compared to the Sun.[48] This indicates how the darkness that he himself is provides an extreme radiance and illumination—*a bright darkness*. This most confidential and intimate exercise of embracing the *Dark Bright Lord* has anciently been referred to as the dark night of the soul.

This concept, originally coined by St. John of the Cross, has universal application to paths other than mystical Christianity. The idea of this dark night basically implies being led into a darker space where deeper healing and learning will take place ("dark" here being the absence of knowing). The dark night of the soul is not an event one passes through and gets beyond, but rather a deep ongoing process that characterizes our very spiritual life. In this sense, the dark night could be seen as a person's hidden life with the Sweet Absolute. St. John of the Cross takes this even further, saying that this dark night is not just the activity of God in our lives, but it *is* God.

He writes, "This dark night is an inflow of God into the soul." In other words, the "dark night" is not primarily *some thing,* an impersonal darkness, like a difficult situation or distressful psychological condition. It is *someone.*[49]

As the reader may probably anticipate, these dark nights will be full of the various sacred elements described in this chapter: doubt, uncertainty, paradox, ignorance, darkness, unknowing, chaos, and mystery. All this is absolutely necessary for us to learn the art of coexisting with a reality beyond our control and discovering how he who is actually in control controls exclusively through the power of unconditional love. In this connection, while during these dark periods it may not be fully clear what may be the way forward, the important thing will be to have a deep faith that *there is* a moving forward by trusting the power of unconditional love coming from the Sweet Absolute. If this quality of faith and its subsequent action are in place, the rest will unfold organically and accordingly. Yes, sometimes we must learn to stay with the pain of life, without answers, without conclusions, and some days even without meaning[50]—but knowing there *is* one, despite our not seeing it. In other words, problems may come and we may not be able to solve them, at least not in the way we solve a math problem. Rather, we must learn to solve them by holding the problem and *allow it to transform us.* We don't need to solve problems; we need them to *solve us.*

These dark nights have been classically seen as periods of incubation, transformation, necessary hibernation, and introspection. We wait in the sacred space of darkness, trusting and allowing the Sweet Absolute to work in those special moments when we are clearly not in control. This can be disturbing or even scary, but in the end, it always works to our benefit. It is during those dark periods that the Divine will heal us most secretly, even without our noticing it. Why is this so? As we already mentioned (and as embarrassing as it may be), if we knew what's actually taking place during our dark nights, we would likely try to sabotage any movement toward true freedom. In other words, if we really knew what we are called to relinquish in our spiritual path, *our defense mechanisms would never allow us to take even the first step.* And that's why sometimes the only way we can enter the deeper dimensions of our journey is by being unable to see where we are going. Therefore, whether we experience it as painful or pleasurable, *the night is dark for our protection.*[51] We can then conclude that darkness can act as a guiding light. Let's thus pray for *a ray of bright darkness.*

As mysteries do not exist only to be solved, darkness is not merely something to be shed light upon. While unsolved mysteries will invoke new epiphanies and deep humility in us, deep darkness will similarly sober our approach to life and God, taking us where we cannot go on our own. These desertlike areas of transition and rebirth are also often referred to as *liminal space*, a threshold zone where necessary displacement and corresponding crisis are induced in the hope of a new point of view. One elementary yet practical way a novice is invited to cross this threshold is in the shape of unconventional codes of physical appearance that help the novice step out of the land of normality and conformity and into a world of possibility. Across spiritual traditions we find departure from the norms of larger society in regard to attire (such as robes, color of garments, head coverings), patterns of facial and head hair (clean-shaven to matted locks and many combinations in between), and bodily markings. The distance created between normal and novel provides enough room to enter the space of liminality, to change, grow, and adopt a new point of view. Ironically, over time those atypical codes themselves become the norm that then need to be shed and redesigned. The innovators of liminality are those who are often considered heretics of a tradition, yet this function is what keeps the door to the liminal zone open for the prophetic community. Each time a new door needs to be fashioned from the old to keep up with the pace of transcendence, a crisis is created—an opportunity to shake loose the confines of normalcy. As it happens with "darkness" (and every other term invoked in this chapter), the very word *crisis* refers to a *decisive point*, and not to something that shouldn't be happening. Therefore, if a crisis experienced in liminal space (either individually or collectively) is properly appreciated for what it is, then such a crisis won't represent any breakdown, but an essential *breakthrough*. This necessary embrace of the underworld of liminality will prove crucial to our remaining realistic and mature while undergoing our darkest nights. Without this, we will simply start idolizing normalcy.

Carl Jung profoundly stated, "No tree can grow to heaven unless its roots reach down to hell."[52] This was his own way to speak about the utter need for the dark night of the soul, or God's waiting room. As intimidating as this journey may sound to some, we need to be introduced to and further educated about such a journey. We need to be taught the language of not only ascending and transcending, but of *descending*, a language that teaches us to enter willingly and trustingly into the dark periods of life.[53] While during these moments we may still remain clueless about the texture of our hearts, this dark brilliance of liminality returns over and over again to make us more familiar with who we are and what we need. In fact, at some point, part of this sacred transition may even include a change in our habitual sense of relationship with the Divine. A common experience is that God has disappeared from our lives. However, what has really disappeared is *the usual way we conceived of God.* All the while he is actually getting closer, but this is happening in the darkness. But since that new proximity is totally new and therefore unknown, some of us may feel that the Sweet Absolute is getting further and further away while he is actually closer than ever. In this way, a new system of perception begins to kick in and allows us to perceive God and *be with him* in a whole different way. In fact, the Sweet Absolute does not *have* unconditional love, but is *made* of it. Correspondingly, to have faith in a God made of unconditional love is to realize how intimately close God is—so close we forget his presence.[54] Therefore, for this dark night to succeed we must be able to relinquish whatever attachments we may have to yesterday's preconceived ideas and/or experiences of the Divine, and today allow him to reveal an even brighter darkness.

As we already mentioned, we may be going through these dark periods as individuals and communally. And perhaps Gaudiya Vaishnavism as a community now finds itself in this particular chapter. What will influence the unfolding of our current communal challenges is our capacity not only to acknowledge such a fact from a distance, but to intimately embrace this holy invitation. We should begin with a foundational "yes" rather than a dismissive "no." Srila Sridhara Deva Goswami described how the mantra *Om* means a yes of grateful assertiveness, trusting that whatever is coming to us will always bring a higher level of purpose and meaning. Conversely, if we start with a no, we deprive ourselves of any actual understanding in our attempt to decode reality. We will be too quickly labeling, analyzing, and categorizing things as in or out, good or bad. Instead, we have to leave the field open.[55] In other words, our initial "yes" will put in context whatever necessary "noes" may eventually be invoked. Those noes will be as sacred as our yeses, provided we begin with a foundational yes. In this way we should learn to begin with a yes of basic acceptance toward reality as well as an openness to its unpredictable unfolding, especially during these dark/bright nights of the soul. We must make friends with the abyss, for it will carry us through the darkest of times, bring us solace when that's most needed, and be the one place where we are truly understood.

The Realm of Contemplative Prayer | 13

The true contemplative is one who has discovered the art of finding leisure even in the midst of his work, by working with such a spirit of detachment and recollection that even his work is a prayer.

— Thomas Merton

THE BLUEPRINT OF RADICAL PERSONALISM entails a crescendo of ever-unfolding possibilities, which cascade on one another, carrying us to our next shore. That shore is the realm of contemplative prayer and constitutes not only an overflowing from our previous chapters and topics but further articulates and integrates many of the crucial aspects we have been talking about. These include vulnerability, individuation, nondual thinking, the guru-disciple relationship, and divine ignorance. For example, any genuine form of prayer will involve a serious dose of vulnerability for it to be fruitful. Similarly, individuation implies being ourselves and allowing the Sweet Absolute to also be himself. This is synonymous with the sacred appeal of contemplative prayer. Nondual thinking runs almost parallel with the notion of contemplation. It's not an activity to do a few moments a day, but an ongoing stance and perspective—a realm—by which we see the relatedness of everything through a participatory state of consciousness. Ideally, the guru and the genuine disciple embody this contemplative attitude toward reality. As to the principle of divine ignorance shared in our last chapter, we could say that without the willingness to inhabit uncertainty and embrace the unknown, there is no possibility of us engaging in prayer—at least not contemplative prayer. That being said, let's begin by describing what this unique realm is not.

WHAT CONTEMPLATIVE PRAYER IS NOT

Unless we want to make the bold case that contemplative prayer is the only possible form of prayer, we should clearly establish the difference between prayer and contemplative prayer. When using the word *prayer*, people generally refer to making a petition. In fact, we find that many people have reduced prayer to a one-time act or something merely functional to get something from God. In these "prayers" we don't allow any form of new and transformed consciousness but remain as egocentric as ever, perhaps even more so. Instead of manipulating others (as we were likely doing before "praying"), during this form of "prayer" we knowingly or unknowingly try to manipulate the Divine.

In contrast, contemplative prayer is always a relationship of dialogue and reciprocal participation. It is a *radically personal* encounter with the Sweet Absolute and fosters an ongoing development of our relationship with him. The essence of any form of genuine prayer (referred to here as *contemplation* or *contemplative prayer*) is an authentic form of expression in which we will never try to manipulate and exploit the Sweet Absolute for our own advantage and ulterior agenda. Contemplative prayer is not an obsessive system for God-domestication; nor is it a moral worthiness contest, an effort-based endeavor, or a calculated approach toward Ultimate Reality. In other words, contemplative prayer has nothing to do with a mainstream idea of prayer, which identifies it as a petition or, if our personal requests have been fulfilled, fills one with gratitude. Why is this so? Because *real prayer is not about problem-solving*. And if we would like to think in that term, then we should say that the only problem that prayer should solve is *us*. And most of us are quite a big problem![1]

Likewise, contemplative prayer is not limited to certain specific actions, nor does it constitute a mere recital of prayers. It mostly has to do with *whatever we may happen to be doing in a prayerful mood.* Prayer is ultimately a mood, a stance, a *realm*, and not a one-act performance or occasional weekend ritual. Real prayer—contemplative prayer—is a way of life to be thoroughly assimilated through dedication and practice. It is something with the potential of becoming second nature. It is something with the potential of becoming not only a genuine source of shelter and divine revelation, but a part of our very identity. In other words, contemplative prayer is not so much something you do, but *something you are.* As someone who writes becomes a writer, and someone who plays becomes a player, *someone who (really) prays becomes a prayer.* This type of natural integration will gradually take place and is an integration through which we will eventually discover how prayer becomes action and action becomes prayer.

WHAT IS CONTEMPLATIVE PRAYER

Contemplative prayer is not foreign to Gaudiya Vaishnavism, although its essence may need to be reframed so we can relate to it. In fact, the very essence and experience of contemplative prayer are related to the core practices of the Gaudiya tradition, such as *smarana* (meditation), *kirtana* (celebratory praise), *sravana* (hearing), and more specifically, *vandana* (prayer). The term *vandana* is connected to the practice of bowing down or, to be more precise, to its corresponding inner mood of permanent veneration toward everything, which is a spirit that also runs parallel to that of contemplative prayer. Apart from bowing down, *vandana* refers to reciting selected prayers from the sacred texts and composing our own spontaneous offerings. However, since praying is ultimately not limited to an official moment of the day, *vandana* is therefore not limited to merely pronouncing words or even having thoughts. It is about going beyond them and presenting ourselves naked before the Sweet Absolute with heart in hand. It means not filtering that act through any preconceived notion and allowing the Divine to introduce himself to us more and more and more. In this sense, contemplative prayer can be described as a particular disposition of the practitioner toward God wherein the practitioner seeks communion with the Divine by offering his own soul as, in, and through prayer.

The word *contemplation* comes from the Latin roots *com* ("with") and *templum* ("temple"). These two terms refer to contemplation as living our life in such a way that we always remain in a temple. This can only be possible if we erect a temple in our heart—if we permanently stand on truly sacred ground through our own lifestyle. Therefore, the very meaning of the word *contemplation* establishes how contemplative prayer cannot and should not be reduced to a one-time act, but conceived as an ever-evolving stance. This important point is repeatedly confirmed in our Gaudiya tradition, as well as in other schools. Sri Gaurahari speaks about "engaging in praise of Hari *always*;"[2] Sri Krishna emphasizes the importance of "*constantly* glorifying me;"[3] and *Srimad Bhagavatam* mandates to "*perpetually* serve" Ultimate Reality.[4] Similarly, the Bible instructs us to "pray *unceasingly*,"[5] among other similar injunctions. If we read any of these instructions on uninterrupted prayer as being confined to the literal utterance of words or to certain concrete acts, these instructions will surely be impossible to follow. Therefore, contemplative prayer is not primarily saying words or thinking thoughts. It is, rather, a stance by which we create a temple through our own life.

While the above is certainly true, contemplative prayer can also be conceived, especially in the beginning, as a concrete practice, where we completely stop whatever activities we may be doing and "just" focus on our connection with the Sweet Absolute, whether through a prayerful recitation of his names, deep silence and introspective hearing, or other forms of prayer. As our practice progresses, however, we will realize that prayer is a mood to carry with us—or *that will carry us*—through our daily life. It is a participatory state of consciousness or, if we prefer, *a feeling*. Even if devoid of words, whatever feelings we may be experiencing in relation to the Supreme will be a prayer unto themselves. As John Bunyan said, "In prayer, *it is better to have a heart without words than words without a heart*."[6] The latter can never be considered prayer, but is perhaps even a way to avoid actual transformative prayer. In fact, if our current way of praying is not leading us to a holy shift in consciousness, it may be counterproductive.

Sadhana, or spiritual practice, is nothing but commitment to one's spiritual maturity. Therefore, *sadhana* has nothing to do with mechanically replicating particular actions but with *awakening to the implications* of those very actions. In other words, by engaging in spiritual practices like prayer we will be transported to the implications of those practices. We will hear more and more clearly the different intimations coming from the spirit of those actions. And we are expected to commit ourselves to such exercise and be willing to admit that the meaning of our practices may be quite different from what we initially thought. An example of this could be equating contemplative prayer with meditation, or *smarana*. In this connection, Sri Krishna said twice to Arjuna in the *Bhagavad-gita*, "Always think of me."[7] Hearing this one-liner, we may rightfully question, How can one think of Krishna *always*? How do you *think* of God, anyway? Therefore, this type of instruction does not necessarily refer to merely sitting and trying to recall the Sweet Absolute's form and attributes, but to ultimately falling in love with him. In love we will always think of the Divine by contemplating the whole of reality with wonder and praise, perceiving our Beloved's presence in everyday life in such a way that we can think of him *always*. Once again, we see how contemplative prayer (meditation, praise, inner hearing) is more a life stance than a fixed act.

THE EXPERIENCE OF CONTEMPLATIVE PRAYER

The essence of contemplative prayer could be described as experiencing the reality of our relationship with the Sweet Absolute. For us to have such experience we need to be present in his presence. Though God's presence is everywhere and always, for us to perceive his presence we have to be present as well. And this can only happen in the here and now, where the import of the moment meets us. Every moment that has ever existed has led up to this one instance that we call the "present moment." Similarly, every moment that will be rests upon this present moment that simultaneously holds and erupts with the potential of all moments yet to be. In this connection, contemplative prayer is the condition of one who presents himself before the Divine and is fully present in the present moment. He empties his mind so that his heart can be filled with a further recognition of his intimate patterns of cadence with his Beloved. For this to happen to us, we should be reminded that the function of prayer is never to influence God or put him in our service, but to modify the nature of us who pray. This requires deep introspection and utter sincerity that will lead us to question not so much where God is but where we are in relation to him.

Prayer is an art. Therefore, in order to pray one has to learn how to pray. And in that attempt and learning, paradoxically one will be praying! What's left for us is to continue refining our prayer through constant practice, until *our practice becomes our life.* We should never consider any spiritual work to be firmly established, and this is especially so in regard to prayer. Our learning can be considered "finished" when in prayer we do nothing but go from one feeling to the other. In fact, that we experience mundane emotions devoid of the Sweet Absolute (and thus pass from one illusory feeling to the other) indirectly indicates that we can do the same thing with God in the center through prayer. And this confirms how contemplative prayer can become a permanent stance and emotional experience—a daily rendezvous with the Divine. Through it we experience ourselves as the best possible version of ourselves in relation to our sacred source.

Despite the thrilling perspective we have shared about a life of prayer, we should be equally realistic and also admit that there may be considerable struggle in our prayer project. This is not because prayer is inherently difficult, but because we are generally *the difficult ones,* presenting abundant ego opposition to all that actual prayer implies. That's exactly why a real experience of contemplative prayer could be defined as a *training in dying*. It means surrender, letting go, learning to lose graciously, and allowing the Sweet Absolute to finally triumph over our stubborn resistance. As difficult as this may sound, the "heart surgery" of contemplative prayer constitutes a truly sacred moment where we are given the opportunity to fully open our own hearts and thus realize how the Divine has been *disclosing his own heart* to us from time immemorial.

In this way, the prayer experience will be an *exchange of hearts*. The Sweet Absolute knows our heart completely and knows everything through his own unconditional heart. If the Divine fully knows our heart through his own heart, we could then conclude that God knows us *by heart*. Even if we ignore who we are and the content of our own heart, the Sweet Absolute knows all these things through his own unconditional heart. This is a crucial thought to rest in during sacred prayer. Without being constantly *re-minded* about God's unconditional approach, we may end up forcing ourselves to serve him "unconditionally" while forgetting his own unconditionality toward us, resulting in various forms of frustration, meritocracy, and even trauma. If we have not experienced ourselves through the reality of unconditional love, then we have plenty of work to do, because that is who we really are. We are constantly seen from above with unconditionally loving eyes. Contemplative prayer deeply revolves around this holy dance of reciprocity between the Divine's unconditional love and the practitioner's awareness of that love. This dance continues as each partner deepens their approach to the other in response to their previous exchange. While we have already elaborated on the principle of unconditional love in our chapter on vulnerability, let's invoke some further musings in relation to how unconditional love plays out in the context of contemplative prayer.

A FEW THOUGHTS ON PRAYER AND UNCONDITIONAL LOVE

While the notion of unconditional love abounds throughout the Gaudiya horizon, it is sometimes exclusively conceived of in relation to how God deals with his unalloyed devotees. While over and over again we find beautiful verses about how the Sweet Absolute is totally in love with (and even controlled by) his own servants,[8] we also hear that, in relation to those who are not his devotees, he remains neutral and unattached.[9] However, if the latter notion is abused or misread, we may conclude that the Sweet Absolute has unconditional love *only* for his devotees and nobody else. And while God certainly loves his intimate servants uniquely and passionately, this doesn't mean he has no unconditional love in any form for everyone else.

The all-inclusiveness of the Sweet Absolute's unconditional love is confirmed in *Srimad Bhagavatam* 6.17.33, where Mahadeva Shiva emphasizes God's impartiality by declaring that the Supreme

Lord holds no one as very dear and no one as inimical. After this declaration, Shiva establishes how this impartiality plays itself out in the context of universal and unconditional love by affirming, "Because he [God] is the affectionate friend of all living entities, *he is very near and dear to all of them*."[10] In other words, God is impartial exactly because he impartially has unconditional love for every living being. A similar point is made in *Srimad Bhagavatam* 10.41.47, where Sudama prays to the Supreme Lord saying, "Because you are the well-wishing friend and Supreme Soul of the whole universe, you regard all with unbiased vision." In his significant commentary on this verse, Sri Jiva Goswami declares,

> *By coming to the house of a low person devoid of* bhakti, *the Lord shows equal vision to all beings. He does not have prejudiced vision thinking "This person deserves mercy and that person does not," since he has unconditional mercy. Moreover, he has affection for the universe. Though he shows mercy to those who worship him, he is equal to all beings, high or low, since he is the Lord of the universe and affectionate to the fallen.*

Likewise, the Sweet Absolute describes himself in *Bhagavad-gita* 5.29 as *suhridam-sarva-bhutanam*, "the friend and well-wisher of all living entities."[11] Similarly, *Srimad Bhagavatam* describes God as "the best friend and well-wisher of all beings, who is equal and affectionate to all" (7.1.1, 7.6.2, 7.6.26–27, 7.7.38, and 7.10.49), as *suparnam* or "he who always stays with the individual soul as a friend," as "he who views nothing as separate from himself" (10.74.24), as "the friend of the whole universe" (7.9.27), and as "the supreme friend and dearmost soul of everyone." In fact, in his commentary to *Srimad Bhagavatam* 7.7.38, Visvanatha Chakravarti says, "The Lord is the friend of the soul, residing like ether in his heart. The *Mundaka Upanishad* 3.1.1 says in this regard *sayujau sakhayau*: the Lord and the soul are two friends in a tree." An even more conclusive statement is shared in *Srimad Bhagavatam* 9.5.11, where the Sweet Absolute is described as *sarva-bhutatma-bhavena*, or "he who has love for all beings as his very self." Likewise, *Srimad Bhagavatam* 10.4.7 declares that God "descends for the benefit of all the souls in the world." In his commentary to this important verse, Sanatana Goswami says, "The Lord manifests specific qualities to benefit each soul in specific ways. Since the souls are unlimited, their natures are unlimited, and their conditions are unlimited, therefore the qualities that God reveals to benefit each of them must also be unlimited." Furthermore, in *Srimad Bhagavatam* 10.29.32 the Vraja gopis refer to the Sweet Absolute as *prestho bhavams tanubhritam kila bandhur atma*, or "the dearmost friend, most intimate relative, and very self of each embodied soul." Likewise, verse 10.87.22 declares that God "always shows mercy to the conditioned souls and affectionately helps them in every way." In his commentary on this verse, Sanatana Goswami declares, "God faces the soul in an inconceivable way because of his natural mercy, and he thus benefits the soul as an unconditional friend, and in this way he shows his affection to the soul." Finally, *Srimad Bhagavatam* 10.46.37 describes the Divine as "indifferent to anyone." In his commentary on this verse, Jiva Goswami declares, "Nobody is completely ignored by him because they have neither good nor bad qualities." Similarly, Sanatana Goswami comments, "God does not notice a person because he is high or ignore a person because he is low, however, he is not neutral." In other words, if someone does not notice or disregard another person because of their good or bad qualities and at the same time he is not neutral, we can thus conclude that such a person only addresses everyone on the basis of unconditional love. In this way, we can see how the Sweet Absolute experiences unconditional love for every single person, and not only his devotees.

To further decrypt this conundrum, we can give the example of a mother. She loves her baby even before meeting him outside of her womb and even during a good number of years that follow, when the child doesn't reciprocate with her consciously, but "only" depends on her. And this dependence is without any awareness (or appreciation) on the part of the child. While the mother's love exists from the very beginning, as the relationship with her child matures and develops he will reciprocate more and more consciously with his mother. And her initial love will then adopt new shapes and expressions in reciprocation with her son's affection. Following this analogy, we can see how the Sweet Absolute already loves each of us unconditionally (even when we dare to deny his existence), since he *is* unconditional love personified. *He cannot but love* in that way. As we voluntarily approach the Divine and attempt to develop our relationship with him, he remains loving us unconditionally, but now in a very specific and different way. Why? Because we have acknowledged our relationship with him and therefore he will correspond (co-respond) with our own reciprocity with the unconditional love he has for us.

For Gaudiyas, the face of the Absolute which has an initial unconditional love for everyone is known as Paramatma. He represents the presence of God's unconditional love residing not only in our hearts, but even in every atom. It is only when we choose to voluntarily reciprocate with that original love that Paramatma "takes the form" of Krishna, Gaurahari, or any of the endless personal expressions of the Sweet Absolute with whom we can have a mutual loving exchange. When appearing in one of these forms, he continues to shower his unconditional love. Then we can eternally reciprocate in a relationship of loving service with that particular form. This same principle is confirmed by Jiva Goswami throughout his *Sat-sandarbha*, where he makes the point that the indivisible nondual Absolute will present different facets of himself according to the level of perception of each respective seeker. But even if we do not seek him, the Sweet Absolute still has unconditional love for each of us. In fact, if God only loves his devotees (those who already love him) then his love would be *conditional* rather than unconditional—the condition being that "I will love you but only after you love me." Therefore, the very meaning of unconditional love has to go beyond these conditions, extending itself not only to God's seekers, but to his non-seekers as well.

We are loved unconditionally by the Sweet Absolute not so much for who we are, but *despite* who we are. In other words, if God loves us even though we challenge or deny his existence (or admit his existence in theory but live our lives as if he doesn't exist), this demonstrates that we have never done anything to deserve his love. And no matter what we might do from now on, we will *never* deserve it. To *de-serve* something is to drag it out of the realm of service, of free-flowing love, and into the world of meritocracy. *Unconditional love is too much to be deserved.* Therefore, to permanently coexist with the principle of undeserved, unconditional love we require the deepest humility. Without it, our ego won't be able to tolerate something that we can never deserve and are never worthy of. For Gaudiyas this unconditional love is synonymous with causeless mercy, which is not the same as *priceless* mercy. There is certainly a price to pay (though we can never deserve unconditional love), and that will be in coins of utter humility. If we are not willing to invest in this department but insist on "deserving," then we will be transferred to the department of justice, or *karma,* instead of the mercy agency. There we will have to pay another price. As ironic as it may sound, it's generally more difficult for us to pay the actual price for causeless mercy/unconditional love than to invest the required currency in the realm of conditional interdependence in the justice system. Apart from the required humility that makes this unconditional transaction so hard for some of us, what makes it even harder is that we are required to also believe in something that for the ego will seem too good to be true. But regardless of our reluctance or current inability to accept love given without conditions, the fact remains that unconditional love constitutes the very nature of ultimate reality: unreserved, unrestricted, unconditional affection.

Since these above implications of unconditional love may not be that easy to embrace in the beginning, it may be similarly difficult to engage in contemplative prayer. Why? Because basically contemplative prayer means to remain aware of our need for and dependence on unconditional love and, on top of that, to realize how such radical grace is already coming to us and has been coming to us from a time without beginning. This radical grace has never been against our will but has always existed *in spite of it.* Therefore, we need to be humble enough to allow grace to happen. This is real prayer, and this is essential spirituality. It is not a punish/reward transactional system where we are merely expected to "play the game right," but a *system of transformation.* It is a sacred space where real conversion can happen. Unfortunately, many of us still think in terms of what we may call "requirement religion" instead of "relationship religion"—*correctedness instead of connectedness.* In many instances, this attitude toward God was formed in childhood by experiences we may have had with parental and authority figures, all of which may carry unconscious fears and create misconceptions for us. Thus, one of the challenges in contemplative prayer is to relate to that Sweet Absolute who really *is* the Sweet Absolute (especially the "sweet" part) and not the Absolute of our childhood imagination, projections, or ethnic and cultural limitations—*most likely not a very sweet one.*

Contemplative prayer is not about changing God's mind, but about *changing our own mind about God*, and about ourselves in relation to him. He is extremely merciful—extremely—and we are to pray with that in mind. No matter how many *anarthas* (false values) we may still carry, the Sweet Absolute's causeless grace is always more powerful than all our *anarthas* put together. Thus, during our practice of prayer, which means our attempt to make prayer our whole lifestyle, we should not lose sight of the unconditionally loving Divine and how he has *already* been loving us much more than we can imagine from time without beginning. This unconditional love verily constitutes our *original blessing*, fully replacing any notion of original sin we may have entertained. Therefore, the idea that we have to first earn God's love by making ourselves somehow lovable for God is basically ridiculous. He already loves us, and his original love will continue evolving and unfolding. But we need to become aware of that, and contemplative prayer can bring that miracle into focus.

THE PRACTICE OF CONTEMPLATIVE PRAYER

If we choose to start thinking of contemplative prayer as a practice more than a permanent state of consciousness (we have to begin somewhere!), then we must first of all become aware of the backdrop behind our starting a life of prayer. As we may already intuit, the Sweet Absolute's unconditional love is the sole reason for this to happen. Therefore, our prayer will be merely an attempt to respond to and reciprocate with God's initial invitation. While we may be seeking him on one level or another, he is and will always be the Seeker of all seekers par excellence—he is the one who always makes the opening move. If we pray, it is not that we pray and sometimes God answers. If we pray, it means that God has already answered.[12]

It is after this sacred kickstart from the Lord himself that we will thus begin our prayer practice, an exercise similar to an alchemical process. Alchemy constitutes a thorough procedure to transform a substance while gently extracting its purest intrinsic potential. This is accomplished through a sequence of distinct stages and even multiple complete repetitions to refine the product to perfect purity. When applied to the practice of contemplative prayer, this sequence could be defined as follows: (1) a recognition of God's position (who he actually is) and a growing awareness of his love and intentions; (2) a recognition of our position (who I am and all I can be in relation to who he is); and (3) a recognition of the shared bond between the two of us. In other words, this holy sequence could be portrayed as (1) him, (2) me, and (3) us—Beloved, Lover, and Love. At this point it is important to note that to recognize God's position and one's own also clarifies that neither can take the place or do the job of the other. The Sweet Absolute may have infinite power and mercy, but he cannot do our job of being receptive or our work of contemplative prayer. As we already explained, this is not a question of being *worthy* of causeless mercy, but of doing our part by being positioned to catch it. Instead of praying for mercy, we should pray in order to realize how mercy has been there forever. That's our role in the sacred alchemy of contemplative prayer.[13]

We begin to attain the ideal of a permanent state of contemplative prayer through "a bunch of momentary behaviors" put together. There is no magical formula or supernatural button to press to attain such a state. We learn to be present in the present moment, aware of who we are and who God is and of how the Sweet Absolute is approaching us. We then open ourselves to receive the gift of God's presence without presenting any opposition. It sounds simple, *and it is*, but due to its very simplicity, prayer is also a struggle, since we are usually very complicated beings. While everything is present already, it is we who are not present yet. Thus, the initial steps of our being present in prayer have mostly to do with what was already referred to previously as *descending religion*: not transcending or even ascending, but first learning to descend. We don't embark upon a journey "up" to ethereal ideas about what we can always be certain of, but we are present to where we are *at present*, and progress from there accordingly. And realistically.

The descending journey needs to be described in phenomenological terms, considering things as they appear in our inner experience. This includes endless stratums of what we may refer to as *descent work.* To begin with, during prayer we need to become aware of our self-image. It is the identity mask we have created for ourselves (and others), and which we may still erroneously identify with as being who we are. Then, if we are attentive and sincere, a further layer of descent will reveal to us our behaviors that proceed from our concocted self-image. In other words, it's one thing to think who we are and it's another to observe our actions and how much they do (or do not) match our preconceived notions about ourselves. After we dismantle these initial layers, a deeper form of descent and presence during prayer will consist of acknowledging what are the underlying motivations and intentions behind each of our actions. In summary, not only do we have to demystify who we think and say we are, we also have to demystify our own actions, since we often hide behind what we do so we don't have to admit the purpose behind our activities. This is the beginning of "presence" during prayer, and yes, it is difficult. But we should remember: *difficult is just the middle point between easy and impossible.* And we are always told to tread the middle path.

DEVELOPING A CONTEMPLATIVE MIND

Just as our physical body evacuates toxins or waste products, contemplative prayer could also be seen as a form of evacuation. However, this evacuation is often prevented by defense mechanisms, repression, and especially *thinking*. Believe it or not, thinking is our biggest defense mechanism against transformation. It's a marvelous way of not facing the real issues of life; it's like a wall of protection against our subconscious. In fact, we could say that if there is anything we are addicted to the most, it is our own thoughts, our own way of filtering reality. However, our real life is not about us and our limited thoughts. Ultimately, we are in response to something much greater than ourselves: God and his unconditional sweetness. This greater thing is looking at us and calling us out, but thinking gets in the way of that call. In order to avoid this—in order to engage in contemplative prayer—we need to develop a contemplative mind.

As we already mentioned, reality is nondual, but we need a nondual mind to deal with such reality. Similarly, we need a contemplative mind to engage with contemplative prayer initially as a practice, and eventually as a full-blown lifestyle. Contemplative prayer is thus synonymous with developing a contemplative mind. This will correspondingly allow us to participate in contemplative prayer. A contemplative mind (basically synonymous with nondual thinking) can be described as *the ultimate assault on the calculative mind* (or fragmented consciousness), which compulsively thinks only in terms of dualistic personal advantage. While this compulsive mind provides quick security and false comfort, it never grants wisdom. Conversely, the contemplative mind can see things in their depth and wholeness instead of just in parts. This is a different way of processing our experience.

The contemplative mind could be defined as a *non-obsessive mind*. Such a mind runs contrary to the dynamics of our current world, which fosters a postmodern, overstimulated, anti-contemplative mind.[14] This obsessive mind is characterized by compulsive patterns of thinking and perception, ninety-five percent of which are said to be repetitive and basically useless. To admit this to ourselves may certainly be humiliating, but we should remember that this is nothing but our false self, so we shouldn't overidentify with it during prayer. This false self needs to be transcended or, in better words, *converted*. And it is no exaggeration to say that the path of conversion will be experienced as nothing but *a series of necessary humiliations to the false self*.[15] However, as terrible as this may sound, there is a beauty in it, and we need to experience the beauty of objective humiliation. This is not a humiliation coming from others, but one experienced by witnessing our own messiness. True witnessing of our wounded side gives rise to genuine compassion toward ourselves, and that in turn spirals into sincere humility. The holding of our human limitations with utter honesty and charity rests in the reality that each soul is a beautiful mystery that the Divine considers more than worthy of being and loving. Yes, this even despite all our present negativity. We can never remind ourselves enough of how the Sweet Absolute doesn't need to eliminate the negative in order to love us, and how we would be best to love back in the same way. How? We can extend this same pattern and experience of unconditional positive regard to those who are in desperate need of learning how to deal with the false self, the "relative identity," which lives by the "performance principle" alone. It's not a bad self; it's just not the real one. We don't need to hate it, *but to convert it.*

During the initial stages of developing our contemplative mind we become aware of the dimension of our noncontemplative mind. This experience will be more like unlearning than learning, more like surrendering than accomplishing. This is probably why so many of us resist prayer to begin with. Because it feels more like the shedding of thoughts in general than attaining new or good ones. It feels more like just letting go than accomplishing anything.[16] In other words, we could say that any in-depth journey into prayer is definitely a training in powerlessness, in what we cannot do, which is why so many of us give up on it.[17] However, we should remain open to this process—*and open continuously*. In fact, contemplative prayer could be described as *a series of openings*. It is a continuous movement of openness, which initially will be focused on letting go of all personal agendas, expectations, desires for divine consolation, and even psychological breakthroughs of any kind. Instead, we will remain open in our minds. This then will allow us to be open in our hearts and relate to the Sweet Absolute from that open space.

Much of the work of developing a contemplative mind has to do with discovering a way to observe ourselves from a compassionate and nonjudgmental distance until we can eventually live our life more and more from this calm inner awareness and acceptance. This implies accepting situations as a whole without rejecting or judging or labeling, but gazing positively at reality while acknowledging its inherent dignity.[18] This gazing and inherent dignity will be disclosed in the present moment, and this is why daily vigilance to be present is the very heart of all spirituality. In fact, the principal fruits of contemplative prayer may be experienced most in our daily life, outside of our official moments of prayer. Therefore, developing a contemplative mind also implies remaining attentive in this regard. A life of prayer requires that we contemplate the truth regularly. It is fundamental that one learns in prayer to be receptive and active simultaneously, harmonizing full dependence with full response-ability.

Contemplative prayer is not a comfort zone; it's a *confront zone*. It's entering our chamber, trying to stop thinking, and then seeing the result of such an experiment. As soon as we take away outside stimuli, all our inner turmoil erupts. Therefore, in the beginning contemplation may not be that consoling; it will "only" be real. We have no choice but to go through this initial stage of what Gaurahari called *cheto-darpana-marjanam*, or cleaning the mirror of our subconscious. If we don't find a way of praying that *invades our subconscious*, nothing will change at any depth.[19] Only when we stop the parade of new voices and ideas will we see the underlying and ever-recurring patterns: voices which are normally negative, paranoid and obsessive, agenda-driven, and insecure. We may want to run away, due to the level of humiliation we'll have to go through.[20] But we should remember in those moments that the word *humility* comes from "humiliation," but a healthy one. And we certainly need humility, because without it there is only false ego—and the false ego cannot pray. To put it bluntly, *in real prayer there cannot be false ego*.

As much as we have to acknowledge the obsessive nature of our thinking patterns, it's equally crucial not to resist these thoughts. We must not repress them, and much less hate them. Rather we need a *joyful* attitude toward them—a friendly attitude toward the most dreadful thoughts. Prayer doesn't mean that we're not going to have thoughts, but that we are not going to *think about* those thoughts. It's one thing is to allow birds to fly above our head; it's another to allow them to build a nest on our head. Therefore, memories and planning can happen as they usually do, but without kidnapping our attention away from whatever else is going on at the time. Instead, they will be experienced as *part of* what is occurring in the moment of prayer. Gradually, we will be able to extend that same pattern to the rest of our day, where we won't be "officially" praying but will be seeing all our life situations as integrated in the context of a bigger picture. This is when prayer finally becomes a lifestyle.

In due time and with proper practice, our contemplative mind will be developed to the point that we are simply present to what is. Nothing will be shut out, nothing excluded. Ideally, there can be no distractions in contemplation because everything is simply a part of what is going on. There is no need to discard reality, since at this point even the profane has become holy by our *centeredness in the present moment.* A contemplative mind implies meeting reality in its most immediate form, that of a sacred relationship in which we will not only talk, but mostly hear.

CONTEMPLATIVE PRAYER AS RELATIONSHIP

We cannot reflect too much on how contemplative prayer is, first and foremost, a relationship. It is a loving exchange between us and the Sweet Absolute. The method—whatever it may be—is totally in the service of that relationship. Deepening trust in any relationship, especially our relationship with God, takes time and commitment. It is a process that moves us from acquaintanceship to friendliness to friendship, and ultimately, if we consent, to intimacy.[21] Ultimately, this relationship (this prayer) is all about immediacy, beauty, intimacy, and depth. However, to develop a relationship with the Divine through prayer presupposes a willingness to listen to him. *And listening is an act of silence.* Therefore, silence doesn't mean "don't speak" but rather "hear attentively." In *Bhagavad-gita* 10.38 Sri Krishna says that among all secret things he is silence. Srila Prabhupada comments that "among the confidential activities of hearing, thinking, and meditating, silence is *most important,* because by silence one can make progress very quickly." In fact, *Srimad Bhagavatam* 7.15.77 declares that the Sweet Absolute is he who is "worshiped by silence." Therefore, we should not only hear attentively, but everything we say should be in response to what we heard in that initial silence.

If we are not silent—if we are making or hearing too much inner noise—we won't be able to listen to God's voice through sacred prayer. That is why Krishna identifies himself with silence in the above *Gita* verse. It is not because he speaks in silence, but because he speaks *through* silence, through our attentive hearing. It is in this connection that Thomas Keating wisely and repeatedly said that God's primary language is silence, "with everything else being a very poor translation."[22] In any genuine conversation, we are listening as well as talking, but mostly listening. Listening is paying attention. It's amazing what people will tell us if we listen. What to speak of what the Sweet Absolute will tell us if we actually listen to him! However, in the initial stages of our contemplative practice, or in our life itself, we will find it difficult to "just hear." As Carl Rogers aptly puts it:

> *The great majority of us cannot listen; we find ourselves compelled to evaluate, because listening is too dangerous. The first requirement is courage, and we do not always have it. ... If you really understand a person in this way [through attentive hearing], if you are willing to enter his private world and see the way life appears to him, you run the risk of being changed yourself: this risk of being changed is one of the most frightening prospects most of us can face.*[23]

Now let's apply this idea to our approach to God and contemplative prayer, which is our attempt to communicate with him, and offer ourselves in an eternal relationship of love and trust with the Divine, with all the risk and transformation this implies. If we do not fully embrace the implications of this relationship, we will construct a false idea of God. We won't take any risk in our relationship with him—and we won't have to be transformed an inch. As it has been brilliantly said, bad theology is like pornography: *the imagination of a real relationship without the risk of one.*[24] However, we have seen how impossible it is to love another without hearing that other, and without being utterly transformed by such a process. Therefore, if we *really* want to love and be transfigured by the Sweet Absolute, we need to pay close attention to him. In fact, this is what contemplative prayer is about. When we actively engage in the silent dialogue of receptivity, we can truly be who we actually are, and acknowledge who the Supreme Lord actually is. Therefore, all we have to do in prayer is "just" stop being who we *think* we are and let God be God for the time being.

Allowing God to be who he actually is and all that he wishes to become in our lives is, as suspected, easier said than done. "Who the Divine is" is more often than not merely an imposition of our own ideas and opinions about who he is and even about how he should be. However, *God is not our idea of God.* Accordingly, contemplative prayer as a relationship implies the permanent willingness to revise and adjust not only our ideas about God but especially our direct experience of him in that relationship. For most of us, God is still a theological concept rather than an actual person we can relate to. But deep prayer is meant for *meeting the person behind the concept*. In other words, a radical encounter with the Divine through contemplative prayer is not the same as *our ideas* about him. In fact, the former will probably undo the latter. To be a personalist—a radical one—doesn't meant to *say* (or even think) that God is a person. It means to *address* him as a person: to have a living, dynamic personal relationship with the Sweet Absolute. Without this disposition, our so-called prayer will be directed to a convenient and imagined idea of who the Sweet Absolute is, which is synonymous with him not being there at all. As Teresa of Ávila has extraordinarily noted, the trouble most of us have with prayer is that *we pray as if God is absent*. We pray as if he is not a real person—as if he does not exist.

THE GREATER WORK

In consideration of the classic template of silent contemplation, the Gaudiya's crucial daily practice of invoking Krishna's names may be seen not as contemplative prayer but rather as something separate from it. However, this invocation is meant to be engaged in with the same contemplative prayerful spirit we have been speaking about. Without the infusion of our prayerful spirit in the recitation of Krishna's names, we will be left with a lifeless and mechanical process rather than the dynamic presence of God in the form of his sacred name. In fact, catatonic repetition of anything is a recipe for unconsciousness—the opposite of any real consciousness, intentionality, or spiritual maturity.[25] Therefore, before our daily practice of prayer (and even during its very first moments) it can be helpful to spend a few minutes focusing our mood and intention of sacred reception, instead of rushing into autopilot and fumbling our beads without any further thought. The example of scanning malicious software could be a good metaphor in this connection. If we do not do a conscious scan of how and why our mind and heart are operating in a certain way at the beginning of our prayer time, often hidden and well-disguised "malware" will end up controlling the entire experience.[26] Conversely, centering our awareness on the proper mood will help us invoke the ideal Gaudiya spirit—the spirit of loving service—during prayer and life itself. That said, "service" refers not only to a specific activity, but more importantly to a specific attitude, which is the intention to keep ourselves in a state of prayer. In other words, the Gaudiya work becomes service (devotional service) proportionately to how much it is based upon an inner life of prayer. Prayer does not qualify us for a "greater work"; rather, prayer itself is the Greater Work.

While contemplative prayer is the Greater Work, we should bear in mind that it always begins ("begs in") at a starting place, proceeds to a continuing place, and finally culminates at an ending place. In the beginning, prayer may be experienced as a practice and even as a struggle. But as we progress in our contemplation, we will eventually realize that prayer is a gift from above that is being given to us. *Prayer is something that happens to us*, much more than anything we privately do.[27] In fact, eventually we will find our reality to be, "Prayer happened, and I was there," more than "I prayed today."[28] In a deep sense, contemplative prayer is not an action that we decide to engage in, but an epiphany. It is a gift that comes to us. Eventually, gradually, it becomes second nature. It's something that *is being done to us*, and the only thing we have to do, so to speak, is *get out of the way*. We have to be there, present, attentive, offering our hands and heart to receive the gift without presenting opposition and trusting the principle of divine radical grace.

Despite whatever stage we may be in, prayer is not to be conceived of as a goal to be attained, but rather as an ever more resolute commitment to our journey. By its very nature, contemplative prayer is a stance that will accompany us into eternity. Correspondingly, eternity can be experienced and discovered through prayer in the here and now. In other words, contemplative prayer is not so much a requirement for entry into heaven—it is much more like *practicing heaven now*.[29] In connection to how the spiritual world (our Gaudiya heaven) can be intimately perceived in our present moment and situation, let's turn to our next and final chapter of this third part.

14 Unearthing Heaven: How Material Energy Hosts the Spiritual World

There are no unsacred places; there are only sacred places and desecrated places.

—Wendell Berry

THE CONTEMPLATIVE VISION addressed in our previous chapter is a stance toward life that allows us to see the truth of things in their wholeness. In this chapter, we will allow the contemplative perspective to continue emerging, brimming, and spilling over by reflecting on how the world is not mundane or profane but, if we have the eyes to see, deeply embedded in holiness and sacred presence. The world of matter is never bad; *it carries an inherently blessed purpose.* This is a pivotal aspect of Radical Personalism. We want to properly venerate and honor every aspect of reality with an ultra-positive approach, including material unfolding. Bearing in mind the nondual foundation of reality (as well as the Sweet Absolute's presence in every atom), we will naturally conclude that the material energy has the potential to reveal and provide the immediacy of transcendence to us *here.* And "here" is not a geographical location, but always a state of consciousness.

In this chapter, we will explain how Gaudiya Vaishnavism promotes the deepest regard for material creation and how this is validated by God himself, who perpetually comes to Earth to execute his divine play, or *lila*. We long to participate in eternal reality, and our participation begins here and now. Before unearthing heaven, however, let's first unearth some typical misrepresentations of the core Gaudiya teaching in this regard.

CLASSIC MISUNDERSTANDINGS ABOUT MATTER IN THE GAUDIYA COMMUNITY

While Radical Nondualism proposes that the universe is ontologically unreal (*jagat mithya*), Radical Personalism, which is synonymous with Gaudiya Vaishnavism, embraces the opposite idea. In fact, essential Gaudiya teachings never promote evading or rejecting anything, but engaging everything in sacred service. The Gaudiya sense of transcendence does not embrace renunciation, but integration. For example, *Srimad Bhagavatam* 11.20.8 mentions that to attain success in *bhakti* one cannot be too attached or too detached. In other words, *nothing needs to be rejected* except our false sense of separateness from our source. Unfortunately, throughout the years an excessive emphasis on asceticism has affected the understanding of a good number of Gaudiya Vaishnavas. It is now common to think that the world of matter is to be urgently dismissed as intrinsically bad, mundane, profane, and even miserable—a place to leave as soon as possible. But the Gaudiya goal is not *mukti* (emancipation from this world), but *prema* (divine love). And the latter does not care for the former *at all*.

Although rejection of this world is not a Gaudiya tenet, Gaudiya teachers and scriptures sometimes speak of the world as devoid of intrinsic value. Such views can benefit both the novice and the accomplished practitioner, but also hinder one's progress if misapplied out of time or context. We will highlight some of these misunderstandings and their effects in this section, but first we will briefly discuss the efficacy of such descriptions.

For the novice, descriptions that seem to negate the value of the world can serve to extricate us, not from the world, but from our limiting conceptions of the world. The more our consciousness is steeped and invested in dualistic thought, the stronger the push must be from the opposite direction in order to free us from our current mindset. In the beginning of our spiritual journey we are embedded in the consciousness that matter is the be-all and end-all. Neither our vision nor our experience goes beyond that limit. It is as if we consider a frozen lake no more than the layers of ice on its surface, and therefore miss the reality of the rich life that lies within the lake. Before we can even begin to think about breaking the ice and entering the water, we must first break our enamored gaze, which is fixed on the notion that all meaning, all value exists on these top layers. Negatively speaking about the created world is meant to break our vacuous catatonic stare upon her. Ironically, this begins the process of honoring Earth's fullest potential to be a conduit of loving exchange. Consider a common occurrence of this process. Although admittedly immature, it is quite normal that after the breakup of a relationship there is often an initial period of speaking badly about the other person, rattling off a laundry list of inadequacies, of failures and bad habits, sometimes rerunning that list over and over again. To be sure, these moments are not our proudest, but they do serve a purpose. And that purpose is not detachment, as one might first construe. Although detachment might come as a result of cognitive pushback, it is not the goal. The purpose of our natural and almost instinctive reaction to speak in ways opposite of how we once felt is to dislodge us from our previous mindset and therefore create the space for a shift to happen. That space, which is often called chaos, allows us to turn things around and over in our mind in order to shake us loose from our previous conceptions and extract the lessons of experience. The final stage of a healthy shift is integration, an assimilation of these valuable lessons into a new and unified way of seeing ourselves, others (including the Sweet Absolute), the world, and the relationships between all of them. So this process that began by speaking as if the world is an undesirable place shook us loose not from the grip of the world, but from our grip on false values and deeply engrained patterns that we had embedded ourselves in. Our vision was near-sighted, our thoughts dualistic, and our sense of self separated from the whole as we misidentifed the top layers of frozen water with the lake itself. As we progress and mature, integrating things we once denied, we are able to be more present. We open ourselves to wider experiences and enter more deeply into that very realm we originally thought we were leaving behind. This is like a heartbroken lover who initially speaks fiercely about her lost love yet with maturity is able to assimilate not what was lost, but what was left after the loss, into a richer experience of all that remains true.

The accomplished might speak about the created world as if it practically has no value, its very existence thwarting the development of divine love. This view allows them to mine their feelings of longing, both mitigating them and, paradoxically, facilitating them. This kind of negative speech about the natural world rises from a deep lamentation by souls who experience the mere thought of being separated from their Beloved even for a portion of a moment as too much to bear. The deepest reach of this kind of lamentation drives the dearest and closest lovers of the Supreme, who are never separated from him, to speak badly of the creator and curse him for giving them eyelids that block their view of their Beloved during the involuntary act of blinking. Please keep in mind that while they are declaring the futility of the created world, it is the utility of that very same creation that serves to inflame their love. Therefore, they continually hanker for such human experience of separation. It is through human experience that their divine love is nurtured, expanded, and expressed. This is what happens when one becomes proficient in swimming deeply within the water of the lake.

In order to survive spiritually and form an initial new sense of identity, at the beginning of our spiritual practice (when dualistic thinking is prominent) we often develop distinctly demarcated conceptions of what's to be accepted and rejected. We do this by conceiving of spirituality mostly in negative terms. In our embryonic stage we may feel the need to flat-out reject many things simply out of our limited capacity to maturely accept them in their proper context. This initial, somewhat required, mental split often continues longer than needed, and so practitioners continue to think and speak and act in terms of "my spiritual life" and "my material life." They see "material life" as a nemesis to be eliminated instead of making it part of a higher integrative synthesis. While we choose to create and maintain such dichotomies, in time all of these patterns need to evolve into a nondual and integral approach to existence, allowing us to retire any childish distinctions still lurking. It's not that religion is holy and the world is profane. Both religion and the secular *can* be holy, and both can be profane as well. It all depends on our vision.

One of the many ways Gaudiyas refer to material energy is by the term *maya-shakti*. This refers to one of the many energies of the Supreme Lord that operate in relation to the material realm. Sometimes *maya-shakti* is misconstrued as some kind of evil personality who wants to keep us from God and intends to make us fall to this planet and suffer here. This pseudo-Gaudiya notion of Christianity's Satan is far from the truth. *Maya-shakti* has nothing to do with an evil, ill-motived, and perverse potency longing to see us fall into her grip. In *Bhagavad-gita* 9.10, Sri Krishna confirms that *maya-shakti*—this world—is not bad or negative, since it works under his direction. *Maya-shakti* is a sacred energy that *we* need to understand and honor properly. If we choose to approach *maya-shakti* in order to exploit her, we will be entangled, but if we proceed toward her with respect and concern, she will naturally point to our common source. *It's all about our approach, not her intention.* That is precisely why the Gaudiya scriptures sometimes describe this world as a perverted reflection of the spiritual realm: to indicate an upside-down perception of reality *on our part.* This world is not in itself an illusion, but the way we may be perceiving this world can be illusory. When properly seen in connection to its source, the world of matter can and will transport us to the other world. It does this not by catapulting us to some other place, but by facilitating the fleshing out of our highest potential. We do this by living fully, wholly, through the pains and joys, triumphs and sufferings. Our spiritual practices will awaken us to such a prospect.

The function of matter and its multifaceted expressions are not bad but highly recommended to meditate on. For example, *Srimad Bhagavatam* 2.7.53 encourages its reader to regularly describe, appreciate, and hear about God's interaction with his material energy, and then concludes saying that by doing so *one will be free from all illusion.* In his commentary to this verse, Sri Visvanatha Chakravarti mentions that "one should have faith that the material energy is *a devotee with the greatest devotion,* and therefore a devotee should hear about such a devotee, since the Lord's *lila* in relation to *maya* [matter] is not *maya* [illusion]. Instead, *it is something transcenden-*

tal." Sri Visvanatha then concludes by quoting *Srimad Bhagavatam* 11.25.25, where the Sweet Absolute himself declares that "residence in a place where I reside is transcendental." Since God is omnipresent and in direct contact with everything at all times, his place of residence is thus everywhere. With this in mind, we are invited to re-cognize how, if properly addressed and conceived, matter hosts transcendence. Therefore, the relationship we seek in transcendence is already here within the fibers of matter.

One of the names through which Gaudiyas conceive of the Divine is *mukhya-sambandha*, or he with whom everyone and everything has a primary relationship. To ignore this crucial fact is to grossly misconstrue this world. Such an oversight is likely the reason we attempt to "transcend" the world, or reject it, by thinking that it is against us or, even worse, that it is against God's will. However, to consider material energy to be separated from the Divine is in itself one of the biggest illusions we could possibly embrace. Like all potencies of the Absolute, material energy is simultaneously one with and different from him, with all differences being rooted in the foundation of nondual reality. This does not say that there are no differences among the energies of God, but rather it fully recognizes the differences and acknowledges that all the variegatedness, regardless of apparent contradictions arising from those differences, exists within the existence of God. In truth, this sacred potency, material energy, is fully dedicated to serving her own source—*much more than we are presently*. Therefore, we should learn from her how to properly dedicate ourselves to our common master. To deeply consider and grasp these essential points will help us enormously. If we misread matter, we may end up trying to exploit it selfishly for our own private agenda or reject it as intrinsically evil. Radical Personalism's definition of a genuine, committed *materialist* is thus someone who does not try to manipulate matter or is indifferent to it, but rather one who cares about, embraces, and even venerates her as a potential portal to infinity. Sri Jiva Goswami confirms this in his commentary to *Srimad Bhagavatam* 10.14.28 saying, "People of good judgment seek only God within the world. According to these people who have proper discernment, the world is an effect of God, the subtle cause, and so the world contains traces of God's qualities." Likewise, *Srimad Bhagavatam* 10.16.46 declares that while God disguises himself with the material qualities, the functioning of those same material qualities ultimately reveals God's existence. In the words of Thakura Bhaktivinoda, "Matter is the dictionary of the spirit."[1]

If we insist on perceiving matter as fundamentally harmful, then we will likely misconceive our body as bad and despicable. This will lead to a poor and premature expression of transcendence by which we attempt to dismiss our physical and psychic selves, which results in many varieties of *disembodied spirituality*. From this unnatural place of physio-psycho-emotional decapitation, we end up conceiving of our body as an unfortunate burden, rather than something with the potential of becoming fully spiritualized and assisting us in the pursuit of our highest ideals. This has been accurately described by Visvanatha Chakravarti's commentary on *Srimad Bhagavatam* 10.29.11, which he concludes by saying, "When one reaches the stage of *prema* [divine love], one's body is *completely* spiritualized, *and no mundane portion remains*." Similarly, in his commentary on *Srimad Bhagavatam* 5.12.11, he says, "All the material objects which give rise to false conceptions *lose their material qualities* by association with *bhakti*. The Lord makes those objects *the highest truth*, favorable to the desires of his devotee. What is impossible for the inconceivable power of the Lord?"

Therefore, our conception and definition of matter may require some rewiring. Instead of seeing matter as vulgar and indecorous, it could be defined as *something with the potential of becoming extremely gross, but also (and especially) extremely spiritualized.* It all depends on our angle of vision. Srila Prabhupada confirms this in his purport to *Srimad Bhagavatam* 1.5.33,

> *The material conception of a thing is at once changed as soon as it is put into the service of the Lord. That is the secret of spiritual success. We should not try to lord it over the material nature, nor should we reject material things. ... Everything is an emanation from the Supreme Spirit, and by his inconceivable power he can convert spirit into matter and matter into spirit. Therefore, a material thing (so-called) is at once turned into a spiritual force by*

> *the great will of the Lord. The necessary condition for such a change is to employ so-called matter in the service of the spirit. ... When everything is thus employed in the service of the Lord, we can experience that there is nothing except the Supreme Brahman. The Vedic* mantra *that "everything is Brahman" is thus realized by us.*

The above quote is a purport on the verse that says, "A thing applied therapeutically cures a disease which was caused by that very same thing." In other words, we can become dis-eased if we approach matter with an eye of exploitation, but we can be cured if we approach that same energy with the proper eye. Accordingly, if everything is connected with the Sweet Absolute—as it is—then our body is also connected to him. Thus, if properly conceived, a connection with our body implies a connection with the Sweet Absolute, because we will be connected with something that is in connection to him. A similar criterion applies to our present ecological crisis, which is in part the result of an unnecessary split between matter and spirit that has been mostly promoted by religion. If this world is perceived as profane and thus separated from the Divine, it becomes negligible.

Matter is not synonymous with *mundane,* although Gaudiyas may often equate these two terms. We reason that a transcendentalist is not supposed to have anything to do with anything mundane, so when we refer to this world as *mundane,* we dismiss the whole topic of our relationship with it out of hand. However, matter is a sacred energy of the Divine, an energy which he himself eternally inhabits in every one of her pores—in every atom. This is confirmed in *Srimad Bhagavatam* 10.30.4, where the Vraja *gopis* describe the Sweet Absolute as he who is "present inside and outside of all created things, just like the sky." Sridhara Swami validates this point even more emphatically in his commentary on *Srimad Bhagavatam* 10.14.56 saying, "The Supreme Lord is not only the Soul of all living beings, but he is also the Soul of all inert things." So how can we call matter *mundane*? What certainly has the potential to be mundane is our own approach to matter; a proper approach will show us matter in a different light. Or, more specifically, *matter itself will show us a different light.*

THE GAUDIYA APPROACH: MATERIAL CREATION AS A BYPRODUCT OF GOD'S JOY

Having explained in brief what the Gaudiya approach is *not*, let's now address what that approach actually is. However, we will do so by considering some possible arguments to our above points, such as abundant sections in the Gaudiya texts which describe the material world as miserable, illusory, temporary, and so on. It is important to clarify that while different scriptures speak in these terms, they also speak in very different tones in many other sections, where they praise all the spiritual opportunities this world offers by being one of God's energies acting in his service. In other words, sacred scripture speaks with different audiences in mind and therefore invokes different expressions. For example, for those who are blindly attached, scriptures will apparently speak about the absolute misery of this world, while they are actually speaking about the misery of being selfish, self-centered, and exploitative toward any of God's energies, this world being one of them. However, for those who see this world for what it actually is—potential paraphernalia to be engaged in sacred service—the Gaudiya scriptures will employ a very different language, as we will see.

We already mentioned in previous chapters how the Gaudiya texts mostly speak about the guru in idealistic terms; they assume that such a person is fully qualified to perform that function. Understanding this backdrop is crucial for us when attempting to discern a situation wherein a guru deviates from ideal behavior. Similarly, we should know that Gaudiya texts speak about the world in different ways because people have very different states of consciousness. Some people need to be dissuaded from wrong action to prevent avoidable consequences; others need to be encouraged to continue deepening their virtuous behavior. A classic example is of a mother threatening her mischievous child so he does not do the detrimental thing she knows he is tempted to do. She wants to prevent him from suffering. When the child becomes serious and mature, then his mother no longer employs threatening language but progresses to more positive language. A scriptural example of these contrasting statements in relation to the material world can be found in

Krishna's words to Arjuna about this world being miserable and temporary.[2] In apparent contradiction, Prabodhananda Saraswati cries out *visvam-purna sukhayate*! "This whole universe is an abode of joy."[3] The fact that different people perceive the world differently and are addressed by the scriptures through different language is also confirmed by Jiva Goswami in *Paramatma Sandarbha* 69, where he declares, "Those whose minds are not fixed on God accept only the unreal aspect of the universe, whose very essence is God. However, those who know God accept only the real aspect." One more time, it is up to us to choose our lens.

The world of matter is *not* against the Divine but is in eternal service to him, and according to Gaudiyas it even manifests as a result of God's own joy. This is clearly stated in *Vedanta-sutra* 2.1.33, *lokavat tu lila kaivalyam*: "The motive of the Lord in creating the world is mere sport only—his *lila*—as we see in ordinary life." Since the word *lila* refers to a celebratory movement on God's part, this *sutra* basically describes the whole material unfolding as a byproduct of God's own maddened bliss—*as an overflowing of his own self.* This unique notion is clearly confirmed in Baladeva Vidyabhusana's commentary on this aphorism. He says, "As in ordinary life, men full of cheerfulness, when awakening from sound sleep, begin to dance about without any object, but from mere exuberance of spirit, such is the case with the Lord. This *lila*, or the sport of the Lord, is natural to him because he is full of self-bliss." If this is not enough, then Sri Baladeva continues his commentary by quoting *Mandukya Upanishad* 1.9: "Some think that the creation is for the sake of enjoyment [of the Creator], while others think that it is for the sake of his recreation. However, this act of creation is God's own nature [he does it without any motive]. What motive can there be for one who has all his desires satisfied?" To conclude, Baladeva Vidyabhusana then quotes *Narayana-samhita* which declares, "The act of creation on the part of God, as well as his other actions, does not depend on any motive: he does so out of sheer joy, as the drunkard dances through frenzy. He who is full of all bliss can have no motive whatsoever. When even the liberated souls have all of their desires fulfilled through him, what unfulfilled desire can there be in the case of the Lord, who is the Self of the universe?" Therefore, if this material world is nothing but an overflow of God's divine frenzy—an outcome of the celebration of his own existence—should we call it "profane" or supramundane?

The idea of God's joy being fully engraved in the DNA of creation is not limited to the above references. The *Chandogya Upanishad*, an even earlier Vedic text, presents a similar backdrop by describing, "In the beginning there was only one Real Entity, only one without a second. That one Real Entity wished: 'Let me become many, let me multiply myself.' "[4] In other words, this foundational Vedic text recounts that in the beginning the One Ultimate Reality was lonely and bored, without anyone to share his joy. Since there is not much fun in playing by oneself, the One desired others to play with and so divided itself. Through this creative method the One produced out of itself the manifold world of all entities, both animate and inanimate, and proceeded to interact with itself in a multitude of forms in order to engage in nondual play, or *lila*.[5] While nonduality leads to an understanding of the infinite in the finite, so does play, as play is one of the consequences of nondualism. Play is nonteleological: it is action in which there is nothing to be accomplished.[6] In other words, the Sweet Absolute does not act for pleasure, but *out of* pleasure. That is his play, or *lila*. This is confirmed in *Bhagavad-gita* 3.22, where Sri Krishna declares how he does not need or desire anything and, in spite of that, he acts. Likewise, *Srimad Bhagavatam* 2.4.7 describes God's interaction with matter with the expression *kridayam kridan*, or "engaging in play," and verse 3.26.4 describes how the Sweet Absolute interacts with material energy in terms of *lilaya*, or "as his divine play." Similarly, verse 8.22.20 declares that the Sweet Absolute creates the entire universe for the enjoyment of his personal *lila* (*kridartham atmana idam tri-jagat kritam te*), and verse 11.29.7 invokes the term *jagat-kridanakah*, describing how the Sweet Absolute employs this universe for his divine play.[7] When full divine presence is everywhere here and now, then joyful play becomes the only option[8]—and God himself engages in such play perpetually. From the nondual perspective that underlies Gaudiya Vaishnavism everything is already *purnam*, or complete. Therefore, nothing remains to be achieved. An *Upanishadic* verse[9] states this well: "That is full, this is full. Fullness proceeds from fullness. When fullness is taken from fullness, only fullness remains."[10] In other words, if the whole is made up of interrelated little wholes—if we are *wholes within wholes, longing for further wholeness*—how can this material realm be seen as entirely unwhole, *unwholy*, miserable, and rejectable?

This same idea is presented with different words by Jiva Goswami in *Paramatma Sandarbha* 102, where he describes how God creates for the sake of his devotees. This is similar to a statement found in *Srimad Bhagavatam* 10.14.37, where Sri Brahma prays to the Sweet Absolute declaring that the Lord comes to this Earth and imitates material life just to expand the varieties of ecstatic enjoyment for his surrendered devotees. We already described how this world is a consequence of God's own inner bliss, but that bliss is mainly experienced by him in relation to his intimate lovers, his devotees. The interaction between God and his devotees is rightfully called *lila*, and thus the overflow of that *lila* into this world is described as *sristi-lila*, or the "play of creation." However, we could argue that while God creates for the sake of his devotees, not everyone is his devotee. While that's certainly true, we could (and should) add that everyone is a devotee *in potential*. And the Sweet Absolute looks upon us not according to who we were or even are, but for all that we can be in terms of our potential. And for every single soul, this ultimate potential entails becoming a lover of God, *becoming his devotee*. Therefore, we can say that the Sweet Absolute sees everyone as his devotee and, since this material creation is manifested for the sake of God's devotees, all of us are therefore included in the ultimate purpose of this earthly unfolding. This is confirmed in *Srimad Bhagavatam* 8.24.29, where Satyavrata Muni prays to the Lord, "All your *lilas* and *avataras* certainly appear for the welfare of all living entities."[11] With this right vision in mind, material creation is no longer our old version of *samsara*—the anxious cycle of repeated birth and death—but a new, deeper form of it. It is *sam-sara*, or full (*sam*) essence (*sara*). When we start in a hole, we never really get out of it, but when we start with an original blessing, life only grows bigger and always much better.[12] This world is not a hole but *something whole*. This world is not bad to begin with, but arises out of God's celebratory madness.

THE ULTIMATE RECYCLING PROCESS

With the above vision in place, the Gaudiya conclusion is that everything can be used and nothing is to be wasted. It is the *ultimate recycling process*. Gaudiya Vaishnavism refers to this as *yukta-vairagya*, or "proper renunciation." The definition of *yukta-vairagya* explains that it is a renunciation that sees everything as part of God and encourages us to relate to everything in connection to him. The opposite of this is called *phalgu-vairagya*, or "useless renunciation." This type of renunciation is useless because everything, including things related to God—and that is *everything*—is rejected in an attempt to transcend matter in unrealistic terms.[13] In other words, proper renunciation means to accept everything in connection to the Sweet Absolute and thus in his service. This position allows us to adhere, without desecration, to the conceptual virginity of all things. In a similar spirit, Jiva Goswami introduces the idea of *sanga-siddha-bhakti*,[14] which implies that things that are not inherently *bhakti* can become such if employed for the pleasure of the Supreme Lord. Peeling potatoes is not intrinsically *bhakti*, but it can become so if we do it while properly acknowledging how those potatoes are one of God's energies, and we relate to them by acknowledging their connection to the Divine. Since everything has a connection to him, everything is potential paraphernalia to be engaged in loving service. In fact, this world of matter is arguably our main paraphernalia. And yes, this world can be pretty messy and chaotic at times, but, above that, a sober vision will appreciate how God's unconditional love is especially present in those wounded places. The Sweet Absolute is *made* of unconditional love, and, him being so, he becomes not only close to us but *absurdly close*. He is so incredibly close that we are forced to either discover him in all the messiness of creation, no matter how confusing and abrasive, or to outright reject him.[15]

In Gaudiya Vaishnavism and Hinduism in general, this ultimate recycling process expresses itself in a variety of ways, one of them being the classic worship ceremony called *arati*. Material elements like incense, flaming lamps, water, and flowers are offered to a form of the Divine made of material elements like wood, stone, bronze, or marble. Instead of sheer idolatry, this sacred ritual teaches us how, through a particular process of transforming our vision, we can see and appreciate that what we conceived of as material is actually transcendental. Ideally, this localized and condensed perception of the sacred in matter is then extended beyond one's altar to the rest of creation—the whole world becoming an altar, our Deity further universalized.[16] To achieve this vision during *arati*, one performs an important preliminary ceremony called *bhuta-suddhi*, through which the worshiper invokes sacred prayers while adopting the ego of a servant. This allows him to approach matter as a portal to infinity. Further preliminary prayers encourage the worshiper to see that the five main elements that make up everything in creation (earth, water, fire, air, and ether) are represented in the items to be offered on the *arati* plate: incense, a lamp, a conch filled with water, a fan, and so on. In other words, the items symbolize the whole of material energy. What does the worshiper then do with this? He offers these items to the Deity, God himself, thus indicating how everything in this world is by its very nature connected to its source. We nonetheless need to become aware of such a sacred bond—we are part of it but have forgotten. This same idea has been clearly established by Srila Bhaktisiddhanta Saraswati:

> *This universe is full of objects for the service of the master of this universe. Therefore, all those objects are adorable. Each of the material elements are truly favorable for Krishna's pastimes and that is why when performing* arati, *the various elements that make up this world are represented there in the incense, lamp, etc. In other words, this world is potential paraphernalia to be used in the service of the Lord, and thus such items will first be offered to him and only newly honored by us.*[17]

Srimad Bhagavatam 12.4.29 confirms this point (and more) thus:

> *This universe and even a single atom within it have no definition without reference to the Supreme Soul. If that is so, then objects related to the Lord are also spiritual and nondifferent from the Lord.*

THE WORLD AS THE FORM OF GOD

Gaudiyas consider Earth one of the seven mothers (along with one's biological mother, the cow, and others), and many Hindus venerate her with mantras at the very onset of each day (before even setting foot on her surface). Throughout the sacred lore we find endless prayers by the personified form of the Earth to the Sweet Absolute for relief and protection, prayers to which God always responds swiftly and accordingly.[18] Even more specifically, verses like *Srimad Bhagavatam* 10.20.48 establish how Mother Earth is an expansion of the Supreme Lord. Likewise, Visvanatha Chakravarti mentions in his commentary on *Srimad Bhagavatam* 10.42.1 how Satyabhama, a form of Krishna's internal energy, is also known as *bhu-shakti* or the potency of the creation of the world, whose expansion is known as Mother Earth. Furthermore, *Srimad Bhagavatam* 3.13.42 describes Mother Earth as the wife of God, in whom he has invested his potency. This investment and empowerment from the fatherlike Sweet Absolute is his very presence, and it can be perceived in and through this motherlike world of matter. In this connection, the Supreme Lord identifies himself in the *Bhagavad-gita* (7.8–12, 9.16–19, and 10.20–38) with different elements and features of this world, indicating how he can be found and perceived through sacred matter.[19] But this is just the beginning. This world is to be seen not only as our divine mother, as God's wife, or as a medium through which the divine presence is to be perceived, but also, from the *abheda* point of view (the perspective through which everything is nondifferent from God, being intrinsically related to him), directly as a form of the Divine.

The aphorism *sarva khalu idam brahma*[20] indicates that absolutely everything, the material world included, is one with the Absolute. Similarly, in *Bhagavad-gita* 9.19 Sri Krishna says, "Both matter and spirit are in me." In his purport to this verse, Srila Prabhupada comments, "For Krishna *there is no distinction between matter and spirit*, or, in other words, *he is both matter and spirit*. In the advanced stage of Krishna consciousness, one therefore makes no such distinctions. He sees only Krishna in everything."[21] If there is no distinction between matter and spirit for God, we are surely to attain such vision at some point. This vision is also portrayed in *Bhagavad-gita*

6.30, which speaks about "one who sees God *everywhere*" and thus hints at the possibility of finding the Divine in this world. There are many, many quotations from the *Gita* promoting what we may call a "religion of immanence." God is described as all-pervading with *everything* situated in him (8.22); *this entire cosmos* is pervaded by the Divine (9.4); the Sweet Absolute is the source from whom *everything* evolves (10.8); *the entire cosmos* is in God's body (11.7); Krishna recommends that Arjuna, who is on Earth, meditate on him, and in that way Arjuna will always *live in him* (12.8); the Sweet Absolute is *everywhere* (13.14) as well as inside and outside of *everyone* and *everything* (13.16); it is *we* who are the cause of our own suffering and not the world (13.21–22); one who sees God *everywhere* does not degrade himself, and in that way reaches the divine abode (13.29); material nature is *our mother*, and God is the seed-giving father (14.4); the Divine *enters each planet* and keeps it in orbit (15.13); this is happening both *in this galaxy and in the three worlds* (15.17). Do we really need further proof to see this material realm as utterly sacred?

For those who still need further evidence, let's now go to a few sections from the Gaudiya central canon, the *Srimad Bhagavatam.* In verse 2.9.35, the Lord mentions how he exists in *everything*. Then in verse 4.31.16, *Srimad Bhagavatam* declares, "Just as the sunshine is nondifferent from the sun, the cosmic manifestation is also nondifferent from the Supreme Lord. He is therefore all-pervasive within this material creation."[22] In his prayers, Prahlada mentions that *God alone is the universe* (7.9.30–31); that he places the universe *within himself* (7.9.32); that *this universe is God's body* (7.9.33); and that the Sweet Absolute (if this has not yet been clear enough) "is the air, fire, earth, sky, and water, the subtle elements, the vital force, the senses, the heart, pure consciousness, and grace as well." Prahlada concludes his prayer to God in the form of Narasimha, "O Great One, *you alone are all things*. There is nothing at all other than you, whether defined by thought or word."[23] In fact, when his atheist father asked Prahlada if his all-pervading God was even in a nearby pillar, Prahlada basically replied, "Where is he *not*?" As a result of Prahlada's faith and vision, the Sweet Absolute appeared from that same pillar in the most astonishing form of Sri

Narasimha—half-man, half-lion. In this way, Narasimha's appearance from a pillar confirms how this world of matter can totally reveal the Sweet Absolute. In this case, matter *literally* revealed the Supreme. In other words, Narasimha's appearance from the pillar proved that God is *immanent in everything*.

How are we expected to respond to God's omnipresence? *Srimad Bhagavatam* 11.2.41 declares that we should "Bow down to ether, fire, air, water, earth, the sun and other luminaries, all living beings, the directions, trees and other plants, the rivers and oceans, seeing them as the body of the Supreme Lord." Sri Jiva Goswami comments on this verse saying, "Seeing ether, air, and all living beings as manifestations of the Lord out of great attachment for the Supreme, seeing all these elements and entities as Syamasundara [Krishna] with his yellow cloth, in the manner that a greedy man sees the world in terms of money and a lusty man sees the world in terms of beautiful women, he offers respects." While this section and commentaries depict the vision of the highest type of personality, one should try to own such vision by making it the goal we want to attain as practitioners. Visvanatha Chakravarti confirms this in his commentary on this verse: "Whatever falls within one's vision, one should see it as the manifestation of the body of Syamasundara. Or the devotee, contemplating his state of perfection, even in the state of *sadhana* or practice, sees in this way." Likewise, in this eleventh book of the *Bhagavatam*, one great personality describes his twenty-four gurus, most of whom are from the natural world—the first one being the Earth.

Verses 10.9.13–14 of the *Srimad Bhagavatam* also describe the Sweet Absolute as having neither outside nor inside, neither front nor back, existing in front of the cosmos as well as behind it, both within and without, and being *the very cosmos himself*. Likewise, verse 10.10.29 presents the Supreme Lord as being everything, and this cosmic manifestation being his form. Similarly, Brahma speaks of *unlimited universes* coming out of the pores of God's body (10.14.11); *nothing* existing outside of his belly (10.14.12 and 10.14.17); and God's body *containing and sheltering the universe* (10.14.15–16). In his commentary on 10.14.21, Visvanatha Chakravarti mentions, "Krishna's unlimited spiritual form is full of all opulences, and though it is not material, *it exists everywhere in the material universe*."

Before we continue, let's stop and meditate on this for a moment: *God's spiritual form exists everywhere in the material universe.*

Similarly, verse 10.40.15 declares that all the worlds travel within the Supreme Lord "just as aquatics swim in the sea," and 10.48.19 describes how God *enters* into the universe. In verses 10.82.45–46, the Sweet Absolute describes himself as existing both within and without all created beings and, therefore, one should see the material creation as manifest within God. In a similar vein, Srutadeva establishes in verse 10.86.44 that he has been associating with the Lord since he created this universe. Likewise, in verse 10.47.29 the Sweet Absolute declares, "Just as the elements of nature are present in every created thing, so I am present within everyone's mind, life air and senses, and also within the physical elements and the modes of material nature." In verse 10.86.48 it is said, "You [God] appear both in your causeless spiritual form *and in the created form of this universe* to uncover the eyes of your devotees." Additionally, a very significant statement is made in verse 10.87.26, which declares, "Just as things made of gold are indeed *not to be rejected,* since their substance is actual gold, so this world is undoubtedly nondifferent from the Lord who created it and then entered within it." Therefore, the world of matter is *not* to be rejected but is to be properly venerated and embraced as one of the unlimited energies *and even forms* of the Lord. In fact, this form is described throughout the *Srimad Bhagavatam* as *virat-rupa,*[24] or the "form of the universe," and it's considered God's very first *avatara* or divine descent—yes, *avatara* means "divine"!—which manifested before any of the other descents. Despite this form being clearly presented as a meditative tool for the yogi, *Srimad Bhagavatam* 2.1.24 describes it as "the personal body of the Absolute Truth." Srila Prabhupada further qualifies this statement by saying, "The omnipotent Lord has his transcendental eyes, heads, and other bodily parts distributed everywhere. He can see, hear, touch or manifest himself anywhere and everywhere, for he is present everywhere." A valid question for all of us at this point is how much time do we spend daily meditating on these astonishing facts?

To clear any remaining doubts, let's conclude this section by sharing some further evidence from other significant Gaudiya sources. In *Bhagavat Sandarbha* 34, Jiva Goswami declares that the body of the Lord *contains even the universe*. In fact, this section explains how Sri Krishna showed his mother, Yasoda, the whole universe within himself, but also showed himself to be within the universe. Similarly, *Bhagavat Sandarbha* 42 describes how Krishna's form can manifest in *innumerable places simultaneously*, as also indicated in *Srimad Bhagavatam* 3.3.8 and 10.69.2. *Gopala-tapani Upanishad* (U. 1.21) glorifies the Sweet Absolute as he who, though living in one place, *is spread everywhere*. In *Chaitanya Bhagavata* 1.7.174–175, while bringing out the truth regarding the differences between the Absolute's energies, Sri Gaurahari nonetheless simultaneously establishes the nondual foundation of reality while sitting on dirty earthen pots and considering everything sacred—in this case material nature—due to its connection with the Divine. Then in verse 1.7.163 the author declares, "This topic is most confidential. *Whoever hears it will attain perfection in devotion* to Krishna." Sri Gaurahari also declares in his second verse of *Siksastakam* that God's name is not only nondifferent from him, but *nija-sarva-shaktis*: all energies (including material energy) are contained within God's name, who is nondifferent from him. Likewise, when teaching Sanskrit grammar, Sri Gaurahari would emphasize how every word of the alphabet is first and foremost a name of God, thus indicating how every object of this world that is addressed by any word is first of all indicating the Divine. This same principle is shared in *Paramatma Sandarbha* 81, where is it mentioned that "God alone is described by all words, *whether secular or Vedic*." And *Skanda Purana*, which describes how the Sweet Absolute is *sarva-nama*, or "addressed by all words," shows how everything we find here is ultimately hinting—or more than hinting—at the Sweet Absolute. Finally, *Vishnu Purana* 1.4.40–41 and *Paramatma Sandarbha* 79 (quoted one after the other below) explain why, despite the overwhelming evidence to the contrary, many of us still see this world as ordinary, rejectable, and divorced from the transcendent:

> *This complete universe is conscious by nature, but the unawakened, seeing only its material form, are lost therein, drowned in delusion. But those who are endowed*

> *with knowledge and intuitive insight, being pure at heart, O Supreme Lord, see distinctly this whole universe as conscious and as your own form.*

> *The world cannot be explained in the least degree independent from the Supreme Lord.*

While the above quotes are mostly connected with the *abheda*, or nondifferent, side of the *bheda-abheda* Gaudiya equation, it is also important to remember how there is also some difference between the Sweet Absolute and the world. If this wasn't the case, the two would become absolutely identical. In other words, the material world does not inhere in God; therefore, it is different from his inner personal identity. This is *bheda*. However, the material world is also an energy of the Lord and is dependent on him for its existence. This is *abheda*. Thus, by emphasizing God's presence everywhere and describing the world as one of the forms of the Divine, we don't do away with his individual existence, but extend its immediacy to our presence in the here and now. *We will not be able to recognize God later if we cannot recognize God now*. Gaudiyas worship a Sweet Absolute who is both immanent and transcendent, simultaneously all-pervading and localized, personal and universal. In fact, a truly transformative God—transformative for both the individual and history—needs to be experienced as both personal and universal.[25] In this section, we have chosen to mainly emphasize the *abheda* side and God's immanence in the world, since many members of the Gaudiya community have emphasized the *bheda* side to the point of seeing this world as disconnected and disconnecting from the Sweet Absolute. But, as we have seen, this is not the case *at all*. Material creation is the result of God's own inner joy and thus points to that same inner joy if properly addressed.

OTHER MYSTICAL TRADITIONS ALSO SEE THE WORLD AS SACRED

The unearthing of heaven in sacred matter is not an idea exclusive to Gaudiya Vaishnavism, but is present in every other mystical tradition. For example, in contrast to Shankara's view Sri Ramanujacharya proposes that the world is not only real but is also the body of God. He illustrates this with the relationship between body and soul. A body (this world) is supported, controlled, and subservient to the soul (God himself). Thus, for Ramanuja, since the world is seen as the body of the Supreme, it is ultimately spiritual and represents one of the unlimited divine attributes of the Divine.

The fifth-century mystical writer Pseudo-Dionysius goes one step beyond by declaring that creation is an erotic outpouring, a divine ecstasy soaking all things. In other words, *passion is the true stuff of the universe.*[26] This notion goes hand in hand with our above Gaudiya thesis of how God's inner bliss overflows and extends itself in the form of material creation. In fact, according to Gaudiya Vaishnavism the highest form of bliss experienced by Sri Krishna is that of romantic love with his female half, Sri Radhika. Thus the world is an erotic outpouring, in the words of Pseudo-Dyonysius. This idea has natural and important implications in what we've addressed in the section on Radical Sexuality.[27] Our human drive for sexual connection is closely tied to the very backdrop of this universe, a drive originating from the Divine and reflected in and through us humans on one level or another. In other words, fully realizing this sacred background frees us from unnecessary and excessive stigmatization of the sexual principle and points to its more essential role. Apart from the function of procreation, sexual connection affords the necessary synthesis of the male-female principles in the building and flowering of our human personality. Although the pureness of love does not require expression through the flesh, becoming more spiritual without ceasing to be physical is also possible and part of the equation.[28] For many of us sex has been reduced to something akin to a videogame, devoid of any depth, intimacy, and commitment. But ideally this powerful drive is to be conceived of as part of the deep religious core of cosmic evolution.[29] However, this is possible only if we first acknowledge how a sacred erotic outpouring invokes and promotes this material world.

Christian mystics are not far behind in conceiving of this esoterica. For them, the whole cosmos is a theophany, or a revelation of God's glory. Or, to be more precise, each aspect of material creation is an instance of the eternal self-emptying of God into creation.[30]

This is also known as *kenosis*, a term that generally refers to the self-emptying of one's own will while becoming entirely receptive to God and his own divine will. However, in relation to this world, Christians conceive of *kenosis* as an explanation of the nature of God's activity and will, this world being an example of God's self-emptying. Gaudiyas will basically say the same while describing this material creation as the overflow (or in this case self-emptying) of the Lord's joy, or inner being, itself made of joy. One well-known Christian example of this self-emptying is when the Bible says, "God is in all things and all things are in God."[31] Likewise, Saint Francis's *Canticle of the Creatures* is another charming example of how to address every aspect of creation as holy and venerable. Teilhard de Chardin, paleontologist and Jesuit mystic, puts it in his own way by declaring, "*The physical structure of the universe is love.*"[32] Similarly, St. John Damascene beautifully declared, "I do not worship matter. I worship the God of matter, who became matter for my sake and deigned to inhabit matter, who worked out my salvation through matter. I will not cease from honoring that matter which works my salvation."[33] Elizabeth Barrett Browning, a Christian poet, similarly said, "Earth's crammed with heaven, and every common bush afire with God."[34] Finally, Richard Rohr writes in *The Universal Christ*, "A mature Christian sees Christ in everything and everyone else. That is a definition that will never fail you, always demand more of you, and give you no reasons to fight, exclude, or reject anyone."[35] In conclusion, every mystical tradition teaches us not only to respect matter, but to love God *through, in, with,* and even *because of* this world.[36]

NO INHERENT PROFANITY, BUT HOLY SECULARITY

As we have seen so far, matter is not just matter. Properly approached, matter includes and fully reveals spiritual sacredness. That's our underlying epistemology as Gaudiyas: all is sacred, including the so-called secular domain, which we'll call *holy secularity*. In fact, if matter is inhabited by God—as it is—then we can say that matter is somehow eternal. Although it is temporary because it's always changing forms, it's also eternal, since it exists without a beginning and without an end. Therefore, we should not get accustomed to thinking in terms of sacred and profane things, places, and moments. As the introductory quote to this chapter teaches, there are only sacred things and *desecrated* things, places, and moments.

Transcendentalizing the mundane is not tantamount to mundanizing the transcendental. Why? Because strictly speaking there is no such thing as "mundane." *Profanity can exist only in our eyes.* As beauty lies in the eye of the beholder, the exact same thing applies to mundanity. It is our ego that tries to decide what's sacred and what's not sacred. Above the ego platform, however, everything is sacred. When we embrace this worldview, there is no longer an honest distinction between sacred and profane. The presence of the Divine is experienced in literally everyone and *every thing*. God is much closer and much more accessible to us in the here and now. According to this sacred perspective—which corresponds to ultimate reality—matter and spirit are no longer as separate as we may like to think. *Matter and spirit will reveal and manifest each other.*[37] In other words, the Sweet Absolute is not found through opposition to matter (anti-matter) or independent of matter (extra-matter), but *through* matter (trans-matter).[38] Therefore, we are not rescued *from* the world by divine grace; we are saved *in and through* the world by cooperating with divine love.[39]

If the Sweet Absolute's presence is everywhere and this world is the body of God, then the matter around us is both the hiding place and the revelation of the Divine, and we can no longer make any significant distinction between the natural and the supernatural, between the holy and the profane. Everything we now see and know is indeed one *uni-verse* revolving around one coherent center.[40] Therefore, instead of conceiving of God as "out there," better we start discovering him *right here.* We discover the Sweet Absolute hidden in the dirt and mud, instead of waiting for him to descend from remote heavenly clouds.[41] *We are not going there until we find him here.* Of course, our naiveté can also lead us too quickly and smartly to say things like, "All things are sacred" or "God is everywhere," but that doesn't necessarily mean we have really *longed for and made space for* this awareness, nor have we really integrated such an amazing realization. Therefore, while we speak about these beautiful things, we similarly need to engage with reality in such a way that we gradually develop this unique vision. We need to learn how to bring together the two apparent opposites of matter and spirit, integrating them into a higher synthesis.

To attain such a vision is of course no easy task. It is a vision that for Gaudiyas belongs to the highest type of devotees, the *uttama-bhagavatas,* who see everything in God and God in everything. By contrast, the view of a novice implies perceiving the Divine in an ultra-localized way (for example, on one particular altar) but not universally yet. That said, those who are in between these two stages—who can no longer remain as neophytes but cannot either imitate the superlative devotees—are advised to trust and follow the vision of the *uttama-bhagavata* and at least accept the vision in theory. By starting to relate with the *uttama-bhagavata*'s vision from a theoretical acceptance, one will gradually advance toward a more mature realization of this theory or type of vision. This is not imitation of those with this highest vision, but what Gaudiyas call "following in the footsteps." How is this so? The vision of the highest personalities most accurately corresponds with how reality is to be seen by all through the lens of divine love. Even if we are not on that level yet, we will know by their vision that this is how reality should look *and should be looked upon.* In other words, we must acknowledge that the vision of the highest lovers is how ultimate reality looks, and then proceed from wherever we are in our inner pursuit of such vision. That's basically the work of a *sadhaka*, or practitioner: acknowledging and appreciating in theory the vision of the *siddha,* or perfected devotee. Then we will acknowledge and appreciate it so much that we cannot help but dedicate our life to live in such vision. And that begins in the here and now by our observing, touching, and loving the physical, the material, the inspirited universe in whatever condition it may be. This is the necessary starting place for any healthy spirituality and any true development.[42] There is no other way, place, or time for becoming a *siddha* or an *uttama-bhagavata*—or *anything at all.*

Everything becomes priceless if it is sacred. And everything is sacred if the world is a temple. *And it is.*[43] Therefore, if we have our heart in the right place, our connection with this world will never prove profane. However, if the heart is not in the right place, even rejecting this world will be another form of hypocrisy. *When there is real love, everything becomes justified. When there is no real love, everything becomes an excuse.*

REPURPOSING HEAVEN: THE SPIRITUAL WORLD IS NOT MERELY A GEOGRAPHICAL PLACE

After having established how the world of matter is not profane but a sacred facilitator, we will now allow this idea to overflow and take us a step further. We will validate matter as intrinsically revelatory of the Divine and reflect on how our ultimate goal as Gaudiyas—to attain what we call "the spiritual world"—is not only about going somewhere else. The spiritual world is to first be gradually attained and experienced right here on Earth. *Here or nowhere at all.* It's *now-here* or *no-where.* Let's open ourselves to a repurposing of heaven.

As shocking as it may sound to some, attaining the spiritual world has nothing to do with transporting to a geographical location as we generally think of it. The Gaudiya heaven is not a place that we can attain by moving physically. The movement is always internal. The spiritual world is a state of consciousness, and whenever we reach the state of consciousness that corresponds with the consciousness permeating the spiritual world, then we have arrived "there." There is no need for geographical transfer or tridimensional movement. In fact, *Bhagavad-gita* 2.24 describes one of the attributes of the soul as being immovable. Therefore, *there is nowhere that we have to go.* Everything is to be found in the here and now.

The ultimate goal of Gaudiya Vaishnavism is not to run away from the material world and retreat to some other planet, like a new episode of Star Wars where the inhabitants flee their tortured existence in a spaceship charted for a perfect planet in a galaxy far, far away. The ultimate goal is rather to attain a particular level of vision in the eternal present moment. We can find the Sweet Absolute when we are fully present in the present moment. And the present moment is the only place where he can be contacted, and where he is *always* available. God is eternal, and therefore he is not a future being. He is always present in the continual unfolding of being into now. In fact, the Gaudiya notion of salvation implies a post-liberated state which, as we will see, plays out eternally on this planet in the form of a perpetual earthly play known as *bhauma-lila*. This does not deny the unlimited realms and dimensions occupied by divinity, but rather recognizes that the very creation that we are a part of is nothing less than one of those unlimited realms. Therefore, for a Radical Personalist salvation has nothing to do with an evacuation plan for the afterlife or a private redemption project where we make a claim on an insurance policy, much less a moral worthiness contest to win entrance into the next world. Instead, the notion of heaven and salvation entails for us a transformation plan on Earth and for Earth. For a mature Gaudiya practitioner, there is no above she needs to get to, since she has already found the top—at the bottom.[44] Therefore, our job is to simply *exemplify heaven now*, and our Sweet Absolute will take it from there. We cannot "get there" without *being fully here*, and "fully here" is the only place we can and need to be. That should be our modus operandi.[45]

The opposite of this, as expressed by different (mis)representatives of all traditions, is the emphasis made on obtaining a reward in this life and in heaven instead of love and union with the Divine and others here and now. While most spiritual traditions speak of heaven, the spiritual world, and enlightenment, their usual mistake is that they push these realities off into the next life. But *if heaven is later, it is because it is first of all now*.[46] And the more room we have to include it in this now, the bigger our heaven will be. Perhaps this is what Jesus meant by there being "many rooms in my Father's house."[47] In this connection, the Gaudiya heaven is known as Goloka and possesses different compartments, all of which appear small to the naked eye only due to the extreme degree of intimacy present there. That's "the place" where we want to go—the consciousness we want to attain—and the heart expansion begins (and continues) right here, wherever we are.

The Gaudiya heaven can be also described as *nara-lila*, or a sacred nondual play in which everyone is both fully divine and fully human. We humans are "created in the image of God," since he is *eternally* fully human, but also fully divine. And this is our highest prospect as well. Therefore, Gaudiya Vaishnavism converges in this zenith of potential known as *nara-lila*. Although technically speaking the soul/consciousness is not human per se, it nonetheless has the potential of being fully human in eternity. In other words, while at present we relate to our humanity as physical and psychic designations, in ultimate reality such humanness will become part of our eternal identity. Therefore, if we want to attain this climactic *nara-lila*—and we do—then we must gradually become more human—fully human—by way of spiritualizing our present existence. Instead of evading our present humanness by too much "heaven talk," we can answer the call to become fully human here on Earth.

Unfortunately, many members of the Gaudiya community portray the attainment of this *nara-lila* as something which has little to do with this world and our present situation as human practitioners. For such people, their eyes are set exclusively on one goal: transcendence and *lila*, leaving the world and other humans behind. This dualistic split has led numerous members of our community to leave the practice altogether; others remain officially, but are unofficially disconnected or dysfunctional members. This situation will be repaired when we understand that this world is not profane, but divine, and we can divinize ourselves as well as *all* our relationships—not just relationships in our group. Doing so will be a crucial testament to our love for the Divine. In other words, we are God's instruments here on Earth, where our Gaudiya heaven is to be ultimately found.

THE PRINCIPLE OF AVATARA: GOD COMING TO EARTH UNINTERRUPTEDLY

Through the lens of Gaudiya Vaishnavism, heaven perpetually comes to Earth to make the above points very clear to each of us. Sri Krishna, Gaurahari, and other endless *avataras* (a term that means "crossing from up to down") come over and over again to this planet and perform their sacred nondual play. As to how much God engages in this play, it is enough to invoke the main Sanskrit word that refers to God. That word is *deva*, a term derived from the root "*div*," which translates as "to sport, to play." The Sweet Absolute is therefore "he who sports." Accordingly, if the Divine is mainly characterized by play, then his most confidential aspect can only be playing, engaging in the most sophisticated form of playfulness as his main activity. For Gaudiyas, this notion of a fully playful God converges in Sri Krishna, who is described as *pranaya-keli-kala-vilasam*, or "he who always revels in the play of love,"[48] and as *Deva-deva*, "the God of Gods," the most playful face of him who is already playful by nature.[49] In this way Gaudiya theology teaches that God is so fond of nondual play that each of his *lilas* is being performed on some planet Earth of some universe nonstop. After the *lila* ends on one planet Earth, it starts on another—forever! Therefore, those who eventually attain participation in such *lila* will be perpetually accompanying the Sweet Absolute in each of his terrestrial exploits. As a consequence, they will remain eternally on Earth as permanent sacred pilgrims, eternally accompanying the Divine and his holy retinue in their earthly garbs.

As endless *avataras*, the Sweet Absolute comes to Earth frolicking in divine intoxication. This is the logical conclusion of God's love affair with his own creation. As we have already shown, the world of matter becomes manifest as an outcome and overflow of God's inner joy—as an extension of his love. Therefore, it's no surprise that such an extended expression of love further expands itself to also embrace and love the very product of such initial love: this world. *God is in love with everything in his creation.* This world was not made as a prison for fallen spirits who were rejected by the Divine. The world was made as a temple, a hidden paradise into which God himself descends to dwell familiarly with the spirits he placed there to tend to it for him.[50] Since the Divine's own heart extends to embrace matter, we could arguably say that God appears not in the heart of matter but *as* the heart of matter. In other words, God and matter are not opposed to each other but are a coincidence of opposites and thus mutually affirming.[51] The Sweet Absolute empties himself in and through the world, pouring his own overflowing heart into all directions, and he himself comes here to play with us *as one of us*. But why does he do so? While God's divine play has no reason apart from celebrating the ever-evolving fullness of his own being, his earthly play naturally invites each of us to relate to him as one of us. This is the type of intimate love he most cherishes and relishes. If the Sweet Absolute would merely remain as a great, remote, and distant figure, we would likely adopt that same template and attempt to make it ours by trying to play God ourselves. The original plan was different.

As the infinite manifests the finite, we could also say that *the finite has the potential to reveal the infinite*. This world will reveal God to us by hosting him, his entourage, and his *lila* perpetually on Earth. In this way, we could say that heaven includes Earth, but, even more specifically, that Earth includes *and reveals* heaven. At this point the Supreme Lord is no longer "out there," but is not just merely "in here" either. For the great mystics of all religions, the great nondual thinkers, the Divine is always experienced as abiding in their own soul and, seemingly in contradiction, totally transcendent and mysterious to them, being both intimate and ultimate simultaneously.[52] So yes, the Sweet Absolute is still fully transcendent, but probably not transcendent in the manner we first imagined! He is "out there" but also eternally "over here," both transcendent and immanent. The same applies to his abode. It is a spiritual realm that can be only inhabited in terms of consciousness—*a state of transcendent consciousness that is immanent to creation*. Someone may be physically next to us but mentally somewhere else. Similarly, while physically in this world, we can experience our Gaudiya heaven. We can be in the world while our consciousness is in transcendence.

A classic example in this regard is given by the founder and Deity of Radical Personalism, Sri Gaurahari. Not only did he experience sacred Vraja while wandering in other sacred spots like Jagannatha Puri, but he even witnessed the Vraja domain in secular jungles like the Jharikhanda forest. By experiencing the Gaudiya heaven in such an "ordinary" place, Gaurahari set the precedent for how to relate to the world. Any corner of this material creation can be appreciated as transcendent. Therefore, "the material world" is nothing but how we choose to perceive reality, or which spectacles we choose to wear, and not so much about where we are geographically. In a similar fashion, when Bhaktisiddhanta Saraswati was asked why he went to Calcutta when his guru told him to never go there, he replied that he never went to Calcutta, but always remained at the lotus feet of his spiritual master. *Calcutta was a state of consciousness for him*, as is every other place. Likewise, when Srila

Prabhupada made plans to "leave" Vraja to go to the Western world, some local Hindus then asked him why on Earth he would ever leave the sacred land of Vraja. Their question clearly showed their own lack of education. They didn't realize that someone like Srila Prabhupada was not replacing Vraja with the West, but *extending* the very presence of Vraja to all shores of the planet. This is further confirmed in *Srimad Bhagavatam* 1.13.10, where saintly personalities are described as personified holy places, since they remain lovingly aware of the Sweet Absolute's presence in their hearts and thus turn all places into pilgrimage sites. In fact, the Sanskrit word for a pilgrimage site is *tirtha*, a term which, according to the *Amara-kosha* Sanskrit dictionary, can also refer to a saintly person. Therefore, if the state of consciousness of a person is to be equated with a sacred abode, we can again conclude that the spiritual world is not a geographical place, but a state of consciousness.

If in this lifetime a Gaudiya Vaishnava attains a consciousness that matches that of the spiritual world, then such a person will already be participating in it. The consensus among Gaudiyas is that such a person will then be transferred to Gokula, or the earthly Vraja in which Sri Krishna will be enacting his terrestrial *lila*. From there, such a soul will attain Goloka, or the celestial Vraja, which exists beyond this Earth. Interestingly enough, Gokula and Goloka are considered nondifferent, as Sri Jiva Goswami declares in Anuccheda 106 of his *Krishna Sandarbha*:

> *Those sacred places existing on Earth [like Gokula] that are well-known by the identical names are understood to be of the exact same nature [as their counterparts in the spiritual world], since they too are described as being beyond the material world, eternal, supramundane in nature, and the eternal abodes of the Lord. ... In this way, the divine abodes of the Lord are manifest simultaneously both above and below, and thus they are not of two different varieties. In reality, because God's abode is the place of his eternal abidance, it is to be understood as being only of one type. This is so because there is no contradiction in its being manifest in both places simultaneously. ... In addition, both locations have been described as having iden-*

> *tical characteristics, names, and forms. ... If, on the other hand, the two abodes were posited to be different, the emphatic particle* eva, *"only," in* Brahma-samhita 5.37, *"Krishna, who is the Immanent Self of all living beings, resides only in Goloka," would contradict the statements of the* Varaha Purana, *wherein the Lord establishes Vraja on Earth as his own eternal place of* lila.

In connection to the above quote, Satyanarayana Dasa has commented, "It is to be noted that by establishing the nondifference between the terrestrial and spiritual abodes of Krishna, Sri Jiva Goswami implies that *the goal to be realized is present right here.* This stands in sharp contrast to the theory of Advaita Vedanta which propounds the visible world as *mithya* or false and, thus, to be spurned. Jiva Goswami *eliminates the gap between the spiritual and empirical worlds*. On this basis, the teachings of the Gaudiya school are concluded to offer the most realistic theology."[53] In this way Gaudiyas consider Goloka and Gokula nondifferent. Therefore, while a perfected being is first born in Gokula before attaining Goloka, since the two places are deemed as identical it is no surprise that those who attain Goloka will be back to Gokula here on Earth time and again with Sri Krishna as he appears, while simultaneously remaining "there" in Goloka. While this may be difficult to understand in our present mindset, a very clear point is being made here: it all begins here on Earth, and *it all continues here as well.* We are not talking about places, but states of consciousness, *states of heart.* This is clearly established by the Supreme Lord himself when he says to Narada that, among other places, *he is not even in the spiritual world*, but right where his loving devotees congregate to sing his glories.[54] The point is again obvious. If the Sweet Absolute is not in the spiritual world but only where his lovers are, then such love *is* the very spiritual world itself—wherever that happens to manifest.

We cannot *go* to the spiritual world if we have not arrived there internally first. As the external circumstances of this world can't change our inner feelings without an internal shift, the same can be said in relation to *being* in the spiritual world. It's not that we "go" there without already having reached there in our consciousness first. This will not be a sudden shift in our consciousness whereby we are relatively ordinary a few minutes ago and then we are miraculously transferred to a magical land without having prepared ourselves in the here and now. Thus, our present challenge is to arrive there from here. In other words, we should not use the highest ideal to avoid our present challenges but rather attain those very ideals *through* our present challenges. Instead of rejecting this world as illusory while over-idealizing a faraway transcendence, we must inject the divine presence into every atom or, even better, realize how such injected and infinite presence is already here from time without beginning. Just contemplate: Infinity is hosted in each atom, and his presence there is another form of *avatara*, or divine descent. *Brahma-samhita* 5.35 depicts this daily miracle by describing how all the universes exist in the Sweet Absolute and *he is present in his fullness* in each one of the atoms that are scattered throughout the universe, at one and the same time. In his commentary on this verse, Jiva Goswami mentions how the form of the universe is also God, and Bhaktivinoda Thakura makes an even bolder statement, declaring, "All the spiritual and material worlds are situated within God, and he is within them." In this way we have clearly seen how the principle of *avatara* shows how the Divine is within both the spiritual and material worlds, and how these two worlds ultimately converge through God's presence and *lila* on Earth. What about God being inherent in *life itself*?

SRISTI-LILA: THE SACRED PLAY OF CREATION

Material creation is described as *sristi-lila*, or "the sacred play of creation," which the Sweet Absolute employs as a dramatic stage to perpetually perform his eternal *lila* on Earth. Let's immerse ourselves in this concept and play out the extended implications.

Sristi-lila implies a bridging of heaven and Earth and is sometimes also known as *bhauma-lila*, or earthly sacred play. Through it, heaven and Earth combine to further expand their own unlimited limits. While we have already analyzed some perspectives for the reasons behind this, let's look at the *sristi/bhauma-lila* in connection to Sri Radhika's unquenchable thirst to satisfy her beloved Sri Krishna. Sri Radhika is the personification of divine love and is obsessed with serving the perfect object of all affection, Sri Krishna.

Her unquenchable thirst to passionately serve Krishna compels her to facilitate Sri Krishna's own desire to express his supremely pure goodness through the bestowal of unconditional grace on the needy. And through such service she has her own perpetual opportunity to expand Krishna's service by infusing endless unique souls with *bhakti*. For this to happen, Sri Radha catalyzes the great theater of *sristi-lila*, or the creational cosmic play. To appease Radhika's need, Krishna wills the genesis of billions of material universes and floods each one with countless souls. He then descends as an *avatara* in each universe in every age to personally teach the sacred path. He intimately accompanies every soul's journey as Paramatma in the heart; he inspires every culture to discover its diverse sacred traditions and revealed knowledge; and he empowers genuine saints, prophets, mystics, philosophers, and sages of every sort to walk with the people and supply every generation with liberal opportunity for connection with Radhika's radical love via multiform devotional ideals. For Gaudiya Vaishnavas, this is yet another perspective—a very intimate one—on the actual background of the *sristi-lila* and the divine descent of heaven to Earth.[55]

This *sristi-lila* is a supreme facilitator for each of us to attain the highest form of love. It is a backdrop and points to the foundational intention of creation which is repeatedly highlighted throughout scripture. For example, *Srimad Bhagavatam* 10.87.2 declares that the Sweet Absolute manifested the different material elements for the welfare of all souls, so they can eventually attain ultimate salvation. Similarly, verse 11.3.3 describes that the material elements and all souls have been "created" (though we know everything exists eternally) so we can choose to enjoy this world or, ideally, embrace ultimate liberation. Sridhara Swami described this liberation in his commentary on this verse: "For what purpose did God create? For the complete fulfillment of the individual self who worships him." Once again, the principle we have already described becomes more and more apparent. Due to the devotion in the hearts of perfected beings in the *lila*, or in those practitioners on Earth yet to attain perfection (or to inspire the *bhakti* in potential in relation to every soul), the Sweet Absolute's joy overflows and this material creation manifests as a result.

In *sristi-lila* God repeatedly comes as an *avatara* to validate the world's existence and purpose in relation to its source, and through that helps us in our own conception of things. Without his presence in this way, we would be tempted to overplay the distance and the distinction between God and humanity. But through the principle of *sristi-lila*, the supernatural is forever embedded in the natural, making the very distinction false.[56] In one sense heaven descends on Earth, and when we "arrive" at heaven, we'll find Earth there as well (since there will also be *nara-lila*). How much can we then speak of these two as being different? There is no scope to dualistically separate the supernatural from the natural. Sometimes we spend too much time trying to get "up there" and we miss God's big leap to come "down here." Therefore, much of our worship and religious effort is the spiritual equivalent of trying to go up what has become the down escalator.[57] Better to realize that nothing is outside the embrace of the Sweet Absolute's love.

Since *lila* is a notion tightly related to that of dramatic performance, it's crucial to understand how the Divine himself engages in it—how he is lost in play while roaming on Earth. While God's descent is described as *avatara*, Gaudiyas are usually careful not to translate this word as "incarnation." This is done to preserve the transcendent ontology of the Divine, presenting him as unmixed with matter even while interacting with it in different ways. That said, the Sweet Absolute is infinite and capable of doing the impossible. So if some may like to define his descent as fully incarnational to the point of God actually inhabiting human flesh, his own divine condition would not be affected or limited by it. More accurately, if he would be affected by inhabiting matter, he would be so in a way that nourishes his *lila* on Earth. It would be in a way that increases his own Godhood, since to be God means to constantly attain new heights of aesthetic sacred rapture in divine love. In this sense only can we speak in terms of *incarnationalism* in regard to our Gaudiya Deity. It is an instance that keeps him fully divine, but now especially close to us. For example, sacred narratives about Sri Gaurahari depict him as inhabiting a body that eats, sleeps, and even sweats blood! In fact, on one significant occasion his divine human body is vicariously, yet "directly," injured as his devotee Haridasa Thakura is whipped. This is an instance of somatic content, and it should be possible to take this at face value without compromising God's ontological position. He remains fully divine, but also fully human.

Highlighting the idea that through his *sristi-lila* the Sweet Absolute comes near us, bringing us to him is crucial for a theology in which our lives and our lived realities matter to God and constitute the starting point of our relationship with eternity. For Gaudiyas, this generous extension is not only clear in faces of the Absolute like Sri Krishna or Gaurahari, but especially in manifestations like Sri Nityananda, a maddened and most compassionate form of the Divine who is at times even found in bars and brothels, getting as close as possible to our most fallen condition. The Gaudiyas' Sweet Absolute redeems the most fallen, and not just the most pious. His name is Patita-pavana (redeemer of the fallen) not Dharmika-pavana (redeemer of the pious). Therefore, this merciful dispensation of the *sristi-lila* constitutes the most golden opportunity in which human existence and mystical reality are bridged and integrated, perfectly and beautifully.

For those who have understood the value of matter and how the highest values are brought to us in the here and now, there is nowhere to go and nothing to do apart from continuing to dedicate ourselves for the pleasure of our Beloved. A verse from the *Srimad Bhagavatam* (6.17.28) describes this fact by declaring that such devotees never fear any condition in life, and for them the heavenly or hellish planets or even liberation are all the same, since they are exclusively interested in divine service. Similarly, in *Srimad Bhagavatam* 10.83.41 Rukmini Devi embodies this same spirit by declaring that devotees not only do not care for mundane opulence or mystical powers, but neither for immortality and, on top of that, they do not even care for attaining entrance into *hareh padam*, or the kingdom of God—they only want to offer divine service, wherever that may be. A very famous example in this regard is Brahma's well-known statement from *Srimad Bhagavatam* 10.14.30, where he prays that in order to engage in loving devotion to Krishna, he does not care being born even in the animal kingdom. Perhaps even more boldly, Bhaktivinoda Thakura prays that as long as he can remain the Lord's servant, he does not care whether he is born as a worm or an insect! However, he despises sophisticated births such as Brahma's if that position is averse to serving the Sweet Absolute.[58] In other words, we can remain as an insect and it won't be a problem, provided we have the proper attitude. This notion is similarly found in *Srimad Bhagavatam* 10.2.37 and even further confirmed in Rupa Goswami's *Bhakti-rasamrita-sindhu* 1.2.187, where he describes a *jivan-mukta* (liberated being) as one who engages in divine service with body, mind, and words. He then adds that such a person "is to be considered liberated in all conditions of material existence, although engaged in many so-called material activities." Likewise, in his commentary on *Srimad Bhagavatam* 9.13.9, Srila Prabhupada confirms this by saying, "Even though a devotee may superficially appear to be in a material body, he is always liberated and is engaged in the same duties of service to the Lord as a devotee in Vaikunthaloka [the spiritual world]. There is no distinction. ... It doesn't matter whether we accept a material body or a spiritual body; our only ambition should be to serve the Supreme Personality of Godhead." This is the fruit of properly understanding that *sristi-lila* is about fully finding the Sweet Absolute and divine love for him right here, without the need to go anywhere.

The above verses depict unique examples showing that a loving relationship with the Sweet Absolute is so comprehensive that conditions of time and place are irrelevant. All time and all space exists within that love. If his devotee is not interested in leaving this world, then the Lord grants such a wish by keeping that devotee eternally on Earth, forever engaged with the Lord in loving *sristi-lilas*. For Gaudiya Vaishnavas, *bhakti* is both *sadhana* (practice) and *sadhya* (goal, or attainment). In other words, their loving service is not only the means but also the goal to attain in ever new ways. In other words, a Gaudiya will already be doing what he projects to do in eternity—*bhakti*. If the practice is thus synonymous with the goal (with both being extremely delightful), then where else would we want to go? Therefore, *sristi-lila* constitutes a love letter written by the Sweet Absolute that is embedded in creation itself. The ultimate aim of this sacred play of creation is to allow each of us to embrace that divine love which sets in motion not only this universe, but our own hearts as well. This ultimate salvation is not some occasional or end-of-life emergency add-on, but God's ultimate intention from the very beginning—something inherent in the very fabric of creation.[59]

THE INFINITE WORLD OF LILA IS RIGHT IN FRONT OF US

The above sections deliver a hopeful but probably still difficult outlook by which we realize how we are already surrounded by everything we need, and even more. To further nourish our enthusiasm to tread this path and discover infinity in what appears to be ordinary, and to show how the highest reality has become accessible to each of us, we will next share some additional reflections to deepen our inspiration along with our commitment to this unique standpoint for the unearthing of heaven.

In various Eastern traditions, including Hinduism and Gaudiya Vaishnavism, the terms *vyavaharika* and *paramarthika* refer to the domain of the phenomenal/relative and the transcendental/absolute, respectively. Although the terms are often applied to the material and spiritual worlds, they actually refer to *realms of perception*, and not physical locations. In other words, two people can be in the same place, but one will be inhabiting the *vyavaharika* dimension and the other the *paramarthika* realm. Therefore, if we inhabit the proper realm by having the proper vision, we can connect with the spiritual world right here. Srila B. R. Sridhara Swami said in this regard, "When you have the proper conception, then you can read Krishna *lila* everywhere."[60] Similarly, his guru, Sri Bhaktisiddhanta Saraswati, repeatedly declared that he wouldn't admit any shortage in this world except for a lack of God consciousness. Thus he was hinting that if we became God conscious we will discover that nothing is lacking. Ultimately, this implies that the spiritual realm is right here but we only lack proper vision to see it. Another way in which this idea has been portrayed by Gaudiyas is by emphasizing how the infinite is contained within the finite, as Srila B. R. Sridhara Swami also described:

> *Everything is full of wonder. If we analyze the atom, we will be in wonder. Only we impose limitations. But when we analyze the atomic parts of wood or stone, we will be in wonder. The infinite is everywhere. Perfection is every-*

> *where. The trouble is that with our limited thinking we have produced a world of limits.*[61]

Through the classic Aristotelian template, we can wrongly conclude that reality can be compartmentalized. However, reality overlaps and does not fit into neat categories; it is expansive, vibrant, alive. The nature of reality is deeply holistic, with everything being interdependent and included. Not only is the finite within the infinite, but vice versa as well. Therefore, when all our illusory conceptions are fully removed, we will find that the Sweet Absolute is everywhere and that *everywhere is him only*. To attain that stage, all planes of limited conception must be crossed. From one level to another, the soul must dive deeper and deeper into reality, and then it will find everything there.[62] As beauty lies in the eye of the beholder, similarly, if conceived of by our illusory perception, this sacred realm of matter will appear as a distorted and perverted reflection of the original. Thus the framework of material nature will end up representing only a blurry echography of spiritual reality. However, the fact is that matter acts intrinsically as a dictionary of the spirit. It is a two-word telegram from the Sweet Absolute directed to every pore of his creation, expressed in the spirit of a holy beggar: *love me*.

We just need to reclaim our loss of perspective and realize how heaven is right here on Earth. As Srila B. R. Sridhara Swami put it, "Everywhere we will find the kingdom of God. Krishna's kingdom, Gaurahari's kingdom, exists. We have only lost the proper angle of vision by which to see it."[63] By acquiring the proper vision through prayer, education, discipline, and inner work, we will realize how this world is not meant to be consumed by us but admired and treasured. In fact, we cannot know things if we don't first of all grant them a foundational respect or don't love them before we grab them with our minds.[64] Gaurahari spoke about this foundational respect through the term *mana-dena*, which speaks about not only offering deep respect to everyone but even to *every thing*, since each atom has the potential to reveal transcendence to us. This principle of revelation is also known as "concrete-to-universal," to which we'll turn next before closing this chapter.

FROM CONCRETE TO UNIVERSAL

The principle of concrete-to-universal implies that, if properly addressed, a concrete object in this world can connect us with a universal principle. It can connect us with the source of that initial object, which is also the source of every other object and aspect of existence, since everything is holistically interrelated. While philosophers tend toward the universals and poets love the particulars, it is the mystics who teach us how to encompass both.[65] And this is what we are expected to do as Gaudiyas. We are not to excessively focus on one at the cost of the other, but to engage in a proper bridging and integration of the concrete and the universal. In other words, Radical Personalism understands how every concrete atom of this world can—and should—ultimately indicate the converging point of Radha-Krishna's loving *lila*. The whole cosmos is not a meaningless explosion, but a *love story*.

If properly approached and integrated, "the concrete" in this material world will reveal "the universal" in the realm of consciousness to such a degree that we will doubt whether to call this world "material." In this connection, Srila B. R. Sridhara Swami has said, "Although some philosophers argue that consciousness is a material thing, I say that *there is no material thing*. If I am to answer the question of whether or not consciousness is produced from matter, then I shall say that *nothing is material*. Whatever we feel is only a part of consciousness."[66] Similarly, when asked if matter will be seen through higher realization as alive, Srila Sridhara Swami replied affirmatively: "In a higher stage of realization we can detect consciousness *everywhere*: within glass, stone, earth, wood—in all the innumerable shapes and colors in which matter may appear. We are always in the midst of consciousness. Consciousness is all-pervading but is situated in different gradations of conception. The gradation of conception may differ, but it is all consciousness, all eternal."[67] As difficult as this may be to conceive in the beginning, we are advised to trust revelation and follow its lead, leaving behind whatever we may have idealized and instead embrace the ideal. In other words, to continue growing we should leave our conceptual comfort zone and change our angle of vision. Our comfort zone means our own agenda—our own idea about almost everything. For heaven to continue happening *in us* here on Earth, that mentality needs to be duly dethroned.

LOVE IS THE BLOODSTREAM OF MATERIAL ENERGY

As we have seen, Gaudiya Vaishnavism is a religion not only of transcendence but of immanence as well, one in which divine love is the very bloodstream of material creation. This is in stark contrast to conceiving of the Divine as utterly indifferent to us in this world or, even worse, as hostile and destructive—and in need of being constantly appeased. The Sweet Absolute is never indifferent to or against humanity, watching, judging, condemning it. But many of us, despite claiming we do not believe in myths that present him as such, still embrace such a mythical worldview by the fearful way in which we live. The truth, however, is that both God and this material energy are on our side, and thus the blueprint of reality can be trusted. Radical grace is not only flowing somewhere, but robustly present *everywhere*.[68]

So this is the ideal Gaudiya conclusion: not only is the world not bad, but it's so much in our favor that the Sweet Absolute himself chooses to descend and remain here eternally, executing his cosmic play while inviting every soul to unearth heaven in the here and now. *The now is the way to the always, the here is the way to the everywhere, the material is the way to the spiritual, the visible is the way to the invisible.*[69] We urgently need a worldview that helps us cultivate meaning in the present moment and remain faithful to the here and now, the only place for us where the spiritual world can really happen.

Every corner is the potential birthplace of the kingdom of God. Everything there is, is potentially accessible from where we are. It's not about going anywhere but *continuing to arrive*—perpetually. If we put on an entirely different mind, then heaven takes care of itself and, in fact, begins now, so it is nothing we have to believe in for later.[70] As St. Catherine of Siena repeatedly said, "It's heaven all the way to heaven, and it's hell all the way to hell." Not later, but now. If we don't touch upon life now, why would we believe in it afterward?[71] The Gaudiya challenge is to thus bridge this unnecessary gap in our own minds to the point that the Sweet Absolute becomes discoverable through matter, and by such an exercise, matter is then brought back to her deserved place of honor. This has been accurately expressed by Shrivatsa Goswami while referring to how Gaudiyas worship God in matter—not in stone but *as* stone, in the form of Mount Govardhan:

> *The world is the body of God, and all nature is divinized. Whereas for many Europeans nature worship is regarded as primitive, the nature worship exemplified in the worship of Mount Govardhan is the highest form of worship; it is the highest form of religion.* The Bhagavata Purana *reveals that Krishna was the first to perform the worship of Mount Govardhan, and in so doing teaches the key to how to celebrate life and survive, as life is always lived in the theater of nature.*[72]

As we can see from the above quote, nature worship has been established by the Supreme Lord himself. And it is a worship that has been deemed the highest form of veneration. Especially for Gaudiyas, the gift available in the worship of Mount Govardhan is an understanding of the divinity of the world. A central point of the mountain's story is realization of divine presence in all nature[73]—*all* nature. While Gaudiya Vaishnavism teaches that a vast and infinite aspect of divinity surpasses the tangible world, the world of finite visible forms is also to be seen as fully divine. In other words, divine presence is here and now, in and *as* concrete entities, which are often considered the most accessible and thus generous forms of divinity.[74] By the inspiration of Mount Govardhan and this highest and most compassionate form of worship, while we had almost concluded writing this chapter an email serendipitously arrived containing the following poem:

> *If I cannot gaze out my window, at the hill rising behind*
> *the house, and see Govardhan, I will not see Govardhan*
> *if standing before him. I will simply see a hill in India,*
> *just like I see a hill in my own hometown.*
>
> *If I do not see the Lord's form in the rocks I meet along*
> *the path, I will not see him in his blooming Deity form,*
> *but will simply see the Deity as a rock.*

If I cannot see the face of the Lord sculpted in the faces of whomever I meet, I will not recognize him even if gazing upon his lotus-eyed blossoming youth. I will simply think, "There is a handsome person."

If I cannot feel the heart of my Lord expressed through the hearts of all living beings, I will not feel the beating of my Lord's heart even if my hand brushed against his lotus chest.

If I do not feel the tips of the Sweet Absolute's toes as I go round and round my prayer beads, I will not do so even if those lotus toes decorated with golden rings and pearl-like moons stepped on my head.

If in the rays emanating from the golden sun and cooling moon I do not see the effulgence of my Beloved,
I will be blind to it even if it lit my eyes.

If I am absent from my Lord in all words, I will not be present with him in each syllable of his holy names. There will be no conversation—no conversion—only an alphabet.

If I cannot meet with my Lord between the grains of desert sand, I cannot meet him anywhere.

All places are one. All spaces are one.
All faces are one. All hearts are one.

All unique expressions in glorious specificity are one symphonic movement of blooming creativity.[75]

This material world is not limited to planet Earth but is a whole environment: an environment formed by consciousness, accompanied and created by a particular angle of vision. The world is an opportunity, the field of activity through which transformation itself will occur and as a result will itself be transformed. We are not meant to be taken out of it, but to engage with it as the very laboratory in which the process of our transformation from being something of it to being *someone in it* occurs. The world is the *place* where we are exposed. It is where our present situation and necessities are exposed to the Sweet Absolute and where we ourselves are deeply exposed, in a very customized way, to that which will lead to the lessons we need to learn—that we are ready to learn—one of them probably being to learn how to be present here and there and everywhere. Everything is already present here, *but are we*?

The God of Radical Personalism is a totally present one, whose abundant grace permeates and sprinkles and soaks every direction. Unless we get the right idea about the Divine, who is the source of everything, all of our remaining conceptions will be colored by such a tragic misreading. Therefore, the actual Gaudiya Deity is someone very different from the one that emerges in a stagnate anti-world theology, where the Sweet Absolute is alienated from this world. That theology leads us to become too otherworldly, thus closing off his free-flowing reach into our lives by making our exchanges based on merit and not a merciful extension from above that reaches every corner of the below. Gaudiya Vaishnavism is interested in God as a person, not as a mere idea. We want to meet *the person behind the concept*. That's the very purpose of the concept. Therefore, we should be careful not to mistake the concept as the person—idealism vs. realism. While some of us may still think in terms of "our practice here" and "the concept (God) over there (above, in the sky)," a proper unearthing of heaven will reveal how material energy deeply contains the spiritual world by being a host par excellence and, thereby, building further bridges of relatability.

Almost reaching the end of our presentation, we have approached our main theme of Radical Personalism in a thousand ways, since most of us—including the one penning these sentences—still have endless levels of unconscious resistance and denial to whatever entails deep transformation. Our main message and our proposal have been shared on the basis of not only sacred revelation from our tradition and other ancient traditions, but especially on the basis of what we may call *uncommon common sense*. An essential aspect of this present work and project is to reclaim our Gaudiya common sense in one way or another. And the best place to begin such exploration is here on Earth, where everything we need will be eventually revealed—including our Gaudiya heaven.

Let's turn next to the conclusion of this work, where we'll share some final reflections while further mining what it means to heroically reclaim our Gaudiya common sense as Radical Personalists.

CONCLUSION: Reclaiming Our Gaudiya Project 15

IT HAS BEEN A LONG, WINDING JOURNEY through hundreds of pages and thousands of words. Multiple approaches have been invoked in our attempt to convey and conceive the notion and implications of Radical Personalism. In the first part of this book, we considered why to stay as Gaudiyas for the right reasons; how to belong to our tradition instead of merely fitting in; where the place is for constructively critiquing one's lineage in committed service to it; why our movement is ideally a living school of prophets; and how to invoke the necessary revival and holy shifts to preserve a bright future for Gaudiya Vaishnavism. We examined all of this while acknowledging our collective unconscious and embracing our wounds in a redemptive way. In Part Two, we presented our Revival Manifesto for Proactive Devotion, which included copious examples of healthy forms of radicality by which the current state of the Gaudiya community could evolve into a more mature, healthy, and sustainable version of itself. The third part of this work dealt with an in-depth articulation of some of the main tenets of our manifesto, including crucial topics such as vulnerability, individuation, nondual thinking, the guru-disciple template, divine ignorance, contemplative prayer, and last but not least, the unearthing of heaven. Having attempted to reach so far and deep into the potential of our excavation project, we will now bring this book to a close by presenting a few conclusive thoughts that will turn this apparent ending into an ongoing invitation for further exploration.

EMERGING AND ANTICIPATORY GAUDIYA VAISHNAVISM

As we already described, Radical Personalism is another way of referring to the emergence of Gaudiya Vaishnavism's ongoing essence and dynamic spirit. Emerging Gaudiya Vaishnavism—an ever-evolving reality—entails the emergence of the tradition's life and soul emanating through the vessel of the tradition's current state as a community. As described by Philip Clayton, the mark of any form of emergence is irreducible novelty, which pertains not only to the properties of the new emerging entity but to the entity itself as being new.[1] Similarly, Emerging Gaudiya Vaishnavism is the very heart of the Gaudiya tradition manifesting itself in ever new and necessary expressions, renewing and reaffirming both its own essence and its current members. This undeniable emergence can be represented only by a deeply avant-garde approach. Members will be innovative enough to explore and experiment with nuanced possibilities that will allow us to reconnect with our tradition from a relevant, relatable, and reliable template. Despite seeming ideologically unacceptable in the beginning, this spirit of Emerging Gaudiya Vaishnavism is the only way we can acknowledge collapsed systems and expired structures in the world and in our own community and update and upgrade them by invoking a new version of them. *It is time to reclaim the Gaudiya project for what it is and for all that it can be.*

Another facet of Emerging Gaudiya Vaishnavism is what we call *Anticipatory Gaudiya Vaishnavism*. In this case, the foundational principles of the tradition will take the shape of a prophetic and visionary quest, through which we will identify ourselves with the ultimate potential of our lineage and strive for it to be attained, whatever it takes. In fact, the very notion of transcendence could be defined as *living up to our potential*. If we need adjustment and repair for actualizing such potential, so be it. If, however, we need comprehensive dissolution and collapse for us to reach whatever shore we need to reach, then so be it as well. "The Christian of the future will be a mystic or will not be at all," Karl Rahner remarked.[2] Likewise, for any mystical tradition to thrive and survive in this world, Gaudiya Vaishnavism included, then *continual doses of further mysticism* are always required. And we should remember that mysticism is intimately tied to mystery. This means opening of ourselves to an unknown future that we are called to embrace, as individuals and as a collective, thus bearing witness to our own mystical heritage. Become a mystic, *or you stop becoming*.

Through the lens of geological time, Gaudiya Vaishnavism is considerably young and the institutionalization of it is even younger—a child. In the present chapter of its history, the Gaudiya community appears to be reaching a point where the collective history of failures is substantial enough to testify to the sources of those failures while begging for progressive, corrective measures. In any laboratory, actual substantive progress is possible only through a process of repeated failures analyzed in relation to each other in order to weed out concomitant factors, to separate substance from form, to see nuances previously undetected. Of course, it is not just the failures, but also the successes that are to be considered in wholistic unity. And part of our success is to see failure as potentially favorable. As Sri Gaurahari has emphatically taught, we must accept what works and reject what doesn't. But how do we know either of those unless we are willing to accept that *failure exists*, that it is a large part of our reality, and that is *not* a bad thing in itself? In fact, failure, breakdown, collapse, and defeat embody a central feature of our progressing forward—probably its very bedrock. If we cannot acknowledge and learn from our mistakes as individuals and a group, then the whole project devolves to the point of devastation, to start all over again. Maybe we need *that* to learn our present lesson. Or maybe we need to first forgive and exonerate ourselves while healing our own history as Gaudiyas, and that will keep the doors open for future creative action and avoid unnecessary disintegration. To deeply ponder these possibilities is to participate in Anticipatory Gaudiya Vaishnavism, without which we will have only the repetition of old patterns and storylines, remembered hurts, and ever-increasing claims of victimhood for all concerned. If you see something, *say* something.

WHERE ARE THE ELDERS?

For the above desired scenario to happen, we need to become Gaudiya elders. However, anyone's initial duty is to first become an infant, then a teenager, an adult, and eventually a mature and revered elder. In other words, part of our elder project is to first integrate each of its preliminary stages, and never skip them in the name of (premature) elderhood. Therefore, while it may not yet be our time to attain elderhood, we at least need to find elders in our own life and community. Without elders, we are basically left with a deadly overdose of unripeness, naiveté, and black-and-white psychology. Conversely, elders can provide maturity, artfulness, and the balancing shades of gray—the grace of grays—to any necessary wholesome equation. That said, for this to happen young people must be willing and open to hear and learn from elders.

While gray is arguably our most important color on the palette of the inner life, it is ironically one of the less popular ones. Why? Because more often than not people mistakenly relate gray with getting old, while it actually speaks of maturity and the act of becoming real adults. Thus, gray could be portrayed as *the color of wisdom*, its appearance inviting us to recalibrate our whole perception of things. It dares us to be broader without ceasing to be profound, more generous without ceasing to be truthful, more compassionate without ceasing to be discerning. Gray (elderhood) represents the exact middle point between black and white. To be more precise, according to some calculations, we have 256 shades of gray—256 *intermediate possibilities and middle paths*. This points to a much more flexible and broad perspective of things. Therefore, to become a Gaudiya elder has nothing to do with white opposing black or black condemning white, but with locating ourselves *right in the middle*, close enough to both ends of the spectrum so we can understand, integrate, and learn from them, even while differing from their perspectives.[3]

Elders are basically synonymous with good leaders, and we *always* need them. Ideally, a Gaudiya Vaishnava leader is deeply embedded and accomplished in the realms of prayer, faith, hope, and love. He or she must have a certain capacity for nonpolar thinking and full-access knowing (*prayer*), a tolerance for ambiguity (*faith*), an ability to hold creative tensions (*hope*), and an ability to care (*love*) beyond one's own advantage.[4] Ironically, although elders are in a position to substantially change people, more so than at any other point in their life, they do not *need to*—and that is what allows them to be true leaders.[5] Due to their strength and lucidity, genuine elders are like diamonds, the hardest of stones. It is one hundred times harder than its closest rival, yet the most transparent. The process through which a diamond becomes all that it can be is through a repeated but sustainable exposure to pressure, heat, and polishing. There is no other way to become a shining, transparent, and empowered elder.

Elders are not seeking fame or followers, but *allies of all ages*. And if there happen to be any followers, elders will immediately see them as part of their committed service and as people to deeply learn from. Elders are ideal mentors and examples when they have inclusive natures and the capacity to challenge everyone by their very loving presence. They are also ideal when they learn from the voices of others, especially the younger voices, while expressing their own individual voices. In fact, if you deprive an elderly constituency of younger voices, it is likely to be regressive and extremist, not merely conservative.[6] Elders have a committed sense of *educational responsibility*, through which they seek to both empower and be empowered by each generation and their unique insights. It has been said that God has no grandchildren, only children. In other words, each generation has to make its own discoveries for itself. If not, we just react to the previous generation, and often overreact. Or we conform, and often overconform.[7] Alternatively, Radical Personalism suggests a reform from the bottom up, where each member of the community is invited to make their own unique contribution under the affectionate guidance of true elders. And those who are being called to become elders themselves should then be provided with whatever is required to master such a crucial skill and be willing to embrace the fire of further transformation. Deprived of elders, Gaudiya Vaishnavism will gradually turn into what we may call Bonsai Gaudiya Vaishnavism, a living organism which, while surviving and even growing, is not growing *as much as it could*. It will be a miniature version of a potential giant.

As expressed in one of our previous chapters, elders are *prophets*—and each one of us is expected to become such at some point. These elderly prophets are those who name the situation truthfully and in its largest context. They shed the light of eternity and its bigger picture so it cannot get pulled into interest groups and political expediency.[8] In fact, one of the gifts of the truth-telling prophets is the crisis they evoke where one did not appear to exist before; where structural violence was inherent in the system, but was denied and disguised until someone was willing to talk about it.[9] Prophets always talk about the untalkable and open a huge new arena of "talkability." Prophets generate a crisis, representing the very point where the fire meets the crucible of collective transformation. It is almost understandable why prophets are usually called troublemakers and oftentimes killed. While others deny and submit their own truth to the popular narrative joining the cheer that the emperor is beautifully clothed, the prophets are willing to say, "No, no, he's naked!" and bring to each heart the decisive point of crisis, that face-to-face encounter with truth. The prophets force us to ask ourselves, "Shall we embrace the responsibility to do what is necessary to flesh out our potential or will we choose to cower behind conformity?" This is where the prophets lead us. In other words, it is the prophet's job to first deconstruct current illusions—the status quo—and then reconstruct on a new and honest foundation. That is why the prophet is never popular with the comfortable or with those who draw power from keeping group-thought and social structures exactly as they are. Only a holy few have any patience with the deconstruction of egos and institutions. The prophets are *radical teachers* in the truest sense of the words. They go to the root causes and root vices and *root* them out, giving us Radical Personalism.[10]

UNCOMMON COMMON SENSE

The proposal of Radical Personalism is based on (but not limited to) sacred revelation. It is also deeply aligned with what we may call our Gaudiya common sense, although such is mostly not a very common one. Common sense refers not to something simplistic, but to something simple, which has become simple by a proper integration of complexity. However, most of us are quite complex and unintegrated beings. Thus we usually have a hard time grasping this uncommon common sense. But this we must.

Any privileged portal into depth and truth needs to be accompanied by common sense, the recognition of the obvious which nonetheless escapes the mainstream eye. In the case of our Gaudiya community and its current global situation, common sense will clearly reveal that we are unnecessarily bearing many outdated structures, external and mental, which are already in rigor mortis. But are we admitting the obvious? In regard to this acknowledgement, how many of our communities include within themselves—or even want to include—a self-investigative branch, where each of these realities can be named and framed through an ongoing fearless inventory? In reply to this, our Gaudiya common sense should be quick to realize our current global situation. We are at an undeniable state of impasse, a space between what was and what can be. We are at a crossroad as a community, a space to reconcile and transfuse the heart of tradition into the minds and hands of convention so that the ways of thinking and moving aren't enacted just because they have been done that way in the past or by the many. Our thoughts and our words and our actions should be selected and crafted to support the vitality of progressive presence into the unexplored land of potential as it is revealing itself at this very moment. What's new disrupts what's stable, and it needs to be integrated with the latter. The dogmatic structure perpetuates the system, while the mystical renews it. And there is always a tension between the two—hopefully a healthy one. These dynamics have been interestingly depicted by Thomas Merton:

> *Tradition is living and active, but convention is passive and dead. Tradition does not form us automatically: we have to work to understand it. Convention is accepted passively, as a matter of routine. Therefore, convention easily becomes an evasion of reality. It offers us only pretended ways of solving the problems of living—a system of gestures and formalities. Tradition really teaches us to live and shows us how to take full responsibility for our own lives. Thus tradition is often flatly opposed to what is ordinary, to what is mere routine. But convention,*

> *which is a mere repetition of familiar routines, follows the line of least resistance. One goes through an act, without trying to understand the meaning of it all, merely because everyone else does the same. Tradition, which is always old, is at the same time ever new because it is always reviving—born again in each new generation, to be lived and applied in a new and particular way. Convention is simply the ossification of social customs. ... Tradition nourishes the life of the spirit; convention merely disguises its interior decay.*[11]

For the more utopian of us, the notion of impasse we Gaudiyas find ourselves in may feel like failure, and success being the exact opposite of that. However, while failure and success may look like binary opposites, if we put them into motion they will actually be more like winter and spring or like mass extinction events and post-event evolutionary explosions of diversity. Together they push the process of growth forward. If we want evolution—and if we still don't want it, then we certainly *need* it—then we have to accept struggle and mass extinction events as an unavoidable part of it. If a mother wants birth, she will have to go through labor that feels as if it's killing her. If we want a new genesis of diversity and beauty, then we have to accept that things may look absolutely hopeless at first. In other words, we must commit to do the right thing against all odds. Otherwise, the systems maintain their equilibrium, and the status quo spins on. And maybe that's the point. Maybe it takes crushing defeat in one generation to create the conditions for the change we need in the next. Maybe death and resurrection, not decline and renewal, is the more accurate model of how change happens.[12] And that's also *uncommon* common sense, isn't it?

CONFRONTATION, TRUTH-TELLING, AND INTIMACY

All of us need the experience of intimacy in one way or another. Without it, we are basically deprived of our very human nature: its vulnerability and empowering prospect. While the experience of intimacy may be idealized as—and limited to—some comfortable amatory episode, a more realistic perspective of it will conceive of intimacy in terms of confrontation and truth-telling. These are not at all divorced from intimacy. If we think about it for a minute, we will naturally conclude that both confrontation and truth-telling are essential components of intimacy, since both of them invoke the very experience of closeness to another. In other words, to be intimately confronted with the truth is not an act of violence but a getting closer to reality and therefore a sign of compassion and affection. As flawed as they may be, each of these pages is a humble attempt at such loving expression.

At least in part, this desirable intimacy entails being confronted with how we want to continue with our life as Gaudiya Vaishnavas. In reply, the voice of Radical Personalism suggests that while there is no need to stay compliantly as a Gaudiya, neither is there a need to leave the tradition defiantly. A sensitive integration of these two is possible. We can *stay defiantly*. In other words, we can stay as Gaudiyas while confronting reality by honest truth-telling, a telling invoked with both integrity and determination. We can do so as best as we can, as long as we can, and at times *as loud as we can*. To stay defiantly in this way will amount to real belonging, instead of merely fitting-in in our tradition. While the very act of fitting-in is based purely on mental constructs, deep belonging is sustained by shared emotional experience of what *actually* moves us. And the more that "thing" moves us, the more we will become uniquely unified with others who are also moved by that same "thing." That's the real participatory movement that Gaurahari's *sankirtana* is meant to be for each of us.

The essential Gaudiya Vaishnavism we all need to see and experience lies beyond ritual, belief, and dogma. Still the question remains: Are *we* willing to go there? Are we ready to embark upon such a journey? In reply to this, we should be reminded of one beautiful Sanskrit word that summarizes our practice and tradition: *abhisara*, or love journey. Yes, to practice Gaudiya Vaishnavism means that we are sent into an adventure—a love journey. Love is both an adventure and a conquest. It survives and develops like the universe itself *only by perpetual discovery*.[13] The toll of that essential journey is to be paid in blood, sweat, and tears, and we are to think of ourselves as nothing less than a pilgrim on such a sacred odyssey. We are to confront reality—to relish intimacy—by opening its enigmatic door and not merely watching through the keyhole. The key to that door has been provided, but we must put it in the right place. Not daring to do so will leave us with an unutilized key, a yet closed door, and a nanoscopic keyhole, a key*hole* devoid of a *key* and therefore remaining nothing more than a *hole* for us. And whatever we see through such a hole will be no different than what we see when we remain in a hole ourselves. The hole is mediocrity and complacency, the norm of the masses through which stagnation follows accordingly. We become conditioned to expect nothing. Conversely, *reality has to be unpacked by insight.*

Truth-telling is a spiritual discipline and requires practice. It begins with being honest with ourselves *about* ourselves, and only then thinking about lubricating our relationships with others. As exaggerated as it may sound, this truth-telling constitutes one of the greatest exhibitions not only of intimacy, but of courage as well. In this connection Howard Zinn once said, "The most revolutionary act one can engage in is ... to tell the truth."[14] Conversely, for us to see shortcomings in our tradition but distance ourselves from them can easily fall into the category of a *cult of innocence*. This means we withdraw from something bad and see ourselves as good and pious people—innocent—*just* by and because of our withdrawal. By distancing ourselves from any discredited religion—which happens to be all of them—we can feel ourselves innocent of its wrongs, weaknesses, and failures. Paradoxically, to acknowledge our collective messiness while not leaving gives us one of the most compelling reasons to stay as Gaudiya Vaishnavas—to leave the cult of innocence.[15] Sri Bhaktisiddhanta Saraswati, one of the most fervent Gaudiya reformers of contemporary times, powerfully and repeatedly expressed the very spirit of confrontation and truth-telling as intimacy that is so much needed in our current times:

> *Without cheating anyone we should boldly proclaim the truth to everyone. If the truth is bitter or unpopular but bestows blessings on the living entities, we must speak it. Unless we fearlessly speak the truth, the Sweet Absolute will not be pleased. ... The aggressive pronouncement of the concrete truth is the crying necessity of the moment, for silencing the aggressive propaganda of specific un-*

> *truths that is being spread all over the world. ... A chanter of the names of God is necessarily the uncompromising enemy of worldliness and hypocrisy ... it is his bounden duty to clearly and frankly oppose any person who tries to deceive and harm himself and others by misrepresenting the truth, whether due to malice or genuine misunderstanding. ... Humility implies perfect submission to the truth and no sympathy for untruth. ... Therefore, the professors of pseudo-humility have reason to fear the preaching of God's servant, one of whose duties is to expose the enormous possibility of mischief inherent in various forms of so-called spiritual conduct when they are prostituted for serving the untruth.*[16]

A NEW VERSION OF GAUDIYA VAISHNAVISM

Earlier this year, some of us had the unique opportunity of personally meeting with Father Richard Rohr, a Franciscan monk, author, and mystic. In our abundant hours of sharing with each other, he and I realized—in astonishment and mutual regret—how all of the main shortcomings surrounding the Christian community are basically the same issues affecting the Gaudiya society (and probably every other religious community). They are ego-centered meritocracy above the unconditional gift of radical grace; ascending vs. descending approaches to religion; an obsession with knowing and certainty instead of holy unknowing; attachment to endless faces of the status quo and religious perks rather than a humble belonging to the essence of one's tradition; being terrified about thinking for ourselves, while stigmatizing those who do so; and so on. In reply to such scenarios, our friend Richard has been deeply engaged for the past half a century in reminding his fellow Christians of their own legacy and how to embrace it in a dynamic spirit. In a similar way, the present manifesto is an attempt to not only learn from other traditions, as we should, but mainly to remind us Gaudiyas about our own treasures in the context of dealing with our current difficulties. In fact, the price for belonging to any tradition is to inherit both treasure and trouble.

If we don't feel identified with the current state of affairs in the Gaudiya community, it is then time for a new version of Gaudiya Vaishnavism. In some cases, this new version will emerge after articulating those specific circumstances that beg for an upgrade, while in other cases we will have to deeply ponder what *we* can do about it. We should pay close attention, focus on our surroundings—inner and outer—and notice what actually bothers and concerns us, and then do something about it. In other words, each of us needs to ask ourselves what bothers us, then question if that is something we can fix, and then inquire if we are willing to do the fixing. If our answer to any of those questions is "no," then we should aim elsewhere, probably lower, until we find something that bothers us, that we can fix, and that we would fix. *And then we should go and fix it.* That might be enough for the day.[17] Conversely, by not taking the initiative, we remain as passive inert consumers of a mere product, not active participants in a living school. But this we should remember: *being committed to nothing and staying on the fence is the worst of all transgressions.*

As with any tradition, Gaudiya Vaishnavism also has a home as well as a fence. It has an essence as well as its outer surroundings. To live inside the fence while not inhabiting home—but thinking we do—is a failed shortcut and a detour from where we need to be. It is only a seemingly spiritual shortcut. However, the only real spiritual shortcut is letting go of having any shortcuts. Instead of trying to quickly move forward, we need to slowly go through whatever needs to be fixed on our journey. There is no rush to go anywhere but *here.* In fact, the greater our hurry to arrive where we think we want to be spiritually, the longer it will take, since our conceptions will still be unrealistic and implausible. Actual spirituality means there is no escape and *no need for escape.* And it also means utter freedom *through* limitation and every sort of difficulty. If we need to experience a breakdown, then let it be and transform into a hugely relevant *breakthrough.* Instead of a shallow relationship with our inner depths, let's become intimate with them—our shadow included.[18]

Gaudiyas who are courageously committed to their own values and ideals of transformation will bravely address the endless issues and tissues that surround any situation in their life. They will follow the fragrance to the garden, *wherever the garden is blooming now*. They are in love with Gaudiya Vaishnavism, and as with any real love affair, they realize that the nature of love is an ever-evolving pattern that demands and engages everyone on a permanent path of transformation. And they also realize that transformation itself cannot be engineered by our own rules and with our own power, which by definition is the opposite of how transformation occurs. If we try to change our ego with the help of our ego, we only end up with a better-disguised ego.[19] Therefore, if we are bothered by some issues in the present Gaudiya community, it doesn't mean that our only option is to abandon Gaudiya Vaishnavism altogether. We can leave *our current form* of it and embrace a better version, one that allows and even encourages the growth we desire and need. In other words, what we may possibly need is *a change of phase, not a change of religion*—an upcycling rather than a discarding. What we may possibly need is not to leave Gaudiya Vaishnavism, but rather to discard all of the layers of immaturity, narrowmindedness, and superficiality through which we continue to approach our own tradition. What we may need is not to leave Gaudiya Vaishnavism, but to transform its early stages and our preconceived ideas of it into a more mature way of being a Gaudiya, one that corresponds with our present thirst. That's the new version of Gaudiya Vaishnavism we are talking about here—whatever that new version will be for each of us.

THE RIGHT AND DUTY TO REDISCOVER OUR TRADITION

To find our new version of Gaudiya Vaishnavism is not something cheap. To begin with, we may have to start by seriously asking ourselves questions like, "What is that single thing that is most worthy of my greatest sacrifice?" After hearing the reply from our deepest inner chambers, we should then proceed accordingly. It doesn't matter how devious and fallen we may still be as individuals or as a collective, the Sweet Absolute can enter us and change whatever is required. Let's have hope, but let's also do our homework. And if something needs to die in order to be reborn, we should allow and respect such a process of loss and renewal as a crucial facet of life's dynamics. Each of us will experience many deaths in a single lifetime only to be born again with renewed force. We will similarly find this pattern on not only a microcosmic level but a macrocosmic one as well. In fact, a necessary experience of loss, failure, and demise is surely to invoke the humility and vulnerability that we may so much need in order to attain the required empowerment. As Rev. Stephanie Spellers wisely said in connection to the Christian church:

> *A church that has been humbled by disruption and decline may be a less arrogant and presumptuous church. It may have fewer illusions about its own power and centrality. It may become curious. It may be less willing to ally with the empires and powers that have long defined it. It may finally admit how much it needs the true power and wisdom of the Holy Spirit.*[20]

We don't need permission to rediscover our tradition. We have the right and duty to do so. This is especially the case with an ever-evolving and eternally discoverable living school like Gaudiya Vaishnavism, whose ideal form is to be uncovered—over and over again. In fact, the earliest form of something is not necessarily its pure or original or best or permanent or ideal form. There really is no pure, original, best, or ideal form, since every form is in process, adapting, evolving, mutating, and changing[21] in an ongoing state of further perfection in the bigger unfolding and deeper flow of love. We can verily call this condition a *flow state*. It is a willingness to remain absorbed, engaged, and open to constant peer review and adaptation. Our individual view of God situated in the Gaudiya conception is no exception to this rule. Therefore, we as a community also need to access this flow state, which is synonymous with wellbeing, and learn to remain in those waters. We are to become multipliers and contributors, experts at recapturing the dynamic roots of our tradition. The capacity to evolve into new forms of expression that are graspable and relevant to the new generation of practitioners is the strength and glory of any movement—ours included—and that strength lies in anonymous, obscure yet sincere and empowered members. There is an increasing minority who are willing to embrace what they see, constantly and vigilantly reevaluating what is being done, lest habits and past wisdom blind us to new possibilities. As Thomas Jefferson is said to have declared, "Eternal vigilance is the price for liberty." Radical Personalism is achieved *one vision at a time.*

Real improvement calls for intelligence and realization coupled with honesty and integrity while remaining deeply aware of how each of our actions has the potential to create necessary change. For Gaudiyas, everything is related to everything (*sambandha*), but without monistic identity or dualistic separation. Therefore, whatever we do (and don't do) will naturally affect everybody else. This aspect of reality is not to evoke neurosis, but realism and responsibility. And if we fail in our attempts, let's be reminded that the rightness is in the sincerity of the process and not in the specific decision. In this connection, Narahari Sarkar Thakura, the author of *Krishna-bhajanamrita* (verses 3 and 4) has the courage to admit that after Sri Gaurahari's earthly *lila* came to an end, all levels of devotees, including the highest ones, "shall always be in anxiety, and it will be at all times." Why is this so? Because "they shall almost feel uncertainty in their hearts regarding the correct understanding of the eternal truths of devotional service." And when there is some doubt about any subject, Bhaktisiddhanta Saraswati taught that "then both sides are needed to reach a conclusion." What are these two sides he refers to? *Purva-paksha*, or the challenging side, and *para-paksha*, or the concluding side.[22] In other words, whatever we deem conclusive today should be duly exposed to whatever we presently feel as challenging, and let these two layers create *a new level of conclusion.* No matter how advanced we are, there is always room for a better understanding of reality. There is always room for an ongoing sense of rediscovery of our own tradition.

LEARN TO SING YOUR SONG

Just as a bird beckons the morning, this book has been a sincere attempt to sing a song. Hopefully it is one that reaches a place where words, like these, cannot. We call that place home. Home is not the name of the tree in which our songbird nests. Home is the name of our song, for that is the place we truly live from and live through. Wherever we learn to sing our song, that is then to be known as home, not because our nest is there, but because our song is. In other words, what matters most isn't staying faithful to the tree, or the nest we've built in it, but rather staying faithful to the song, to the song of Gaudiya Vaishnavism. Some Gaudiyas will remain in their old familiar tree and sing their song from there. Others will stay in that tree but, tragically, give up singing entirely. And some others will leave that tree and continue to sing their song somewhere else.[23] The motto of Radical Personalism, given by Sri Gaurahari himself, is *kirtaniyah sada harih*—never ever give up your song!

The honest attempt of this Revival Manifesto has been to kindle a necessary thinking *process*. While thinking starts in our head, it continues through further dialogue, hearing, and ongoing articulation. Thus, the present treatise is not meant to be a finished product, but an embryonic approach to a permanent conundrum with a thousand faces. *And it's okay* for this to be an ongoing evolution of thought and heart. Evolution is, after all, the very being of life—a process of becoming. A common ground of all becoming is participation, and common in all participation is integrity and responsibility, since actual participation involves a concern with making things better, and things can only get better by assuming commitment to our own ideals. Therefore, if becoming responsible makes us—and everything—better, then what could be the limit of that?

We have tried not to push our readers toward any predetermined answer but rather provide ideas and inspirations for each of us to discover an answer on our own, to participate in our own way in this unique celebration of existence called Radical Personalism. "How are we conceiving and embodying Gaudiya Vaishnavism?" Asking ourselves hard questions like these are not meant to be whips of shame and guilt used to beat ourselves or others into fitting in, but rather, like the true constant of the North Star, introspective questions are meant to be guides used to chart our journey toward Radical Personalism. Each question begins with our own heart and the answer ripples, knowingly or unknowingly, into the fabric of society.

- How vulnerable am I, willing to acknowledge my brokenness and frailty, and courageously accept what needs to happen to bring about the best version of myself?

- How whole am I, willing to integrate the beautiful and messy components of my humanity—my body, emotionality, and psychology—in service to my unique potential in *bhakti*?
- How willing am I to grow into the role of an elder, to consciously pass down to the next generation the wisdom of my lessons born through healing, rather than trickle down the pain from my unresolved traumas?
- Do my loyalties belong to my faith or have I sold them to an institution in exchange for membership?
- How much am I willing to accept divine guidance and unconditional love flowing through the accompaniment of an affectionate inspired mentor?
- How much am I willing to walk with such a mentor, responsibly dedicating myself to my own progress rather than riding on the glory of his or her endeavors?
- How much am I willing to follow my faith regardless of the place from which it calls to me or the shape it takes for reasons of its own?
- Am I willing to enter deeply into conceiving and reconceiving of the Gaudiya conception, even if that requires my deeper commitment in response?
- Am I willing to individuate myself from the foundation of my group, defining and following a *Rule of Life* that enables me to bring into flesh the unique gifts and inspirations the Sweet Absolute has placed in my care?
- Am I willing to be socially responsible by reaching out to others as a natural overflow of my inreach, sharing the unconditional love of a transformed heart?
- How willing am I to walk in the world from the inside out, actively listening in silent contemplation to the presence of Divinity in all I see and don't see?

- How willing am I to coexist with the mystery of that all-present Sweet Absolute, to allow him to be unendingly more than I can ever conceive?
- How willing am I to develop my relationship with the Sweet Absolute, to be involved with him through the sacredness of this world by seeing every atom as an embassy of his expression?
- How resolved am I to accept, integrate, and embody the principles of Radical Personalism in ongoing evolution into eternity, beginning right here and right now with the unfolding possibilities of the present moment?

If we accept all the responsibility we are capable of and face everything we need to, who would we become? And how would the world transform around us?

I would like to personally invite you to participate in the continued exploration of Radical Personalism, establishing a branch of the Gaudiya *sampradaya* in the *heart*quarters of each of us. Gaudiya Vaishnavism fully revolves around the idea of love. Love is not merely an emotion or a feeling. *It is an existential stance of commitment in binding with a significant other.* And the source of that significance is the Sweet Absolute. This is Gaudiya Vaishnavism. This is Radical Personalism.

Srimad Bhagavatam 11.19.39 mentions that *dakshina* (religious remuneration) constitutes not merely giving a monetary donation to others, but "informing friends after a festival of one's realization of bliss." This Revival Manifesto for Proactive Devotion, which ends now, is my attempt of such *dakshina.* All the complexity and pain experienced in this journey has gradually but mystically turned into a genuine festival of true joy and insight as each page filled with the churning of experience that only chaos can so thoroughly provide. My commitment to the ideal of Gaudiya Vaishnavism has been nourished by this experience. Thus, I am hoping to inform my friends of such a festival in glorification of the Sweet Absolute.

For the purpose of further evolving and refining this celebration, we have established a Facebook forum where we can come together in rich dialogue and discuss our adventure as pilgrims on this most beautiful path of loving devotion. Please visit the online group,

Gaudiya Reform Forum:
A Platform for Dialogue, Reflection & Healing
(https://www.facebook.com/groups/gaudiyareformforum).

Thank you for trusting me and opening yourself to the sacred journey of Radical Personalism.

Acknowledgments

Our whole life can be seen as a large, abundant book, either an autobiographic one or, even better, a confession letter. In fact, we often speak about our life in terms of its "different chapters." In this way the writing of this book, Radical Personalism (every single chapter), is to be considered one of the many crucial sections of the book of my life. Therefore, my initial gratitude is offered to those most unexpected but sacred circumstances that recently came into my life that made the present work possible. As the best version of ourselves is always coauthored by love, this book (and its author) have similarly been coauthored by love—a love that came to me in the form of life and its serpentine dance. After completing his first commentary on the *Bhagavad-gita,* Srila Prabhupada mentioned that he could write a second one. Perhaps he said this due to no longer being the same person who began the first edition, he himself having become a new edition, having been written by the pages of his commentary. Certainly, I'm no longer the same individual who began writing this book, being considerably edited by life's circumstances. Therefore, I offer this manifesto in the service of this inscrutable turn of events, as well as to the persons who were instrumental in them, with a hope that I have learned my lessons properly and am ready for the next version of myself.

This book has sprung from so many influences, inspirations, and contributors that I find it especially difficult to put only my name on its cover as the author (God bless those who invented the acknowledgments section!). To begin with, however, all copyrights go always to the Sweet Absolute himself, residing in everyone's heart and expertly orchestrating every episode that made this book—and everything else—what it is, according to his sweet will and unconditional affection. Next, I wish to express deep gratitude and indebtedness toward my dear sister Bhaktirasa dasi, who graciously helped me not only with in-depth editing, peer review, layout, and further details of the publication of this book, but also with caring support and ongoing inspiration for the whole concept of Radical Personalism to emerge as it has. In a similar light, Sumati dasi is to be deeply acknowledged for her sweet comradeship and ongoing encouragement at each step of this book's writing—and beyond. These two saintly elders have been uniquely remarkable pillars during the main six-month period through which this work came into being.

Another special mention goes to my friend, brother, and elder Richard Rohr, whose example and teachings have been particularly and powerfully influential—*electrifying*, to be more precise—during these liminal times of my life and during the writing of this book, as you can easily detect by seeing the endnote section. Likewise, Pranada dasi (Pranada Comtois) has been extremely supportive not only by writing an insightful foreword to this book, but also through her fellowship, peer review, and editing. Likewise, her husband, Nagaraja das, has helped immensely with his thorough and substantial editing. Similar appreciation goes to further friends and peer reviewers like Radhamadhav das, Deva Madhava das, Kalakanthi dasi, and Arcana-siddhi dasi. Their rapport and affectionate critique broadened the scope and depth of the book you now hold in your hands.

Deep gratitude is also extended to Krishna-kumari dasi for her assistance with the proofreading, as well as to Kali-yuga-pavana das for his help in finding specific textual references. My friend Juan Manuel Tavella is to be applauded for the beautiful cover art that depicts the very Deity of Radical Personalism—Sri Gaurahari—along with those who embrace his sacred mission of divine exploration. For a second time, Inword Publishers has been in charge of the publication of this work, and I would like to thank each of its members for facilitating the publication of this book. Finally, I extend my indebtedness and affection to my old friends Swami das and Govinda dasi as well as other well-wishers who have continually spread out their hearts and voices in my life.

To those I forgot to mention, my sincere apologies. Please contact me so we can talk about it.

About the Author

At an early age, Swami Padmanabha delved deeply into the theology of diverse mystical traditions. After taking up Gaudiya Vaishnavism in 1999 at the age of 19, he has dedicated himself to an extensive study of the Gaudiya scriptures under the guidance of his various mentors. Fluent in English and Spanish, Swami has written hundreds of articles in both languages, with his first two books published in English and in the process of being translated to other languages. For the past twenty years, he has traveled around the world and lectured in universities, ashrams, and yoga studios. All of his numerous talks and seminars are available online for free at swamipadmanabha.com. As a leader of spiritual retreats and communities, he inspires both practitioners and visitors with his penetrating teachings and personal example.

Bibliography

A. C. Bhaktivedanta Swami Prabhupada. *Bhagavad-gita As It Is.* Sanskrit text, translation, and commentary. Los Angeles: The Bhaktivedanta Book Trust. Vedabase.

——. *Srimad-Bhagavatam.* Sanskrit text, translation, and commentary. Los Angeles: The Bhaktivedanta Book Trust. Vedabase.

Anonymous. *The Cloud of Unknowing.* Translated by Carmen Acevedo Butcher. Boulder, CO: Shambhala, 2009.

Barrett Browning, Elizabeth, *Aurora Leigh.* London: J. Miller, 1864. Reprinted by Chicago Academy Printers, 1979.

Berry, Wendell. "How to Be a Poet (to remind myself)." Found in *Wendell Berry New Collected Poems.* Berkeley: Counterpoint, 2013.

Billings, Josh. *Josh Billing's Encyclopedia and Proverbial Philosophy of Wit and Humor.* Hartford, Connecticut: American Publishing Company.

Bonhoeffer, Dietrich. *I Want to Live These Days with You: A Year of Daily Devotions*. Louisville, KY: Westminster John Knox Press, 2007.

Boyle, Gregory. *The Whole Language: The Power of Extravagant Tenderness*. New York: Simon & Schuster, 2021.

Brahma Sutras: with Govinda-bhasya commentary of Baladeva Vidyabhusana. Translation by Bhanu Swami. Independently published, 2018.

Brown Taylor, Barbara. *Holy Envy: Finding God in the Faith of Others*. New York: HarperOne, 2020.

Brown, Brené. *Daring Greatly: How the Courage to Be Vulnerable Transforms the Way We Live, Love, Parent, and Lead*. New York: Avery, 2015.

Bucko, Adam and McEntee, Rory. *The New Monasticism: An Interspiritual Manifesto for Contemplative Living*. Maryknoll, New York: Orbis Books, 2015.

Chandogya Upanishad. Translated by Muni Narayana Prasad. Delhi: D. K. Printworld, 2006.

Chariton, Igumen. *The Art of Prayer*. New York: Farrar, Straus and Giroux, 1997.

Clayton, Philip, *Mind and Emergence: From Quantum to Consciousness*. New York: Oxford University Press, 2006.

Dasa, Purnachandra. *Unspoken Obstacles on the Path to Bhakti*. Independently published, undated.

Dasa, Radhamadhav. *Perfect Imperfection: On Guru's License to Err and on Friendly Criticism*. Independently published, 2022.

Dasa, Tamal Krishna. *Gaura Yuga*. Independently published, undated.

Damascene, St. John. *On Holy Images: Followed By Three Sermons On The Assumption*. Translation by Mary H. Allies. London: Thomas Baker, 1898.

Delio, Ilia. *The Unbearable Wholeness of Being: God, Evolution, and the Power of Love.* New York: Orbis Books, 2013.

Eliot, T. S. *The Dry Salvages by Four Quartets.* New York: Harcourt, Brace & World, 1971.

Einstein, Albert. *Living Philosophies.* New York: Forum Publishing Company, 1931.

Frankl, Viktor. *Man's Search for Meaning.* New York: Beacon Press, 2006.

Freud, Sigmund. *Civilization and Its Discontents.* New York: WW Norton & Co., 1969.

Fromm, Erich. *Psychoanalysis and Religion.* New York: Open Road Media, 2013.

Gopala-tapani Upanishad. With commentaries of Vishvanatha Chakravarti and Baladeva Vidyabhusana. Translated by Bhanu Swami. Chennai: Tattva Cintamani Publishing, 2022.

Goswami, Jiva. *Sri Bhagavat Sandarbha.* Translation and commentary by Satyanarayana Dasa. Vrindavan, India: Jiva Institute of Vaishnava Studies, 2014.

——. *Sri Bhakti Sandarbha.* Translation and commentary by Satyanarayana Dasa. Vrindavan, India: Jiva Institute of Vaishnava Studies, 2021.

——. *Paramatma-sandarbha.* Translation and commentary by Satyanarayana dasa. Vrindavan: Jiva Institute of Vaishnava Studies, 2017.

Goswami, Krishnadasa Kaviraja. *Sri Caitanya-caritamrita.* Sanskrit text, translation, and commentary by A. C. Bhaktivedanta Swami. Los Angeles: The Bhaktivedanta Book Trust. Vedabase.

Goswami, Raghunatha Dasa. *Sri Manah-siksa.* With the commentary of Ananta dasa Babaji. Translated by Advaita Dasa. Independently published, 2000.

Goswami, Rupa. *Bhakti-rasamrita-sindhu* with *Durgama-sangamani-tika,* the commentary called "Resolving the Difficult," of Srila Jiva Gosvami, and *Bhakti-sara-pradarsini-tika,* the commentary called "Revealing the Essence of Bhakti," of Srila Visvanatha Chakravarti Ṭhakura. Translation by Bhanu Swami. Chennai: Sri Vaikuntha Enterprises, 2006.

——. *Sri Laghu Bhagavatamrta.* Translation by Gopiparanadhana Dasa. Sweden: Bhaktivedanta Book Trust, 2017.

——. *Ujjvala-nilamani.* With commentary by Srila Jiva Gosvami and Srila Visvanatha Chakravarti Ṭhakura. Translation by Bhanu Swami. Chennai: Sri Vaikuntha Enterprises, 2014.

Goswami, Sanatana. *Sri Brhad Bhagavatamrta*, translation and summary of the author's commentary by Gopiparanadhana Dasa. Sweden: Bhaktivedanta Book Trust, 2003.

Goswami, Srila B. R. Sridhara Deva. *Sri Guru and His Grace.* Nadia, West Bengal: Sri Chaitanya Saraswat Math, 1999.

——. *Subjective Evolution of Consciousness: The Sweet Play of the Absolute. Nadia,* West Bengal: Sri Chaitanya Saraswat Math, 1989.

Haberman, David L. *Loving Stones: Making the Impossible Possible in the Worship of Mount Govardhan.* New York: Oxford University Press, 2020.

Jung, Carl G. *Aion: Researches into the Phenomenology of the Self* (Collected Works of C. G. Jung Vol. 9 Part 2). New York: Princeton University Press, 1959.

——. *Man and His Symbols.* New York: Random House, 1968.

——. *Modern Man in Search of a Soul.* New York: Harcourt Brace, 1955.

Keating, Thomas. *Invitation to Love: The Way of Christian Contemplation.* London: Continuum, 2012.

King, Thomas M. *Teilhard's Mysticism of Knowing*. New York: Seabury Press, 1981.

Mahabharata. Gorakhpur: Gita Press, 1987.

Maharaja, Narayana. *Brahma-samhita*. Fifth Chapter. Vrindavan: Gaudiya Vedanta Publications, 2003.

Maha-Upanishad. Publisher and date unknown.

Malone, Patrick. "A God Who Gets Foolishly Close." America Magazine, May 27, 2000.

Manu Samhita. Translated by Manmatha Nath Dutt. Andesite Press, 2015.

May, Gerald G. *The Dark Night of the Soul*. New York: HarperOne, 2005.

Masters, Robert Augustus. *Spiritual Bypassing: When Spirituality Disconnects Us from What Really Matters*. Berkeley, CA: North Atlantic Books, 2010.

McLaren, Brian D. *Do I Stay Christian?: A Guide for the Doubters, the Disappointed, and the Disillusioned*. New York: St. Martin's Essentials, 2022.

——. *Faith after Doubt: Why Your Beliefs Stopped Working and What to Do about It*. New York: St. Martin's Essentials, 2021.

Merton, Thomas. *New Seeds of Contemplation*. New York: New Directions, 2007.

——. *No Man is an Island*. New York: A Harvest Book, 1983.

——. *Spiritual Direction and Meditation*. Collegeville, MN: Liturgical Press, 1960.

——. *The Silent Life*. New York: Farrar, Straus, and Giroux, 1975.

Mundaka Upanishad. Publisher and date unknown.

Narasingha, Swami B. G. *Evolution of Theism*. San Rafael: Mandala Publishing, 2004.

Nietzsche, Friedrich. *Beyond Good and Evil*. New York: Penguin, 2003.

Padmanabha, Swami. *Inherent or Inherited?: Bhakti in the Jiva According to Gaudiya Vedanta*. North Carolina: InWord Publishing, 2022.

Panikkar, Raimon, et al. *Blessed Simplicity: The Monk as Universal Archetype*. New York: Seabury Press, 1982.

Pascal, Blaise. *Pensées*. Translated by W. F. Trotter. "Section XIV Appendix: Polemical Fragments," 894. London: Dent, 1908.

Peterson, Jordan B. *12 Rules for Life: An Antidote to Chaos*. New York: Penguin, 2019.

Rahner, Karl. "The Spirituality of the Church of the Future," in *Concern for the Church*, vol. 20, Theological Investigations. Translation by Edward Quinn. New York: Crossroad, 1981.

Rilke, Rainer Maria and Kappus, Franz Xaver. *Letters to a Young Poet*. Letter 4. New York: W. W. Norton & Co., 1993.

Rohr, Richard. *Breathing under Water: Spirituality and the Twelve Steps*. Cincinnati, OH: Franciscan Media, 2011, 2021.

——. *Everything Belongs: The Gift of Contemplative Prayer*. Chestnut Ridge, PA: Crossroad, 2003.

——. *Falling Upward: A Spirituality for the Two Halves of Life*. San Francisco: Jossey-Bassan, 2011.

——. *Just This*. New Mexico: CAC Publishing, 2017.

——. *The Good News According to Luke: Spiritual Reflections*. Chestnut Ridge, PA: Crossroad, 2002.

——. *The Naked Now: Learning To See As the Mystics See*. Chestnut Ridge, PA: Crossroad, 2009.

——. *The Universal Christ: How a Forgotten Reality Can Change Everything We See, Hope For, and Believe*. Colorado Springs, CO: Convergent Books, 2021.

Rohr, Richard and Morrell, Mike. *The Divine Dance: The Trinity and Your Transformation* (large print edition). New Kensington, Whitaker House, 2016.

Rosen, Steven. *Sri Chaitanya's Life and Teachings: The Golden Avatara of Divine Love* (*Explorations in Indic Traditions: Theological, Ethical, and Philosophical*). Lanham, MD: Lexington Books, 2017.

——. *Vaishnavism: Contemporary Scholars Discuss the Gaudiya Tradition*. New York: Folk Books, 1992.

Rumi, Jalal al-Din. *The Essential Rumi*. Translation by Coleman Barks. New York: HarperOne, 2004.

Sarasvati, Prabodhananda. *Caitanya-candramrta*. With commentary by Sri Anandi. Translated by Sarvabhavana dasa. Edited by Kunjabihari dasa. Vrindavan: Rasbihari Lal & Sons, 2004.

Singh, Avinash. *All about Prayer: Basic Aspects to Higher Aspects* (*Part One*). Delhi: Indian Society for Promoting Christian Knowledge, 2014.

Skanda Purana. Translation by Bibek Debroy. Delhi: Books for All, 2016.

Solzhenitsyn, Aleksandr. *Archipiélago Gulag I*. Barcelona: Tusquets Editores S.A, 2015.

Spellers, Stephanie, *The Church Cracked Open: Disruption, Decline, and New Hope for Beloved Community*. New York: Church Publishing, 2021.

Teilhard de Chardin, Pierre. *Human Energy*. Translation by J. M. Cohen. New York: Harcourt Brace Jovanovich, 1962.

——. *The Divine Milieu*. New York: Harper & Row, 1965.

——. *The Future of Man*. New York: Image Books, 2004.

Thakura, Bhaktisiddhanta Sarasvati. *Amrita-vani: Nectar of Instructions for Immortality*. Translation from Bengali by Bhumipati dasa. Vrindavan: Touchstone Media, 2011.

Thakura, Bhaktivinoda. *Harinama Chintamani*. Translation by Bhanu Swami. Self-published, undated.

——. *Caitanya-siksamrta*. Translation by Bhanu Swami. Independently published, 2017.

——. *Sajjana-toshani* Periodical 4/1, Independently published, 1892.

——. *Sri Bhaktyaloka: Illuminations on Bhakti*. Translation by Bhumipati Dasa. Vrindavan, India: Vrajraj Press, 1996.

——. *The Bhagavata: Its Philosophy, Its Ethics, and Its Theology*. Calcutta: Bagh Bazar Gaudiya Math, 1936.

Thakura, Narahari Sarkara. *Sri Krishna Bhajanamrita*. Translation by B. P. Puri Maharaja. Publisher and date unknown.

Thakura, Visvanatha Chakravarti. *Sarartha Darsini: Tenth Canto Commentaries to Srimad Bhagavatam*. Translation by Bhanu Swami. Vrindavan, India: Mahanidhi Swami, 2004.

Thakura, Vrindavana Dasa. *Sri Chaitanya-bhagavata*. Translation by Bhumipati Dasa. Vrindavan, India: Vrajraj Press, 1998.

The Bible, King James Version. Vero Beach, FL: Christian Art Publishers, 2017.

Vishnu Purana: Sanskrit Text and English Translation according to H. W. Wilson. Edited by K. L. Joshi. Delhi: Parimal Publication, 1986.

Wallace, Dave Foster. *This is Water*. Transcript of speech delivered at Kenyon College, 2005, published on Kenyon College website, http://bulletin-archive.kenyon.edu/x4280.html. Accessed January 2023.

Watts, Alan W. *The Wisdom of Insecurity*. New York: Vintage Books, 1951, 1968.

Weil, Simone. *The Simone Weil Reader*. Kingston, RI: Moyer Bell Ltd., 2007.

Zinn, Howard. "Marx in Soho: A Play on History," in *Three Plays: The Political Theater of Howard Zinn*. Boston: Beacon Press, 2010.

Endnotes

Introduction: Should I Stay or Should I Go?

1 Brian McLaren, *Do I Stay Christian?*.
2 Blaise Pascal, *Pensées*, p. 894.
3 Swami Padmanabha, *Radical Personalism Video Series*, https://www.youtube.com/playlist?list=PLGVblgfMMnT-B6KXsRdm2sWIZDYkqpBsQO.
4 Swami Padmanabha, *Inherent or Inherited?*, p. xxxv.

Chapter One: Why Radical Personalism?

1 For more on the different schools of personalism throughout history, see https://plato.stanford.edu/entries/personalism/.
2 See Raghunatha Dasa Goswami, *Sri Manah-siksa*.
3 Adapted from Swami B. R. Sridhar, *Subjective Evolution of Consciousness*, pp. 24–29.
4 Throughout this book, I will often refer to God as "the Sweet Absolute," as does one of my main teachers. Although God is by definition absolute, he is nonetheless also sweet—in fact, the sweetest. But this sweetness does not at all deprive him of his

absolute status. Veritably, it allows for the uncommon experience of absolute sweetness.

Chapter Three: Upgrading My Loyalty by Critiquing My Own Tradition

1 This is a term coined and usually invoked by Richard Rohr.
2 A. C. Bhaktivedanta Swami Prabhupada, purport to *Chaitanya-charitamrita* 2.10.182.
3 Robert Augustus Masters, *Spiritual Bypassing*, p. 3.

Chapter Four: A Living School of Prophets: An Urgent Need for Proactive Revival

1 Richard Rohr, *Everything Belongs*, p. 134.
2 Richard Rohr, *The Universal Christ*, p. 156.
3 This and the next three paragraphs have been inspired by Brian McLaren's introduction to The Future of Christianity, an online presentation: https://www.youtube.com/watch?v=jGl7yqYC35s.

Chapter Five: Holy Shift!

1 The last two sentences have been adapted from Richard Rohr, *The Divine Dance*, pp. 46–47.
2 The last two sentences have been adapted from Richard Rohr, *Just This*, p. 12.
3 *Srimad Bhagavatam* 2.9.34.
4 The last two sentences have been adapted from Richard Rohr, *The Divine Dance*, pp. 61–63.

Chapter Six: The Collective Unconscious

1 Bhaktivinoda Thakura, *Sajjana-tosani* 4/1.
2 This definition of trauma has been taken from Gabor Maté, https://humanwindow.com/dr-gabor-mate-interview-childhood-trauma-anxiety-culture.
3 Richard Rohr, *Falling Upward*, p. 158.

4 Friedrich Nietzsche, *Beyond Good and Evil*, p. 168.
5 This last sentence has been adapted from Rory McEntee and Adam Bucko, *The New Monasticism*, p. 164.
6 Ewert H. Cousins as quoted in *The New Monasticism*, p. 34.
7 Brian McLaren, *Do I Stay Christian?*, p.157.
8 The last two sentences are an adaptation from Thomas Keating, *Invitation to Love*, pp. 30–31.
9 Viktor Frankl, *Man's Search for Meaning*, p. 77.

Chapter Seven: The Manifesto

1 Thomas Merton, *New Seeds of Contemplation*, pp. 29–30.
2 Based on Pierre Teilhard de Chardin, *Future of Man*, p. 126.
3 Aleksandr Solzhenitsyn, *The Gulag Archipelago*, quoted by Paul Levy, *Wetiko: Healing the Mind-Virus That Plagues Our World*, p. 168.
4 Dave Foster Wallace, *This Is Water*, speech delivered at Kenyon College, 2005, published on Kenyon College website, http://bulletin-archive.kenyon.edu/x4280.html.
5 For more on this, see my article *The Most Empowered Vulnerability*, https://swamipadmanabha.com/archive/rpm/most-empowered-vulnerability.pdf.
6 For more on this, see my lecture *Personalism vs Impersonalism Explained*, https://youtu.be/cp5UwZVgdIo.
7 For more on this see my article *Loyalty, Institutions, and Identity*, https://swamipadmanabha.com/archive/rpm/loyalty-institutions-identity.
8 For more on this see Bhaktisiddhanta Saraswati Thakura's article *Putana*, http://daivasangam.weebly.com/warning-by-srila-bhaktisiddhanta.html.
9 The paragraphs from this particular section have been inspired by Purnachandra das, *Unspoken Obstacles on the Path to Bhakti*, ch. 10.
10 For more on this, see my article *Is It Possible to Think for Oneself Within the Framework of a Transrational Experience?*, https://swamipadmanabha.com/archive/rpm/think-for-oneself-within-framework-transrational-experience.

11 This whole paragraph and the last three sentences from the previous paragraph have been adapted from Radhamadhav das, *Perfect Imperfection*, ch. 10.

12 For more on this, see my article *What is Critical Thinking for a Devotee*, https://swamipadmanabha.com/archive/rpm/what-is-critical-thinking-for-devotee.pdf.

13 These biases have been taken from a list shared by Brian McLaren, *Do I Stay Christian?*, p. 93.

14 These last three paragraphs have been adapted from Thomas Keating, *Dismantling the Emotional Programs (part 2)*, https://www.contemplativeoutreach.org/wp-content/uploads/2021/09/31_Dismantling-the-Emotional-Programs-Part-2.pdf.

15 This last paragraph has been adapted from Radhamadhav das, *A Progressive Spirit is the Default Setting of Nature*, https://www.facebook.com/groups/483833409168760/permalink/756123921939706/.

16 For more on this, see my article *Anachronic Proselytism: When Time Advances, but One Does Not*, https://swamipadmanabha.com/archive/rpm/Anachronic-Proselytism.

17 An interesting online presentation in this regard is *ISKCON University* by Deva Madhava das, https://www.youtube.com/watch?v=Q7RuQ2BDB2o&t=13s.

18 Thomas Merton, *New Seeds of Contemplation*, p. 35.

19 For an interesting series of articles depicting different levels of dysfunctionality in the name of spirituality, see Satyanarayana Dasa Babaji, *Delusional Disorders (part 1)*, https://www.jiva.org/vedic-psychology-on-delusion/.

20 I thank Deva Madhava das for his insight about reframing "false ego" as "intermediary identity."

21 For more on this, see my lecture *4 Regs 2.0: Updating our Approach to the Four Regulative Principles*, https://www.youtube.com/watch?v=BusH9yvNeoY.

22 For more on this, see my lecture *Bhakti & Social Media*, https://www.youtube.com/watch?v=yZSP-LhgWIE.

23 This last sentence has been adapted from Richard Rohr, *The Prophets* (San Antonio, TX: Catholic Charismatic Bible Institute, 1980), audio recording.

24 Tamal Krishna das, *Gaura Yuga*, p. 82.
25 Part of this paragraph has been adapted from Richard Rohr, *The Good News According to Luke: Spiritual Reflections*, pp. 140–141.
26 This could be one interpretation for verse 10.38 of the *Bhagavad-gita*, where Sri Krishna says that among secrets, he is silence.
27 This section has been adapted from Purnachandra das, *Unspoken Obstacles on the Path to Bhakti*, p. 25.
28 See Ephesians 6:5–8, Colossians 3:22–24, 1 Timothy 6:1–2, and Titus 2:9–10, among other examples.
29 Examples of this are verses 2:213, 3:239, 9:15, and 9:78, among others.
30 Carl G. Jung, *Man and His Symbols*, p. 91.
31 Adapted from Richard Rohr, *The Divine Dance*, p. 213.
32 This paragraph has been adapted from Robert Augustus Masters, *Spiritual Bypassing*, ch. 16.
33 For more on this, see my article *What to Do with the Varnasrama? Scope and Purpose of Our Horizontal Development*, https://swamipadmanabha.com/archive/rpm/What-to-Do-with-Varnasrama.pdf.
34 Richard Rohr, *The Universal Christ*, p. 63.
35 For more of this, see my lecture *Can Sex Be Bhakti?*, https://www.youtube.com/watch?v=3vaf9ZfgGXM.
36 Bhaktivinoda Thakura, *Sri Bhaktyaloka*, purport to verse 4.
37 This paragraph has been adapted from Robert Augustus Masters, *Spiritual Bypassing*, ch. 14.
38 *Srimad Bhagavatam* 11.21.2 and 11.20.26.
39 For more on this see my podcast on *Has Monasticism Reached its Shelf Life?*, https://www.youtube.com/watch?v=Ce7yl-8UzOY.
40 For more on this, see my article *My Greatest Difficulty as Swami*, https://swamipadmanabha.com/archive/rpm/My-Greatest-Difficulty-as-Swami.pdf.
41 For more on this, see my article *The Sannyasa of Kali-yuga vs. the Sannyasa in Kali-yuga*, https://swamipadmanabha.com/archive/rpm/The-Sannyasa-of-Kali-yuga-vs-the-Sannyasa-in-Kali-yuga.pdf.
42 Thomas Merton, *The Silent Life*, p. 140.

43 See Raimon Panikkar, *Blessed Simplicity: The Monk as Universal Archetype*.

44 For more on this, see my article *Activate Your Monastic Side!*, https://swamipadmanabha.com/archive/rpm/Activate-Your-Monastic-Side.

45 For more on this, see Rory McEntee and Adam Bucko, *The New Monasticism: An Interspiritual Manifesto for Contemplative Living*.

46 This sentence has been adapted from Richard Rohr, *Universal Christ*, p. 125.

47 https://www.andrewharvey.net/sacredactivism.

48 For more on this, see my article *How Much Do We Really Understand Compassion?*, https://swamipadmanabha.com/archive/rpm/How-Much-Do-We-Really-Understand-Compassion.pdf.

49 For more on this, see Steve Rosen, *Sri Chaitanya's Life and Teachings*, ch. 8.

50 A recommended reading in this regard is *Holy Envy: Finding God in the Faith of Others*, by Barbara Brown Taylor.

51 Vrindavana Dasa Thakura, *Sri Chaitanya-bhagavata, Adi-khanda* 16.76–78, 80–81.

52 Simone Weil, last letter to Father Joseph-Marie Perrin, (26 May 1942), as translated in *The Simone Weil Reader*, edited by George A. Panichas, p. 111.

53 These last two sentences have been adapted from Brian McLaren, *Do I Stay Christian?*, p. 307.

54 This whole paragraph has been adapted from Purnachandra das, *Unspoken Obstacles on the Path to Bhakti*, pp. 11–12.

55 A. C. Bhaktivedanta Swami Prabhupada, letter to Karandhara on December 22, 1972.

56 A. C. Bhaktivedanta Swami Prabhupada, purport to *Srimad Bhagavatam* 1.6.37.

57 A. C. Bhaktivedanta Swami Prabhupada, purport to *Srimad Bhagavatam* 1.6.37.

58 *Bhagavad-gita* 18.63.

59 This sentence has been adapted from Purnachandra das, *Unspoken Obstacles on the Path to Bhakti*, p. 10.

60 The last two sentences have been adapted from Gregory Boyle, *The Whole Language: The Power of Extravagant Tenderness*, pp. 80–85.
61 For more on this, see my article *Have We Already Reached the Goal, Are We on the Way Or Will We Never Reach Them?*, https://swamipadmanabha.com/archive/rpm/Have-We-Reached-the-Goal.pdf.
62 Sajjana-tosani 4/1.
63 This conversation appears in Krishnadasa Kaviraja Goswami, *Chaitanya-charitamrita* 2.8.
64 This was a common phrase invoked by Srila B. R. Sridhara Deva Goswami.

Chapter Eight: Vulnerability & Empowerment

1 Brené Brown, *Daring Greatly*, ch. 2.
2 Rupa Goswami, *Ujjvala-nilamani* 15.102.
3 The last two sentences have been adapted from Richard Rohr, *Just This*, p. 55.
4 Richard Rohr, *Just This*, p. 42.
5 Sigmund Freud, *Civilization and Its Discontents*, p. 29.
6 Some sections of this and the previous paragraph have been partly adapted from Brené Brown, *The Call to Courage*, https://www.netflix.com/title/81010166.
7 *The Bible*, Romans 5:20–21.
8 Adapted from Richard Rohr, *The Divine Dance*, p. 247.
9 Adapted from Richard Rohr, *The Divine Dance*, p. 286.
10 Richard Rohr, *The Naked Now*, p. 142.
11 The last two sentences have been adapted from Robert Augustus Masters, *Spiritual Bypassing*, pp. 163–164.
12 The last two sentences have been adapted from Robert Augustus Masters, *Spiritual Bypassing*, pp. 165 and 168.
13 Richard Rohr, *Falling Upward*, p. xxii.
14 Jordan B. Peterson, *12 Rules for Life*, p. 345.
15 The beginning of this paragraph till this point has been an adaptation from Jordan B. Peterson, *12 Rules for Life*, p. 343.

16 Jordan B. Peterson, *12 Rules for Life*, p. 345.
17 Eliot, T. S., *The Dry Salvages*, p. 39.

Chapter Nine: Individuation: Carving Out Our Full Humanity in Divine Service

1 *Srimad Bhagavatam* 10.29.11. Emphasis added.
2 Examples of this are *Srimad Bhagavatam* 11.20.17, among others.
3 The last three sentences have been adapted from Purnachandra das, *Unspoken Obstacles on the Path to Bhakti*, p. 51.
4 Ilia Delio, *The Unbearable Wholeness of Being*, p. xiv.
5 Richard Rohr, *Just This*, p. 59.
6 Richard Rohr, *The Universal Christ*, p. 65.
7 For verses which describe how Krishna executes human divine play, see *Srimad Bhagavatam* 10.23.37. For verses which confirm how this *nara-lila* is supreme, see *Chaitanya-charitamrita* 2.21.101.
8 This paragraph has been adapted from Swami Sadananda, https://www.sadananda.com/txt/en/text_downloads/en/vasudeva_datta-en.pdf.
9 *Srimad Bhagavatam* 11.21.2.
10 Tamal Krishna das, *Gaura Yuga*, p. 15.
11 Adapted from Richard Rohr, *The Naked Now*, p. 23.
12 Sanatana Goswami, *Brihad-bhagavatamrita* 2.1.110 (commentary). A similar idea is hinted in Sanatana Goswami's purport to verse 2.5.51.
13 Some examples of this are found in *Srimad Bhagavatam* 10.48.19 and 11.7.20.
14 The last seven sentences have been adapted from Satyanarayana dasa, https://www.jiva.org/theory-evolution-dialogue-scientist/.
15 The analogy of the tricyle has been adapted from Richard Rohr, *The Universal Christ*, p. 213.
16 *Srimad Bhagavatam* 11.11.41. Emphasis added.
17 Adapted from Richard Rohr, *Just This*, p. 64.
18 Some of the ideas from this subsection have been adapted from Robert Augustus Masters, *Spiritual Bypassing*, chapters 3 and 5.

19 While the first part of this quote comes from Srila Prabhupada's purport to *Srimad Bhagavatam* 3.15.31, the second part of it comes from his commentary to *Srimad Bhagavatam* 4.10.4.

20 Some of the ideas from this subsection have been adapted from Purnachandra das, *Unspoken Obstacles on the Path to Bhakti*, ch. 8.

21 This quote is an adaptation from two different letters by Swami Sadananda, found in https://www.sadananda.com/txt/en/text_downloads/en/inner-en.pdf and https://www.sadananda.com/txt/en/text_downloads/en/joy-en.pdf.

Chapter Ten: Nondual Thinking: Everything is One, But Never Impersonal

1 A few of these examples could be *Srimad Bhagavatam* verses 2.6.40, 3.27.11, 8.12.8, 10.14.18, 10.51.16, 10.84.33, and 11.9.31, among others.

2 Adapted from Shrivatsa Goswami, *Vaishnavism: Contemporary Scholars Discuss the Gaudiya Tradition*, p. 250.

3 For more on panentheism, see https://plato.stanford.edu/entries/panentheism/?fbclid=IwAR0L6sGhtlg4Cogiz350hMEgpO85x0wYLzuuhB9UHvGRUiBUFyKY1f0EXe8.

4 *Srimad Bhagavatam* 1.9.42.

5 Jiva Goswami, *Bhagavat Sandarbha* 31, commentary by Satyanarayana Dasa, p. 291.

6 Swami B. R. Sridhara, *Subjective Evolution of Consciousness*, p. 50.

7 The first part of this quote (till "resistance") comes from Richard Rohr, *The Naked Now*, p. 160. The second part of it comes from Richard Rohr, *Falling Upward*, p. 147.

8 Adapted from Richard Rohr, *Universal Christ*, p. 215.

9 Richard Rohr, *Everything Belongs*, p. 52.

10 This quote has been adapted from Bhaktivinoda Thakura, *The Bhagavata: Its Philosophy, Its Ethics, and Its Theology*, https://bhaktivinodainstitute.org/the-bhagavata.

11 A similar statement is found in *Srimad Bhagavatam* 7.15.65.

12 For the full story, see Krishnadasa Kaviraja Goswami, *Caitanya-caritamrita* 2.9.178–217.

13 For the full exchange between Gopa-kumara and Hanuman, see *Brihad-bhagavatamrita* 2.4.

14 Rupa Goswami, *Bhakti-rasamrita-sindhu* 1.2.269 and 1.2.309.

15 For more interesting expositions on different types of interreligious dialogue, see https://irstudies.org/index.php/jirs/article/view/499/521?fbclid=IwAR1itrx4z3nu3BZUSls6jdyvxmYB-NgOd9Oiq8jxXB-V47DFA8C1s8gLmtog.

16 This analogy has been taken from https://www.sfgate.com/news/article/FINDING-MY-RELIGION-Religious-scholar-Huston-3302971.php.

17 Bhaktivinoda Thakura, *Sri Chaitanya-siksamrita, First Shower*.

18 This paragraph has been mostly adapted from Rory McEntee and Adam Bucko, The New Monasticism, p. 125.

19 This analogy has been taken from https://cac.org/daily-meditations/the-holy-water-we-share-2022-11-08/.

20 Part of this paragraph has been adapted from Rory McEntee and Adam Bucko, *The New Monasticism*, pp. 79–81.

Chapter Eleven: Issues & Tissues Between Guru and Disciple

1 See Bhakti Raksaka Sridhara Deva Goswami, *Sri Guru and His Grace*, ch. 11.

2 For an example of this, see Krishnadasa Kaviraja Goswami, *Chaitanya-charitamrita* 2.22.54. Another similar statement is be *Srimad Bhagavatam* 4.24.57.

3 For an example of this, see Sanatana Goswami, *Brihad-bhagavatamrita* 3.34–35 or 11.322–328. Another similar statement is be *Srimad Bhagavatam* 5.1.35.

4 Krishnadasa Kaviraja Goswami, *Chaitanya-charitamrita* 1.1.44.

5 Some of the main verses where these attributes are mentioned are *Bhagavad-gita* 4.34, *Srimad Bhagavatam* 11.3.21, and *Mundaka Upanishad* 1.2.12.

6 A. C. Bhaktivedanta Swami Prabhupada, purport to *Srimad Bhagavatam* 4.15.23. A similar statement is found in *Srimad Bhagavatam* 4.15.24.

7 This particular subsection and the following one will revolve considerably around Radhamadhav das, *Perfect Imperfection.*
8 Interestingly, this verse is repeated exactly in the same way at the very end of this book in verse 12.12.52, all of which speaks of its utmost significance.
9 See Sanatana Goswami, *Hari-bhakti-vilasa* 1.73–76.
10 Bhakti Raksaka Sridhara Deva Goswami, *Sri Guru and His Grace*, p. 80.
11 Adapted from Richard Rohr, *The Divine Dance*, p. 147.
12 See Sanatana Goswami, *Hari-bhakti-vilasa* 1.64–68.
13 The letter is from November 23rd, 1967, and can be found in https://prabhupadabooks.com/letters/calcutta/november/23/1967/umapati.
14 A similar situation in which the guru asks his disciple to leave his sight but does not necessarily reject him is found in *Srimad Bhagavatam* 12.6.62–63.
15 One example is Hemalata Thakurani's rejection of her disciple Rupa Kaviraja, which is mentioned in Visvanatha Chakravarti's commentary to *Bhakti-rasamrita-sindhu* 1.2.295.
16 For similar statements, see *Srimad Bhagavatam* 6.9.43 and 6.16.46.
17 Commentary to *Srimad Bhagavatam* 8.24.53.
18 This point is first mentioned in Rupa Goswami, *Bhakti-rasamrita-sindhu* 1.2.74.
19 These last two sentences have been adapted from Richard Rohr, *The Universal Christ*, p. 143.
20 This paragraph has been adapted from Purnachandra das, *Unspoken Obstacles on the Path to Bhakti*, p. 79.
21 The last three sentences have been adapted from Robert Augustus Masters, *Spiritual Bypassing*, pp. 147–148.
22 This term has been originally referred to by Erich Fromm in his book *Psychoanalysis and Religion.*

Chapter Twelve: Divine Ignorance: Knowing Through Darkness, Doubt, and Paradox

1 Carl Jung, *Modern Man in Search of a Soul*, p. 111.
2 Alan W. Watts, *The Wisdom of Insecurity*, p. 24.

3 Thomas Merton, *New Seeds of Contemplation*, p. 134.
4 Adapted from Tamal Krishna das, *Gaura Yuga*, p. 19.
5 Rupa Goswami, *Ujjvala-nilamani* 15.102.
6 Quoted in *Josh Billing's Encyclopedia and Proverbial Philosophy of Wit and Humor*, p. 286. Emphasis added.
7 For other verses about God's unknowability, see *Bhagavad-gita* 10.2, among others.
8 *Srimad Bhagavatam* 1.9.16. A similar statement can be found in *Srimad Bhagavatam* 7.9.49.
9 *The Bible*, 1 Corinthians, 3:18.
10 Richard Rohr, *Falling Upward*, p. 112.
11 Caltech Science Exchange, *What Is the Uncertainty Principle and Why Is It Important*. California Institute of Technology. https://scienceexchange.caltech.edu/topics/quantum-science-explained/uncertainty-principle.
12 Adapted from Brian McLaren, *Do I Stay Christian?*, p. 292.
13 Anonymous, *The Cloud of Unknowing*, p. 21.
14 The last two sentences have been adapted from Rainer Maria Rilke and Franz Xaver Kappus, *Letters to a Young Poet*, p. 23.
15 These last two sentences have been adapted from Brian McLaren, *Faith after Doubt: Why Your Beliefs Stopped Working and What to Do about It*, pp. 116–117.
16 The last four sentences have been adapted from Jordan B. Peterson, *12 Rules for Life*, p. 218.
17 The complete letter can be read in https://sadananda.com/txt/en/text_downloads/en/bhaktisiddhanta's_words_of_advice-en.pdf.
18 Richard Rohr, *The Divine Dance*, p. 220.
19 See *Bhagavad-gita* 2.29.
20 The last two sentences have been adapted from Richard Rohr, *The Naked Now*, p. 11.
21 Swami Padmanabha, *Inherent or Inherited?*, pp. xxxvii–xxxix.
22 Adapted from Richard Rohr, *Falling Upward*, p. 111.
23 Anonymous, *The Cloud of Unknowing*, p. 94.
24 Satyanarayana Dasa, purport to *Bhagavat Sandarbha* 31, p. 298.
25 Richard Rohr, *Falling Upward*, p. 112.
26 Jordan B. Peterson, *12 Rules for Life*, p. 41.

27 The last two sentences have been adapted from Richard Rohr, *Everything Belongs*, p. 97.
28 The last three sentences have been adapted from Jordan B. Peterson, *12 Rules for Life*, p. 36.
29 Jordan B. Peterson, *12 Rules for Life*, p. 278.
30 Adapted from Richard Rohr, *The Divine Dance*, p. 33.
31 The last two sentences have been adapted from Anonymous, *The Cloud of Unknowing*, p. 217.
32 Albert Einstein, *Living Philosophies*, p. 6.
33 Adapted from Richard Rohr, *Falling Upward*, p. 51.
34 Dietrich, Bonhoeffer, *I Want to Live These Days with You: A Year of Daily Devotions*, p. 365.
35 Adapted from https://www.youtube.com/watch?v=osJjn6pgvu4&list=LL&index=126.
36 Richard Rohr, *Everything Belongs*, p. 24.
37 Paul Louis Metzger (2016) *"If you see a Buddha on the road, kill him." What about Jesus?* Patheos. https://www.patheos.com/blogs/uncommongodcommongood/2016/05/if-you-see-a-buddha-on-the-road-kill-him-what-about-jesus.
38 Adapted from Richard Rohr, *The Divine Dance*, p. 316.
39 See *The Bible*, Exodus 20:21.
40 See *The Bible*, 1 Kings 8:10–12.
41 See *Bhagavad-gita* 9.2.
42 This term has been coined by Rudolf Otto.
43 *Mahabharata* 12.336.20.
44 *Srimad Bhagavatam* 10.14.38.
45 For more on this, see http://www.centeringprayer.com.
46 Richard Rohr, *Everything Belongs*, p. 29.
47 Other similar verses in this connection are *Srimad Bhagavatam* 2.6.36, 3.2.12, 3.6.39, 10.51.36, and 11.16.39.
48 For an example of this, see Krishnadasa Kaviraja Goswami, *Chaitanya-charitamrita* 2.22.31.
49 The last five sentences have been adapted from Gerald G. May, *The Dark Night of the Soul*, pp. 95–96.
50 Richard Rohr, *Everything Belongs*, p. 41.
51 The last four sentences have been adapted from Gerald G. May, *The Dark Night of the Soul*, p. 72.

52 Carl Jung, *Aion: Researches into the Phenomenology of the Self*, p. 78.
53 Richard Rohr, *Everything Belongs*, p. 41.
54 Adapted from Ilia Delio, *The Unbearable Wholeness of Being*, p. 91.
55 The last two sentences have been adapted from Richard Rohr, *The Naked Now*, p. 49.

Chapter Thirteen: The Realm of Contemplative Prayer

1 The last three sentences have been adapted from Richard Rohr, *Just This*, p. 39.
2 See *Siksastakam* 3.
3 See *Bhagavad-gita* 9.14.
4 See *Srimad Bhagavatam* 1.2.18.
5 See *The Bible*, 1 Thessalonians 5:17.
6 John Bunyan, quoted in Avinash Singh, *All About Prayer*, p. 43.
7 See *Bhagavad-gita* 9.34 and 18.65.
8 Examples of this could be *Srimad Bhagavatam* 9.4.63–68 and *Bhagavad-gita* 12.13–20.
9 An example of this could be the first half of *Bhagavad-gita* 9.29.
10 Emphasis added.
11 Emphasis added.
12 Adapted from Richard Rohr, *The Divine Dance*, p. 238.
13 Most of this paragraph has been adapted from Tamal Krishna das, *Gaura yuga*, pp. 21, 57, and 62.
14 Adapted from Richard Rohr, *Just This*, p. 95.
15 This is a classic expression of Thomas Keating, quoted for example in https://cac.org/daily-meditations/sharing-gods-one-spirit-2016-08-07/.
16 The last four sentences have been adapted from Richard Rohr, *The Universal Christ*, p. 222.
17 Adapted from Richard Rohr, *Just This*, p. 71.
18 Adapted from Richard Rohr, *Just This*, pp. 58 and 60.
19 Richard Rohr, *The Universal Christ*, p. 222.
20 The last two sentences have been adapted from Richard Rohr, *Everything Belongs*, p. 66.

21 Adapted from https://www.contemplativeoutreach.org/course/9-prayer-as-relationship/.
22 Adapted from Thomas Keating, *Invitation to Love: The Way of Christian Contemplation*, p. 90.
23 Carl Rogers, *Communication: its blocking and its facilitation*, pp. 9 and 83–88.
24 William Paul Young (2016). Foreword in Richard Rohr & Michael Morrell, *The Divine Dance*, p. 21.
25 Adapted from Richard Rohr, *Just This*, p. 97.
26 Adapted from Richard Rohr, *Just This*, p. 111.
27 See *The Bible*, Romans 8:26–27.
28 Richard Rohr, *The Naked Now*, p. 102.
29 Richard Rohr, *The Naked Now*, p. 23.

Chapter Fourteen: Unearthing Heaven: How Material Energy Hosts the Spiritual World

1 Bhaktivinoda Thakura, *The Bhagavata: Its Philosophy, Its Ethics, and Its Theology*, https://bhaktivinodainstitute.org/the-bhagavata.
2 See *Bhagavad-gita* 8.15 and 9.33.
3 Prabodhananda Saraswati, *Chaitanya-chandramrita*, verse 5.
4 *Chandogya Upanishad* 6.2.1 and 6.2.3.
5 Last 3 sentences adapted from David Haberman, *Loving Stones*, p. 229.
6 Last 3 sentences adapted from David Haberman, *Loving Stones*, p. 232.
7 Similar verses are *Srimad Bhagavatam* 10.57.15 and 10.60.2, among others.
8 Adapted from David Haberman, *Loving Stones*, p. 232.
9 This verse can be *Brihad-aranyaka Upanishad* 5.1.1 as well as the invocation of *Isopanishad*.
10 Last 2 sentences adapted from David Haberman, *Loving Stones*, p. 232.
11 For a similar statement, see *Srimad Bhagavatam* 10.14.7.
12 Adapted from Richard Rohr, *The Divine Dance*, p. 258.
13 See Rupa Goswami, *Bhakti-rasamrita-sindhu* 1.2.255–256.
14 See Jiva Goswami, *Bhakti Sandarbha* 225.

15 Patrick Malone, *A God Who Gets Foolishly Close*, p. 23.
16 A section that clearly makes this point is *Srimad Bhagavatam* 3.29.21–27.
17 Adapted from Bhaktisiddhanta Saraswati, *Amrita-vani* 2.71 and 1.4.
18 An example of this can be found in *Srimad Bhagavatam* 10.59.25–30 and 12.3.1–13.
19 A similar section can be found in *Srimad Bhagavatam* 11.16.9–37.
20 *Chandogya Upanishad* 3.14.1.
21 Emphasis added.
22 A similar idea can be found in *Srimad Bhagavatam* 11.21.28.
23 Similar statements can be found in *Srimad Bhagavatam* 7.9.20 and 7.9.48.
24 See *Srimad Bhagavatam* 2.1.26–37, 2.5.37–42, 8.20.21–29, and 10.85.7–17 as examples of this description.
25 Adapted from Richard Rohr, *The Universal Christ*, p. 36.
26 The last two sentences have been adapted from Ilia Delio, *The Unbearable Wholeness of Being*, pp. 60–62.
27 See Part Two of this book.
28 Adapted from Teilhard de Chardin, *Human Energy*, p. 77.
29 Adapted from Ilia Delio, *The Unbearable Wholeness of Being*, p. 63.
30 Adapted from Richard Rohr, *Just This*, p. 101.
31 Colossians 3:3, 11 or 1 Corinthians 15:28.
32 Pierre Teilhard de Chardin, *Sketch of a Personal Universe*, p. 72.
33 St. John Damascene, *On Holy Images: Followed By Three Sermons On The Assumption*, p. 17.
34 Elizabeth Barrett Browning, *Aurora Leigh*, p. 821.
35 Richard Rohr, *The Universal Christ*, p. 33.
36 Adapted from Richard Rohr, *The Universal Christ*, p. 112.
37 The last two sentences have been adapted from Richard Rohr, *The Universal Christ*, p. 239.
38 Adapted from Thomas M. King, *Teilhard's Mysticism of Knowing*, p. 66.
39 Adapted from Ilia Delio, *The Unbearable Wholeness of Being*, p. 78.
40 The last two sentences have been adapted from Richard Rohr, *The Universal Christ*, p. 15.
41 Adapted from Richard Rohr, *The Universal Christ*, p. 119.

42 Adapted from Richard Rohr, *The Universal Christ*, p. 113.
43 Adapted from Richard Rohr, *Everything Belongs*, p. 52.
44 Adapted from Richard Rohr, *The Divine Dance*, p. 294.
45 The last three sentences have been adapted from Richard Rohr, *The Divine Dance*, p. 297.
46 Adapted from Richard Rohr, *Falling Upward*, p. 95.
47 *The Bible*, John 14:2.
48 *Brahma-samhita* 5.31.
49 *Bhagavad-gita* 10.15.
50 Adapted from Thomas Merton, *New Seeds of Contemplation*, p. 198.
51 The last two sentences have been adapted from Ilia Delio, *The Unbearable Wholeness of Being*, pp. 77–78.
52 The last two sentences have been adapted from Richard Rohr, *Just This*, p. 64.
53 Adapted from Satyanarayana Dasa's commentary on Anuccheda 106 of *Krishna Sandarbha*, pp. 612–613.
54 Verse of unknown source quoted in Srila Prabhupada's purport to *Srimad Bhagavatam* 4.30.35.
55 This paragraph has been adapted from Tamal Krishna das, *Gaura Yuga*, p. 10.
56 The last two sentences have been adapted from Richard Rohr, *The Universal Christ*, p. 87.
57 The last two sentences have been adapted from Richard Rohr, *The Universal Christ*, p. 110.
58 Bhaktivinoda Thakura, *Saranagati* 11.
59 Adapted from Richard Rohr, *The Divine Dance*, p. 42.
60 Swami B. R. Sridhar, *Subjective Evolution of Consciousness*, p. 17.
61 Swami B. R. Sridhar, *Subjective Evolution of Consciousness*, p. 53.
62 Adapted from Swami B. R. Sridhar, *Subjective Evolution of Consciousness*, p. 56.
63 Adapted from Swami B. R. Sridhar, *Subjective Evolution of Consciousness*, pp. 71–72.
64 Adapted from Richard Rohr, *The Divine Dance*, p. 156.
65 Richard Rohr, *Just This*, p. 11.
66 Adapted from Swami B. R. Sridhar, *Subjective Evolution of Consciousness*, pp. 68–69.

67 Adapted from Swami B. R. Sridhar, *Subjective Evolution of Consciousness*, p. 78.
68 The last three sentences have been adapted from https://cac.org/daily-meditations/is-the-universe-on-our-side-2022-12-11/.
69 Richard Rohr, *Just This*, pp. 10–11.
70 Richard Rohr, *Just This*, p. 18.
71 Adapted from Richard Rohr, *Everything Belongs*, p. 140.
72 Dave Haberman, *Loving Stones*, p. 242.
73 Adapted from Dave Haberman, *Loving Stones*, p. 242.
74 The last two sentences have been adapted from Dave Haberman, *Loving Stones*, p. 230.
75 Deep gratitude to Bhaktirasa dasi for sharing this gift of a poem.

Conclusion: Reclaiming Our Gaudiya Project

1 Philip Clayton, *Mind and Emergence: From Quantum to Consciousness*, p. 39.
2 Karl Rahner, *The Spirituality of the Church of the Future*, p. 149.
3 This paragraph has been adapted from Swami Padmanabha, *Gray: The Most Important Color*, https://swamipadmanabha.com/archive/rpm/Gray-the-Most-Important-Color.pdf.
4 Adapted from Richard Rohr, *The Naked Now*, p. 158.
5 Adapted from Richard Rohr, *Falling Upward*, p. 123.
6 Adapted from Brian McLaren, *Do I Stay Christian?*, p. 109.
7 The last three sentences have been adapted from Richard Rohr, *Falling Upward*, pp. 2–3.
8 Adapted from Joan Chittister and Richard Rohr, *Prophets Then, Prophets Now*. The audio version can be found here: https://store.cac.org/collections/all/products/prophets-then-prophets-now-mp3.
9 Adapted from Richard Rohr, https://cac.org/daily-meditations/disrupting-the-status-quo-2023-01-15/.
10 The last seven sentences have been adapted from Richard Rohr, https://cac.org/daily-meditations/disrupting-the-status-quo-2023-01-15/.
11 Thomas Merton, *No Man is an Island*, pp. 106–7.

12 This whole paragraph has been adapted from Brian McLaren, *Do I stay Christian?*, pp. 120–125.
13 Adapted from Teilhard de Chardin, *Human Energy*, pp. 74–75.
14 Howard Zinn, *Marx in Soho: A Play on History*, p. 115.
15 The last two sentences have been adapted from Brian McLaren, *Do I Stay Christian?*, p. 180.
16 All these quotes have been adapted from Radhamadhav Dasa, *Perfect Imperfection*, pp. 89–90.
17 The last four sentences have been adapted from Jordan Peterson, *12 Rules for Life*, p. 108.
18 The last six sentences have been adapted from Robert Augustus Masters, *Spiritual Bypassing*, pp. 40–42.
19 Adapted from Richard Rohr, *Breathing under Water: Spirituality and the Twelve Steps*, pp. 4–5.
20 Stephanie Spellers, *The Church Cracked Open: Disruption, Decline, and New Hope for Beloved Community*, pp. 22–23.
21 The last two sentences have been adapted from Brian McLaren, *Do I Stay Christian?*, p. 151.
22 Commentary by Bhaktisiddhanta Saraswati to Vrindavana Dasa Thakura, *Chaitanya-bhagavata* 1.10.8.
23 The last five sentences have been adapted from Brian McLaren, *Do I Stay Christian?*, p. 310.

Made in the USA
Middletown, DE
11 April 2025

73978093R00262